Praise for the First Edition

"This book is brilliant! Professor Macfarlane analyzes the changes in the legal profession as fewer and fewer cases go to trial and legal information (and misinformation) abounds on the internet. *The New Lawyer* is a fascinating analysis of the shifting public perception and expectations of lawyers as well as ways that the practice of law has changed in recent years ... This is an extraordinary research-based analysis of the past, present, and future of the role of lawyers in our society. Thought-provoking for anyone interested in the future of the legal profession."

– Susan Hansen, Hansen & Hildebrand, Milwaukee;
past president, International Academy of Collaborative Professionals

"This is a remarkable book. I recommend it to all as a profound explanation of the somewhat glacial revolution in legal services that began in the 1970s. It is a landmark book that speaks to the entire legal profession about itself. Professor Macfarlane's empirical research and laser-like observations show how the distinctive threads of legal and facilitative approaches to conflict interrelate and form the fabric that is emerging from their confluence. A real-life vision of a changing landscape."

– Chip Rose, lawyer and mediator; director, The Mediation Center, Santa Cruz

"Building on her cutting edge research on lawyering, with *The New Lawyer* Professor Macfarlane has established her place as a leading thinker in the areas of legal access, negotiation, and dispute resolution. With an easy-to-read style breaking down complex and nuanced issues and the use of interviews with practising lawyers, Macfarlane eloquently educates the reader on the problems facing legal services and proposes workable solutions for the future. This book should be required reading for law students, practising lawyers, and policy makers in legal education and the organized bar."

– Forrest (Woody) Mosten, collaborative lawyer and mediator; adjunct professor at UCLA School of Law; author, *Collaborative Divorce Handbook* (2009), *Mediation Career Guide* (2001), and *Unbundling Legal Services* (2000)

"For anyone who is considering going to law school, who is presently in law school, or who is already in legal practice, *The New Lawyer* is a must-read. Dr. Macfarlane paints a compelling picture of the future of lawyering and the significant role of legal education in helping create that picture. If the experience of my students reading the book at the University of Victoria is any indicator, Macfarlane's description of the new lawyer will resonate with all persons interested in a progressive and honourable legal profession. The book might even signal an end to lawyer jokes!"

– Andrew Pirie, professor, University of Victoria Law School

"The legal profession needs a wake-up call, and *The New Lawyer* resoundingly provides it. Macfarlane persuasively critiques the outmoded habits of the profession and lays the foundation for the new settlement-oriented, problem-solving approach to lawyering."

– David Hoffman, founding member of Boston Law Collaborative, LLC; John H. Watson, Jr. Lecturer on Law, Harvard Law School; and Boston's "Lawyer of the Year" 2016 in the field of mediation

"A provocative and hopeful vision of the 'new lawyer' who has chosen to embrace a more inclusive calling ... With Macfarlane's guidance, it may be possible to reclaim the pragmatic nobility of the legal profession."

– Nancy A. Welsh, Professor of Law, Dickinson School of Law, Pennsylvania State University; chair of the Section of Dispute Resolution of the American Bar Association, 2016–17

THE NEW LAWYER

Law and Society Series
W. Wesley Pue, General Editor

The Law and Society Series explores law as a socially embedded phenomenon. It is premised on the understanding that the conventional division of
law from society creates false dichotomies in thinking, scholarship, educational practice, and social life. Books in the series treat law and society as
mutually constitutive and seek to bridge scholarship emerging from interdisciplinary engagement of law with disciplines such as politics, social theory,
history, political economy, and gender studies.

For a complete list of the titles in this series, see the UBC Press website,
www.ubcpress.ca.

JULIE MACFARLANE

THE NEW LAWYER

How Clients Are Transforming
the Practice of Law

Second Edition

UBCPress · Vancouver · Toronto

26 25 24 23 22 21 20 19 18 17   5 4 3 2 1

Printed in Canada on FSC-certified ancient-forest-free paper (100% post-consumer recycled) that is processed chlorine- and acid-free.

Library and Archives Canada Cataloguing in Publication

Macfarlane, Julie, author
    The new lawyer : how clients are transforming the practice of law / Julie Macfarlane. – Second edition.

(Law and society series, ISSN 1496-4953)
Includes bibliographical references and index.
Issued in print and electronic formats.
ISBN 978-0-7748-37071 (hardcover). – ISBN 978-0-7748-3583-1 (softcover). –
ISBN 978-0-7748-3584-8 (PDF). – ISBN 978-0-7748-3585-5 (EPUB). –
ISBN 978-0-7748-3586-2 (MOBI)

    1. Practice of law – Canada. 2. Practice of law – United States. 3. Dispute resolution (Law) – Canada. 4. Dispute resolution (Law) – United States. 5. Compromise (Law) – Canada. 6. Compromise (Law) – United States. 7. Attorney and client – Canada. 8. Attorney and client – United States. I. Title. II. Series: Law and society series (Vancouver, B.C.)

K120.M33 2017   347.71'09   C2017-900577-4
                                                              C2017-900578-2

Canada

UBC Press gratefully acknowledges the financial support for our publishing program of the Government of Canada (through the Canada Book Fund), the Canada Council for the Arts, and the British Columbia Arts Council.

Printed and bound in Canada by Marquis
Set in Myriad and Minion by Marquis Interscript
Copy editor and proofreader: Francis Chow
Indexer: Christine Jacobs
Cover designer: Will Brown

UBC Press
The University of British Columbia
2029 West Mall
Vancouver, BC V6T 1Z2
www.ubcpress.ca

This book is dedicated to the upcoming
generation of New Lawyers – those who are just
entering legal practice, graduating from law school,
or perhaps still dreaming of becoming a lawyer.

To you falls the greatest challenge,
but in you I have the greatest hope.

Contents

Contents

Foreword

KARI BOYLE AND JENNIFER MULLER

We live in interesting times. The legal profession is facing multiple internal and external challenges, including disruptive legal technologies, competition from other professionals and service providers, changing demographics, insourcing of legal expertise, and financial pressures. The environment in which lawyers practise is changing more quickly than ever and many lawyers are struggling to keep up. In addition to a reasonable income, lawyers are seeking meaningful work and an opportunity to make a difference in the world. A review of the first edition of *The New Lawyer* (2008) confirms the prescience of Julie Macfarlane's observations and predictions about forces of change affecting the profession and the role of the lawyer. A decade later, the pace of change has accelerated and new types of forces are coming into the picture.

There has been significant dialogue recently regarding the accessibility of the justice system. Issues related to access to justice are a growing concern throughout the world's developed nations as fewer and fewer middle-income earners are able to afford legal services. Self-represented litigants now outnumber those with legal counsel in many of Canada's family courts, with as many as 80 percent of parties in urban family courts unrepresented by legal counsel. Meanwhile, clients of all kinds, corporate and personal, are increasingly capable of accessing legal knowledge and information on their own, and are interested in new professional relationships that foster partnership and a collaborative approach. Twenty-first-century legal consumers are seeking partnerships with their lawyers based on transparent dialogue, including frank conversations about cost and value for money.

What are the implications of these challenges for the legal profession? How can these profound issues be addressed? In particular, how can lawyers respond in ways that are practical and accessible? What will the lawyer of the future look like? Julie Macfarlane addresses these key questions in this second edition of *The New Lawyer*, and it is hard to imagine anyone better placed to do so. She has been a leading researcher, legal educator, and alternative dispute resolution professional for decades, and was the initiator and leader of the National Self-Represented Litigants Project, which published its seminal report in 2013 and continues to inform justice dialogue across the country.

Macfarlane creates a cogent picture of the New Lawyer that challenges past and current thinking and practice. To provide a sense of the helpful insights found in this book, we'd like to highlight a few important issues and predictions that correlate with our experience.

First, lawyers will need new skill sets that have not, to date, been priorities in legal education or legal practice. A viable "partnership" relationship will require excellent listening skills, empathy, patience, interpersonal communication skills, and a willingness to share responsibility and decision making with the client. The lawyer's first job cannot be to mine the client's story for legal issues. Instead, the lawyer needs to start by exploring and understanding the client's needs and goals, and then identify process options, consider how the law applies to the situation, and allow the client to make informed decisions about how his or her matter proceeds.

Second, in addition to new skill sets, new business models and process tools are needed to refashion how legal services are provided. One example of a new business model is "unbundling" (often referred to as the "limited scope retainer"). Unbundling offers significant benefits to both lawyers and clients. For lawyers, potential benefits include flexibility, greater and more stable revenue, work that is amenable to creative pricing options and reduced accounts receivable, improved lifestyle, and greater personal satisfaction. Such attributes will go a long way towards meeting the dual goals of income and meaningful work. For clients, potential benefits include price certainty, a stronger voice and greater empowerment – through what Julie Macfarlane describes as legal coaching – in their legal matter, and, of course, access to legal services that would otherwise be beyond their reach. Lawyers will develop other equally promising business models.

Third, although we need a strong court system to support the rule of law, the courts will no longer be the default process in many disputes. Instead, lawyers will need to consider and advise their clients on a variety of process options, including those that focus on settlement, such as mediation and collaborative law, as well as judicial settlement programming. Lawyers and clients will be jointly creating custom-made pathways for swifter, problem-responsive dispute resolution.

These new relationships, business models, and process designs will require a significant shift in, and even a reinvention of, the current practice paradigm as well as the legal education provided by most law schools. Julie Macfarlane offers unique and penetrating insights into these and many other difficult issues.

We welcome the second edition of *The New Lawyer,* which offers a thoughtful response and viable approaches to the broad changes facing the legal profession and individual lawyers, including the challenges posed by the access-to-justice crisis. *The New Lawyer* should be required reading for everyone contemplating a career in law, for all law students, for all young lawyers, and for experienced lawyers who are trying to understand the whirl of change around them. This book both captures and inspires a movement towards the New Lawyer. Turn the page to begin to learn more ...

Jennifer Muller is a former self-represented litigant and Kari D. Boyle is a retired British Columbia lawyer, consultant, and dispute resolution professional.

Acknowledgments

When I was first starting to talk to UBC Press about revising and updating *The New Lawyer*, it was summer 2014 – six years since the first edition had appeared. I had completed my research on self-represented litigants the previous year, and was still absorbed with these issues (the National Self-Represented Litigants Project). Updating *The New Lawyer*, I thought, would be relatively simple and would focus on the development of conflict resolution advocacy and settlement practice, and I could review new data and how much progress had been made.

Of course, that was not at all how this panned out. First, life threw me a few curve balls in the form of a second cancer (late 2014) and then a recurrence (2016).

But the time it has taken me (and many helpers) to bring out this second edition of *The New Lawyer* has been a very good thing. It has meant that the new edition is not a simple updating of the first, but instead reflects the interconnectedness of many different aspects of change in lawyers' roles – in settling cases fairly and expeditiously, but also in providing affordable, relevant legal services to a new generation of clients who are not interested in an open-ended approach to legal costs. The self-help revolution and the consumer empowerment movement produced by the continuing, astonishing expansion of the Internet has converged with an enhanced awareness of the importance of settlement advocacy. The result – illuminated by new data on the self-representation phenomenon – has led to an impatience for different types of legal services and has created an urgent need for new approaches to lawyer/client collaboration, new financial structures for paying for legal services, and much more.

This is really just a long-winded way of saying that the fact that this process took me more than twice as long as I had imagined has allowed me to write a much better book. The same themes remain, but they are more than simply internally updated. Now there is an integration, I hope, between the skills and tools that the New Lawyer needed in 2008 and what lawyers need in order to properly serve clients in 2017 and beyond.

Among the many people to whom I owe thanks, my greatest debt of gratitude remains to my hundreds of research subjects – lawyers, clients, judges, and now also self-represented litigants – who were generous and patient as they subjected themselves to my interrogations. Many of them told me that they hoped that describing their knowledge and experience would be valuable for others, and I hope that they see that goal somewhat achieved in this book.

My supportive and stimulating professional community has been further deepened and enriched in the last nine years. I find myself drawn increasingly to the ideas of my younger colleagues (or maybe everyone just seems young to me now). I want to acknowledge in particular the exceptional insights of Brady Donohue, Nikki Gershbain, Rob Harvie, Michaela Keet, John Kleefeld, John Greacen, Lisa Nakamura, Sue Rice, Kadey Schultz, David Tanovich, Justice David Price, and Noel Semple. I benefited enormously during this time from a stream of capable and committed research assistants who have worked with me on one or another of my projects, especially Mackenzie Falk, Tamara Thomas, Gurleen Gill, Erin Chesney, and Lidia Imbrogno, who has helped me bring this new edition across the finish line. And I want to reiterate my thanks to first-edition researchers Hena Singh and Raong Phalavong.

A special thank you is due to Cynthia Eagan, who has edited my blog and other materials published by the National Self-Represented Litigants Project for the past four years. Cynthia has enhanced my writing enormously, and I am the beneficiary of her intelligent, perceptive, and nuanced way with words. Cynthia's edit of this new edition will have also improved the readability and accessibility – and the sheer common sense – of the text. I also want to thank Ann Macklem, my UBC Press editor, with whom it was a delight to work once again.

For their continuing personal support, strategic analysis, and important provocations, I want to call out special thanks to my longstanding colleagues Bill Bogart and John Manwaring. My singularly most important colleague of all is of course my husband, Bernie Mayer. Bernie is the best thinker I have ever known (I mean, I'm always right when we disagree, but he's still a smart guy). Thank you, Bernie, for letting me be me. Without you, I think I might have spontaneously combusted by now.

Finally, I want to thank those who support and nurture me on a daily basis and make all things possible for me. Some of you are my family – my amazing children, Sibyl, Ellie, Mark, and Hopey, and of course Bernie. Some of you make it possible for me to do what I do while you take care of what is beloved to me (Joyce Chapman, everyone at Cidermill Farms, and Lynda Woodison), and some of you are my special teachers (Melodie Queenen, Brendon and Hilary Laing, Jennifer Irwin). All of you are part of my friendship family across the world. As a cancer survivor, I take a whole new meaning from the old adage "I couldn't do it without you."

THE NEW LAWYER

1

Changes in the Legal Profession and the Emergence of the New Lawyer

"You're giving a speech about lawyers and *conflict resolution?* Huh?
I don't usually connect lawyers with conflict resolution."

– Waiter in Vancouver hotel

"The two lawyers were just saber rattling, seeing who
could piss the other off the most."

– Former client, now a self-represented litigant[1]

The disassociation between lawyers and conflict resolution expressed in these two statements reflects a public culture that increasingly regards lawyers as irrelevant to the practical solving of problems, and an individual experience that is unfortunately all too common. Both publicly and privately in our culture, lawyers are more often associated with conflict than with conflict resolution.

There is a growing divide between private citizens and the delivery of legal services. Over the past thirty years, legal services have increasingly focused on corporate and institutional clients, diminishing their relevance for ordinary people with domestic disputes (and without the resources to pay for expert aggression or defence). At the same time, legal aid and public assistance have dramatically declined and now assist only the very poorest in family and civil cases.[2] The disassociation between lawyers and conflict resolution does not work for commercial clients either – those who need to solve their business conflicts without unnecessary expense, delays, obfuscation, and posturing. Spending vast sums of money and scads of time on "fighting" is no longer acceptable to major corporations and institutions. In any case, this strategy was never pragmatic enough in terms of results to be fully compatible with a business culture.[3] The huge costs of protracted litigation and the delays in accessing judicial hearings increase a sense of profound disconnect between what the legal profession offers and attainable, expeditious conflict resolution.

If lawyers do not represent affordable and effective conflict resolution in our culture, then what is their function? What unique services and skills can they offer clients to justify their hourly rate? What value and advantage do legal representation bring? And what is it that twenty-first-century clients want lawyers to do for them? In order to answer these questions, the legal profession needs to adapt to changes in the professional environment – where the frequency of settlement in civil and family cases means a growing emphasis on processes such as mediation and settlement conferencing – and new social and economic conditions in the public sphere.

Prospective clients now have access to the World Wide Web: as one self-represented litigant put it, "Google is my lawyer."[4] Google may not be a very skilled or effective lawyer, but it is a lot less expensive than a "real" lawyer. Numerous studies now show that the cost of legal services is out of reach for many, and an unappealing big-ticket investment even for those with a reasonable income.[5] Domestic clients – accustomed to shopping in the limitless environment of the web – now evaluate legal services against the standard of an expeditious, practical solution at a reasonable cost, and are far less likely than the previous generation to defer to their lawyer's directions. This demand for "value for money" is coming from all client groups, and the phenomenal explosion of access to legal information facilitated by the web sets a new benchmark.

The consequences can be seen most dramatically in the exponential rise in the number of people going to court without a lawyer at their side. Self-represented litigants now account for at least half the docket in many family courts, and 30–45 percent in the civil courts.[6] Many of these litigants cannot afford to even contemplate paying upwards of $350 an hour for legal assistance. Many others reach a point at which they can no longer go on paying for a lawyer, long before their matter is concluded.[7] Spending decisions differ in an era when Internet information is ubiquitous and proprietary information less walled off – there is a new sense of consumer empowerment. Some who may have taken their business to a lawyer – perhaps by using up their savings or forgoing other expenses such as a vacation or a new car – ten or even five years ago now regard legal services as out of their reach.

The New Lawyer of the twenty-first century must find creative, practical, and affordable ways to meet his or her clients' expectations and aspirations. This means a shorter time frame for achieving effective, appropriate, and sustainable outcomes. It means greater transparency about likely outcomes – and more frank talk about what can and cannot be achieved in the current justice system. It means offering the client tangible progress at a suitable price.[8]

Some of the consequences of a movement away from using lawyers include the development of web-based self-help legal services;[9] a larger role for paralegals in areas delegated to them by the legal profession;[10] new interest in "unbundling legal services," so clients can purchase a particular service from a lawyer rather than retain the lawyer for full representation;[11] and a developing market for all types of vaunted "cost-effective" dispute resolution processes, including collaborative law and mediation.

Governments and policymakers have begun to take action. Placing a priority on cost savings and efficiency, jurisdictions across North America have introduced a variety of new systems (e.g., case management) and processes (e.g., mandatory mediation, settlement conferences) into civil and criminal justice systems, many focused on reaching an agreed-upon resolution. Some of these new approaches have been forced on lawyers by policymakers who recognize the inefficiency of a conflict resolution model in which almost everything resolves before trial but only after years of expending money on legal fees and accumulating paperwork, much of which is never used in the construction of a settlement. Increasing numbers of "access to justice" initiatives – such as court-based legal information services and online resources – are being introduced to assist the vast numbers of self-represented litigants.[12]

This book describes and analyzes the changes both inside and outside the legal profession that are driving a transformation in the role of lawyers, the nature of client service, and the fundamental principles of legal practice.

Economic and Demographic Changes inside the Profession

The first site of change for the legal profession is internal. The structure of the profession – particularly its economic footprint, and hence its practice emphasis – changed dramatically over the final twenty-five years of the twentieth century.

An obvious place to begin this analysis is the size of the bar. The number of lawyers has almost doubled in both Canada and the United States since the 1970s.[13] The Canadian bar has grown tenfold since 1951, and it is estimated that the profession grows by another fifteen thousand lawyers every five years.[14]

The Canadian Bar Association recently reported that the number of practising lawyers in Canada is growing at a faster rate than the general population.[15]

The employment market for lawyers is not growing at the same rate, however. The last five years have seen law firm mergers – creating "mega-firms," discussed below – and even firm closures.[16] For the first time in thirty years, new law schools are opening in Canada,[17] but in the United States there is a significant decrease in law school applications due to tuition costs and employment prospects.[18] The likelihood that supply has outstripped demand – at least for traditional "full-representation" legal services priced using a billable-hours model – looms over much of this book's analysis and discussion.

The Rise of the "Mega-Firm"

The practice of law has become increasingly directed to the service of corporate and institutional clients, which reflects the expanding influence of increasingly large corporations, who in turn impel the search for more efficient economic models, such as the increasing "outsourcing" (also known as legal process outsourcing, or LPO[19]) of document review, drafting, and physical appearances at hearings. While sole practitioners are still entering the marketplace, the proportion of practice conducted in larger organizations has risen at a much sharper rate, often at the expense of sole practitioners or small firms that do not enjoy the economies of scale available to larger units. Sole practitioners and small firms now face growing competition in their "core" areas – divorce, landlord and tenant issues, simple wills, and consumer bankruptcies – from a barely regulated market for paralegals, contract lawyers working for low salaries in larger firms, and even from advertised "legal help" services on craigslist.[20]

While much of the data used as evidence of these changes originate in the United States, it is broadly applicable to other common law jurisdictions with similarly developed market models, legal professions, and legal systems. The profession in both Canada and the United Kingdom, for example, has experienced very similar patterns of economic restructuring over this period. Two studies that examined work patterns among lawyers in the Chicago bar have been especially influential in highlighting these changes. The first Chicago study, published in 1975, suggested that two "hemispheres" of legal work were emerging, one related to delivering services to personal clients and the other dedicated to serving commercial clients.[21] A second study, sponsored by the American Bar Foundation and published in 1995, found a similar separation between personal and commercial work, although there was some overlap – for example, a tax lawyer might have both personal and corporate clients – and generally a much higher level of specialization among practitioners.[22] These conclusions were broadly accepted by Canadian researchers John Hagan and Fiona Kay, who recognized that the two hemispheres were typically represented by different models of law firm, with larger firms representing commercial clients and smaller firms or sole practitioners representing personal clients.[23] Most significant is the fact that in the last quarter of the twentieth century the corporate legal sector grew at a far greater rate than the personal sector. In the second study, 61 percent of Chicago lawyers' time was spent on work for corporate clients, compared with 53 percent in the first Chicago study, while the figures for personal client work dropped from 40 percent to 29 percent by 1995.

To meet the expanding demand from commercial and institutional clients, the so-called mega-firm has emerged. These firms can more effectively respond to corporate client needs by offering specialized departments and teams of lawyers dedicated to serving particular clients. The second Chicago study found that the average number of lawyers in a firm had rocketed from 27 in 1975 to 141 in 1995. Ron Daniels and Hagan and Kay have found a similar trend towards larger units and the absorption of sole practitioners in Ontario in the early 1990s.[24] Firms that serve mostly commercial clients can now offer them a range of highly specialized legal services in new or emergent areas that were unheard of thirty years ago, including international trade law, e-law, and a range of intellectual property disciplines. Professional regulators increasingly offer specialist qualifications and designations that recognize areas of special expertise. Law school curricula also offer a larger range of subjects representing many new specializations, especially in business law.

With the decline in their market share and workload, the earnings of sole practitioners have declined significantly over the last thirty years, and the earnings of lawyers (and especially partners) in large firms have risen exponentially. The profitability of larger firms is maintained by the concept of the billable hour; as a result, targets are set for lawyers at all levels, and younger associates in particular are required to work extremely long hours. Competition for the best young lawyers also means that in some cases earnings rise at a faster rate than profits,[25] which simply increases the pressure to bill more hours to make up the shortfall.[26]

The billable-hours model has significant consequences for the culture of the mega-firm. By separating fee generation from salary calculation, the firm establishes and maintains a hierarchy within that is tightly controlled by the partners. Some firms now encourage consolidation of the power of the partners by establishing two levels of partnership – one of which enjoys only limited rights – in order to delay the achievement of full partnership status for associates.[27] Mobility within the firm is difficult other than by embracing the given criteria (not only the volume of billable hours but also the various social requirements, such as client contact and networking).

The dominance of the mega-firm market model within the professional culture has had a profound impact on professional identity. Law students quickly learn to regard articles on Bay Street or a job on Wall Street as the ultimate mark of status and success at law school. However, once they begin working within a large firm, their self-image is often challenged by the realization that the economic conditions of their labour constrain the types of professional autonomy and responsibility for decision making that they assumed would come with the dream job for which they had competed so fiercely. In order to be economically successful within this model, lawyers must also accept significant limitations on their personal autonomy and decision making.[28]

The Rise of Corporate Counsel

Paradoxically, another consequence of the increasing emphasis on corporate legal services in the second half of the twentieth century has been the establishment of corporate legal departments and the emergence of a new professional role: in-house corporate counsel. Almost unheard of prior to the 1950s, the number of in-house positions has grown rapidly and demonstrates the significance large corporations attach to keeping a firm handle on their legal strategies and costs. Where litigation is still contracted outside the corporation, in-house counsel acts as a highly informed client asserting the company's interests. Business analysts agree that the power and prestige of general counsel within any given corporation is greater now than ever before, and reflects a desire to take control over outside legal fees and strategy.[29]

The numbers of corporate counsel appear to be growing at a faster rate than in any other sector of the profession.[30] According to Mary Daly, there was a 40 percent rise in the numbers of in-house counsel between 1970 and 1980, and a further 33 percent rise from 1980 to 1991.[31] Robert Nelson found that the proportion of lawyers in corporate positions had risen from 4.4 percent in 1948 to 9.8 percent in 1988.[32] According to a survey conducted by the Association of Corporate Counsel (ACC) in 2004, there were 71,702 corporate counsel working in 23,540 corporations in the United States. This number represents approximately 10 percent of the total number of practising lawyers in the United States.[33] In Canada, the Canadian Corporate Counsel Association was established as a conference of the Canadian Bar Association in 1998 and now has almost 9,000 members.[34]

A More Diverse Legal Profession

Besides structural and economic changes, the profession has experienced dramatic change in demographic composition during this period, at least at the entry level. Women and minorities are entering law school and the profession in unprecedented numbers, and law school classrooms and associate levels in law firms have taken on a different gender and ethnic composition as a result. For example, in the 1950s just 4 percent of law school entrants were female. By the 1990s, the numbers of men and women in law school classrooms had become virtually equal.[35] Lesser but still significant increases have also been recorded in the numbers of minority students attending law school, which rose from 4.3 percent of enrollment in law schools approved by the American Bar Association in 1969 to 13.1 percent in 1990.[36]

It seems, however, that previously excluded groups have not yet acquired sufficient power to affect the organizational culture of the law firm. Research shows that these newer members of the profession also leave at higher rates than established white males. When they stay, they rarely acquire the power and status their white male counterparts continue to enjoy. Fiona Kay and John Hagan's work has highlighted the marginalization of women in practice, even when they reach partner level.[37] The systemic barriers, including the lack of role models and mentors and inflexible and anti-social working hours, were chronicled in the 1995 report *Touchstones for Change: Equality, Diversity and Accountability*, which concluded that the consequence is a "glass ceiling" in the legal profession for women and minorities.[38] Women are also leaving the profession in greater numbers than men.[39]

This means that despite some efforts at diversification, especially at the level of law school recruitment, the legal profession in Canada continues to be overwhelmingly white and underrepresents minorities. A 2004 survey sponsored by the Law Society of Upper Canada reported that less than 1 percent of the sample described themselves as African-Canadian, South Asian–Canadian, or Aboriginal.[40] It is well known that minority law graduates face greater obstacles to securing articles than Caucasians. Lawyers of colour face many structural barriers similar to those of women lawyers, including a lack of mentoring opportunities and difficulty achieving partnership status. Like their female colleagues, minority lawyers are often marginalized in particular roles within the profession, with an assumption that they will prefer and adopt certain positions.[41] The consequence is that minority lawyers are well represented in legal clinics and government positions, but underrepresented in the megafirms that are the economic engine of the profession.[42]

The structural changes of the last thirty years have profoundly reshaped the business model of the profession. The dominant market model of lawyering is moving towards larger and larger firms, providing increasingly specialized services to primarily corporate and institutional clients, and a growing corporate counsel sector. These changes have transformed the organizational and economic structure of the profession, and helped to shape its practice norms. The limited impact to date of a generation of women and minority lawyers should alert us to an apparent contrast between the relative ease with which the profession accommodates changes to its structure and organization and its resistance to deeper challenges to dominant norms and values.

Changes in Dispute Resolution Processes

A second site of change is the transformation of many civil and family – and, to a lesser extent, criminal – dispute resolution processes that has been changing practice for many, if not most, lawyers since the late 1980s and early 1990s. Pressure for justice reform has come and continues to come from government, from the largely dissatisfied and often disenfranchised public, and from influential members of the bench and bar. Some of the calls are for simplification of procedures; some are for expedited processes and the reduction of delays in reaching resolution. Many are for greater emphasis on early intervention and assistance with resolution, enabling cases that will settle anyway before trial to settle earlier, at lower cost and with less damage to the parties. In 1994, the Ontario Civil Justice Review estimated the cost to each party for bringing a case to trial (assuming three days) in the Superior Court to be $38,000. The average family income in the same year was $44,000.[43]

The widespread introduction of court-connected and private mediation programs, case management, and judicial mediation into courts throughout North America –programs that encourage and facilitate early negotiation and assessment of resolution possibilities – is testament to concerns about costs and delays in justice. Civil and family justice innovations throughout North America, especially over the past twenty years, have focused on changing the procedural context within which settlement might occur, including case management programs (setting timelines, encouraging the early exchange of documents) and court-annexed mediation programs (assigning a neutral third party to facilitate settlement discussions and/or to evaluate potential legal outcomes). As a result, all courts now function differently from twenty-five years ago, with at least some shift towards the judicial management of cases and their settlement.

While settlement before trial has long been the norm, the rate of resolution before trial has risen to 98.2 percent.[44] Even before the initiation of major procedural reforms designed to divert civil cases into early settlement negotiations, the number of full trials had been steadily declining for several decades. Data collected by Marc Galanter show that, in spite of the growth of all aspects of the legal system (more law, more lawyers, more judges, more court personnel, and bigger budgets), the absolute number of trials has declined significantly since 1962.[45] The phenomenon of the "vanishing trial" is not limited to the United States. The proportion of civil cases that proceed to full trial in Ontario has also been falling over the past twenty years. One study using a sample of approximately six hundred cases a year shows that recourse to full or partial trials fell from 4.9 percent in 1973–74 to 3.2 percent in 1993–94.[46] The decline in the number of full trials appears to have had little overall impact on the accumulation of cases on trial lists, however, since, when trials do take place, they are often longer and more complex (using more expert witnesses and taking up more courtroom time).[47]

Outside the courts, some of the most significant innovations in developing early dispute resolution processes for clients have grown out of the dissatisfaction felt by some members of the profession with the frequent inability of traditional litigation to bring peace and closure to their clients. Some sectors of the bar are experimenting with practice models that focus on practical problem solving and have reduced their reliance on complex, expensive, and time-consuming procedures. A few initiatives – such as collaborative law, where counsel is retained only to negotiate and is disqualified from litigating the case, in an effort to incentivize negotiation – have developed out of the frustration of lawyers who want to offer their clients a faster, less expensive, and more pragmatic and realistic approach to conflict resolution.

How This Changes the Lawyer's Role

The shift away from full trials – and the growing importance and credibility of processes designed to facilitate the settlement of issues that are unlikely ever to be argued in a courtroom – has many layers of significance for the legal profession. Recent scholarship examining the phenomenon of the "vanishing trial" has pulled back the curtain on the small amount of time litigators now spend on trial work and opened a debate over academic and professional training.[48] Lawyers and judges are increasingly involved in legal tasks that are not related to trials. Lawyers are offering different kinds of services to their clients and performing different tasks. Some of these tasks, such as negotiating with the other side or providing the written forms of advocacy required for pleadings and other litigation documents, are familiar but acquire new significance in a legal culture that is increasingly conscious of the need to offer practical problem solving and resolution. Lawyers are also spending more time on newer and less familiar forms of advocacy, such as judge-led settlement conferences and pre-trials as well as representation in mediation.

There are more opportunities for lawyers offering services within a different financial structure. Best known among alternative billing practices is "unbundled legal services," where lawyers offer expertise and assistance on an hourly as-needed basis to individuals who will undertake some tasks themselves in order to save money.[49] The closer a matter gets to trial, the more difficult it becomes for self-represented litigants to handle their case alone, yet they often lack the financial resources to pay counsel for full representation.[50] The stress and difficulty of conducting a trial as a person without a legal background is immense, as attested to by data collected from individual self-represented litigants.[51] In some jurisdictions, rules on the appearance of paralegals have been relaxed to enable a less costly alternative to trial representation, whereas in others restrictions remain.[52]

The combination of the decline of the full trial with the development of new processes to facilitate dialogue about settlement (some of them mandatory) has changed the environment within which much contentious legal practice occurs. While the impact of these changes is greatest on civil litigators, it also affects lawyers who specialize in administrative law matters; most administrative tribunals now require or recommend an early settlement meeting, pre-trial, or mediation. In corporate legal services, there is growing emphasis on dispute resolution clauses that enable parties to retain control over future disputing processes, as well as other strategies that anticipate and reduce the costs of future conflict.

Criminal Justice

Reform is also taking place within the criminal justice system. Interactions between the public and the criminal justice system demonstrate similar patterns of dissatisfaction and diminishing trust, and a disconnect between the work of lawyers and the courts and real-life problem solving. There is manifest evidence for the failure of the retributive model to reduce crime or increase public safety in light of recidivism rates.[53] Overcrowding in prisons and inadequate resources for rehabilitation programs mean that incarceration often compounds tendencies towards crime and antisocial behaviours. Disillusionment with the retributive model has led to legislative and other initiatives to encourage restorative justice processes and outcomes that rest on the offender's acceptance of responsibility and agreement to cooperate with a sanctions regime.

As or more important, the criminal justice system is losing credibility as an unbiased and fair means of social control. For example, First Nations people make up 2 percent of the population of Canada but 10.6 percent of its prison population.[54] In the United States, African Americans make up 12 percent of the population and 44 percent of the prison population.[55]

These startling statistics, along with the rise of victims' movements asking for greater involvement in the punishment process, have generated momentum to look beyond traditional models of crime and punishment to community panels, victim/offender mediation, and sentencing circles. In Canada, legislation now places responsibility on criminal court judges to consider the possibilities of a restorative justice process for "all offenders, with particular attention to the circumstances of aboriginal offenders."[56] The 2002 *Youth Criminal Justice Act* introduced a new regime described as "extra-judicial measures," which promotes the use of earlier, preventive alternatives to incarceration for juvenile offenders, where the offender pleads guilty and the victim is willing to participate in a dialogue.[57] Both of these innovations reflect the same trends seen in the civil courts, with an effort to reduce judicial time spent on hearing arguments and a corresponding emphasis on broadening the responsibility of the parties, with the assistance of counsel, to negotiate an appropriate outcome. All of these processes are based on principles of dialogue, information exchange, and agreed outcomes, as are civil justice processes such as mediation and settlement conferencing. The universality of these norms is a reminder of just how closely related some types of criminal behaviour are to civil torts, especially where personal relationships are affected.[58] Just as civil litigators are having their legal practice changed by civil mediation and other settlement processes, so too are criminal lawyers seeing their responsibilities, their relationships with client offenders or victims, and the strategies they may pursue altered by the introduction of restorative justice processes.

How Have These Changes Affected Legal Practice?

How much impact have changes in dispute resolution processes and norms had on the legal profession? Just as we saw in examining economic restructuring within the profession, there is plentiful evidence of significant external changes – in this case, in the ways in which contentious matters are managed by lawyers and the courts. The sheer volume and extent of civil justice reforms suggest that a settlement orientation is here to stay. As well, some evaluation data indicate deeper systemic changes measured by the acceptance of these new processes by both lawyers and their clients.[59] While there is less clarity about the effectiveness of restorative justice programming (e.g., in bringing about lower levels of recidivism), early experiments have produced good results.[60] Some civil and criminal programs have been in existence now for almost two decades, and we are beginning to see the mid-term impacts of an emphasis on facilitating early settlement wherever possible. A deeper level of acceptance and change may be a matter of time.

One conclusion drawn from studies of more established dispute resolution programs is that continued exposure to mediation and other settlement processes, even where these are initially resisted by the bar (especially where they are mandatory), generally builds recognition of the usefulness of the process and commitment to its continued use. Several studies now demonstrate that the attitudes of counsel become more positive with time as a result of repeated experiences with mediation. Some lawyers have even described themselves as "converts" or "believers."[61] In less melodramatic terms:

> My experience has now belied my original idea that counsel can always do this themselves ... I recognize that in some cases what happens would never have happened that way without a mediator ... Without a mediator we often stop [negotiating] on hearing first offers.[62]

Another lawyer summed up what these studies are showing:

> I think it's fair to say that my experience with mediation has improved every time, and I suspect it will continue to improve.[63]

Similar changes over time are illustrated in data on changes in lawyer/ client relationships in settlement processes. What is initially an unfamiliar and often uncomfortable shift in practice – for example, working with clients at the table rather than holding them at arm's length from mediation – becomes more comfortable over time, enabling lawyers to explore its potential benefits. Many find that their commercial clients welcome the opportunity to take a more hands-on and active role in managing the file. Others point out that mediation can provide a welcome reality check for less experienced clients:

Mediation can ... put things into a different perspective, including seeing the shades of gray that were always apparent to the solicitors.[64]

The frequency with which lawyers now encounter various court and private dispute resolution processes is also reflected in cultural norms around a "mainstream" style of practice. Lawyers who are vocal about opposing settlement and gunning for trial are more likely to describe themselves as "dinosaurs," whereas they would once have regarded themselves as part of the mainstream. Related to this, there is some evidence of a growing acceptance of the importance of taking an earlier look at settlement, in contrast to a system where settlement most often took place right before trial, and lawyers who eschew this newer approach feel the need to justify their position.[65]

While these findings suggest that familiarity and experience with dispute resolution is having an impact on professional norms and values, other data suggest that change is still often superficial. In criminal law, attitudes towards restorative justice and the actual use of alternative measures in the sentencing of juveniles and other offenders varies widely between prosecutors and courts. Civil justice reform that does not resonate with the local bar association is often reassimilated into more familiar process models and outcomes (or, in Ontario, "downgraded" to a far less interventionist model that allows lawyers complete control over the timing of mediation[66]). We know that lawyers are critical in influencing their clients' attitude towards mediation or any other mandated settlement process, and in determining the amount of effort and goodwill that is invested in the process.[67] Given the reality that settlement efforts require good faith, and of the influence of lawyers over their clients, it is easy for the claim that these processes are a waste of time to become a self-fulfilling prophecy.

Other strategies for resistance include belittling mediators and other "softies" (colleagues) who are supportive of mediation, using mediation and settlement conferencing to obtain a strategic advantage (such as informal discovery) rather than entering into them with an intention to settle, and "going through the motions" by showing up but being unprepared to negotiate. The creative capacity of lawyers to find ways to frustrate the purpose of mandatory settlement procedures if they are convinced that mediation is unhelpful or useless is apparently boundless. In Ontario, the pioneering early mandatory mediation program (requiring mediation within ninety days of the filing of the statement of defence) has been altered to allow mediation to take place any time before trial, arguably in part as a result of pressure from the bar as well as an under-resourced case management system.[68] Also in Toronto, lawyers boasted openly about defeating the random assignment case management system that existed in the mid-1990s by closing a file that was selected for case management and refiling it in the hope of escaping assignment. It is important to remember that formal procedural reforms are typically driven by legislators and policymakers and only rarely by lawyers themselves. Unsurprisingly, imposed change, such as the introduction of case management or mandatory mediation, has not been welcomed by many bars, which regard such initiatives as encroachment on their professional autonomy.

Other lawyers accept the formal imposition of a mediation consideration but do not see this as having an impact on their practice.[69] There is still a belief among some that they do not need to be concerned about any new knowledge or skills training that might equip them to function more effectively in dispute resolution processes, and law school curricula address these issues only through electives. There is still a widespread assumption that, of course, a law-yer knows how to negotiate or advocate effectively in a mediation or settle-ment conference, without an acknowledgment that this requires a different skill set from appearing in an adversarial hearing. These lawyers do not believe that any special training or the acquisition of new skills and knowledge is necessary to function effectively in a range of dispute resolution processes as well as in traditional adversarial proceedings; indeed, they may not see these as different in any important way.

Some lawyers continue to express discomfort with processes that require a different approach to advocacy and negotiation, that diverge from the trad-itional advocacy skills that they are comfortable with and that have become central to their self-image. As one put it:

> I mean, we're trained as pit bulls, I'm not kidding you, I mean we're trained pit bulls and pit bulls just don't naturally sit down and have a chat with a fellow pit bull, the instinct is to fight and you just get it from the first phone call. I'm big-ger and tougher and strong and better than you are.[70]

Change? What Change?

This chapter invites the conclusion that the legal profession embraces some types of change and resists others. While the profession has historically been adept in responding to changing marketplace conditions, its core norms and values are much more resistant to change. Earlier, I suggested that the continuing difficulty faced by women and minorities in reaching the same levels of status and influ-ence as their white male peers is a good example of the profession's ability to make structural adjustments without challenging or changing internal norms and values. The profession cannot resist the integration of women and minorities, but it can maintain its traditional systems of status, hierarchy, and evaluation in order to keep them "in their place."

Another example of the limits of structural change in altering deeper professional values is the entrenchment of traditional attitudes towards practice, as shown, for example, in the image of the pit bull in the quote at the end of the previous section (or, as one female lawyer put it, "a bulldog with lipstick").[71] The types of strategies and attitudes implied by the pit bull and bulldog analogies are still widely regarded as appropriate and even normative lawyering behaviour – this despite the fact that justice reforms mean that lawyers are increasingly asked to explore an early negotiated settlement through the intervention of a mediator or a judicial officer, and that commercial clients in particular are more likely to press for expeditious settlement in place of protracted litigation.

It is certainly true that problem-solving styles of negotiation are more widely understood and used now than they were thirty years ago. This is in part the result of a growing market for continuing legal education programs and publications that teach models of problem solving and principled negotiation. There is also evidence, however, that the traditional values of advocacy and adversarialism have, if anything, become more entrenched as a result of the increasingly competitive environment of the 1980s and 1990s. Extreme versions of these traditional values are common in larger firms in big cities, which promote competition and believe that they need to cultivate a macho image, particularly for their commercial clients.[72] The consequence is a notable decline in civility and a rise in adversarialism in civil litigation, exemplified by the increasing use of the unfortunately named "discovery" process to delay, obfuscate, obstruct, and badger.[73]

Possibly the most conclusive evidence for the assertion that despite sweeping structural changes, the profession's underlying norms and values remain relatively unchanged is to be found in our law school classrooms. Despite important curriculum innovations – primarily the addition of specialized substantive courses, mostly in the business area but also in human rights, international law, and critical legal theory – the philosophy and substance of legal education, particularly its implicit ideal of what makes a "good" or "successful" lawyer, has been easily sustained without major challenge for the thirty years that I have taught in law schools. There have been some calls for a renewed commitment to professionalism[74] and some work on enhancing the practical nature of aspects of the law school curriculum.[75] However, legal education continues to be focused on the teaching of substantive knowledge, in an adversarial normative framework, and within the dominance of adjudicative decision making. Considerations that are irrelevant to the making and proving of a legal case are ignored, and students are not taught how to assess or deal with such issues – the "client" is a purely hypothetical construct to most law students. The lawyer's "philosophical map" continues to include certain skills, knowledge, and values and to exclude others, and what are included and excluded have remained largely unchanged.[76] Over the past decade, important reports – such as the American Bar Association's MacCrate Report[77] and the Canadian Bar Association's *Futures* reports[78] – have called for change, but despite the repeated calls for a more responsive legal education curriculum, laws schools continue to focus on the "old" skills: appellate advocacy via mooting, and traditional doctrinal pedagogies and assessments. The practice values promoted by legal education in North America continue to emphasize technical skills, client control models, and the discounting of non-legal and emotional considerations in disputing. These remain the profession's dominant values.

In summary, although significant change has taken place in the structural, economic, and procedural character of legal practice, these changes have had far less impact than one might expect on the core practice norms and values or on the ways law students are prepared to enter practice. One can see the impact of a growing focus on corporate clients and the power of the mega-firms in the business orientation of many law school curricula, but this emphasis does not extend to a re-examination of the lawyer's role, and even further entrenches a traditional model of client advocacy founded on argument and assertion. There is a growing disconnect between traditional adversarial advocacy and the pressure to participate in early settlement processes – a tension experienced by many litigators and met with anything from outright resistance to demands for an entirely different approach to legal training.

Despite the speed and scope of change, both internal and external to the profession, there seems to be only patchy interest in a serious mainstream debate over what these mean for the skills and services lawyers sell to clients. Procedural, demographic, and business changes within the profession appear to have had little, if any, impact on the types of practice knowledge valued by the larger firms who serve an increasingly corporate-dominated client base; technical specialist knowledge is still widely regarded as vastly more important than process experience or resolution expertise. At least at the point of hiring, there seems to be little interest in other skills and qualities, such as empathy, wise counsel, creativity, and conflict resolution. In this largely unaltered world, legal education continues to be functionally efficient: the image of lawyering promoted by the law schools fits with the qualities emphasized by many law firms at the entry level.

At the other end of the legal services market, as the gap between those who are eligible for public legal assistance and those who can afford lawyers widens,[79] it may be that lawyers are losing the battle for public regard. Public skepticism about the cost of legal services is now widespread. Historically, negative public attitudes towards the legal profession as a whole – exemplified in lawyer jokes – has been balanced by the fact that most clients report that they are satisfied with their own lawyers.[80] Some have reasonably concluded that there is no apparent threat to the assumptive status of lawyers as the authoritative agents of conflict resolution in our communities,[81] but this may no longer be the case.

A consistent critique is emerging among those who are now self-representing of how they were served by the lawyers whom they had previously retained, identifying in particular poor listening skills and insufficient consultation and transparency over fees and costs.[82] Both developments suggest a widening gap between what the public wants and can afford and what lawyers continue to offer.[83] When they retain a lawyer, clients and potential consumers of legal services have limited information about alternative models of lawyering, such as work based on a limited-scope retainer, legal "coaching," or fixed-fee services. They just know that they want a speedy and affordable solution. A very large number of middle-income litigants are self-representing because they feel that legal representation is too expensive, represents poor value for money, and does not give them enough personal agency.

There are of course exceptions to the largely passive response of the bar to these potentially critical challenges to its legitimacy. At senior levels of the bench and bar, there are individuals who increasingly recognize the need for adjustment and for acquisition of new skills for negotiation, consensus building, and settlement. However, these voices have not yet been able to challenge the traditional benchmarks for what makes a "good" lawyer that law schools and the recruiters continue to use – namely, high grades for memorization in technical courses and success in competitive mooting, rather than strong interpersonal and communication skills or successful clinical experience. At the critical point of entry into the profession, there is a continued failure to recognize the skills and qualities that are needed by a new generation of lawyers in a new environment of dispute resolution, facing a new set of client expectations (including, increasingly, affordability and value for money). The disconnect that occurs once these students become lawyers operating in the real world is plain to see.

The absence of real change in underlying values and norms should not really surprise us. Lawyers are an extraordinarily powerful professional group, whose clients hire them for their superior expertise and rarely question their judgment. Jokes denigrating the profession at large abound on the Internet, but how many clients – even sophisticated ones – can constructively and knowledgeably critique their lawyer's strategy and demand a specific alternative course? As in any professional field sustained by its high social status, much of what lawyers do as a matter of course – diagnosis, strategy, argument, and, eventually in most cases, settlement – has gone unquestioned and unchallenged for decades, despite the possibility of alternative approaches, potential efficiencies, and new ideas.

The Evolution of the New Lawyer

I first argued in the 2008 edition of this book that what we were seeing was the evolution of a new form of lawyering, one that would be more effective and realistic in an evolving disputing landscape in which trials are a rarity. Eight years on, this continues to be my view. However, another, critical aspect of the evolution of the lawyer's role has become increasingly important since the first edition of *The New Lawyer*: how the profession responds to an increasingly empowered client, both corporate and personal.

These clients can access knowledge through the Internet, can carry out some tasks associated with their matter themselves, and are looking to their professional advisers for more than technical assistance or courtroom advocacy. The empowered twenty-first-century legal consumer directly challenges the ingrained paternalism of the profession. Many clients no longer want to be told that lawyers know better what is good for them; they want to be talked to as peers. Many are no longer content with "trust me, I'll take care of it"; they want to know exactly what they are paying for, and why. This decline in deference is a phenomenon not limited to lawyers – it is taking place across all aspects of professional services – but it may be an especially bitter pill for the legal profession to swallow. Status – as an expert, as a person of social stature in their community, and as an earner – is a core element in the identity of many entering the legal profession. The historical assumption that lawyers must "take care of" their clients needs to be replaced with an open, working partnership in which there is full transparency and shared decision making.

What would it take for a new professional identity to evolve and emerge from these multiple layers of change – in the profession's internal structure, in the practice of litigation, and in external conditions (e.g., the Internet-savvy empowered consumer)? What would happen if, in addition to reorganizing the way it does business and manages client files, the profession also examined its core values and skills in light of the changes of the last thirty years?

Rethinking Practice Habits

A prerequisite in any change process is a willingness to take a long, hard look at cherished habits and modes of operation. Many elements of the practice habits of lawyers, like those of any other professional, are fairly routine and go largely unquestioned. Every lawyer can identify some routinized habits in his or her particular practice. Some of these habits relate to negotiation, which is used as a detailed case study in Chapter 3.[84] There are also parallel sets of habits and routines for litigation drafting, courtroom advocacy, corporate deal-making, and so on. Some of these habits are useful, important, and often successful. Others need re-evaluating in light of contemporary conditions. All need to be responsive to the needs of the individual client.

Practice habits arise from, and are sustained by, norms and values that form the ideological backbone of the lawyer's professional identity. These norms and values are in turn sustained by beliefs, many adopted unconsciously long ago. The evolution and modification of beliefs is an incremental process that should continue over the course of an individual's professional life and over the centuries-long development of the legal profession. In order to challenge beliefs, it is necessary first to recognize and understand them. The hallmark of a vibrant and responsible profession is the ability to re-evaluate itself without fear and in anticipation of offering enhanced service.

Re-examining old habits does not mean starting from scratch. Effective representation of clients in settlement-oriented processes require some new "habits" of action and thought, but many of these will build on existing skills and values, including client loyalty, information assimilation, and analysis. The discourse over just what needs to change has sometimes been misleading and even polarizing. A popular expression is "paradigm shift." A call to lawyers to embrace paradigm shift assumes that real change requires the elimination of the old paradigm (characterized by the old lawyer) and its replacement with a new one (the new lawyer).[85] However, many of the traditional tools that lawyers use to protect client interests remain important, for example, the evaluation of possible outcomes, the development of strategy, and the firm assertion of bottom lines (supported by legal advice). The core value of protecting and advancing client interests is not changed by dispute resolution processes that help focus the parties on the potential for settlement.

The introduction of consensus-building processes into legal disputing structures does not mean an elimination of the old system of litigation. Rather, litigation continues to travel alongside efforts to settle legal disputes using settlement processes. Although trial work makes up a much smaller part of legal practice than in the past, many trial advocacy skills are similar to, or congruent with, the skills and techniques that the New Lawyer needs in order to practise conflict resolution advocacy. For example, good litigators are extremely capable of assimilating large amounts of new information, analyzing and synthesizing data, and moving between strategies and options in order to maximize their clients' gains (often by providing expert legal advice). The New Lawyer needs these same skills. But fewer and fewer lawyers are now regular litigators, especially at a trial level. In working towards a just and expeditious settlement, the New Lawyer will be making different choices about what information to prioritize, how to use data (exactly how that information is used), and what strategies are most effective in bringing about a good outcome for the client.

The profession needs to be willing to challenge its present assumptive habits of practice and belief if it is to evolve a new professional identity – the New Lawyer – that accepts and responds to all these new challenges. This includes a willingness to take some risks, to cautiously experiment with new dispute resolution processes, and to consider offering services to clients who may do some of the work themselves and who are, in the spirit of the contemporary consumer, looking for "coaching" rather than directing. These new experiences will in turn lead to a demand for training that meets the challenges of this new environment by addressing the skills and knowledge gap.

Filling the Skills and Knowledge Gap

The way that legal services are now offered as well as demands for further change require new skills and knowledge that those who entered the profession one or more decades ago did not encounter in their own legal education and training. While most law schools now offer some training in dispute resolution – basic negotiation and mediation skills – as electives in the curriculum, many law students still graduate without knowing the difference between a mediation and an arbitration; what it takes to be an effective advocate in a settlement process; the numbers of potential personal clients who are now self-representing in family and civil court; or the range of (fully indemnified) possible retainers that can enable clients to pick the legal services they can afford to pay for.

Some lawyers are especially effective in settlement processes but others come ill prepared and, as a result, are sometimes wrong-footed. The most effective ones can identify special new skills and knowledge – albeit often built on more familiar practices – that are valuable and relevant to them and their clients. Much of this they have developed on a need-to-know basis, having been thrown into mediation or similar processes and discovering that these processes offer a genuine opportunity for advancing client interests:

> My role has significantly changed and now I don't think a litigator can be a litigator without also being a ... person who has advocacy skills relevant to conducting the process of mediation ... How do you do an opening statement? How do you identify issues? How do you know to prepare yourself for what issues you want to give up? What issues do you want to hold on to? How do you best present your client's case? *All of those things are done quite differently at the mediation.*[86]

As yet, relatively little writing or training has focused on the skills of counsel in settlement processes.[87] There are complex and sophisticated skills and qualities involved (e.g., persuasive oral advocacy, effective interpersonal communication, patience and attention to detail, the ability to rapidly assimilate large amounts of new information), as well as new knowledge required (e.g., basic negotiation theory, how to choose the right mediator for your case). Our current understanding of these skills and new areas of knowledge for lawyers is as yet underdeveloped. As the use of settlement processes continues to grow, the expectation and the market value of skillful performance will rise. Similarly, as commercial and institutional clients increasingly look to counsel for advice on process design in large and complex cases, the skills and knowledge associated with dispute systems design will become a commodity of consequence. If obtaining these new skills and the knowledge that underpins them ensures continued professional income and status, then the profession will buy in.[88]

The same can be hoped for new skills and knowledge that anticipate and respond to the expectations and needs of twenty-first-century clients. In order to work with clients as peers and to respect them as decision makers and problem-solving partners, lawyers need to learn to talk less and listen better. Respecting the terms of the new professional "contract" between legal expert and a savvy, sophisticated client will be necessary in order to market legal services. Lawyers may find that they need to take seriously client desires – for empathy, for shared decision making, and for affordable financial arrangements with realistic cost caps – that they may have previously considered an optional add-on.

Changing the Norms of Legitimacy

The ultimate step in any process of change is altering the norms of legitimacy. Here, this means changing our understanding of what "good lawyers" do. In the old model, a good lawyer is a zealous advocate, asserting the best-case outcome for as long as possible, neglecting negotiation and continuing to assert rights claims until a final "compromise" is reached on the courthouse steps. The good lawyer of law school mythology spends every day in appeals court arguing obscure points of law.

Or are good lawyers those who see themselves as conflict resolvers, providing efficient, realistic, principled, and empathetic dispute resolution with constructive and practicable results? Real change follows when these norms change. For example:

> Good lawyers, in this town, understand what mediation's about ... I think that's what is accepted in the system, so lawyers have made the change.[89]

The challenge is to create credibility and legitimacy within the profession itself for both new dispute resolution processes and a modernized lawyer/client relationship. Lawyers who choose to practise in a settlement advocacy model need a supportive community within which to work. One indicator of change would be a situation where lawyers in a community find themselves regularly facing opponents who have a similar level of skill and commitment to engaging in serious settlement processes. Many lawyers presently describe the frustration they experience when a negotiation or mediation meeting reverts to the lowest common denominator – when the lawyer on the other side is poorly prepared, or unskilled, and/or unwilling to take the negotiation process seriously. They cannot gain traction. Exasperation with the predominance of settlement-averse lawyers in their community has led collaborative family lawyers to form their own networks that over time have provided critical mass for their alternative process.

Outside the voluntary networks of like-minded lawyers, a critical mass of support for settlement processes can be achieved only by changing the types of practice associated with good lawyering. This shift may be accomplished faster in smaller communities, where the legal culture is often more cohesive, with stronger prevailing norms and a relatively homogeneous client base.[90] In larger communities, the role of the most influential players in the wider legal community – and their leadership role in encouraging innovation and change – is

Changes in the Legal Profession and the Emergence of the New Lawyer critical. Local professional leaders include not only members of the judiciary but also seasoned litigators.[91]

A similar level of normative change is required to confront the challenges of a new generation of legal consumers, both corporate and institutional as well as personal. Public confidence in legal services and the legal system is at an all-time low.[92] Corporate and institutional clients want to control decision making; experienced commercial litigators have seen this trend coming for many years.[93] So do personal clients, who expect their lawyers to treat them as peers and partners (and not as an ATM) – there is growing public pressure for lawyers to offer affordable legal services. This requires changing the norms of not only how legal services are offered but also who offer them (e.g., paralegals, other specialists).[94]

The New Lawyer

It is more urgent than ever that the legal profession not be passive in the face of these changes. Lawyers and their professional organizations should take a proactive approach to managing the new disputing environment and continuously assessing the need for new skills and knowledge. This includes developing new financial structures that offer affordable services to more Canadians. The profession needs to respond to client expectations for faster, less costly, and more effective legal services, negotiated between lawyer and client and fully transparent in relation to costs.

If the legal profession is to rise to these challenges, it must be willing to reappraise some of its sacred tenets, including the traditional notion of zealous advocacy and the primacy of rights-based dispute resolution processes. Lawyers need to start thinking about the public as "users" who are increasingly participating in legal processes without a lawyer's assistance. They need to view the contemporary consumer as a prospective client and partner.

Which brings us to the need for a "New Lawyer." The New Lawyer will have evolved and responsive professional values and beliefs, and new habits of practice. The rest of this book focuses on three core dimensions of the New Lawyer's practice that distinguish her from the old lawyer.

The first is the elevation of negotiation skills. Lawyers have always negotiated on behalf of their clients, but they have used a model of arm's-length communication between agents using a bargaining dynamic framed exclusively by legal positions. Despite the regularity with which negotiation closes a dispute, negotiation has not been regarded as a primary area of expertise for lawyers.

But negotiation skills are critical to the effectiveness of the New Lawyer, and she will place a far greater emphasis than her predecessors on becoming a good (intentional, educated) negotiator. The old tools of positional bargaining, often ritual bluff and bluster represented by a terse exchange of offers, are ineffective in building a consensus. They are being replaced by problem-solving strategies and more effort to directly include the client in face-to-face negotiation.

Second, communication skills such as listening, explaining, questioning, and establishing rapport and trust have always been important for lawyers who work directly with clients or as oral advocates. In the litigation model, however, effective interpersonal communication takes second place to making substantive and procedural arguments. Courtroom eloquence – the convincing presentation of arguments – has been regarded as the pinnacle of communication. For the New Lawyer, a different type of communicative eloquence is necessary. Interpersonal communication is the primary vehicle for the resolution of conflict, whether through negotiation, mediation, or another settlement process. In this model, interpersonal communication skills have the potential to set one lawyer apart as particularly skillful and ultimately successful. This model also elevates the importance of so-called emotional intelligence, as well as legal knowledge, including attributes such as empathy, self-awareness, optimism, and impulse control – all important qualities in an effective negotiator.[95]

Demonstrating the importance of persuasive interpersonal communication in reaching a good agreement requires paying more attention to what the other side in a dispute needs and wants. One experienced litigator describes this as follows:

> I call it the new lawyering role. You do have to be in tune to the other side's interests. For instance, I've seen counsel do it for a plaintiff in a personal injury action, a lot of it is they just want to be able to look at my insurance client and vent, and money is not always what they want; they just want the other side to feel their pain and to understand what they've gone through. You start thinking about what their interests are, and what they really need out of this mediation and a lot of times it's just that, in order for them to understand or for them or your client just to see the other side and hear their side of story and see what's driving them and their personality. You have to be more attuned to the interests of the parties and what's going on between them.[96]

Third, the New Lawyer considers her client a partner in problem solving, to the extent that this is both feasible and desirable (for the client) in any one case. Ideally, there is a new mutuality of both purpose and action between lawyer and client. The client will participate more actively in planning and decision making, while the New Lawyer will offer a participatory model of compassionate, client-centred, professional service instead of the traditional "trust-me" detachment of the old lawyer. The New Lawyer needs to earn and establish trust with a client who is no longer satisfied with being told to "just leave it to me." This requires good listening skills and genuine empathy. Conflict resolution advocacy accepts the potential for human connection in lawyer/client relationships. The hard lines that have traditionally been drawn around the lawyer's professional demeanour of detachment and even coldness are beginning to blur as power shifts in the relationship between lawyer and client.

This is a new model of legal practice and client service. It should be diverse, responsive to client context, and vigorously debated, both inside the profession and also with the public. The rest of this book examines the challenges of new lawyering in the light of research data from hundreds of interviews with lawyers and clients, as well as with judges and self-represented litigants.

Can the legal profession remake itself as a valued public good, relevant and important to more than a small fraction of the general public? Can lawyers really be conflict resolvers? And can the profession support the development of a new model of legal practice and client service that really embraces change at the deepest level of all – the professional identity of the New Lawyer?

2

The Making of a Lawyer
How Professional Identity Develops

Although well aware of the structural and procedural changes occurring around them, lawyers often seem unreflective about the deeper impact of these changes on their professional role and practice values. Nonetheless, every lawyer in practice has a sense of their professional identity – their purpose, mission, or vocation – which motivates them and gives meaning to their work.

Lawyers also have a set of values and beliefs that guide their practice choices and decisions and that are consistent with their sense of professional identity. Such values are often formed early in personal or professional development, absorbed at an unconscious level from the professional (or family or societal) milieu or "culture." They may go largely unexamined and subsequently unquestioned. For many lawyers, their value system is implicit, buried beneath the decision making of their busy practices. Nonetheless, personal and professional values operate as an invisible and unarticulated driver for their practice behaviours and choices. Whether explicit or implicit, values guide lawyers on how to serve their client, and also justify and rationalize practice and conduct choices.

This chapter examines the origins of professional identity for lawyers. Professional identity is constructed from many sources, some of which are personal (e.g., the influence of family members, life experiences, and role models outside one's chosen profession); some are professional (e.g., working in particular practice contexts, professional mentors, and education and training), and some are both (e.g., professional experiences, participation in social media).

For most lawyers, their professional identity reflects their practical experience of practising law and serving clients. However, the development of that identity actually begins before they practice law or even enter law school. It begins with the narratives and images of lawyers and their work that form part of our public culture. It begins, in short, with the ever-growing collections of "lawyer jokes" that circulate in conversation, and now on the Internet.[1]

The Adversarial Stereotype

The popular stereotype of lawyers focuses on several behaviours: aggressive argument, positional bargaining, formalistic rituals and procedures, and the conduct of a single strategy (to win). Equally important but more elusive are the values that determine (and justify) these behaviours. These include beliefs about the purposes of law, the role of the lawyer, the agency and self-determination of the client, the value of argument and assertion in the resolution of conflict, the potential for interest-based solutions, the extent to which conflict resolution is a public or private process, the responsibility of the individual for the collective good versus individual self-maximization, and many other issues close to the heart of legal practice.

Almost anyone you ask – whether a law student, a member of the public, or a practising lawyer – is familiar with the popular lawyer stereotype. Earlier movie and television images of lawyers were often positive – for example, Atticus Finch, Clarence Darrow, and Henry Drummond.[2] Contemporary public opinion on the subject of lawyers is highly negative; lawyers are frequently characterized as greedy, self-interested, aggressive, and even dishonest.[3] The general dislike that the public feels towards lawyers as a class has historically not been reflected in individual lawyer/client relationships, where evaluations of personal experiences have tended to be somewhat more positive.[4] More recent studies, however, suggest widespread moderate to significant dissatisfaction with legal services.[5]

Whether or not generalized negative stereotypes of lawyers are accurate or fair, they are unquestionably prevalent. Those outside the profession of law have access to ample information (accurate or not) about lawyers, generated by popular culture and headlines, on which to base their assumptions and opinions, even when they have never had professional contact with a lawyer themselves. Judging by the attention paid to lawyers in media and popular culture, the general public has a real fascination with the profession of law. James Elkins, who taught one of the first law school courses devoted to studying lawyers and film, observes that the media's portrayal of lawyers is a "cultural phenomenon – lawyers and law have never been more prominently featured in popular culture (television, movies, novels, journalistic accounts in newspapers, and radio talk shows) than they are today."[6] Some scholars draw a strong correlation between public opinion and public culture, seeing the media as expressing views that are deeply held within the community's psyche.[7] The contrary argument is that media portrayals themselves establish certain stereotypes in the public's mind.[8] In either case, stereotypical images, once solidified by constant broadcast, are highly resistant to change.[9]

The stereotype of the adversarial lawyer – sometimes depicted as having substance abuse issues as well as a susceptibility to depression[10] – also tells the public that this is the type of behaviour that they should *expect* from a lawyer. There is a paradox here. Some aspects of the stereotype – lawyers as fighters who will use their superpowers to win their client's case – are exactly what many members of the public believe they want when they ask a lawyer to help them in a conflict. It is human nature to want to win over one's adversary and not accommodate or compromise, and the adversarial stereotype satisfies this basic need.

This truism helps to explain how the populist stereotype is influential for young people considering entering the legal profession, because the negative stereotype presented by popular culture is open to a more positive interpretation by those who believe they understand the "special" role of lawyers. Students entering law school have often developed their initial ideas about practising law from many of these same stereotypes; the difference is that their image of the adversarial lawyer is the glamorized image of the courtroom lawyer battling for individual rights. Law students tend to see assertiveness rather than aggression, determination and tenacity rather than close-mindedness, entrepreneurial values rather than money-grabbing, and zealous advocacy for their client rather than unethical or even illegal conduct. Positive images of lawyers focus on the determined pursuit of justice by all available means and uncompromising attitudes. These people are rarely "good" in the sense of being well adjusted. Indeed, they are often pictured making "wrong" choices about family and career. However, their drive, tenacity, and determination are depicted as admirable.

This line of characters, beginning with John Mortimer's "Rumpole of the Bailey," continues today with the media portrayals of real-life lawyers like Gareth Pierce and paralegals like Erin Brockovich,[11] as well as fictional superheroes from the pages of John Grisham novels.[12] Positive images emphasize the special nature of lawyering as a tough career that requires a strong personality in order to succeed. These assumptions are evident in legal education, where students are inculcated from the outset with a sense of elitism and are encouraged to be highly competitive. These fictional characters also encourage the belief among law students that their life as a lawyer will be spent in trials, leading to frequent disappointment when they learn that most cases settle.

Lawyers themselves are naturally aware of the prevalence of negative public opinion and of the adversarial stereotype associated with their public image. While rejecting suggestions of dishonesty or corruption, some lawyers embrace these fierce primitive stereotypes, taking delight in describing themselves as a "barracuda," a "bad ass," or a "shark." These lawyers point out that clients seem less offended by aggressive and borderline unethical practices when their own interests are being promoted. Other lawyers actively reject any association with the adversarial stereotype by committing themselves explicitly to non-adversarial forms of legal practice.

The glamour of the adversarial stereotype may be rooted in popular entertainment rather than the reality of legal practice. A reputation for unpleasant and uncooperative behaviour, once made, is difficult to shake off. It affects professional relationships with other lawyers and has more negative than positive consequences. Nonetheless, the stereotype reflects a reality that most practising lawyers both recognize and acknowledge: that lawyers are expected to be argumentative, pedantic, and unyielding, and that many lawyers believe themselves to be well suited to legal practice if they possess these qualities (and, conversely, ill suited if they do not).[13] I am still exasperated by the number of applications to law school that assert that "because" this candidate is aggressive, argumentative, and opinionated, he or she must be a natural fit for the legal profession.

Popular culture may shape initial expectations and career aspirations, but by the time lawyers are called to the bar, they will have been subjected to a far more lasting and significant influence on their sense of professional identity – law school.

Legal Education and Professional Identity

Law school, with its overriding curricular emphasis on appellate advocacy and legal argument, does remarkably little to correct or even modify the images of lawyers presented in popular media. If anything, it revels in the stereotype of the tough, aggressive, single-minded litigator. The glamorized picture of courtroom advocate is rarely challenged in law school – and so the beliefs and values implicit in this image are barely if ever discussed or held up for scrutiny.

Legal education seldom raises issues of professional norms and values in anything other than a formal positivistic frame (i.e., by teaching the rules of professional conduct). Despite its significance in the early development of professional identity, much of what prospective lawyers learn about purpose and mission at law school appears accidental or assumptive rather than an intentional effort to offer some alternate norms for future practice. For decades, there has been a complacent assumption that young lawyers will absorb the "correct" norms and values by osmosis as they progress through law school and into practice.

I have often begun one class I teach to upper-year law students (The Lawyer as Conflict Resolver) by asking students, "What type of lawyer do you want to be?" The first problem is always that they assume the question refers to what substantive area of law they would aspire to practise in – family law, commercial law, criminal law. When I explain that my question implies a much broader and deeper meaning of "type" – incorporating their vision of client service, what they would like to achieve through their practice, and how they hope that their work will bring them meaning – they scratch their heads. No one has asked them this before in law school. The ensuing conversations are always fascinating and energizing – but I often feel that they are too little, too late.

When we do talk about professional identity issues at law school, we do so almost exclusively through the prism of rules (the jurisdictional code of conduct; see the further discussion below). Professional educators caution against assuming that values and a sense of purpose can be simply taught and imposed without any regard for their integration with personal values, especially in a professional environment where the exercise of personal discretion is so central.[14] Leaving out a discussion of personal goals and mores from the development of individual professional attitudes renders any teaching of ethics that does take place even more fragile and superficial.[15] There has been talk of a "pervasive approach" to integrating discussion of professional ethical values and identity into the legal curriculum, but it is unclear that any schools have yet been able to achieve this.[16]

In the hierarchy of knowledge presented by legal education, a low priority is placed on awareness and sensitivity of professional identity and purpose, compared with knowledge of substantive law and procedure. Students are rarely motivated to concern themselves with such questions beyond a formal analysis and what their individual professors are interested in examining them on. Just what "correct" values are can only be discerned by observing what types of law student behaviour bring rewards from the professoriate: evidently hard work, strong and well-researched assertions of positions, a willingness to jump into an argument, deference to professorial opinions, and an appetite for the cut and thrust of student mooting.

That these norms are ubiquitous in legal education appears paradoxical given that many members of the academy strongly reject the assumption that the legal profession rests on a set of universally shared norms and values that law school should promulgate. The recruitment of feminist, critical race, and other critical legal scholars into the law schools over the past fifteen years has impacted law school curricula, including the introduction of both courses and teaching methods that critique notions of universal norms and values. Yet these important hirings and critical curriculum additions do not seem to present a serious challenge to the norms of "good law student" behaviour described above – indeed, they have continued many of the same norms. The focus of critique is generally on the state and society rather than on legal education or the practice of adversarial advocacy. Invaluable though these courses are in broadening the intellectual foundation of the law school curriculum, their critique is often highly abstract and rarely applied to the practice of law itself. The intellectual critique thus generally coexists with an uncritical acceptance of adversarialism as the best approach to conflict resolution.

Law school also encourages certain behavioural norms. The intensity of the law school experience permeates all dimensions of student life, both inside and outside the classroom. Hierarchies flourish in an environment that constantly "grades." Law school students learn that it is important to be competitive, since they are continuously compared with one another (the law school bell curve ranks students in relation to one another, not in relation to what they have achieved).[17] Judgment and evaluation are constants in the law school experience, both formal and informal, which is apparent even in "academic street-corner talk at which one is informally tracked as excellent, good, fair, poor or terrible."[18] As one law student put it, "there are a lot of judgments passed around in the law school, [law school] is a capital for that."[19]

Law students quickly assimilate this norm. One student who was surprised at how guarded her peers were about asking questions or offering answers in class commented that "other students ... told me that in law school you don't let anyone know how intelligent or stupid you are." Any sign of weakness often results in cruel nicknames and teasing or banishment to the "retard room." While one might assume (and studies show) that many students who make it into law school are likely to be highly individualistic and competitive, the acceptance of peer-on-peer competition means that students who wish to reject this model need to make a conscious effort to do so, in the face of an assumption that "real lawyers" will "suck it up."

Instrumental and often condescending attitudes towards clients are also promoted by law school teaching and learning methods. Students rarely discuss conflicts in terms of real people but rather in terms of rules and principles. They are seldom if ever asked to imagine what the clients' goals might be but, instead, to develop a strong legal theory for their case. Law students learn that facts are more important than emotions, and that emotions are a distraction from real lawyering work. What is most important about clients is their potential to provide facts that will fit a theory of the case. The other parts of what they need or may have to say are an unwelcome distraction from the real work of advocating for the "theory of the case."

Legal education is highly efficient at doing what many would argue is its core function – teaching the intellectual values that are congruent with a traditional approach to professional advising and decision making in law. The structure of legal education, particularly its approach to "legal reasoning," where the internal definition of "relevancy" excludes certain types of argument and includes others, reflects the traditional values of rights-based expertise and a complete deference to this approach.[20] The "adversary method" of argument,[21] in which positions have more significance than interests or needs, pervades legal education. In this way, the intellectual focus of legal education once again entrenches a particular system of values and beliefs – one that holds that there will inevitably be winners and losers in conflict and that a good lawyer is always on the winning side – and this assumption goes largely unquestioned and unchallenged.[22]

The assessment model that has been widely adopted throughout legal education reinforces these same values.[23] The most prevalent assessment model in law school is still the "unseen" examination, in which students regurgitate information and sometimes take a position on a hypothetical situation or issue. In line with the dominant values, grading rewards comprehensiveness and persuasiveness (with good reason), but entirely overlooks an analysis of the causes of conflict, meeting non-legal needs, the consideration of negotiation strategies, or any other analysis that fails to adopt the adversarial model. Further examples include the differential valuation of student contributions to class discussion (for instance, "emotional/intuitive" input usually carries far less weight than the "rational/logical" comment) and standards for research papers (valuing the descriptive/analytic over the narrative/discursive). In this way, the culture of legal education emphasizes a particular form of technical knowledge above all other learning goals.

How much choice do law students have in either avoiding or modifying these norms and values? Law students are rapidly assimilated into the culture of law school. The norms are reinforced by upper-year students, who quickly "initiate" first-year students into the appropriate expectations and modes of behaviour. Unless students participate in the assimilative process, they will remain "an out-law, an outsider, a victim until s/he becomes assimilated into the genre."[24] There is extensive documentation of the high levels of stress experienced by law students.[25] High levels of stress make fighting the system even more difficult. The competitive job market may further weaken resistance to assimilation. Standing apart from the competitive culture becomes very difficult when it excludes one not only from the most prized social and economic rewards but perhaps also from any employment at all.[26]

It should come as no surprise that a number of studies show that students typically start law school with idealistic and often altruistic visions but that these decline rapidly.[27] Susan Daicoff reports that personal characteristics that appear to be developed or amplified in law school include a decrease in altruism and an increase in interest in private practice (coupled with a decrease in interest in public service); an increase in cynicism about the legal profession; and an increase in insecurity, defensiveness, anxiety, and sometimes psychological distress.[28]

Communities of Practice

Once out in practice, there are many influences on the young lawyer's professional identity. The first of these is the culture of her own firm or practice environment, described by Lynn Mather, Craig McEwen, and Richard Maiman as a "community of practice."[29] These authors argue that such communities play a critical role in defining professional norms and values via the mediated influence of collegiality.[30] Membership in any one or more of these multiple worlds – for example, a law firm, a practice group within a firm, or the local family/employment/personal injuries bar – contributes directly to professional development "by translating the general and often contradictory professional identities and norms into guiding principles for daily application."[31] Mather, McEwen, and Maiman argue that "communities of practice" are at least as significant in the development of professional identity as formal codes of conduct. A community of practice, sometimes consciously selected but more often simply a matter of chance, will determine the acceptable and unacceptable ways to practise, the appropriate professional goals, and how to relate to clients, set fee levels, establish billing practices, and so on.

An increase in specialization, and the growing divide between larger firms and solo practices gives rise to myriad subcultures and "communities within communities." Any one lawyer may belong to more than one community, but will probably establish a primary loyalty to one in which she is most comfortable. That comfort comes from knowing the rules and expectations of conduct, and there is a predictable nature to professional interactions. Each of these community subcultures has its own norms and values, sometimes described as "local legal culture."[32] Local legal culture is more than simply differences in formal rules or practices. It reflects a "how we do things here" perspective in relation to particular rules and practices. These perceptions arise from local expectations and assumptions – for example, about another lawyer with whom one has worked before (or not), an assumption that a particular judge will be flexible on a particular issue (or not), shared mores on the timing and type of exchange of information, and so on. Approaches to negotiation provide a good example of practice norms that are mediated by the conventions of local communities of practice. Is negotiation in this community usually hardball or cooperative? Does counsel habitually speak privately and frankly with counsel for the other side, and, if so, in what setting, business or social? (Community norms might even extend to attending a particular pub or restaurant favoured by the local bar association.) Are local judicial settlement conferences, mediations, or pre-trials seen as an important resolution opportunity, or do counsel attend simply in order to go through the motions? Can settlement become a subject of serious discussion only after discoveries, or can negotiations proceed earlier?

Practice community characteristics often reflect the size and social relationships of the local bar. For example, in smaller communities, litigators sometimes establish conventions that allow for the sharing of information without unnecessary procedural formalities that may be routinely expected in larger and more competitive bars.[33] The social networking that tends to follow professional relationships in smaller communities provides an incentive to adopt and follow the community norms and may enable them to become rapidly stable and predictable.[34]

In most law firms, practice bars, and geographic legal communities, the norms of expected behaviour are fairly clear (though often implicit), and most lawyers adopt them without question. These norms are critical to professional socialization. For young lawyers in particular, there are costs associated with not following the local norms – more experienced lawyers often act as gatekeepers to more interesting and profitable types of work. Acquiring knowledge about local legal culture is often (and understandably) a higher priority for a junior lawyer than challenging or questioning it. Knowledge of local legal culture, whether it is based on a firm, a practice area, or a geographic region, is what distinguishes an "insider" from an "outsider" – and is an important source of power.

The influence of local legal culture is evident in the continuing resistance in the family bar to providing unbundled legal services to family litigants. Despite research showing that a large majority of family litigants cannot afford extended legal services in a full-representation model, and that many are searching for limited but affordable assistance that enables them to move forward,[35] many family lawyers are, at best, lukewarm towards unbundling, and some are outright hostile. When younger lawyers approach a mentor or senior lawyer with the idea of including limited-scope retainers in their practice, they are frequently discouraged from pursuing this idea. It is extremely difficult for newcomers to challenge what is sometimes presented as the "holy grail" of legal practice – the traditional retainer, full-representation model. As a result, we see growing numbers of family lawyers offering limited services when requested to by a former client, but without advertising this to avoid criticism from other lawyers in their communities.[36]

When a lawyer representing one party arrives from out of town, or a newcomer joins the local bar, the community may take on the role of educating them in "the way we do things here." Lawyers are often very aware of the distinctive norms of their own community of practice. For example, Ottawa lawyers often comment on the different approach to mediation they see when they work with Toronto lawyers:

> Certainly in the Ottawa area I would say that lawyers are much more amenable to mediation and non-traditional court methodology of settling cases now ... I find that the Toronto lawyers in general are resistant – even if you ask the mediators they'll tell you that. They're resistant to mediations, they feel that they can't settle them, and they feel they're unable to put their skills forward and properly advise their clients.[37]

Clients also have an impact on the culture of a community of practice. For example, the orientation and outlook of family lawyers is affected by the high levels of emotion and anger experienced by their clients. As one family lawyer bleakly put it, "you're seeing people at their absolute worst."[38] Constant dealings with highly emotional and angry clients take their toll on family practitioners and result in many "community" strategies to blunt the impact, including an emphasis on remaining detached, the use of (often sardonic) humour, and sometimes a cynical attitude towards marriage and family life.

Lawyers who serve particular client constituencies, especially when these represent a significant proportion of their work, recognize that this may place them under particular constraints or expectations. For example, lawyers working for corporations will be obliged to adopt the "company line" on negotiation and settlement. Some organizations intentionally foster a reputation for being tough and unwilling to negotiate and expect their legal counsel to embrace this approach.[39] Lawyers project an image that – rightly or wrongly – they believe fits with the expectations of appropriate behaviour from their main client group. For example, one lawyer states that

> in my community I see my role as a lawyer as just being a hired gun to take a fight.[40]

Other corporations want legal agents who will embrace a settlement orientation. As another lawyer explains:

> A lot of my clients want to settle. They're business people, they're not litigators ... they didn't choose my profession, they chose theirs. So they want an excuse to settle and if you have mandatory mediation it gives them a reason to continue talking.[41]

Virtual Communities of Practice

Since the first edition of this book was published in 2008, the impact of social media and networking has grown.[42] This impact is seen in law school and in legal practice, as real-time communities of practice based on location are extended into virtual communities, connected by the World Wide Web.

From the moment today's law student is accepted to law school, social media plays an integral role in networking and building an online professional identity. Students "clean up" their existing social media to befit their new status as prospective lawyer – they "untag" old photos, adjust listed interests, and maybe even delete some old statuses or posts. Some students wipe the slate clean by opening new social media accounts.

Their online profile is important as they begin to establish themselves in the competitive environment of law school and to look for work. In 2015, CareerBuilder.ca reported that nearly one in two employers had researched a job candidate on social media.[43] Platforms such as LinkedIn allow students and working users to create professional identities, list experience, awards, interests, and more. Social media allows for a living resume that is capable of constantly being updated and improved. Unlike a traditional resume, tucked safely away in a laptop folder, it lives online for others to see.

In identifying and connecting with virtual communities of practice, lawyers can introduce themselves, obtain information, and assess the practice profiles of others without ever having to attend a networking event. The online nature of these platforms enables lawyers to follow what their colleagues are working on without ever having to have a conversation. As of 2009, over 70 percent of lawyers surveyed had social media accounts.[44]

Life and Practice

So far I have described three important external sources for the development of professional identity. Practising lawyers also bring their personal experiences – their membership in a particular cultural, generational, religious, or other group, for example – to their professional identity, along with their experiences at work. Exposure to clients, cases, colleagues, opponents, and judges inevitably shapes individual values and norms. The range and variety of our personal experiences means that we do not all understand the world in the same way. Instead, we create meaning as we "connect" experiences to what we already know in a process of implicit comparison.[45]

Some lawyers can still recount a life event that took place before they started law school – typically, an experience of a family member with the legal system – that provided the original inspiration for their decision to enter the field. This particular event, while followed by many subsequent experiences (perhaps quite different) and shaped by formal legal training, may continue to contain their deepest attitudes towards law and legal practice. For others, more recent events may have shaped their approach to practice. For example, a large number of lawyers who practise collaborative family law (where the parties retain counsel for the negotiation only and are disqualified from continuing with the same lawyer into litigation) have been through a messy divorce themselves. As a result, their motivation is often to ensure that the experience is less distressing for their clients. As one lawyer explains:

> I went through a divorce myself several years ago, well four years ago, and I just thought it's such an emotional time and I'm suffering so much and I wish that this process [collaborative family law] was available to me ... because I thought this is perfect. Because people are already just haemorrhaging with their

emotions and we're flipping from anger to guilt to sorrow to all kinds of emotions – and I thought why should attorneys get involved and turn these parties into war people, instead of just getting them through the process and the transition period?[46]

The range of disputing processes now available in litigation adds further potential experiences to the development of professional identity. Different processes will raise different expectations about how lawyers play their roles, and offer different models of effective client service. For example, when a lawyer meets with her client in order to obtain instructions to file a statement of claim or defence, her goal is to secure sufficient information to make an arguable case. She also needs to know about any potentially prejudicial information. The lawyer may discuss possible settlement options (although probably not at the pleadings stage), but the assumption is that any negotiations will be handled directly by the lawyer herself. The lawyer can be confident that her relationship with the client is a privileged one, in which she will take information and use it to make decisions in her client's best interests. In contrast, if the lawyer is preparing to involve her client in direct negotiations, mediation, or a judicial settlement conference, her goals and consequently her interaction with her client will be quite different. She needs to ask more questions – in order to gain a broader picture of her client's understanding of the conflict, including issues that may not bear directly on the strength of the legal case – and should review what the client will say at the meeting and what will not be talked about. Lawyers experienced in preparing clients for mediation characterize this dialogue as deeper and broader than the discussion that would precede either the planning of a litigation strategy or preparation of the lawyer to negotiate on the client's behalf. In these and many other ways, professional experiences affect the development of identity.

When lawyers do things differently, their sense of role and purpose inevitably changes also. Social psychologists have long posited a dynamic relationship between changing behaviours and changing values and attitudes.[47] Changing behavioural practices, even by diktat, allows for new and different experiences. This remains the strongest argument in support of mandatory mediation processes, which require lawyers to have experiences that they would probably not otherwise have.[48] Lawyers who have had significant exposure to court-connected mediation (e.g., in Ottawa, Regina, or Saskatoon, or in the United States within the Florida and California state court systems),[49] or family lawyers practising in jurisdictions where family mediation is a regular occurrence, are generally more positive about it than their counterparts with less experience.[50]

An evaluation of the Saskatchewan program uncovered many accounts of lawyers who described themselves as being resistant to the legislature's introduction of mandatory mediation in 1994, but whose views have changed over time. As one senior practitioner put it, "after ten years [since the introduction of the mandatory mediation program in the Queen's Bench], mediation is no longer a dirty word."[51] One Ottawa lawyer acknowledged:

> We've had it [mandatory mediation] 100 percent now since 1 January 1997 so we've been three years into this. So ... a lot of us who do a lot of work have done literally hundreds of mediations ... It's a learning curve about the value of this process.[52]

Mentors

All professions need inspirational role models who can draw new recruits and motivate those who are already insiders. Individuals tend to seek out sources of socialization – they are not passive – and this is especially true of those contemplating membership in an elite profession. For many, the influences they gravitate towards – a family member, a practitioner mentor, a cultural icon, or even a law school professor – draw them towards particular practice goals and values.

In his book *The Lawyer's Myth: Reviving the Ideals of the Legal Profession*, Walter Bennett laments the demise of powerful role models in the legal profession such as the "lawyer-statesman," the lawyer as a "champion of the people and causes," and the lawyer as a "paragon of virtue."[53] Bennett argues that without modern heroes, the profession is doomed to drift without direction. Both archetypal heroes and mentors are crucial motivators who can also be sources of practical advice and encouragement. They also maintain an essential storytelling narrative that transmits professional ideals to the next generation.

What kinds of mentor models are out there for young lawyers? Some might be inspired by Alan Dershowitz, who urges young lawyers to consider that "if everybody likes you ... you're not being tough enough" (from his book *Letter to a Young Lawyer*).[54] The choice of others might be a high-profile litigator who has become wealthy and influential. Still others may look for a more low-key role model who encompasses their values. One student described an important role model thus:

> She is compassionate, understanding and objective. She is a person who I could trust with personal issues but whom I could equally rely on to handle professional problems in a holistic and professional way.

Others go outside the legal profession for their heroes and role models, finding no one within the profession who meets their ideals.[55]

Mentoring has always taken place informally within the legal profession, often with an emphasis on social events and guidance regarding professional behaviours. Several law societies and law schools offer volunteer mentoring programs, but these focus on providing advice on substantive issues. Some law firms adopt strong mentoring systems that pair young lawyers with associates or partner mentors. Equally important today are the informal relationships that are expedited through the use of social media, which offers an easier means of connecting. Social media also opens up a virtual network of other potential "silent" mentors whom the mentee may not know personally but who can be followed on social media in order to gain insight into their practice.

Inevitably, mentoring can be pretty hit-or-miss. At worst, it can be a damaging or disillusioning experience for the mentee. Sometimes a mentoring relationship is little more than a front for exploitation of the junior's work by the senior colleague.[56] Sometimes the "wisdom" that is passed along to the mentee does not appear to meet any standards of professional integrity or respect, and does not invite comment or discussion. A student summering in a large city firm described the most significant moment of his experience as a conversation with his mentor about the fact that a young associate was intending to take paternity leave when his partner's baby was born. The mentor commented that this would be the end of that person's career prospects at the firm. The message to the summering student was clear and chilling. There was no further discussion because the student felt that he could not question or challenge this statement. It may be time for the legal profession to consider a more formal and structured approach to mentoring, including some threshold qualifications and guidelines in offering mentoring in a way that is genuinely altruistic rather than self-serving.

Another concern is the difficulty experienced by women and minority lawyers in finding mentors. These groups are often disadvantaged in terms of patronage and promotion within their firm.[57] This reflects in part the association of mentoring with social settings, which those with family responsibilities or those less comfortable with the particular setting may prefer to avoid.[58] Shortage of peer mentors for these groups is also a reflection of the limited number of senior female and minority lawyers available to mentor their younger colleagues. These groups are already experiencing the pressures of a marginal group in a workplace (typically, to perform better and conform completely) and have little time or energy left for mentoring less-experienced

The Making of a Lawyer

peers.[59] If the potential of mentoring to motivate and guide the development of professional identity for young lawyers is to be maximized, it is important to ensure that opportunities exist for relationship mentoring – and not just for social patronage – for as many lawyers as desire this.

So far, this chapter has considered five sources that influence the professional development of lawyers. I have intentionally left until last an examination of the influence of professional codes of conduct. This is not because codes of conduct are unimportant; however, I do not share the view of some in the profession who may see them as the *primary* vehicle for the development of professional identity (I explain why below).

So what part do codes of conduct play in the construction of professional identity for lawyers?

Professional Codes of Conduct

There is a general sameness about the various codes of conduct for legal professionals operating in common law jurisdictions. The codes that operate in the United States and Canada are similar in language and tone, and historically have in most respects paralleled the conduct rules promulgated by the Law Society of England and Wales.[60]

Lawyers' codes of conduct are underpinned by a set of fundamental and consistent moral values, including the importance of upholding the rule of law, a commitment to integrity in relationships with other lawyers and the courts, and the central value of dedication to clients' interests. For example, each of the many codes that exist in North America includes a statement about advocacy and uses a variety of adjectives to describe the principled stance taken by lawyers towards the promotion of their clients' interests, such as zealous, resolute, fearless, dedicated, loyal, and partisan. Rule 4.01 of the Law Society of Upper Canada's *Rules of Professional Conduct* reads:

> When acting as an advocate, a lawyer shall represent the client resolutely and honourably within the limits of the law while treating the tribunal with candour, fairness, courtesy, and respect.[61]

The original *Canons of Professional Ethics* set down by the American Bar Association (ABA) in 1908 states that

> a lawyer should represent a client zealously within the bounds of the law.[62]

In practice, such general statements of principle are interpreted in different ways by different practitioners, and are always affected by context. When the codes try to offer more concrete and less generic advice, some differences of nuance and emphasis emerge. For example, the Ontario code tries to provide further specific guidance on the application of Rule 4.01 in its commentary section, stating:

> The lawyer has a duty to the client to raise fearlessly every issue, advance every argument, and ask every question, however distasteful, which the lawyer thinks will help the client's case and to endeavour to obtain for the client the benefit of every remedy and defence authorized by law.[63]

The ABA's *1908 Canons of Professional Ethics* has been revised many times over the past century, becoming more detailed and specific each time. In the *2007 Model Rules of Professional Conduct*, an entire section is devoted to an elaboration of the advocacy role:

> A lawyer shall not bring or defend a proceeding, or assert or controvert an issue therein, unless there is a basis in law and fact for doing so that is not frivolous, which includes a good faith argument for an extension, modification or reversal of existing law.[64]

So how do these sample clauses help to clarify the lawyer's advocacy role, a critical component of overall professional identity? A student comparing the Ontario and the ABA codes might understandably ask: When does the responsibility to "advance every argument ... which the lawyer thinks will advance the client's case" (Ontario) become a "frivolous" argument (*Model Rules*)? Further, when the law itself is uncertain, how can one know that one is making an argument "authorized by law" (Ontario) or for which there is "a basis in law and fact" (*Model Rules*)? We can speculate, but in practice the lines are not clear.

Let's add one further example. The Law Society of British Columbia's *Canon of Legal Ethics* offers the following language to describe and explain the parameters of the advocacy responsibility:

> A lawyer should endeavour by all fair and honourable means to obtain for a client the benefit of any and every remedy and defence that is authorized by law. The lawyer must, however, steadfastly bear in mind that this great trust is to be performed within and not without the bounds of the law.[65]

This approach is a little less strident and sets a more positive tone than the earlier examples. However, is it really saying anything substantively different than the other two provisions?

These examples illustrate both the usefulness and the limitations of codes of conduct in establishing a shared understanding of the lawyer's role and core identity. The principal appeal of codes is that they can identify some core principles. The similarity between the statements made about advocacy in each code is an example of a measure of consensus around this core principle. But as the examples above show, there are also nuances and arguable distinctions.

The diversity of individuals who make up the legal profession and the work that they do means that in order to sustain a broad consensus, the language used in codes of conduct needs to be very general and somewhat abstract. When codes start to become more concrete, as in the explanatory provisions quoted above, they inevitably become less consistent and are more likely to raise objections or controversy. Without any direct contradiction between the texts, the Ontario commentary on Rule 4.01, the British Columbia *Canon of Legal Ethics,* and the ABA's *Model Rules of Professional Conduct* each reflect a somewhat different approach to client advocacy.

Practitioners must interpret how such texts relate to their own work. Anthropologist Clifford Geertz describes the given rules and texts as the "material" elements of a practice culture, which he contrasts with the "immaterial" elements – the precise meanings and interpretation given to the norms by the individual players.[66] Lawyers understand their advocacy role within the context of their clients, their practice, and the forum – an administrative tribunal, a motions hearing, a mediation, or a negotiation – in which they are acting as advocates. Since codes describe absolutist rather than contextualized standards, they tend to be highly non-specific and subject to multiple interpretations.

The ability to use personal judgment and discretion in interpreting rules is a core value for non-routinized professions such as medicine, engineering, and law. "Good judgment" is a frequently cited characteristic of those lawyers who are widely admired by their peers. The exercise of discretion itself rests on often tacit beliefs about appropriate professional behaviour. However, most codes of conduct for lawyers – in contrast to those of other professions – do not describe the role of discretion in professional decision making, and instead maintain the fiction that the rules will suffice.[67] For example, a code of conduct may articulate a procedural basis for when to terminate a relationship with a client, but is less concerned with criteria for making that decision, any significant contextual factors, or the value implications of different decisions. These are serious limitations when – as in legal practice – ethical dilemmas characteristically arise from the management of human relationships rather than from procedures (e.g., accounts auditing) or events (e.g., trading in insider information). Ethical dilemmas that arise in the course of managing client relationships are both difficult to anticipate and subject to numerous contextual variables, which often render codes of conduct and general rules less than helpful. Codes also provide little or no guidance on how to resolve tensions or conflicts between different rules (e.g., the rule on confidentiality and the lawyer's duty to the court).

Furthermore, it is obvious that knowledge of the rules contained in codes of conduct does not guarantee good behaviour. Donald Schon warns about the distinction between "given" or stated norms of conduct and how lawyers actually behave.[68] Knowledge of a generalized formal rule may replace the process of individual reasoning and the weighing of alternatives until the moment when an intuitive and immediate response is demanded. Research suggests that the existence of formal codes of conduct may limit or inhibit individual reflection and reasoning about moral problems by limiting assessment to whether or not a formal rule has been broken.[69] Instead of exploring the moral basis for decisions, a lawyer is more likely to take down the code of conduct and try to "look it up."[70] In essence, codes are more significant in theory than in practice and may be a poor substitute for "real thinking" about the development of professional roles and identity.

Because of their absolutism, codes are also limited in assisting with the identification of new and emerging dilemmas for the profession as a result of changes in practice. A later chapter in this book will explore the emerging ethical dilemmas that are part of the movement towards a settlement-oriented model, as well as a consequence of the larger and larger numbers of litigants who come to court without counsel. Current codes offer limited guidance in both these areas of rapid change.

All the influences on the making of a lawyer described in this chapter deserve to be taken seriously. A hard look at the sources of lawyer socialization is critical to the future of the legal profession and should be a subject that concerns law schools, bar associations, and lawyers' organizations, rather than simply being left to chance. In legal education, this means confronting the more damaging and inaccurate stereotypes of so-called good lawyering, and providing alternatives. Instead of allowing law students and young lawyers to unconsciously absorb any number of influences, there should be an effort to assist them with the conscious development of role identity, including a discussion of how this can continue after they have completed their formal training.

The impact of communities of practice and varieties of personal experience are often highly significant in the professional development of a young lawyer. The more structured opportunities there are for reflecting on these influences and for gleaning the lessons for future practice, the more self-aware, open-minded, and ultimately sophisticated we become about professional identity, role, and purpose. Mentoring is an important means of encouraging such reflection, and higher standards should be expected throughout the profession. Finally, codes of conduct are an important, but insufficient, element in the construction of professional identity, values, and norms. They certainly have symbolic importance in setting benchmarks and parameters for appropriate conduct. At best, codes may provide a common set of fairly anemic values and a starting point for thinking about ethical choices, but they offer little in the way of operationalization of these values as behaviours.

Despite the myriad influences on young lawyers as they develop a sense of professional identity, my research with lawyers over twenty-five years suggests a set of core beliefs and attitudes that are held – admittedly along a continuum – by most practitioners. The next chapter describes three key beliefs that have historically been front and centre in the lawyer's professional identity, and asks whether these should be re-evaluated in light of the changing conditions of legal practice.

3

What Lawyers Believe
Three Key Professional Beliefs

What core beliefs are promoted and sustained by the socialization of young lawyers? In order to be a legal profession "insider," what norms of behaviour are expected? What, if any, tacit consensus exists over the fundamental principles of lawyering? And how do these beliefs reflect and reinforce underlying values about the role of law and lawyers?

Even as significant changes take place – in the business structure of legal practice, the composition of the profession, and legal procedures – and as pressure for improved access to justice stimulates debates over new models of legal services, a handful of broadly recognized values continue to dominate the legal culture. The sources of professional identity described in the previous chapter coalesce to promote and reinforce a set of core beliefs about the practice of law. These beliefs enjoy widespread acceptance among lawyers and are well defended against revision and renewal.

This chapter describes three of these core beliefs – which I identify, by default, as rights-based dispute resolution, an emphasis on justice-as-process, and the assumption that an expert (the lawyer) will guide and direct a novice (the client). I shall show how these beliefs flow naturally from the present structure of the legal system, and are sustained by a set of assumed values about the role of law and the responsibilities of the legal profession. They have been constant in legal practice for a long time, at least since the professionalization of legal services and the opening of law schools. At the same time, I shall evaluate the signs of erosion of these dominant values, modifications, and even alternate beliefs.

Articulating the core beliefs that have underpinned the practice of law for so long offers some insight into the challenges facing young lawyers who have inherited these values and norms, and now must manage change while trying to meet the real needs of their clients. The core beliefs were established long before the changes in the legal environment described in Chapter 1 came about, and appear in many respects to be out of step with the new disputing culture and contemporary client expectations. Despite this disjuncture, the core beliefs continue to be reinforced in some communities of practice and mentoring relationships – for example, discouraging young lawyers from offering unbundled legal services – as well as in legal education (where the "lawyer-in-charge" model is frequently offered uncritically). Certainly some communities of practice – for example, the collaborative law movement or lawyers committed to "mindfulness" in their practice – explicitly offer an alternative view of the core values and beliefs. Despite these minor rebellions, a set of foundational beliefs remains solidly established at the heart of legal practice – beliefs that express the purpose of the practice of law and against which all other beliefs and practices are still compared.

A Common Core

Clues to the common core of what lawyers believe can be found in the most common, oft-repeated mantras of legal practice and legal education. Examples include "thinking like a lawyer" (translation: examining a conflict in a logical and technical fashion through the lens of legal rules); "my clients wants his day in court" (translation: I am pursuing a rights-based claim and am not interested in negotiation); and "the only thing I don't love about legal practice is the clients."

The empirical basis for "what lawyers believe" as described in this chapter comes from analysis of data I have collected through hundreds of interviews with lawyers, as well as many hundreds of hours of professional training and observation. But they are neither scientific nor uncontentious. Making an argument for a set of dominant values for legal practice in all its diverse forms inevitably involves generalizations and simplifications. I do not assume that each and every member of the legal profession subscribes to these beliefs to the same degree, or holds them with the same depth of conviction. An attempt like this one to extrapolate core beliefs cannot possibly account for the multiple variations in the way in which these beliefs may be interpreted and applied by individual practitioners and their communities of practice. This range of influences inevitably produces nuanced individual "takes" on the core mission of the profession.

Despite individual idiosyncrasies and variations among local legal cultures, there are common threads that link different communities of practice and the lawyers who practise within them. The result is less than universalism, but neither is it a diffuse collection of unrelated values and norms. Identifiable differences between "arenas of professionalism" such as substantive specialization, client base, firm culture, and the culture of the local bar association are generally maintained within a limited spectrum of alternatives.[1] The extent of digression from the core beliefs is carefully contained. The core beliefs represent the mainstream, and determine what is an "outlying" (or aberrant, deviant) position.

The common core of what many lawyers believe also represents a force for stability – a level of coherence that may be essential to maintaining a unified profession. To a large extent, our values have been barely revised or challenged since the formal establishment of the profession almost two centuries ago.[2] The most important and fundamental is a belief in rights-based processes of dispute resolution.

The Default to Rights

First introduced in law school, am unwavering belief in the primacy of rights-based conflict resolution is reinforced by most communities of practice and memorialized in professional codes of conduct. Rights strategies are characteristically presented as the default approach that a competent lawyer should adopt. In this model, there can only be a winner and a loser.

The default to rights means that the heart of lawyers' work (and, before that, their education in the law) is rights-based research and advocacy. Despite the fact that most cases will in fact resolve short of a full adjudication, preparatory work and communication with the other side is focused on claims of legal entitlements and defences – a sort of endless rehearsal for a show that will probably never open. Moreover, there is a disconnect between this model and many client goals and interests (such as expeditious resolution, relationship preservation, and the potential for pragmatic trade-offs). So what is its appeal?

Rights, Rules, and Expertise

Given the structure of the North American legal system, with its hierarchy of courts, system of precedent, and vast volumes of primary and secondary sources for legal argument, it is hard to imagine a more functional core belief for lawyers

What Lawyers Believe

than the primacy of rights-based advocacy. Western justice systems emphasize an individualist approach, in which the rights of the individual will be recognized and upheld, or the converse, in which the individual will be protected against the oppressive assertion of the rights of others (including the state).[3]

This commitment to individual rights means that the primary responsibility of lawyers is the furtherance of their clients' goals framed as legal ends. These legal goals are understood as principled and legitimate and sustained by moral rationalizations. Strong advocacy is therefore equated almost exclusively with a strong assertion of positional arguments over rights claims. This belief both flows from and sustains the substantive knowledge base of legal education and training.

Similarly, the focus on rights sustains substantive knowledge of law as the key expertise lawyers offer clients. For advocates to function effectively within a rule-based system of dispute resolution, they must focus their energies and talents on convincing decision makers – real or imagined – that they have the stronger rights-based argument. As one lawyer put it, "It's just brain power in a particular niche, in our case it's litigation ... we're just salesmen, in our case, brain salesmen."[4] Because the eventual "winner" will be the party whose arguments are judged – formally or, more often, informally – to be the most compelling, breadth and depth of legal knowledge are critical to expertise and winning (or getting the better deal in a settlement). Regarding negotiation and settlement through the lens of rights-centred expertise places little value on communication skills, rapport building, or creativity. The most frequent use of rights-based arguments is in beating down the other side and carving out a settlement. Law school continues to focus on the development of substantive expertise, with barely a passing glance at effective negotiation strategies or other "person" skills or problem-solving approaches.

As Richard Bell points out, "to have bought into rights language is to believe that power can be counterbalanced by power."[5] Because the navigation of a rule-based system requires substantive (technical) expertise, outcomes are always vulnerable to subversion by a more powerful and better-resourced party. This party can choose to use their resources to purchase superior legal expertise, which will enable them to impose their will on the other party by persuading them that they can best them at trial. This reality is echoed in the following statement by a litigator:

> Remember our job, our duty is to our individual clients to fearlessly assert the
> clients' rights – and if we have a client where they have more economic might

or other weapons in their arsenal, they (can) win or prevail just as they do in the business world, over people with less weapons and a smaller arsenal.[6]

The volume of litigants now proceeding without legal counsel makes this power inequality even more dramatic. As studies begin to emerge comparing outcomes between those with and without counsel, they point to markedly different results for those without legal representation.[7] This is discussed further under justice-as-process, below.

"A Matter of Principle"

Focusing on a rights-based analysis assumes the essential moral basis of any conflict. Once the conflict becomes "objectified" in this way (sustained by an appeal to moral standards claimed to be "objective"), it becomes inevitable that the aggrieved party will press his or her moral claim.[8] This is one of the most seductive aspects of rights-based approaches for clients, who want nothing more than to be told that they are wholly "right" and that the other side is wholly "wrong." A natural tendency to elevate our conflicts to the level of "a matter of principle" is further aggravated by a model that holds out the potential of moral victory to every disputant.[9] Focusing on rights raises the stakes for clients, whether or not they realize this, by offering only two possible outcomes: winning or losing. Obviously no one – no lawyer and no client – wants to be the loser.

When the moral language of legal arguments becomes attached to a conflict and transformed into a fight over rights, it often obscures or disguises the underlying issues. We are accustomed to this transformation, and accept the disguise in many cases. The moral appeal of claiming that one's conflict is a matter of principle is highly seductive. But lest we forget, while any particular outcome can always be advocated as the most expedient, the most logical, or even the most fair, not every conflict can plausibly assert the moral superiority of a particular resolution. For example, "When IBM and Xerox square off against each other in court over the issue of controlling shares of some market in computer hardware, the issue of justice may be very remote. The battle is a cold-blooded struggle over resources."[10]

"Real" Lawyering

Rights-based approaches often go hand in hand with declarations of machismo and strength. Successful marketing strategies promote lawyers as "fighters," "warriors," and even "sharks."[11] The (sometimes explicit) claim that this is what "real" lawyering is all about is still not commonly challenged, either in law school or in legal practice. As a consequence, for many lawyers a rights-based approach is less about situational appraisal – assessing a particular case as best suited to a rights-based strategy – and more of an ideological approach that they are unaccustomed to questioning. Lawyers working as mediators, collaborative lawyers, and others who focus less on rights and more on negotiating among needs and priorities may be derided as having "a soft, dreamy approach to the world."

> There are a lot of lawyers who probably shouldn't be litigators because they don't grow up before they get to court and they get too nervous, they don't like it, they don't want to put in the time because going to court takes up a tremendous amount of time – you work night and day when you're in trial.[12]

In the characteristic single-mindedness of adversarial rights talk, there is no midway point in the making of arguments. Rights claims are never asserted as "maybe" or "perhaps" we will win, or "maybe" or "perhaps" this is the best strategy for you, but are always put forward with unwavering certainty, even when counsel knows better – for example, when business factors favour the pragmatic resolution of a long-running stalemated dispute, or family ties make preserving relationships and saving face a higher priority than winning. In a rights model, every other approach, including business experience, is "soft."

> I'm the softy of our litigation group. I think it may be because I've got more of a business-type background.[13]

The pervasiveness of this attitude and the widely accepted focus on rights-based conflict resolution mean that for many lawyers, an adversarial approach to client advocacy is the most comfortable place for them to situate themselves. Younger and less experienced lawyers also say that in "proving" themselves, it is expected that they show themselves to be "tough" (positional and unyielding over rights).[14] No one wants to be called out as a softy.

Challenges to Rights-Based Conflict Resolution

How far is a default to rights being questioned by a new generation of clients and lawyers, and by the fact that the vast majority of cases will settle before trial?

In reality, many disputes that are brought to lawyers do not require, and may even be unsuited to, a rights-based solution. Many conflicts are precipitated by incompatible aspirations involving access to finite resources, principally money. And in fact they may easily and perhaps unnecessarily escalate when viewed exclusively through the prism of rights.

Disputes also become significantly more difficult to resolve once a series of (rejected) rights claims have been traded back and forth. Notwithstanding the push towards institutionalized and sometimes mandated settlement processes, the undertow towards stalemate is a profound limitation for rights-based dispute resolution. Once made, positional statements are hard to rescind without appearing weak. After the lawyers' original assurances of a merit-based argument – often taken to heart by clients when it may more accurately reflect a best-case scenario and a heavy dose of wishful thinking in the first client meeting – clients are frequently baffled and even resentful of later admonitions to settle. The extreme likelihood of a negotiated accommodation before trial means that clients are set up for disappointment when their "strong case" (as originally appraised by their counsel) is almost always ultimately compromised in a negotiated settlement. This will look and feel to clients like capitulation, and even betrayal.

A tendency among lawyers to assimilate the arguments they advance on behalf of their clients may have contributed to their overly optimistic view about the likelihood of success, having been convinced by the brilliance of their own argument.[15] There are many dangers with this when it comes to managing clients' expectations and meeting their needs. As one senior litigator reflected:

> There's a tendency in our profession to go from step to step without standing back, taking an overall look at what's this all about, and what does the client hope to get? One of the single biggest criticisms of lawyers that I would make as a result of that is that they have not been realistic with their client as to what their client is going to get out of this litigation.[16]

Overreliance on a rights-based approach carries the risk of blindness to alternative strategies. Many disputes can potentially be resolved by a negotiation to divide the resource "pie" (e.g., money, influence, status, and market control) among the parties. There are no outright winners, but the loss of moral vindication may be replaced by closure, an end to a significant financial cost, and at least some of what had been wanted in the first place. Collaboration over solutions also allows for solutions that "expand the pie"[17] – for example, by generating solutions that have value to one or both sides but that fall outside what is formally claimed; examples include future business arrangements, apology and acknowledgments, or the bestowal of some other valued outcome by one party on the other. These and many other options for resolution may be important to the client, but an exclusively rights-focused strategy will limit these opportunities and may ultimately disappoint. Moreover, even the "winners" may ultimately feel disillusioned when they receive their final legal bill.[18]

Access to Justice and the World Wide Web

Having the best and the most costly legal counsel and the means to conduct extensive investigation and discoveries obviously makes a big difference to one's chance of success. Having no counsel at all often places a litigant at a significant disadvantage.[19]

On the other hand, open access to the resources of the World Wide Web means that some aspects of legal expertise are now accessible without a lawyer. In the age of the Internet, being a "brain on a stick" (as one lawyer once memorably described his role to me) is an incomplete professional role for a lawyer, rapidly being replaced by Google. At the same time, simply giving individuals access to legal information does not help them with its complex comprehension and application. Nor does Google allow access to the cultural dimensions of navigating the legal system – what some self-represented litigants call "the club" of legal representation.[20] Many self-represented litigants describe how frustrating it is to realize the limits of legal information without the context or background to explore and apply it to their own conflict.[21]

Despite these limitations – by the end of their experience, few self-represented litigants would prefer Google to a real-life, affordable, competent lawyer[22] – the World Wide Web and the glimpses it affords into a hitherto inaccessible world has ignited a public pushback against lawyers as the gatekeepers to a rights-based system. In addition, the development of new legal technologies – platforms for accessing and sharing information, digital communication, global outsourcing of legal tasks, online filing – is disrupting the old system that lawyers are accustomed to.[23] Access to legal knowledge changes everything for members of the profession as well as for the public. A closed system has just become an open one.

None of this is to say that a right-based model deployed by experts is not an essential component of access to justice. Despite its limitations, the rule of law requires the possibility of a rights-based process for dispute resolution.

Adjudication according to rules is an appropriate approach for dispute resolution over "public goods"[24] and a critical way to both reinforce and extend principled protections and entitlements. The problem lies in the belief in the universal application and superiority of rule-based adjudication, which makes advocacy via rights claims a dominant value for lawyering practice. The New Lawyer needs to recognize the limitations of an overreliance on a rights-based approach. Rights-based processes and strategies will continue to be crucial to the services offered by lawyers, but they should not, and in practice cannot, be the sole or default approach. Rights-based processes should never be an ideology ("I always go to court/fight to the last ditch") but rather a chosen, intentional strategy in particular cases. As a default, rights-based conflict resolution is insufficiently practical, responsive, and affordable to meet the need of contemporary justice system users.

Justice-as-Process

Sustaining and reinforcing the dominance of rights-based approaches to conflict is a set of values that assume the authority and respect associated with the formal legal process. These values are in turn sustained, at least historically, by a belief in the ultimate fairness and impartiality of the justice system.

A belief in the inherent fairness of the legal/judicial process is widely shared among lawyers as well as deeply embedded in public attitudes towards the legal system (more on this below). A strong consensus has been established over centuries among lawyers over those elements of process that are necessary to ensure fairness and thoroughness in the search for truth in both civil and criminal processes.

For example, Thomas Church found significant agreement among prosecutors and public defenders over case disposition (whether or not a trial was necessary).[25] In contrast, he found clear disagreement between prosecutors and defenders over sentencing norms, but these differences are easily explained within the pattern of role and traditional adversary theory – that is, prosecutors ask for harsher sentences than defence lawyers.[26] What is interesting about Church's work is that it shows that despite disagreement over substantive issues like sentencing outcomes, there is widespread consensus among both prosecutors and defence counsel over what constitutes procedural fairness. Different actors within the legal system have different roles to play, but they appear to share a basic moral and practical commitment to the system of justice itself.

One way in which we see this consensus continue to operate – minor incremental changes aside – is the unity of the profession in opposing significant procedural rule reforms and simplifications.[27] Despite the efforts of numerous commissions and task forces to propose measures of rule reform and simplification, relatively little has been accomplished. The story of rule reform in British Columbia – where recommendations for process streamlining, the greater use of judicial case management, simplifications of certain procedures (e.g., discovery), and the development of information hubs for the public were intensely resisted and eventually defeated by the Trial Lawyers Association of British Columbia – is a case in point.[28]

So just why does justice-as-process remain a core belief for lawyers?

Predictability and Control

In order to understand this preoccupation with process, it is important to recognize that legal procedure is the only aspect of justice seeking, and the only part of the client experience, that lawyers can manage and predict with some certainty – in a way, legal process is the only certain "product" that a lawyer can "sell." A few might argue that this control is being eroded by the introduction of mandatory mediation and an enlarged role for judicial case management – underscoring the strong sense among lawyers that they should be in charge of procedural matters.

All other aspects of the system can be anticipated but not controlled – for example, a loss at trial or a compromise in settlement, an unsympathetic judge or a dilatory and hostile opposing side. Thus, for many lawyers, it is their commitment to legal process and procedures – rather than the actual outcomes of legal action – that is the practical realization of their commitment to "justice." In this way, lawyers appear to understand process and procedure as the central public good of the legal system.

At law school, what seems important is that the final result – generally presented in the form of an appellate court decision – is "fair." In practice, most cases do not end up in appellate court. In fact, most do not end up before a decision maker at all. As law graduates move into practice, they realize that the uncertainty and ambiguity that characterize adjudication, especially at the lower court levels, make a reliance on outcomes as a measure of justice a risky proposition to sell to their clients. Instead they promote and defend justice-as-process.

One lawyer explains:

I really believe in justice. I think it's an indispensable part of the process, but I don't think of results as justice. I think of process as being a just process. If somebody wants to settle a case for a five-year deal in carrots, then so be it. If that's what they wanted I can't say that that's not just, if they've had a fair hearing or they've had a fair mediation if the process is just. That's where I attach the word justice.[29]

The formal adjudicative system and its procedural rules are widely regarded by lawyers as being inherently fair and equal – or, more simply, tried and tested and the best that we have. Each step towards reducing complexity and the central role of judicial discretion in applying procedural rules is met with concerns that this will reduce the fairness and safeguards of the process.[30] Detailed procedural rules and regulations (civil, family, criminal procedure) require every disputant to follow the same steps – filing requirements, timelines, and appearances – in pursuing or defending a claim. This notion of procedural equality is sacred to the adjudicative system, which assumes that a significant component of fair process is the sameness of procedures for each disputant.

Faith in justice-as-process, rather than in justice as a particular substantive outcome, is an extension of the belief in rights as a means to resolve human conflict. Whereas justice-as-outcomes is both abstract and subject to uncontrolled variables, justice-as-process is a concrete, rational, and more reliable means of advancing or defending a claim because it rests on the procedural integrity of the system that makes the "same" formal demands on everyone:

I think it's an enormous mistake to confuse a procedurally sensible, reasonable, system with a fair system of justice. Justice is not a concept that can be measured by meanings ... to measure justice you must take certain values and apply them to ... the procedural system. You may well have a system that leads to a result quite appropriately but that is not just according to the abstract criteria of justice.[31]

Given these realities, following through on a clear and predictable process is more sustainable for lawyers than an abstract commitment to justice in terms of results. This expectation – if lawyers take the trouble to explain it – is also more realistic for clients, who of course come to lawyers bent on achieving a substantive "justice" outcome. Practitioners know that even the best legal arguments can be defeated or an unforeseen challenge made – and that unexpected and uncontrollable variables can disturb what they might consider to be the "right"

What Lawyers Believe

outcome. Many also recognize that even a good legal result at the end of a protracted process may be less beneficial for their client than an earlier settlement, which would reduce their costs and shorten their involvement in litigation.

Some lawyers do a better job than others in describing this reality to their clients and evaluating the potential of the legal system to offer "real" or "ultimate" justice. A fascinating example of this discussion is seen in the interaction between a divorce lawyer and his client recorded and analyzed by Austin Sarat and William Felstiner. The client wishes to secure a restraining order against her husband.[32] In his effort to explain to his client the inherent uncertainties of the legal system and how they might affect her case, the lawyer describes an experience he had in the past where a restraining order was granted in apparently inappropriate circumstances by an inattentive judge. The lawyer tries to redirect the client to a discussion of what demands they might make in a possible negotiated settlement. The client keeps coming back to the question of the restraining order, confused and alarmed that an injustice was done in the case that the lawyer described. Sarat and Felstiner observe:

> To the client, "justice" demands that the error of the restraining order be righted. For the lawyer, *that kind of justice* [emphasis added] simply gets in the way of what for him is the real business of divorce: to reach a property settlement, not to right wrongs or vindicate justice. There is, if you will, a particular kind of justice that the law provides, but it is not broad enough to include the kind that the client seeks.[33]

Eventually the client "gets it," saying: "As you say if you want justice in this society, you look somewhere other than the court, I believe that's what you're saying."[34]

Lawyers can manage their clients' expectations by replacing an aspiration for a particular outcome with a commitment to steer them through the (complex, impenetrable, formalistic) legal process that they must navigate. Lawyers offer clients a process (which in practice might be disturbed by multiple variables, including the attention span of the judge and the personal relationship between the judge and the lawyer) and not an outcome. In this way, lawyers project their own commitment to process, rather than to certain outcomes, onto their clients:

> I attempt to find a way of developing a person's expectations, so that they will in the end feel that they've got justice. Usually when I do that, I achieve those

expectations, and once they achieve those expectations then I think they feel they've received justice.[35]

This lawyer appears to be saying that clients should trust the process, as managed by their lawyers, to produce fair results.

Procedural Justice

Research on procedural justice examines how process affects perceptions of outcomes, especially in terms of fairness and inclusivity. In its simplest form, this research is highly congruent with lawyers' belief in justice-as-process. This corpus of work suggests that the experience of *how* a result is reached is often as, or even more, important than the substantive "rightness" of the outcome itself in fostering a sense of fairness or justice among participants. So, for example, in a properly conducted democratic election, the result will be far more acceptable to those voting for the losing candidate than if they discovered that there was evidence of electoral fraud or simply mismanagement.[36]

The work of John Thibaut and Laurens Walker has established (and later studies have confirmed) that perceptions of fair treatment are as important as outcome when disputants appraise dispute resolution processes.[37] While there is an intuitive relationship between fair process and a favourable outcome, this work indicates that these judgments are substantially independent.[38] One study even suggests that procedural fairness is *more* significant than distributive fairness (i.e., outcomes) in determining the attitudes of litigants towards the courts.[39]

Lawyers might argue that their belief in justice-as-process reflects the importance of procedural justice values for their clients. However, lawyers are differently invested in the value of legal process than their clients. Having been trained in the legal model, they are comfortable with formal procedural rules. There is a strong consensus in legal practice, created in communities of practice over decades if not centuries, that centres on the formal rules of procedure (on the other hand, we often see practice communities resisting procedural innovations that offer flexibility with less clearly stipulated "rules," such as mediation and settlement conferences). Lawyers are familiar with the legal processes and procedures they use every day and can confidently counsel their clients about the procedural steps that lie ahead of them. However, lawyers' commitment to justice-as-process may place them in a parallel universe, because their clients as well as many self-represented litigants, will often find the same procedures confusing, inexplicable, and unfair. I return to this problem below.

There are other problems also.

What Lawyers Believe

Challenges to Justice-as-Process

The Superficiality of Formal Equality

Formal equality in legal procedure is a limited means of ensuring fairness. In practice, procedure can be used to great advantage by those with greater resources, knowledge, and staying power, and defendants represented by superb criminal lawyers may be acquitted more often than those defended by duty counsel. Even fair and reasonable procedural rules raise a risk of exploitation by those with greater power and resources, just as substantive rules raise the risk of manipulation.

This problem takes on even greater significance in light of the large numbers of individuals who lack legal assistance and who are entering the labyrinthine pathways of the courts alone, often making mistakes and finding themselves overwhelmed with elaborate procedural requirements. Initial development of resources to assist those without counsel – such as guides to procedures, court form instructions, and online legal information – reflects a failure to understand the experience from the perspective of someone with no legal background and training. The National Self-Represented Litigants Study (2013) found that such resources were almost always inadequate to enable self-represented litigants to understand enough about the procedure to be really effective.[40] The study concluded that

> SRLs who anticipated that the proliferation of on-line resources would enable them to represent themselves successfully became disillusioned and disappointed once they began to try to work with what is presently available on-line. In particular, they identified the following weaknesses: an emphasis on substantive legal information and an absence of information on practical tasks like filing or serving, advice on negotiation or a strategy for talking to the other side, presentation techniques, or even legal procedure; often directed them to other sites (sometimes with broken links) with inconsistent information; and multiplicity of sites with no means of differentiating which is the most "legitimate."

Substantive equality for those without counsel is further reduced by the culture of procedural tactics, widely practised by legal counsel and not regarded by them as inconsistent with justice-as-process. Procedural tactics are simply the way the game is played. Procedural rules and regulations set the scene for many skirmishes as each side struggles to use the process to its tactical advantage. Despite the efforts of codes of conduct to set limits on "sharp practice,"[41] it is normative to use such tactics to one's advantage wherever possible – for example, taking advantage of an expired time limit for filing, moving to strike a claim before critical information can be obtained, or using mediation as "a fishing expedition."[42] There is a broad tolerance for these and other forms of procedural "gaming" as long as they fall within the given norms of the community of practice – and those without lawyers are not part of this community.

Justice? What Justice?

Reflecting procedural justice research in other areas of public participation, researchers describe a number of procedural justice values that appear to be important to those using the court system. These include the importance of "voice," seeing one's perspective recognized in any decision making, whatever the outcome, and a minimal level of comfort in one's own role in the proceedings.[43] What procedural justice theorists term "decision control" requires some level of direct client involvement, such as planning, anticipating, strategizing, or reviewing options. Some writers highlight the importance of a feeling of control over the outcome – or at least a sense of personal agency – as well as the potential to accurately anticipate outcomes.[44] Related to this is the need to coordinate experience with expectations, including expectations that are the result of subjective evaluations of outcome (usually provided by counsel). Finally, a number of studies of the experiences of litigants emphasize the importance of being treated with respect and dignity.[45]

The problem with claims that lawyers and courts can offer clients quality procedural justice experiences – a positive experience of justice-as-process – is immediately apparent. Even where lawyers do a good job of managing client expectations by discouraging them from overanticipating certain outcomes, there is still the problem that procedures may not "feel" fair. Where a poor job is done of managing client expectations, or where clients feel left out of decision making by their lawyers – both experiences commonly reported by clients[46] – the disconnect with a sense of procedural justice is clear.

Whereas earlier studies have reported high levels of satisfaction with respectful treatment by judges and courts,[47] this may be challenged by growing public skepticism about the role of the courts, judges, and lawyers. "Diffuse support" – the perceived legitimacy and credibility of the courts in the eyes of the public – may be declining, especially among those who come to court alone and often feel treated disrespectfully and harshly by judges and others.[48] As a consequence, perhaps the most important challenge to the concept of justice-as-process comes from the growing divergence between what lawyers understand and accept as "fair process" and the experiences of both represented and self-represented litigants. Unlike some lawyers, clients and self-represented litigants are not sentimental about the "good old days" (when the legal process was more widely respected). They are not as invested in the idea of the legal system as lawyers and other justice system professionals are, and often complain of feeling disempowered, confused, and frustrated.

Settlement Processes and Justice-as-Process

For many lawyers, their commitment to justice-as-process does not include a commitment to settlement processes. They may be especially resistant to processes in which their clients will directly participate, such as court-ordered mediation, and judge-led settlement conferences). Their belief in justice-as-process, and their commitment to a rights-based model in which they are the expert, does not include a role for clients.

Even when clients do participate in settlement processes, the results are mixed in meeting their procedural justice needs. Certainly some clients attest to a positive experience. One client described his experience of mediation over child access this way:

> I walked out as a big fan ... You control your own fate there whereas if you stand in front of a judge for an hour, they don't really know you, they are deciding between two lawyers – this was far better for (X) and far better for us.[49]

However, other research suggests that even when they are directly included, clients do not always have an opportunity to participate fully. Nancy Welsh notes that "disputants in consensual processes often do not perceive themselves as wielding real control over outcomes achieved in those processes."[50] Lawyers often continue to play not just a lead but a dominant role in settlement meetings, and in some cases do little to prepare their clients to contribute to a mostly legalistic discussion. Traditional adjudication may appear more familiar to clients looking for justice-as-process – especially one-shotters – than more informal procedures such as mediation or settlement conferencing.[51]

It is questionable whether the profession's faith in its idea of justice-as-process, and its place as a core belief in legal practice, can survive the transformation taking place in the legal system as more and more litigants come to court without counsel. Can a belief in justice-as-process provide a credible alternative to justice-as-outcome that will persuade the public that it can continue to believe in justice? Compare these two comments, one from a litigator and the second from a self-represented litigant, on the nature of justice:

> Justice has nothing to do with it. I'm sorry – that may sound very jaded – but in my view, as I say to my clients, there's only one person who dispenses justice, (and) he doesn't live on this earth.[52]

> No matter how right your cause is, you do not get the justice you deserve because it is about your resources.[53]

Lawyers in Charge

> Look, we're big people and we can settle the darn thing, what do we need a third party for and why do our clients have to be there?[54]

This statement reflects the sense of entitlement held by some lawyers that their training and expertise allow them to assume authority and a large degree of autonomy in decision making. In this quote, a third-party mediator and her clients are regarded as being unnecessary, irrelevant, and possibly obstructive to her task. While this may be an extreme statement, there is a pervasive assumption in the legal profession that things "go better" when lawyers can work together without their clients "in the way" or "getting emotional."

The third belief that has become a core, unifying value for the legal profession is that their expertise means that lawyers are "in charge" – both of the lawyer/client relationship (expert/novice) and in the management and direction of the case. Few lawyers would say this out loud (the opinion above may have been unguarded but honest). In ethics classes, law students are taught that final decisions are always the purview of the client (on their "advice"). Once they begin to practise, however, those working with corporate clients and repeat players quickly learn that these clients are sensitive to staying "on top of" how their matter is progressing. If they work with personal clients, they are also likely to experience higher expectations of how involved clients should be in decision making than they were prepared for at law school – particularly in relation to understanding how their fees are being spent. Contemporary legal clients of every type are now accustomed to gathering fast and easy second opinions on everything via the World Wide Web. This single fact has dramatically altered consumer culture in professional services.

Despite these changes, a persistent air of paternalism and "we know best what is good for you" continues to dominate the legal culture, as if suspended in time. Clients who want to be closely involved in the development of case strategy and who may question or even sometimes reject their lawyers' advice are still universally regarded as troublesome – life is generally smoother if the lawyers can sort things out between themselves (as the opening quote in this section illustrates perfectly).

Douglas Rosenthal's now classic work on the dynamics of lawyer/client decision making suggested two models of lawyer/client relations: the "traditional," in which the client is passive and the lawyer is fairly autonomous, and the "participatory," in which the client plays a more active role. Rosenthal's analysis suggests that the passive client, the one who follows the lawyer's instructions and is detached from the problem-solving process, is the conventional model, and that departures from this norm – for instance, clients who want to participate actively in anything other than the established areas of client input – are seen as aberrant and even disruptive by many lawyers.[55]

Rosenthal's study is now dated but its conclusions still ring true. Many contemporary clients describe this attitude in their lawyers, and while some may be content to relinquish direction to their counsel, many more are uncomfortable with the assumption of lawyer control over *their* matter. From the National SRL Study:

> There was a general feeling among many self-represented litigants that their former lawyers did not listen to them, either disregarding their specific instructions or, more commonly, not paying attention to what was really important to them. At minimum the narratives of these respondents suggest that their lawyers were not effective (perhaps did not give sufficient time to) explaining and evaluating different strategies with the client as a full partner in that discussion. Instead the lawyer appeared to the client to disregard their views and focus on taking charge.[56]

Even if lawyers have not significantly changed their attitudes about being in charge since Rosenthal conducted his study in the early 1970s, their clients have. Tolerance among clients for the lawyer-in-charge model is far lower now than it was then. While historically many clients chose to nominate their legal representatives as both managers and agents in disputing,[57] sophisticated commercial clients, and especially repeat players, are far less prepared to be passive and are more inclined to assert their wishes. Whereas domestic clients may have once been more passive,[58] they too are now increasingly likely to assert their needs, wishes, and concerns. Some of the many reasons for the client rebellion against the lawyer-in-charge model are examined below.

But first, just as we did with the first two core beliefs, we should ask why the lawyer-in-charge model continues to exert such a strong hold on lawyers, including those just graduating from law school.

Training Experts

The roots of assumptions about power and control in the lawyer/client relationship lie in the epistemology of law school and professional legal training. The model of knowledge promoted in legal education views technical expertise as the single most powerful and significant element in the professional relationship, to the exclusion of all other elements of professional service (e.g., communication, empathy, and problem-solving abilities). Legal education, in common with many other professional disciplines, continues to focus on what Donald Schon calls a "technical-rational" model of knowledge.[59] To be an "expert" in a technical-rational model requires the ability to implement the goals of the client via a legal strategy – by default a rights-based strategy – as determined by the application of the lawyer's legal knowledge to the client's "story."[60] Other types of skill and competence (negotiating skills, interpersonal communication and rapport building, empathy) appear unimportant and even irrelevant.

This culture also affects how lawyers understand their role in relation to other conflict professionals. Partnering with and referrals to other professionals are at best regarded as secondary. Even when there is collaboration with other professionals, such as in a multidisciplinary collaborative law model, lawyers still generally expect to be in charge.[61]

The technical-rational model in professional education was functional and sustainable for as long as the professional adviser remained the sole gatekeeper to the area of specialist knowledge, and therefore the most powerful person in the professional relationship. But this is no longer the case. The fact that their clients can now access legal information via the World Wide Web – and even use legal databases such as CanLII[62] – is not something that lawyers' legal education has prepared them for.

Limiting the Lawyer's Role

In a traditional adversarial model that centres on substantive legal advice – even the ubiquitous "taking instructions" actually often means telling clients

What Lawyers Believe

what is best for them – the lawyer's professional role is limited to that of technical expert. This role definition limits the intrusion of emotional and other less predictable dimensions of conflict resolution into both decision making and the lawyer/client relationship, and sets down clear boundaries in that relationship.

The extent of commitment to the "brain salesman"[63] model is reflected in attitudes towards other tasks and skills. For example, talking about the lawyer's counselling role almost always provokes the comment, "But we're lawyers, not therapists." In this way, the lawyer's primary function is as a technician rather than as a counsellor or, to use Anthony Kronman's analogy, as the predictor of weather patterns.[64] Similar discussion of the need for lawyers to be empathetic is often met with derision and an assertion of the boundaries described above.

By the time many young lawyers enter practice, they have spent three to four years being educated in law without any significant experience of clients. Clients are rarely, if ever, mentioned in law school classrooms; they are invisible as real or even straw people. It is not surprising, then, that the arrival of real-life clients who are experiencing anxiety, uncertainty, and fear of conflict is an unwelcome intrusion for many. In a law school class, I once sent a group of students to interview a "client" actor as he was sitting and weeping in an office. The students immediately returned to me horrified, saying that they had no idea what to do. They understood their role as providing legal advice (in this simulation) and not as offering Kleenex or understanding the impact of the matter on their client. For many lawyers in practice, the detached "lawyer-in-charge" model appears much more attractive than trying to be a "counsellor," a task for which we equip graduating law students with few tools, if any.

Dispute Ownership

A rights-based model of dispute resolution assumes that lawyers acquire some form of ownership – and not simply stewardship – of their clients' conflicts as a consequence of their professional expertise. This is especially apparent where the relationship is understood as being one of expert/naïf, which is usually the case for a first-time client. There is little for the client to do other than place himself or herself in the lawyer's hands. A rights-based paradigm reinforces this attitude because it identifies the lawyer as a technician "fixing" the problem by applying the law.[65] As William Simon describes this model of advocacy, "the litigants are not the subject of the ceremony, but rather the pretext for it."[66] One client described the process of "interviewing" prospective legal counsel as follows: "A lot of lawyers told me what they wanted to do as if it was *them* making the decision"[67] (emphasis added).

This assumption of ownership by lawyers is both practical and emotional. Only certain types of client input – those deemed to be relevant to building a strong legal argument – are sought. Where other issues, such as a client's emotionality or sense of urgency, intrude, the message is that these fears should be assuaged and controlled so that the lawyer can get back on track. The widespread resistance to the intrusion of emotional issues into the management of a file is epitomized by the quip, "The only thing I don't love about legal practice is the clients." Like the most enduring jokes, this comment is not without candour. There is an underlying belief that clients are secondary to and ultimately detached from their legal problem – or, put another way, that the job of the lawyer is to deal with the legal problem rather than with the client.

Challenges to the Lawyer-in-Charge Model

The lawyer-in-charge model may still be firmly entrenched in the culture of legal practice, but it is a belief destined to become extinct in the face of societal changes in consumer values. As litigation wanes in its attraction to commercial clients and is replaced with strategic approaches to negotiating resolution, and as personal clients feel increasingly empowered by greater access to legal information via the World Wide Web, lawyers can no longer assume the traditional relationship of expert/naïf. Both commercial and personal clients are coming to expect not only technical legal advice but also assistance with negotiation, strategic appraisal of options, and practical problem solving. These same clients also expect to be more involved in the progress and perhaps the conduct of their case, and are far less content than in the past to hand over control to the lawyer and sit on the sidelines. Some clients will always prefer to have their lawyer take on their problem for them, but increasingly New Lawyers are finding themselves negotiating a working partnership with their clients, rather than being able to assume the traditional lawyer-in-charge arrangement.

The increasing unaffordability of legal services for most personal clients, combined with the demise of the assumption that the lawyer must be in charge, has resulted in a growing call for limited-scope services in which lawyers will "coach" sometime clients, sometime self-represented litigants to take forward their own cases as much as possible. The demand for this type of unbundled legal services, where the lawyer works with the on-again, off-again client on discrete tasks (for example, reviewing a document or preparing the client for a hearing) rather than completing assigned tasks more autonomously, is driving

What Lawyers Believe

the development of a new conceptual framework for "legal coaching."[68] Legal coaching is an important manifestation of new consumer expectations about both the lawyer/client relationship and its costs.

The World Wide Web

The single most powerful change agent is almost universal access to the World Wide Web. Access to the web has transformed the power relationship in many professional services. Consumers want to see what their money is buying in a tangible, results-oriented frame. Mystifying legal bills are no longer simply paid but increasingly questioned.[69]

Web-based resources have created a culture of "disintermediation"[70] – doing it yourself and cutting out the "middle guy" (realtor, investment adviser, travel agent) – which is changing the way virtually all personal services are now marketed and delivered (with law being a rare exception). Consumers see the information they can gather for free on the Internet as a substitute for expert advice. There is a proliferation of self-help approaches to, for example, financial investment, house sale and purchase, and even legal services (self-representation). Moreover the desire for value for money[71] leads to the view that anything that appears to be accessible via Google is not worth paying for. This results in a different equation of "affordability" – paying for a lawyer to represent you is no longer essential, especially if it means sacrificing many other things, but instead is weighed against, for example, an overseas vacation, a college fund, or a new car.

Client Dissatisfaction

A number of consistent themes relating to dissatisfaction with their lawyer's handling of their case are emerging from research with personal clients.[72] These include dissatisfaction with sharing decision making; insufficient attention to settlement opportunities; and a general feeling that nothing very substantial is resulting from the expenditure of a large amount of money.[73]

Some clients who bring their dispute to a lawyer feel that their original problem becomes transformed into something they do not readily recognize, moulded into a "stock story" via a statement of claim or defence.[74] The burning issue that originally belonged to the disputants, both intellectually and emotionally, becomes detached from them on both levels when it is placed in the hands of a legal representative. This leads to a sense that the lawyer is not really "on their side," or that the lawyer "does not get it" – a disconnect that sometimes persuades clients to stop paying for a lawyer and try to represent themselves. One self-represented litigant who had previously retained a lawyer until he ran out of funds described this as follows:

> [They] did not want me involved in the case ... they wanted to ensure that they would do it their way, and my input would be not a significant part of the case.[75]

This assumption of control contributes to an "empathy deficit" that sees some lawyers operating in a universe of technical-rationalism that seems unconnected to their clients' real interests.[76] Limited to the role of technical expert, lawyers often neglect to pay attention to their clients' practical goals and emotional needs. In fact, this is not what their clients really want from them in many cases. An American Bar Association survey found that many clients felt that their lawyers – especially litigation counsel – often acted unempathetically and in an uncaring way towards them.[77] It may come as a surprise to some, but "what clients want most from their lawyers is a sense that they really care about them and their problem."[78]

Despite significant consistency in client complaints about lack of communication, empathy, and action,[79] there is a significant disconnect in practice. Few law firms have a system for systematically gathering and channelling client feedback to lawyers (another sign of presumptive paternalism). Even if regular client feedback were built into the process of file management, questioning or challenging the lawyer's approach is fraught with difficulties in a model that assumes that the lawyer is the most powerful player in the relationship. Moreover, the inevitable risks and uncertainties of litigation (which only the lawyer can really assess) make it possible for the lawyer to justify almost any decision or choice of tactic.

Other Sources of Client Power

Default to a rights-based strategy has historically enabled lawyers to assert the power of their expertise, no matter how powerful or wealthy (or knowledgeable in another area) their client is. There is growing evidence, however, that high-profile and high-billing client accounts can assert their own forms of social power.

In relationships with commercial clients, particularly those who account for a significant percentage of the lawyer or firm's business, lawyers often feel they have limited autonomy in exercising personal judgment or discretion or in making a decision about whether to take on a file in the first place. In a

What Lawyers Believe

Chicago study, John Heinz and Edward Laumann asserted that there was an inverse relationship between client status and lawyer autonomy.[80] Robert Nelson and others have since shown that lawyers working for corporate clients frequently experience a reduced sense of personal autonomy and decision making. Nelson's study of corporate lawyers in four large Chicago firms found that lawyers rarely refused a client assignment, and even smaller numbers of individuals turned down a file because of personal values or principles, for example, refusing a client assignment for personal reasons. Many lawyers felt that they had little or no control or influence over the choice between different strategies on a client file.[81]

Domestic clients engaging a lawyer for one time only do not have the same monetary power in the relationship as repeat corporate players, but they have other ways of asserting their power as consumers. There is growing recognition that the complaints of many domestic clients that their lawyers did not listen, that they did not receive service that reflected their original expectations, or that they were not billed transparently demand the attention of the profession. While these dissatisfied customers still largely feel powerless (there is also widespread dissatisfaction with lawyer complaints systems), there is greater attention in the media to access-to-justice issues that often focuses on problems with private legal services. In another sign of the incremental erosion of the lawyer-in-charge model, the profession is forced to defend itself against an increasingly vocal critique of many of its core services and assumptions.

Role, Values, and Resistance

However much comfort lawyers find in the familiarity and sometimes self-serving nature of the three key beliefs, without re-examination and some modification they seem inadequate to meet the challenges of legal practice in the twenty-first century.

Nonetheless, these beliefs appear highly resistant to change. This is obvious if one attends a handful of law school classes, observes a series of client consultations, sits in on a partners' meeting in a law firm, attends a professional conference, observes a pre-trial hearing or settlement conference or even a mediation – or goes for drinks with a group of lawyers at the end of their day in the office. The three beliefs described in this chapter are very much in evidence in each of these settings, largely unaltered by shifts in client and societal culture.

Perhaps as a reflection of this paradox, growing numbers of lawyers are talking about the disconnect they experience between the contemporary culture of the legal system and their personal beliefs. Legal education and the traditional values of legal practice have conventionally forced a separation of personal and professional values, with personal beliefs usually subsumed within overriding professional duties (such as the right of representation, the obligation to follow client instructions, and so on). Law school has traditionally discouraged students from concerning themselves with the relationship between their personal moral values and the values they adopt in pursuit of justice for their clients.[82] Personal moral scruples are discouraged or even derided as "soft," a message reinforced by the adversarial culture of legal practice. Instead, lawyers are excused from any feeling of moral responsibility because their choices and actions are necessary to "play the system" for their clients.[83]

More lawyers are starting to question the assumption that they must acquiesce in this moral bargain. A desire for the realignment of their personal values with their professional ones is a constant theme in research conducted with lawyers who decide to move to a collaborative model of family practice.[84] For example, some collaborative lawyers are highly sensitive to what they see as the inevitability of adversarial behaviour and hurtful consequences in the traditional litigation model, and their discomfort with being drawn into this situation. Some of them complain that the adversarial system distorts their personal value system. For example:

> It's about winning. And you don't care. I'm a pretty moral person but in the old system you want to win for your client and that's it.[85]

> I would find myself encouraging ... grossly inflated and unrealistic expectations on the part of the client as you prepare for trial. You file settlement conference statements that ask for the moon and stars because you know you're only going to get a half to a third of what you ask for so you have to do that ... You're taking a complex life situation and you're reducing it to cartoon characters of black and white.[86]

As a result, growing numbers of lawyers are actively seeking alternative ways to practise law that are more congruent with their personal values and original goals. This is evident in networks of lawyers considering holistic practice, the application of therapeutic jurisprudence, and other non-adversarial approaches to the practice of law.[87] Others are choosing to leave the profession altogether.[88] The emphasis on a narrow technical role, while still appealing to some, and the diminution of autonomy undermine the potential for fulfillment and satisfaction and may account for disillusionment among some lawyers, who find that the expectations of practice that were encouraged in law school are not realized within these professional structures.[89] There appears to be a diminishing sense of pride and purpose among some of those entering legal practice, and a lack of realization of the ideals that originally motivated them to go to law school.[90]

Growing criticism of legal services and of lawyers has prompted a somewhat defensive backlash in some parts of the profession. Instead of exploring what clients really want from them, professional organizations tend to trivialize criticism as a culture of "lawyer hating," exemplified by the proliferation of "lawyer jokes." Others in the profession are beginning to express real concern about the failure to provide legal services in a way that ordinary people can both afford and value. Much of this debate centres on how to provide affordable legal services to those who do not qualify for public assistance but who cannot realistically commit thousands of dollars to paying for legal representation; the group that is stuck in the middle, without services, comprises an increasingly large proportion of the general public. These discussions are overshadowed, however, by the widespread retention of traditional models of legal services, including the retainer model, the billable hour, and the full-representation model.

The disconnect between the profession's core beliefs, changes in the external environment, and clients' expectations is a symptom of a wider malaise – a stalled and outdated concept of professional identity. Lawyers need to be able to make sense of change in a way that is congruent with their perception of their skills and expertise and that enables them to establish a sense of purpose. They need to listen to the public and consider new models for delivering legal services. They need to identify and develop new areas of skill and knowledge that build on the old, just as the evolution of the modern legal profession builds on 150 years of legal practice.

The next chapter explores what this disconnect looks like in practice, using an activity that all lawyers engage in – the conduct of legal negotiations – as a case study. It describes how the three key beliefs interact with the traditional structures of legal negotiations to produce highly inefficient negotiation norms and practices. It goes on to propose a realistic and responsive approach to legal negotiations that rejects the constraints of the three key beliefs and enables New Lawyers to properly serve their twenty-first-century clients.

4

Legal Negotiations

The conduct of legal negotiations offers a case study for how the three key beliefs – a default to rights-based conflict resolution, justice-as-process, and the assumption that lawyers are in charge in the lawyer/client relationship – are translated into everyday choices about counsel's behaviour and practice. These beliefs underpin behaviours, since norms, or standards of behaviour, derive from beliefs and values.[1]

The structure of legal negotiation – taking almost every case to "the courtroom steps," where it is then settled by discussion between agents – is consistent with the assumptions of an adjudicative system that frames every move in litigation as a rehearsal for trial. This pervasive assumption that each case must be handled as if it is going to trial is memorably summed up by Marc Galanter's description of negotiations over litigation as "litigotiation," where negotiation is the real, but secondary, work of the litigator.[2]

"Litigotiation" is a structural and conceptual creation of the litigation model. The anticipation of future steps in litigation determines the manner in which lawyers approach the negotiation of lawsuits on their clients' behalf. This anticipation drives not only appraisal of potential settlements but also decisions along the way, including whether to disclose information, what information to request from the other side, how to frame and prioritize arguments, the strategic use of delay – in effect, all communications with the other side. In this way, the strategic framework for legal negotiations is dominated by the anticipation of an event – a full trial – that will almost never occur.

There are obvious deficiencies with this model of negotiation. A focus on preparation for trial when trial is extremely unlikely is often inefficient, resulting in the expenditure of time (and therefore client money) on activities that are necessary for trial but less important for negotiating a good settlement. As one litigator confessed:

> If only 3 percent of the cases actually go to trial, that means 97 percent of the time all the pre-trial stuff is wasted to a large extent – so therefore 97 percent of money I make is from wasted time.[3]

The "litigotiation" strategy also exacerbates the problem of divergence between lawyer and client interests in the pursuit of settlement, since lawyers can bill for each hour they spend on the file, whereas clients want to minimize expenses in pursuit of settlement, and there is little accountability for the relationship between expenditure and eventual settlement. As one lawyer puts it:

> At times, you see a file that was going to keep you into discoveries for three months and it just got settled on very good terms for the client and you kind of go: "Wait a minute, is that the wildest thing I ever did?" I think there's a certain tone of that, especially among senior partners that goes: "Wait a minute." Then there's a tension there. You can't deny that there's tension there.[4]

Keeping a laser-like beam on the potential for a best-case adjudicated outcome – where an adjudication is statistically highly unlikely – produces mediocre and unimaginative settlements at a point at which the parties are exhausted and embittered, and settle in order to avoid further expense, not because they are satisfied with the outcome.

Despite these and many other problems with this model, the practice of legal negotiation continues to be dominated by the three key beliefs described in the previous chapter. In a study of legal negotiations among New Jersey litigators, Milton Heumann and Jonathan Hyman show that although the structure of legal negotiations perpetuates systemic problems of inefficiency and lack of creativity – and although many lawyers state a preference for problem-solving approaches that seek out mutual gains – rights-based positional bargaining in the shadow of the law remains the dominant model.[5] Heumann and Hyman suggest that the difficulty of changing this approach is embedded in the "habits" that lawyers form around negotiation behaviours, principally a focus on entitlement assertions rather than real-life events, and the control exerted by lawyers (who are in charge) over both their clients and the negotiation process.

The Norms of Legal Negotiations

As Heumann and Hyman observe, when lawyers negotiate, their dominant values and beliefs drive their choice of strategy and behaviour, even at an unconscious level. While Donald Schon and Chris Argyris remind us that many professional judgments are intuitive rather than learned or conscious, the tacit norms of legal negotiations are especially fascinating because most lawyers have not been professionally trained to negotiate.[6] Their instincts, experience, and wits – and the traditions of their community of practice – are all they have to go on.

There is some evidence of differences in negotiation norms – mostly minor conventions of bargaining – specific to particular practice areas, such as those described by Hazel Genn in her work on personal injuries litigation,[7] or by John Baldwin and Michael McConville in their study of plea bargaining.[8] Lynn Mather, Craig McEwen, and Richard Maiman suggest that the norms of "reasonableness" in negotiation are more strongly established in the family bar than in other areas of practice, such as commercial litigation.[9] Other research, however, suggests that family lawyers are more adversarial and less committed to problem solving than other practice groups.[10] In general, despite some practice-related differences, research on legal negotiation strongly suggests more similarities than differences in the culture of such negotiations.[11]

The following are broadly similar norms of legal negotiations found across many practice areas. Each of these norms reflects, and is reinforced by, the three key beliefs.

Playing to Win (Legal Negotiations Are a Zero-Sum Game)

In a rights-focused system, there is in theory only one winner – and everyone wants to be a winner. This belief that negotiation is a zero-sum game affects how both lawyers and clients approach legal negotiations. In a zero-sum game, one side's loss is inevitably the other side's gain, and vice versa. There are no mutual gains, only the distribution of a fixed resource. This approach to negotiation means that all or both parties are assumed to want the same thing and that the only way to settle is to divide up what is at stake (money, market share, intellectual property rights, child custody, and so on) in some acceptable way. In this classic distributive model of negotiation, the goal of all competent professionals is to claim and take as much as they can, thereby increasing their share and reducing their opponents'.

One lawyer describes his client's approach to negotiation, the moral force of "playing to win," and the techniques that the client uses to achieve her goals:

> She uses the blunt force of her own power ... her disapproval and the word "no" as tools to get what she wants as she goes for the win, that is, capitulation.[12]

Of course, this lawyer also knows that he and his client will eventually compromise to some degree, and settle. The assumption is that the harder they play to win, the better the settlement they will eventually achieve.

In legal negotiations, a claim is asserted in relation to a likely legal outcome. Hypothetically, the more credible the legal argument, the better the outcome via trial (despite the fact that there probably will be no trial). Because legal settlements customarily mimic likely legal outcomes, this means an almost exclusive reliance on monetary remedies and little creativity or diversity in settlement outcomes.[13]

A zero-sum approach to bargaining fits perfectly with the belief in a default to a rights-based approach, driven by legal expertise. Expert knowledge of the law becomes critical to developing a so-called winning strategy. Assuming that legal negotiation is a zero-sum game elevates substantive legal expertise, because a credible prediction of outcome is critically important. "Litigotiation" therefore privileges the role of the "lawyer-in-charge" who has the required expertise for this bargaining model, with the clients' underlying interests, and more creative solutions, sidelined. A zero-sum approach is also consistent with the traditional model of "zealous advocacy" discussed in the next chapter. Advocates who "play to win" are intent on maximizing their clients' outcomes at all costs (including negotiation bluff and bluster, making inflated demands, and so on). Here again, underlying beliefs about a lawyer's purpose and goals play out in the way the lawyer handles legal negotiations on behalf of the client

Is it inevitable that legal negotiations play out as a zero-sum negotiation? Taking the position that the lawyer's goal is a "good," but not necessarily "the very best," outcome for the client would allow lawyers to look beyond the zero-sum assumptions of traditional "litigotiation."[14] Looking for a good instead of a "maxed-out" outcome also reduces the heavy reliance on legal expertise in evaluating a settlement offer, and allows for other factors to be considered that might be important to the client, such as future relationships, timing, and emotional cost.[15]

In many legal disputes, the parties want different things, in different ways, and for different reasons, and there is plenty of potential for intelligent and strategic bargaining that recognizes this. In reality, the substance and issues at stake in legal disputes are rarely zero-sum. For example, disputes over commercial influence and market share, or the co-parenting of children, or the ending of an employment relationship, are not zero-sum. Each of these examples admits of many possible creative outcomes in which giving one side some of what it wants does not *have* to mean less for the other. Lawyers provide better service to their clients when they explore the "integrative potential" of a deal,[16] looking behind positions to understand a variety of possible interests that may be not be zero-sum. Different priorities may allow trade-offs – for example, one side may need cash flow whereas the other may need long-term security – where it first appeared that the parties' goals were in direct conflict. Or one side may want an outcome that effectively costs the other nothing, such as an apology or an explanation. Effective negotiators review all the options, ideally to the point of "Pareto optimality."[17] The result is more choices, a better and more complete understanding of how to meet both sides' needs, and a more constructive and creative bargaining climate.

Despite the potential for problem solving – and as Heumann and Hyman point out, this is the declared preference of many litigators – legal negotiations are still often begun *as if* they are zero-sum, in which there will be a winner and a loser. Transition to a settlement mindset is a benchmark for whether or not enough work has been done to maximize the chances of "winning." The question that the lawyer asks at this juncture is: "Have I played hard enough at winning now to be able to make a good deal?" Put another way: "Have I been unyielding long enough to secure the best possible deal?"

Stick to Your Position

There is an obvious relationship between a win/lose approach to dispute resolution and the tendency to deploy the tactics of positional bargaining. If one is playing to win, the rules of shadow adjudication require the articulation of a strong, unyielding position based on the best legal arguments. In order to demonstrate strength, lawyers adopt a stance of conviction that their arguments are certain to succeed at trial. A certain amount of hardball tactics and failure to cooperate with the other side is *de rigueur*. Acknowledging weakness on any issue or even articulating a priority from among a list of demands is widely regarded as "soft" advocacy. Hence, counsel quickly defaults to a positional approach to bargaining.

Positional bargaining is somewhat like the verbal exchange between two people who do not share a common language but who believe that by constantly restating their needs in an increasingly loud voice, they will eventually get what they want. No effort is expended in understanding the other side or obtaining more information about their needs. Instead, there is simply an increasingly insistent, repetitive restating of one's own position.

Threats, bluffs, and posturing are common in legal negotiations. Many lawyers acknowledge that the positions they take at the beginning of negotiations are inflated. They are conforming to the ritual dance of legal negotiations, when each side gradually evolves its opening position towards something more reasonable and realistic. There is always the risk that a positional approach drives the dynamics of legal negotiations towards an impasse or, at best, a lengthy period of negotiation and the significant adjustment of expectations. This potential is well illustrated in the following quote, in which a lawyer contrasts positional bargaining with a more open, mutual-gains approach in which information is exchanged and expectations clarified:

> In a traditional litigation file, if I thought my client's claim was worth $50,000, I'd ask for $100,000. If the other lawyer thought the claim was worth $30,000, they would say it's worth zero. In a collaborative law file, I have the confidence to say to my client: "Let's not talk about the 50 to 100, it's a waste of your time, it's not going to happen. Let's concentrate on the 30 to 50 that we all can agree on and make some creative options that suit you both within that 30 to 50."[18]

A "dance" towards an acceptable proposal, beginning with extreme positions from both sides, may be inefficient and time-consuming. It may be further impeded by the need of one lawyer or the other to show strength by holding tenaciously to his or her original position. Less experienced counsel are especially susceptible to this concern. Many lawyers regard tenacity over a legal position, which often means resistance to any movement away from a winner-take-all result, as characteristic of strong (zealous) advocacy. As the lawyer quoted in Chapter 2 said, "our duty ... to our individual clients [is] to fearlessly assert [their] rights."[19] Since in legal negotiations there is no third party to rule on the reasonableness of any particular arguments or proposals, the best way to assert them is to show unyielding confidence.

Many lawyers fear that they – and their case – will appear weak if they do not adopt a confident or even aggressive approach. Andrea Schneider has noted that this concern particularly affected younger, inexperienced lawyers facing off against more experienced counsel.[20] This dynamic drives even lawyers who recognize at some level that positional bargaining is blind to the clients' underlying goals towards this style of negotiation:

I struggled to get that adversarial model to begin with. It never felt right. I always felt that I wasn't giving as good service to my clients as I could be giving, but I was forced into it because [that] is what the system required.[21]

Just how aggressive counsel might be in advancing a position may depend in part on whom they are dealing with. One lawyer, describing a case with an experienced counsel on the other side, anticipated position taking in the following way:

I know them, and they're going to put every obstacle in my path. It's going to be obstructive, difficult, cranky. You know, a joyless, lifeless, adversarial, somebody's got to win, somebody's got to lose type situation.[22]

At its most extreme, a commitment to positionality at the expense of settlement appears to be ideological rather than strategic; as one lawyer memorably put it to me, "the objective is to destroy the opponent."[23] The most adversarial lawyers are so focused on working for a win that they do not consider it their responsibility to explore settlement, or to talk to their client about settlement either.

INTERVIEWER: What if the client starts for whatever reason to get cold feet and says to you: "I want you to go to them and ask them if they'll talk settlement," how might you respond to that?
INTERVIEWER: Very badly!
INTERVIEWER: What would you say to the client?
INTERVIEWER: I would say to the client: "If you're interested in settlement, you go and talk to the other side about it, I'm very bad at it, my job is to manage a war, not to manage a peace."[24]

Lawyers frequently use war metaphors to describe legal negotiations. Settlement is "giving up on fighting."[25]

This level of adversarialism is characterized by an aggressively uncooperative and rigid approach to negotiations in which all cards are held firmly to the chest, and is often accompanied by frequent tactical use of motions procedures, lengthy discovery processes, and the withholding of information. Rather than a conscious strategy calibrated to the individual case, fighting reflects a blind adherence to the idea of the lawyer as a warrior who must eliminate the other side. Adversarialism turns "stick to your position" into "defeat the other side at all costs."

Despite its prevalence in popular culture, this type of extreme adversarialism is much less common in close-knit communities with small bar associations – where it may have direct social costs – and far more common in larger (and hence more anonymous) and more competitive bars. In either case, successful marketing of reputation via negotiation style is important.[26] Depending on that market, establishing a fearsome reputation as a highly adversarial lawyer may be seen as a branding opportunity:

> Mainly people come to me because I'm known as a son of a bitch. I'm not afraid to go to trial. I won't cave in and go and settle. I have clients who know that and don't mind losing. They want to fight, so they expect me to be a son of a bitch.[27]

Legal practice in urban settings is increasingly competitive and has been described as "a nasty business" that is "no longer fun."[28] This competition extends into law school, where students vie for the best-paid and highest-status jobs. A more competitive environment persuades many lawyers that they need to be mean to survive, and meaner still to do well.[29] Andrea Schneider's research on how lawyers negotiate suggests that both the number and the "nastiness" of "adversarial" lawyers have grown.[30] Schneider attributes this in part to the culture of competition in law school and in legal practice. She describes the reality bluntly: "Given the choice between being too soft and too hard, most lawyers would opt for too hard."[31]

Information Is for Winning

The zero-sum assumptions of legal negotiations also have implications for the way in which information is used in legal negotiations. In a winner-take-all model, access to information is focused on using it to win – often to "ambush" the other side – rather than on developing a better understanding of the particular needs of each client, developing shared facts, or identifying areas of possible mutual interest.

When information is only about winning, a culture of secrecy and non-disclosure develops in legal negotiations that borders on the paranoid. Disclosure of almost any information is assumed to give an advantage to the other side. As a consequence, "litigotiation" is often conducted on the basis of very limited information about the other side's motivations, goals, or priorities. Lack of information – about the other side, about what is important for settlement, and even about opposing counsel's negotiation strategy – tends to further ramp up adversarial behaviour, as counsel and client assume the worst and may adopt a protective/defensive stance as a demonstration of strength.

The tendency towards this type of defensive entrenchment in the absence of key information about the other party's goals, intentions, or motivations is noted by game theorists in numerous iterations of the Prisoner's Dilemma, described by Robert Axelrod in his book *The Evolution of Co-operation*.[32] In the Prisoner's Dilemma game, two friends are held in adjacent cells and questioned separately about an alleged crime in which both of them participated. Each has to decide whether to confess and turn in the other or deny their involvement and hope that the other does the same. They are dependent upon one another for determining the best strategy, but ignorant of each other's decisions to confess or deny. The game illustrates the difficulty of interdependent decision making, or negotiating, when there is little or no information about the other: What are they thinking? What are they planning? What do they really want? The ensuing dynamic is generally defensive/reactive because without information to the contrary, each prisoner must assume that the other will do likewise.[33]

The Prisoner's Dilemma helps to explain how the norms of legal negotiation are pre-emptively competitive rather than presumptively cooperative. If both sides share information, there is a greater chance of mutual benefit. If both sides refuse to share information, negative results ensue. If one side shares information but it is not reciprocated, it gives a real advantage to the receiving side. Assuming the worst and protecting oneself perpetuates a culture of secrecy in which even apparently innocuous information – for example, about goals and motivations – is routinely withheld.

Instead of being seen as an obstacle to settlement, withholding information in legal negotiations is often seen as an important assertion of power and control. Information is seen as a means of gaining power over the other side, with a high value placed on secrecy and the potential for an ambush of the other side with a brilliant legal argument, relevant precedent, or startling new fact.[34] The value placed on secrecy here highlights the function of information in legal negotiations; in preparing a case for trial, counsel must collect information that makes the rights-based case, and this information (aces up the sleeve) becomes relatively less valuable if it is shared with the other side.[35]

The ironically named "discovery" process illustrates this well. Discoveries are principally concerned with what information can be dragged from the other side, and what can continue to be concealed. Litigation requires the collection of information – large amounts of it. Plaintiffs drive their case forward by collecting as much data as possible that are advantageous to them. Defendants stall the process – and any possible judgment against them – by requesting further and better information from the plaintiff.[36] The emphasis on rights-focused case development encourages the collection and concealment of as much information as possible, and discourages the early exchange of information about needs and interests.

There are other potential inefficiencies with seeing information as exclusively about creating a win. Legal negotiations privilege certain types of information (deemed relevant to the legal argument), and diminish others (deemed irrelevant). Because information sought is focused on strengthening the clients' rights-based case, it rarely includes information about what either side really wants and needs in order to settle. "Irrelevant" information that is routinely discarded or ignored includes the emotional context, business needs and interests, information about the bargaining context and strategy of the other side, including the cultural context (e.g., the culture of bargaining in a corporation or the conventions of settlement for a particular insurer). These types of data may be very important to building a good settlement, but they are not associated with building a winning case. A focus on information for the purpose of winning impedes the possibility of developing a shared understanding of priorities and issues among the disputants or enlarging the scope of settlement alternatives.

Commitment to a model of asserted rights also requires that information always be presented as fact. There can be no suggestion of ambiguity, or circumstantial or contextual interpretations. Any acknowledgment of uncertainty, the possibility of diverse interpretations, or even missing information undermines the assertion of a winning argument. Conversely, this requires the exploitation of any ambiguity in the "facts" as presented by the other side, so that when one side presents information, it is routinely attacked by the other.

Is this approach to obtaining and presenting information inevitable in legal negotiation? In common with playing to win and sticking to your position, it is a logical and rational approach if the assumption is that there will be a single winner, determined by the strength of the legal arguments. Lawyers are extremely nervous about exchanging information – any information, it sometimes seems – that they believe might give the other side an advantage in the ambush/aces-up-the-sleeve model of legal negotiations. There is significant pressure, especially on junior lawyers, to play it safe and hold their cards close, even where sharing information about client needs and priorities would make a good settlement far more likely. Nonetheless, in some smaller communities informal conventions of information exchange – sometimes before discoveries – are starting to emerge. Some lawyers see this as an important aspect of their responsibility to advance a case towards a possible settlement. This is discussed further later in this chapter.

Playing to win, sticking to your position, and using information to win are all strategies that are consistent with the belief in the primacy of rights and the need for the lawyer to be in charge of the negotiation process. Because of the well-established and well-documented practice habits of "litigotiation," the same behaviours can be presented as justice-as-process (this is the way things are done; this is how we shall serve you) to the client. Because these behaviours are normative, they are expected, assumed, and rarely challenged.

The norms of legal negotiation also give rise to, and sustain, the structure of how bargaining takes place. These structural characteristics, some of which are described below, are highly predictable and stylized across all sectors of legal practice involving litigation.[37] Just like the norms of behaviour, they are compatible with the three key beliefs. However, it is also in the structure of negotiation that we can most easily observe some signs of change in negotiation norms that challenge the three key beliefs, such as the greater inclusion of clients and earlier negotiation openings.

The Structure of Legal Negotiations

Traditional approaches to legal negotiations are being superseded by alternate norms and processes that offer more efficient and creative negotiations and better outcomes for clients. The New Lawyer's effectiveness as a negotiator, and his or her ability to develop expeditious and fair outcomes, lie at the heart of a renewed professional role.

Preparing for Settlement, Preparing for Trial

The glorification of positionality and playing to win, along with constraints on the exchange of information between the parties, make it surprising just how many lawsuits are settled by negotiation. Civil trials were just 1.8 percent of United States federal court filings in 2002,[38] but as some writers have pointed out,[39] we do not really know how many of these are settled by negotiation.

We do know, however, that there are very few full trials in civil and family cases.[40] The phenomenon of the "vanishing trial" is apparently here to stay,[41] yet cases settled by negotiation do not necessarily reach a result independently of the courts. There has been a significant increase in motions activity and other forms of pre-trial adjudication.[42] In other words, lawyers are still using the litigation process and the authority of judges to settle cases, but they are doing fewer trials. Moreover, significant numbers of cases leave the civil system without a clear outcome – perhaps one party simply gave up, or litigation fatigue took over?

However, while negotiated *or* non-tried outcomes are the overwhelming norm in civil litigation, the practice of negotiation remains a mere adjunct to the practice of litigation. Lawyers spend far more time preparing for litigation than preparing for or holding negotiation sessions. Studies consistently show that negotiation is a low-intensity activity for most lawyers, who devote significantly more time to the procedural aspects of litigation (drafting court documents, preparing motions, and conducting discoveries) than to negotiating settlements.[43] The amount of dollars that clients invest in settlement preparation and negotiation, compared with what they expend in taking procedural steps in litigation, seems disproportionately small for something so important to an eventual outcome.

Settlements appear as if by magic once the parties have exhausted (and perhaps bankrupted) themselves with the legal process. Researchers have found that most settlements result from one or two exchanges of offers only.[44] This exchange is characteristically at arm's length, not by face-to-face contact, and is almost always a monetarized solution reflecting the anticipation of likely legal outcomes (consisting of primarily monetary remedies) rather than creative or original solutions or outcomes (see the discussion later in this chapter).[45] This means a limited role for the client, who must defer to the lawyer in matters of legal knowledge. It also maintains the primacy of rights-based conflict resolution and preserves the technical control of the lawyer, whose specialist knowledge is the sole or dominant currency of the settlement process.

Preparation for negotiation is seen by many lawyers as virtually identical to the preparation of a strong litigation file. This means legal research to maximize the strength of the legal arguments (developing a legal theory); fact gathering that supports those arguments but neglects anything contradictory to, or outside the scope of, the legal theory; minimal information exchange ("hiding the ball"); and the presentation (usually at arm's length, via correspondence) of a strong, confident front.

This focus means that clients are not offered intentional negotiation strategies (such as reciprocal information exchange or an exploratory face-to-face meeting) that could expand the range of available outcomes and increase the possibility of a good settlement before the last-minute agreement typical in civil cases. Instead, negotiation proceeds along the predictable path of an exchange of inflated offers and counter-offers, until the distance is bridged via a modest meeting point. This helps explain why negotiated outcomes seem to fall within such a narrow range and focus so heavily on monetarized compromises, without the "value-added" components that would require a more creative approach.

This approach to settlement negotiation often leaves clients facing an unexpected collapse in their expectations when settlement offers do not match up with the lofty initial claims and demands made by their counsel. Whereas lawyers are accustomed to lowering expectations in order to make a deal that averts the costly and uncertain possibility of a trial, their clients (especially one-shotters) are generally less familiar with this pattern. Since the strength of a negotiating position in litigation is characterized by its assertion of convincing legal argument, the eventual compromise, which probably abandons at least some legal arguments, is for many clients wholly incommensurate with earlier conversations with their counsel. Especially when the client has been only minimally involved in any strategic dimensions of the negotiation, the presentation of a settlement proposal may come as something of an unpleasant shock. Having been initially advised that they have a good case that counsel will vigorously pursue for them, clients are now told that they should face the reality of the costs and uncertainty of trial and settle for something less than their original claim.

Instead of preparing for trial, could lawyers be preparing – and preparing their clients – for the likely reality of settlement? What would that look like, and how would it challenge the three key beliefs?

Signs of Change

Clients' legal bills reflect the time and energy put into preparing for adjudication, and they acutely experience the consequences of a legal strategy that anticipates a trial yet settles in advance of one. This is no longer acceptable to many clients, who want value for money in their dealings with lawyers.[46] Personal clients are now more questioning of costs and want to know how their limited resources are being spent. In particular, experienced corporate clients are no longer as willing to accept counsel's advice that they must expend more money on, for example, expensive discoveries in order to maximize their outcome. There is increased client scrutiny of expenditures and more onerous reporting requirements, leading one outside counsel to complain that "the old 'just fight-at-all-costs' and don't look at it [the legal bill], don't even think about an approach [opening negotiations], [that attitude] just doesn't seem to exist anymore."[47]

Government litigators, conscious of controlling legal costs, describe a similar change in attitude towards preparing for settlement. In a 2009 study conducted shortly after an audit critical of lack of constraints on legal costs, a significant majority of Canadian Department of Justice counsel indicated a growing institutional commitment to using appropriate settlement tools and planning for negotiation. As one counsel put it, alternative dispute resolution is "the general wave of how people like to do things now."[48] One senior litigator described himself as a "dinosaur" in the "new culture of settlement."[49] His own, traditional approach to case preparation was "not even to indicate that we are interested in discussions that might lead to a resolution until we have about the strongest position we can muster."[50] Departmental clients, on the other hand, are conscious of where their dollars are going and associate earlier settlement with lower costs. "We have a particular responsibility to safeguard public funds, safeguard taxpayer money on reasonable claims."[51]

While client impatience with legal costs without clear returns is perhaps the most important pressure for increased attention to work that supports settlement readiness, another is the frequency with which counsel must now prepare for discrete events such as (mandatory) court-based settlement processes, including mediation and case management. Preparation for such events changes both the type and the timing of work that counsel must put into a file if they are to be effective and well prepared for such fora. Does this mean that counsel is now investing time and energy in developing an intentional negotiation strategy – for example, the exchange of important information or consideration of settlement options with the client? The best place to look for concrete signs of change is in the timing of serious settlement discussions.

When to Begin Legal Negotiations

Research shows that the actual back-and-forth pattern of bargaining tends to be of low intensity and fairly short.[52] The contested point is exactly when bargaining should commence. In the absence of a requirement to negotiate early, many counsel continue to insist that they generally cannot be ready to negotiate until close to the time of trial. They will resist opening negotiations until a point at which they feel they have collected sufficient information to be able to make a strong legal case. Like the litigator quoted above, they feel that they need to be in the "strongest position we can muster" before opening serious settlement discussions. The calculation of value to the client is further complicated by counsel's perception that he needs to protect himself against professional negligence claims that he has not met an ambiguous standard of "due diligence."

> I think that a lot of lawyers just react as a knee jerk reaction [saying], how the hell can you mediate something when you haven't even had discovery?[53]

For many litigators, the milestone represented by the costly and time-consuming discovery process brings a belief that they have met their due diligence requirements. My study of commercial litigators in Toronto and Ottawa in 2000 found that for many lawyers, this means not even considering settlement negotiations before discoveries.[54] In jurisdictions where mediation is mandatory but can take place at any time before trial, most lawyers will wait until after discoveries to schedule mediation.[55]

The argument, of course, is that without the information obtained in discoveries, counsel is unable to put forward the strongest possible case for his client. While this may sometimes be true, the real question is whether it is always true and whether this timing should be a default – especially in light of evidence that suggests that discovery materials are rarely read until the eve of trial.[56] The widespread reluctance to engage in any type of settlement discussion before discoveries may be less practical, and more ideological. One lawyer characterized this practice norm in this way:

> There is an almost fetishistic obsession with knowing everything about a file before you can say anything about it.[57]

Opening negotiations or attending mediation does not presuppose that the only positive outcome is a settlement – there may be secondary benefits, including eliminating or resolving "outlier" issues, or simply learning more about the other side's interests and priorities. A more intangible but important benefit of an earlier effort at negotiation may be a shift in mindset. Without an event that requires counsel to seriously consider possible negotiated solutions, they may get all the way to trial without having done so. "I was involved in one case in which it was halfway through a trial before some of the lawyers really turned their minds to what this case was about."[58]

It has long been speculated that the monetary difference between an original offer of settlement, made perhaps one year or eighteen months into a lawsuit, perhaps before discoveries but certainly before trial, and a final agreement may be negligible, especially when legal costs are factored in. An example of a high-profile Canadian case that illustrates this perfectly is the legal action brought against Stockwell Day in 1999 by lawyer Lorne Goddard. Goddard sued Day – who was at that time the leader of the Canadian federal opposition – over a letter that Day had written while a minister in the Alberta government to a newspaper in Alberta, in which he accused Goddard of supporting child pornography because he had acted for a client accused of possessing child pornography. Goddard sued for defamation, asking for damages of $600,000.

Day was provided with legal representation by the Alberta government, further increasing public interest in the outcome of this case. In December 2000, one month before trial, government lawyers settled with Goddard out of court for $60,000 and some of his legal costs. The total legal costs paid by the Alberta government for both Day and Goddard was $732,000. It was disclosed that an original offer of settlement had been made at an early stage by Goddard's representatives for the sum of $70,000 – just $10,000 more than Goddard's final settlement – *including* legal costs.[59]

In 2008, a quantitative study in California established that trial awards for many plaintiffs (and a slightly smaller number of defendants) in civil suits are actually lower than their previous best offer, and if legal costs are factored in, they do worse when they proceed to trial than if they take that earlier settlement offer.[60] This study raises questions about the predictive ability of lawyers to advise their clients when spending more money might give them a return. Risk assessments appear to be especially flawed in cases involving contingency fees, such as medical malpractice.[61]

Since most civil and family cases will eventually settle – most on them on the courtroom steps – the challenge for the New Lawyer is how to open negotiation earlier in the process. Can settlement be negotiated before the legal costs have escalated and the parties have become even further entrenched in their respective positions?

Signs of Change

There is some evidence that the last-minute approach to the timing of negotiation described above is changing as more and more counsel and clients are exposed to mandatory early settlement procedures. The introduction of mandatory mediation in Saskatchewan and Ontario during the 1990s provides useful case studies.[62] One of the strongest sources of resistance to the new programs in both provinces came from lawyers who felt the required timing of mediation – early in the litigation process – to be premature. The timing issue proved to be a particular battleground in Ontario, where it has been amended several times over the last decade.[63] Despite the pushback from the bar, evidence quickly accumulated in both provinces that early mandatory mediation had a significant positive impact on the timing of settlement. For example, my 1995 study of the original Ontario mandatory mediation pilot contrasted the mean number of days from filing to settlement for both mediated cases and a matched control group of litigation cases, and found that cases that were mediated (a requirement to be met within ninety days of the filing of the statement of defence) were consistently settled in a shorter period of time than those without any mediation intervention.[64] A second study of the same program found that a substantially higher proportion of cases that went through mediation resolved within three, six, nine, and twelve months.[65] Similar data are reported elsewhere.[66]

Lawyers with experience of early mandatory mediation have started to modify their assumptions about the need for certain types and depth of information.[67] They have begun to question whether particular types of detailed information are really necessary in order to negotiate responsibly and effectively in some files. They note that at least some of the information they have assumed to be essential to the initiation of serious settlement discussions might not in fact be relevant to the type of solution that could emerge, and sometimes has emerged, from these very early negotiations.[68]

Professor Bobbi McAdoo's study of the impact of Minnesota's Rule 114 – a "mandatory consideration rule" that requires counsel to formally consider the possibility of alternative dispute resolution, and allows judges to impose a requirement of such in some cases – suggests a similar shift in attitudes towards how much information is necessary before opening settlement negotiations. Although Rule 114 does not require mediation to take place before discoveries,[69] some lawyers reported that they now consider settlement negotiations before discoveries. Others suggested that Rule 114 has sped up the discovery process, with counsel trying to complete this before mediation.[70]

There is some emerging evidence of a more systemic reorientation towards earlier negotiations, even without the pressure of mandatory mediation. A 2009 study of settlement patterns in cases handled by Canadian federal litigators revealed that where files were settled via negotiation, the most common time to open negotiation was immediately after the filing of the statement of claim, and the second most common was after production of documents. In this sample, opening negotiations after discoveries was relegated to third place as the choice of timing.[71] While most litigators interviewed expressed a preference for choosing their own timing for negotiation (or mediation), a number commented that some files were resolvable at an early stage. For example:

> The timing can occur at any time. It could be earlier on, when you have less information and both sides take a chance mediating because ... they may get less or they may pay more. But on a small claim, sometimes it's just better to go ahead with less information because it's not cost effective to actually get all the records or do all the interviews, if you're only talking about a claim that might only be worth $15,000, $20,000 or something like that.[72]

Keeping costs down is crucial to this evaluation: "If there is a possibility of settlement before discovery then it's a good thing to ... try and do that because of the cost associated upfront with legal expenses."[73]

Bargaining by Agents

> We decided the lawyers could settle this easier. So every two months, I took them to Canoe [an upscale Toronto restaurant] upstairs for drinks, or they would take me, and we would try to settle. We're getting close, we're now extremely close, but we're not there yet.[74]

This quote perfectly illustrates the assumptive control and ownership that lawyers exert over negotiation, as well as its social/professional context. The implication is that in a comfortable environment, such as an expensive restaurant, the lawyers can have a civilized, rational negotiation in language and terms they all understand. Just how efficient regular meetings over drinks are for the resolution of the client's problem is, of course, less clear.

A third and well-established structural characteristic of legal negotiations is that clients are generally excluded from the bargaining process. Many lawyers would argue, with some justification, that they are better able to accommodate and resolve differences between disputing parties than the clients themselves. After all, the lawyers can remain emotionally detached from the burning issues and understand what is and is not relevant as a matter of law. With regard to negotiating, lawyers must remain firmly in charge, and this is the way things are done (justice-as-process).

While experienced commercial clients have become accustomed to being included in formal face-to-face discussions, many informal negotiation meetings still take place between lawyers in the absence of their domestic clients. Austin Sarat and William Felstiner make the following observation on settlement work in divorce cases: "The major ingredient of this settlement system is the primacy of the lawyers. They produce the deals, while the clients are limited to initial instructions and the after-the-fact ratification."[75]

Bargaining by agents entrenches the lawyer-in-charge model. Even where alternative paradigms are emerging – where there is an intention of "client-centredness"[76] or where commercial clients rein in the independent decision making of their lawyers – clients are rarely immune to the influence and paternalism of their professional advisers. This effect is strengthened by the relatively passive role of the client and the active role of the agent in legal representation.

Of course, rising rates of self-representation throw a curveball into the field of representation by agents and create challenges for lawyers who are accustomed to talking with one another, and not with someone outside the guild, when they believe that the time is right for negotiation. How lawyers are managing this phenomenon, and how it changes the dynamics of legal negotiations, is discussed further below.

Agency representation in negotiation has significant consequences for clients, many of which are not good. First, it makes it more difficult for clients to assert a position independent of or contrary to the lawyer's advice, since they can always be told that they cannot fully appreciate or comprehend the dynamics, context, personalities, or other factors at play. For example, a lawyer may also be using what he or she knows about the negotiation reputation of the other counsel to formulate a strategy and a set of predictions.[77] This information is rarely accessible to clients. Clients are at a similar disadvantage in evaluating proposals presented by the agent resulting from a meeting from which they were absent. Counsel is the sole source of information and can frame it in multiple ways.

As well, the transmission of instructions from client to lawyer to the other side inevitably distances initial instructions from their ultimate final presentation. Once a position or proposal is filtered through the agent, delivered by the agent to the other side, and then passed on by opposing counsel to their client, its tone, even if not its content, may have been altered quite significantly. Where there are, as Jeffrey Rubin and Frank Sander put it, "extra moving parts" in a negotiation, there is less control and more uncertainty for a principal.[78] The net result may be greater reliance by the client on the agent than the client might have originally wished or intended (although some clients remain happy to hand over management of negotiations to their lawyers).

Agency representation also prolongs the time needed to effect a settlement. It is more time-consuming for an agent to go back and forth between principals, especially when there are agents on both or all sides, than to undertake direct negotiations. Some argue that excluding those individuals who are in conflict enables counsel to discuss the options more frankly and to move the dialogue forward more efficiently. This may sometimes be the case, and it is a plausible argument for using agency representation in some types of bargaining. At the same time, the time taken to seal a deal where agents carry messages back and forth drives up legal costs, and may extend the time to disposition and settlement.

Signs of Change

The requirement that clients attend mediation, and in some cases settlement conferences, has begun to change assumptions about lawyers-only bargaining.[79] Negotiation by agents in the absence of clients excludes some of the potential creative energy that clients can bring by their direct involvement. Sometimes lawyers hear their business clients proposing new and innovative solutions for the first time at mediation, while working with their counterparts on solutions that match the business context. Such solutions are less likely to arise from traditional lawyer-to-lawyer negotiations. Counsel describe mediation outcomes where commercial clients are present that include the continuation of a commercial relationship; a new commercial relationship such as trade partnership or joint venturing; the completion of a (disputed) sale and purchase agreement; access to the preferred terms of a new supplier; agreement to a forbearance period; consent to judgment for a lesser sum; agreement to vacate in order to avoid eviction proceedings; and a settlement structured to maximize tax advantages for the parties.[80]

Many counsel recognize that these types of solutions necessitate the direct participation of their commercial clients in mediation. As one lawyer put it, "the clients take much more of an active role because they understand their business better than I do. I understand it the least."[81]

Personal clients also can raise issues and solutions that would be impossible or at the least very time-consuming for counsel to develop without their direct input. Examples include creating a flexible parenting schedule; agreement on a structured payment schedule; an agreement to substitute payment of tuition fees or purchase of a car for a portion of spousal support; or the writing of a testimonial letter following a termination of employment. Having personal clients at the table can assist in the creation of trade-offs between elements of an agreement. Having clients present can also generate momentum and even motivation towards immediate closure:

> Both of them can end it that day. No letters going back and forth, that you receive five days after you sent something to some other lawyer, then the other lawyer goes to somebody else and gets back two weeks after ... On that day, this whole thing can be over with. That day you don't have to talk to your lawyer anymore if you're the client. That day you can easily walk out ... with this problem over.[82]

In judicial settlement conferencing, the degree to which clients are expected to participate depends on the approach of the individual judge, although there are signs that as experience grows with this forum, judicial attitudes may be changing. Particularly in family matters, judges are increasingly convinced of the value of having the client speak up and be spoken to.[83]

The movement towards the inclusion of clients in negotiation challenges the primacy of legal agents in the bargaining process. Nowhere is this challenge more evident than in counsel's relations with a self-represented litigant on the opposing side. Self-represented parties now account for up to 40 percent of those appearing in civil cases, and well over 50 percent in family court.[84] Many self-represented litigants (SRLs) report that they find it difficult to communicate with opposing counsel. SRLs experience the possibility of negotiation with opposing counsel as an intimidating prospect and an uneven contest. "I'm scared because I doubt myself and there is a lawyer sitting on the other side."[85] A common theme in interviews with the 253 individual SRLs who participated in the Canadian National SRL Study was a complaint that opposing counsel was not willing to discuss and seriously explore settlement with them.[86] In addition, many SRLs complain about behaviour and tactics by opposing counsel that appear to them to be highly adversarial, and report being threatened with costs and encountering refusal or delays in providing information.[87] A small group of SRLs who were lawyers themselves described stark differences between the way they were treated by opposing counsel when they appeared as legal representatives and when they appeared as self-represented litigants.[88]

At the same time, many lawyers have preconceived notions about SRLs, particularly the reasons why they are representing themselves, which widens the miscommunication gap and creates further obstacles to negotiation. Some counsel appear to believe that SRLs are representing themselves because they think that they can do as good a job as, or better than, a lawyer.[89] While some SRLs have complaints about how much money they expended on earlier legal services without a final resolution, the vast majority of SRLs are representing themselves because they cannot afford legal services, do not qualify for public assistance, and see no other alternative.[90]

The assumption that self-representation is a choice rather than a necessity stereotypes SRLs, and this affects how lawyers relate to them. Some believe that many or even most SRLs are mentally unstable, emotional, and obsessive about their cases. Facing a self-represented litigant on the other side, some counsel assume that this individual will be unable to function effectively in the justice system, and also be unwilling to work to advance the matter. While there is evidence that SRLs are under considerable stress and that many struggle to navigate the justice system, individual SRLs often work very hard to get it right, including looking for opportunities to open negotiations. More importantly, neither assumption is helpful to the development of a healthy working relationship and progress towards a negotiated solution.

It would be unfair to underestimate the extraordinary additional complexities of managing a file where the other side is self-represented, particularly negotiating with a self-represented litigant. A big challenge for lawyers is the uncertainty that this situation brings. Some lawyers have an underlying fear that their own clients will lodge a malpractice complaint if they see them "assisting" the SRL. Others believe that working opposite an SRL will create extra work and delays for their client. For example:

> Managing a file with a self-represented (unrepresented) opposing party can be challenging – in some cases, misunderstandings, protracted proceedings, and additional expense to the lawyer or paralegal's client result.[91]

There is also the concern that if counsel participates in a negotiation discussion with an SRL without a third party present, they expose themselves to being called as a witness if there is a future disagreement about the content of the discussion.

The central dilemma for counsel facing an SRL in negotiating a settlement is how to balance service to their client with the need, in the interests of their client, to advance a case towards resolution. Working with an SRL on the opposing side may mean offering them some assistance. Counsel will be in a relatively powerful position with a deeper understanding of the legal and procedural issues, but they are also obliged not to take advantage of the SRL's lack of knowledge and familiarity.[92] At the same time, counsel should not provide legal advice to anyone other than their own client. The balance is a difficult one.

Some counsel would prefer not to negotiate at all when there is a self-represented litigant on the other side. This is not a reasonable or realistic approach, and is unlikely to be in the interests of their own client. There are ways to reduce, if not eliminate, the risks described above. One is to ensure that clients are fully briefed on the implications of facing off against an SRL, and the possibility that their own lawyer may need to offer assistance if the matter is to move forward. This is not a conversation that counsel are accustomed to having with clients, but it is essential. Relatively simple practices to obviate risks include ensuring that a third party is present in any negotiation discussions, committing any potential negotiated settlement to writing at an early stage, and ensuring that the SRL on the other side fully understands the terms and consequences of any such agreement (the same applies to agreements overseen in a settlement conference with a judge). A self-represented person may be able to afford a few hours of so-called unbundled legal services, such as a review of a proposed settlement agreement, and it may be in the interests of counsel's own client to both suggest this and, if possible, make an appropriate referral.[93]

Obstacles to Change, and Some Promising Ways Forward

The structure of legal negotiations, combined with the dominant values of legal practice, results in predictable, almost ritualized norms of bargaining behaviour between lawyers. The status quo may be comfortable for lawyers as long as they remain in control of this format, but it is much less popular with their clients and of questionable effectiveness in achieving their goal.

This chapter has tried to show that the relationship between the structure of legal bargaining and the norms that sustain it is the result of a conflict resolution model in which the slightest possibility of adjudication overshadows every activity and decision. Lawyers, of course, often exacerbate and sometimes exploit the worst excesses of the dominant model. They do this through unnecessary and prolonged delay, protracted time and dollars spent on discoveries, failure to digest material in a timely manner with a view to settlement,[94] and even posturing as an alternative to working at settlement. As well, there are certainly obvious financial advantages to the profession of settling after, rather than before, the costliest steps in litigation (usually discoveries).

Traditional legal negotiations are not inefficient and expensive because lawyers plan them this way. They proceed in this way because there is a functional congruence between the way that legal negotiations are usually structured and the three key beliefs. It is therefore easy for lawyers to continue to operate in this way, despite the deficiencies of the process and its outcomes and the many disadvantages for their clients.

However many good reasons we can come up with, from both research and practice, for changing the dominant ethos of legal negotiations, fundamental change is a complex and probably long-term endeavour. It means challenging the historical conflation of "good" (zealous, strong) advocacy with positional bargaining. Lawyers who propose negotiations with a view to settlement are often perceived as being weak or are assumed to have a poor legal case. One lawyer described colleagues who liked to use mediation as "gun shy."[95] As one lawyer attending mediation training put it, "all the other lawyers I see here are wimps – that's why they're here." Another lawyer described the culture of the senior bar as follows:

I think that listening to the more senior people the whole concept of litigation is the more comfortable forum. They're used to fighting and taking things to trial and often mediation seems like a soft lovey, dovey approach to the world that they are not accustomed to.[96]

The core question is how to change the norm from fighting to settling. What are some of the most promising ways forward?

Mandatory Settlement Processes

Mandatory mediation (as well as mandatory settlement conferencing and, to a lesser extent, mandatory case management) has enabled some lawyers to overcome this bias against negotiation as a sign of weakness. One lawyer explains:

> I think what [mandatory] mediation has done is made it easier to try and negotiate a settlement or discuss settlement without doing so from a point of view or giving the perception that you're doing so because you're worried about your case, or it comes from a point of weakness because you can just say everybody does it, so you want to do it.[97]

Settlement-Only Counsel

With an eye on a changing and increasingly dissatisfied consumer market, some practitioner organizations are developing specific strategies for reinventing the ritual of legal negotiations, with the goal of including clients, creating space for creative solutions to emerge, and reducing hostility and negativity. One such approach is the development of law firm branding that emphasizes settlement expertise (e.g., the establishment of an alternative dispute resolution department within a firm). Another approach that some larger firms are experimenting with is to separate the litigation and the negotiation function by formally designating certain lawyers as specialist "settlement counsel." Working alongside litigation counsel on the same file, settlement counsel can offer clients special expertise in the negotiation of early settlements and can conduct negotiations, represent clients at mediation, and generally offer assistance in relation to the development of consensual solutions at an early stage in the litigation.[98] If their best efforts fail, their place is taken by "litigation counsel" who will proceed to trial.[99]

Despite scholarly interest and some experimentation within larger law firms with the creation of alternative dispute resolution departments, the development of specialist settlement expertise to date has been largely limited to the work of one or two individuals rather than affecting the broader culture of the firm.[100] Moreover, settlement counsel are usually only retained on very large files when it is possible to fund both settlement and litigation counsel. This reality limits the range of cases in which specialist settlement counsel is available.

Cooperative Pledges

A different approach to changing the culture and practice of legal negotiation is membership in a community of practice that seeks to promote a more collaborative approach to negotiations (e.g., corporations that have signed on to the CPR [Conflict Prevention and Resolution] Pledge).[101] One such approach is to ask lawyers to make an advance commitment to the principles of cooperative bargaining. Instead of having to guess at and perhaps assume the worst about the opponent's negotiation style, there is a shared commitment to the disclosure of information, a respectful and timely response to communications, and an effort to build rapport and trust.

Such an approach reduces the unknowns of the Prisoner's Dilemma and allows lawyers to negotiate on the basis of shared understandings about process. It institutionalizes the assumption of beginning cooperatively, which Axelrod proposes,[102] and changes this approach only if there is bad faith. The growth of cooperative lawyering groups promotes this approach, which sees cooperative tactics in negotiation as part of an overall mindset and a professional commitment rather than something that requires formalizing in a contract.[103]

Collaborative Family Law

Others argue that in order to change the norms of bargaining, it is necessary to go further in altering the fundamental structure of legal negotiations. The collaborative lawyering movement has focused on removing the spectre of litigation from bargaining. In a collaborative law case, the responsibility of counsel to facilitate settlement is directly traded for the traditional core responsibility to win in litigation, a trade that is undertaken by all lawyers participating on a single file. The basis of the retainer agreement in a collaborative law file is a contractual commitment between lawyer and client *not* to resort to litigation to resolve the client's problem. The legal services provided by counsel are limited to advice and representation regarding the non-litigious resolution of the conflict, and the focus is on developing a negotiated, consensual outcome. There is no parallel litigation strategy. If the client does decide that legal action is ultimately necessary in order to resolve the dispute, the retainer stipulates that the collaborative lawyer (along with any other collaborative professionals, such as divorce coaches or financial planners) must withdraw and receive no further remuneration for work on the case.[104] This device is described as the "disqualification clause/agreement."

The collaborative lawyering model's premise is the belief that without the possibility of litigation in the background, lawyers will adopt different strategies in negotiation. For example, in anticipating negotiation, counsel will not need to be "papering" the file as they would when approaching litigation. The argument is that once a legal action commences, the temptation to use a legal discourse and paradigm for analyzing and resolving disputes is irresistible – first with threats and then with action.[105] Instead, the objectives of collaborative lawyering are to change the context for negotiation itself and to provide a strong incentive for early, collaborative, negotiated settlement without resorting to litigation. One of the earliest proponents of collaborative retainer agreements (often described as a "participation agreement" because of the emphasis placed on client participation) argues that it changes the context for negotiations by enabling "a way to approach a person with whom one has a perceived conflict with a request for an honest and detailed examination of the problem in a way that also offer[s] an absolute and irrevocable commitment to do so in a non-adversarial manner."[106]

Some lawyers, including but not limited to the cooperative lawyering groups, regard the approach of the collaborative lawyers as overly formalistic and process-oriented. The disqualification agreement, they argue, is unnecessarily constraining when the client and the lawyer can simply agree to use a cooperative approach.[107] This claim has not yet been tested by research comparing the two models. An examination of the collaborative lawyering process provides some evidence to support collaborative lawyers' claims that the use of a formal collaborative retainer agreement, including a disqualification clause, reduces posturing and gamesmanship of traditional lawyer-to-lawyer negotiation, including highly inflated and low-ball opening proposals.[108]

Communities of Practice

Changing the norms of legal negotiations also requires the development of communities of practice that can support and nurture a different type of bargaining culture.

In both collaborative and cooperative lawyering groups, the commitment to cooperative negotiation is strengthened by the "club" culture of the groups or networks and a sense of shared values. The collaborative group, for example, becomes a critical community of practice for individual collaborative lawyers, which is highly influential in shaping and maintaining informal practice norms and behaviours.[109] It also offers the potential for informal mentoring and monitoring of member practice. For example, "the lawyers watch one another and we will catch ourselves doing it [positional bargaining]."[110]

A supportive culture has also developed in some centres where the bar and the bench have embraced mandatory civil mediation. Reputation in negotiation is an extremely important resource given the degree of strategic uncertainty and lack of information that accompanies classic legal negotiations. This reputation includes not only behaviour during the actual negotiations but also honesty, competence, the ability to work constructively and effectively with one's client and reach a firm decision, and follow-through in drafting a memorandum of agreement and meeting subsequent obligations. A personal reputation for collaboration becomes a commodity that carries positive consequences – for reputation and for earnings – when a critical mass within one's community of practice embraces mediation and settlement processes as mainstream and reflective of good lawyering.[111]

Changing the Culture of Legal Negotiations: Revisiting the Three Key Beliefs

One lawyer who preferred to settle early reflected as follows on the widespread habit of leaving negotiation until an advanced stage of a lawsuit:

> My radar is very much in tune to a deal that I think accords with the clients'
> wishes ... what fits with the client, and is probably pretty close to what I would
> have otherwise got two years hence, after thousands of dollars of money down
> the toilet in litigation. By the way, that toilet is my pocket.[112]

In striving for a more noble model of professional service than flushing client dollars down the toilet, the New Lawyer needs to re-examine the assumptions of traditional legal negotiations that flow from the three key beliefs.

A first step is to challenge the assumption that all conflicts necessarily implicate rights. Some do, and these need to be addressed, ideally within an adjudicative model. Saying that not all conflicts implicate rights does not mean that none do. Interests-based bargaining can and must coexist with negotiation over rights entitlements. Adopting an interests-based approach to finding a feasible long-term solution does not exclude bargaining for a clear rights-based threshold (e.g., payments in line with or above child support guidelines, or structured settlement payments for breach of contract). The key to effective lawyering lies in distinguishing between different types of conflicts and the appropriate means of addressing and resolving them, in order to meet both the needs of the disputants and society's interest in fairness.

Lawyers should be able to apply their professional judgment to this question rather than adopting without question the characterization of every client's problem as "a matter of principle." The claim of "principle" is attached to many disputes that, in their origins at least, appear to be wholly or primarily about the sharing of resources, including property, business interests, or time with children, and implicate power, status, material wealth, reputation, and other desired social symbols. While a principled argument can be, and usually is, constructed for each side's moral position, this analysis may miss both the core of what the conflict is and the potential solutions or accommodations. Even when the conflict is over a moral difference – for example, the custody of children or decisions over their schooling – determining who is right through the application of legal principle may not address the core needs of the parties.

Similarly, few cases merit the singular application of either interests-based bargaining or negotiation over rights entitlements. Effective bargaining on behalf of the client requires the identification of those issues that require a rights-based benchmark to ensure that power does not violate rights or overwhelm interests; which elements of a deal require distributive (dividing up the pie) bargaining; what extra value can be created for both sides; and what aspects of a conflict can be resolved using principles developed and embraced by the parties themselves.[113]

An exclusive or overwhelming focus on a rights-based model is an inadequate, inappropriate, and simply impracticable means of resolving every type of dispute. It is time for lawyers to learn how to handle other types of conflict resolution. That means thinking strategically not only about your own clients' interests but also what the other side needs in order to be persuaded to settle.

> You can posture and advocate until you're green in the face, but unless you're trying to solve the other person's legitimate issues, you're not going to succeed.[114]

Second, in the context of negotiation, lawyers' long-standing belief in justice-as-process may be more concerned with justifying professional legal services than with understanding and meeting client needs. Lawyers are right to discourage their clients from assuming that they have a lock on judge-dispensed justice, but their habits of discouraging an early exchange of information – even innocuous information about motivations and priorities – delaying serious negotiations until after discoveries, and behaving as if the final outcome will be adjudicated even when it almost certainly will not do not feel satisfactory for many clients, particularly when instead of directly participating in these decisions themselves, clients are presented with these strategies as "the way we do legal negotiations." Procedural justice research suggests not only that participation in decision making over negotiation strategies is important but also that there are values surrounding the way in which the negotiation process unfolds – did the other side listen and take their concerns seriously? were they civil and polite? did they acknowledge some fault or ambiguity? – that have an impact on a disputant's sense that justice was done.

Third, negotiation strategies that respond to the needs and expectations of contemporary clients – whether commercial or personal – must reject the lawyer-in-charge model that keeps clients at arm's length from the settlement process. Decisions regarding when to open negotiations, how to appraise potential solutions, what information to exchange, what type of process to use (mediation? client four-ways? lawyers-only meetings?) should be made by lawyers and clients together, on the basis of all necessary information – well beyond just legally relevant information – that may affect these considerations.

A rejection of the old top-down hierarchy is also important as a recognition of the shift in power that is manifest in all types of professional service in the age of the World Wide Web. Clients demand a stronger sense of personal agency than their professional advisers have been accustomed to in the past. It is important that the consumers of legal services create their own sense of justice that enables them to live with the outcomes they choose, both practically and emotionally. This means that they should be able to participate in shaping processes that give them a voice, that they have the chance to be listened to and taken seriously. Clients are increasingly unwilling to hand over control and ownership of their dispute to their lawyer. They want to know how their money is being spent, and what concrete progress towards their goals is being made. They will no longer meekly accept the traditional norms and given structure of legal bargaining.

Changing the culture of legal negotiations by questioning its assumptions and developing alternative behaviours and practices is a formidable challenge, especially for new members of the legal profession. Participation in the status quo rather than challenging it is a way for junior lawyers to demonstrate to their colleagues that they understand and accept "the way things are done." Becoming part of a profession brings with it implicit obligations to maintain its central claims to professionalism and special expertise. For many lawyers, this continues to mean a commitment to defining disputes through the lenses of rights, believing in the justice of legal process, and taking ownership of clients' conflicts. Challenging these values may be seen as disloyal to the profession – a betrayal of the claims that sustain the profession's image as well as bolster the economics of legal practice. There is pressure to conform at least in part to the dominant norms that the profession has established for clients and for collegial relationships.

But change in the way that lawyers manage legal negotiations is not only necessary but inevitable. For too long, the legal profession has been disassociated from practical problem solving and conflict resolution in the public consciousness. Contemporary clients – including a growing group who are part-time clients and self-represented litigants – are demanding a different approach to the provision of legal services. This does not mean the rejection of the expertise that lawyers have developed over generations in negotiating their clients' conflicts but a reformulation building on existing skills, knowledge, and attitudes. Lawyers spend a lot of time negotiating, and whatever the deficiencies of the structure and norms of "litigotiation," they have much practice wisdom. It is time to take this to a new level of intentionality in a system that resolves almost every dispute before a full trial.

Changing the culture of legal negotiations – and for new entrants to the profession, landing in a place where they feel comfortable and confident – requires the thoughtful and skillful development of alternative behaviours and practices that reflect and enable new norms. This must include creating both a model for strong cooperative bargaining and sensible conventions on disclosure and information exchange. It also means the creation of negotiation models that emphasize and incentivize early negotiation in some cases, the direct participation of clients, and perhaps even coaching of clients to conduct their own negotiations.

Although changing the process does not in itself change attitudes, there may be a longer-term relationship between process and attitude change.[115] Mandatory mediation may secure lawyers' compliance without necessarily changing their minds and hearts, but the changed conduct may, with further practice and exposure, affect a lawyer's normative values and attitudes towards mediation.[116] The use of the disqualification clause in collaborative practice may appear to some as an overzealous imposition of a collaborative commitment, but it also normalizes and supports behaviours that historically have not been habitual in legal negotiations. As more lawyers propose early negotiation, it becomes more acceptable and can be taken increasingly seriously. As more clients insist on participating in the negotiation process, it seems like a natural step. Gradually, the model of what is good lawyering practice in negotiation evolves and changes.

Changing how they think about and approach legal negotiation is just the first of many challenges for New Lawyers, but it is a central one. New Lawyers also need a model of advocacy that meets their clients' goal of effective conflict resolution rather than absolute victory. Their relationship with their clients is profoundly altered by a reconfiguration of roles and expertise in which both contribute expertise and each takes responsibility for aspects of planning, negotiation, and decision making. A new roadmap of values and norms sets up a new set of questions for ethical professional conduct, challenging the stability of conventional lawyer/client expectations and introducing new challenges, not least of which is working with the self-represented. The remainder of this book will examine each of these challenges in turn.

5

The New Advocacy

Advocacy is at the heart of how lawyers understand their role. It is also at the heart of the changes facing the New Lawyer.

The essence of advocacy is strong dedication to a given set of goals and ends that can be moved forward by the advocate's expert advice and experience. The particular style of advocacy historically associated with lawyers is more fiercely adversarial and positional – and perhaps less noble and dignified – than this ideal. In the hands of lawyers, advocacy sometimes veers into a wild caricature of someone who seems prepared to behave in uncivil, immoral, and even barely legal ways in order to achieve client goals. In such instances, the core principles of dedication and strength morph into blinkered single-mindedness, rigidity, and aggression.

Paradoxically, the attribution to lawyers of this particular style of advocacy – often analogized to heavy weaponry such as cannons, boxing gloves, or fierce animals with large teeth[1] – appears to be both effective marketing ("let me fight for you"[2]) and a source of public opprobrium. Consumers seem to still want to hire tough lawyers, although many clients complain about the needless escalation of hostilities that often results from involving adversarial lawyers. As one client put it, "a lawyer should have the wisdom and skill to modify their approach, instead of putting fuel on the fire."[3]

Adversarial tactics and behaviours are rarely what is most effective in the resolution of a dispute. In fact, the role of an adversarial advocate is extremely limited. However single-minded and aggressive, the advocate cannot guarantee his client any particular outcome and may end up getting his client less rather than more – for example, permanently ending a relationship or running up costs that cancel out or seriously offset any monetary gains. Clients do not always confront these risks until they are facing the consequences of escalation.

Clients want someone to help them articulate and validate their concerns and to protect them and their interests, perhaps because they are fearful and/or vulnerable. A good advocate has a number of choices for how to meet these fundamental needs. Many are more effective than adversarial bargaining.

In this chapter, I shall argue that the central role of advocates, in a legal system in which most cases settle, is to help clients continuously reassess what they need and want in light of what is possible (including costs) – and to advance that goal. This means regularly assessing the potential for resolution. To do this well, advocates must apply their negotiation skills and, in some cases, draw on their ability to convince a decision maker of the superiority of their legal argument. I shall describe as "conflict resolution advocacy" the work of lawyers in exploring and advancing fair settlement, which may mean pursuing multiple strategies but with the same goal of realistically maximizing client outcomes, both short- and long-term.

To be effective as a conflict resolution advocate, a lawyer must listen carefully to what clients say they really want, and what they are prepared to give up in order to achieve resolution. In bringing his or her specialist knowledge to the problem faced by the client, the New Lawyer must be cognizant that the client's perspective will be affected by many factors other than legal arguments, and meeting the clients' needs may, or may not, require a maximized legal outcome. A negotiated settlement should always be considered. An effective conflict resolution advocate should be firm, but not hostile and uncivil, about bottom lines, and creative about negotiable issues. This does not mean abandoning strong advocacy but retooling these principles for a different type of engagement with the problem, and with the other side.

In order to develop a model of conflict resolution advocacy, lawyers need to redefine what is meant by advocacy in legal practice. Populist notions of "legal advocacy" are characterized by noisy argumentation and table banging. The idea of being both committed to the client – "on their side" or "in their team" – while also being committed to promoting mutual peace and resolution seems impossible in this model. It is not only in law where that tension exists; there are other examples in the field of social justice, where activist advocacy is often framed as being at odds with efforts to promote peace. We seem stuck with the idea that only neutrals can be "real" conflict resolvers.[4]

In fact, this polarization between conflict resolution and advocacy is a relatively new development. The earliest community-based conflict resolution initiatives – in areas such as policing, racial conflict, and public policy – were social activism that promoted awareness and progress on important issues, while at the same time modelling non-violent resistance.[5] Historically, notions of legal advocacy among small-town general practitioners did not assume that having the client's interests at heart – transparently, *not* being neutral – precluded counsel from the promotion of peace and understanding.[6] However, the last thirty years have seen mainstream professional values and norms, driven by larger corporate firms, evolve to reflect a more zealous version of advocacy, which in some cases is explicitly adversarial. This conception of advocacy sets the promotion of peaceful resolution at odds with many widely expected behaviours and attitudes.[7]

"Zealous Advocacy"

Any discussion of the meaning and practice of legal advocacy must begin with the ubiquitous expression "zealous advocacy," which is included in professional codes of conduct for lawyers throughout the common law world. Just what the expression means, and what obligations flow from it, has been the subject of debate ever since its original articulation in the American Bar Association's *Model Rules of Professional Conduct*.[8]

The most literal formulation of zealous advocacy means doing anything and everything that is lawful in order to advance the clients' interests. Described by William Simon as the "dominant view," this understanding of advocacy assumes that "the only ethical duty distinctive to the lawyer's role is loyalty to the client."[9] The interests of the other side, third parties, or the public are secondary and extraneous to this loyalty, and the client's position must be asserted unambiguously.[10] Any attention paid to outside interests may distract or undermine the lawyer's focus on the client.

This perspective on advocacy also implies that the time for talking is past. Zealous advocacy is not concerned with scrutinizing, questioning, or reassessing the client's interests or positions. Instead the lawyer-advocate is focused on acting to further the clients' given (legal) goals. So, for example, zealous advocacy in legal negotiations means positional bargaining that simply asserts, rather than discusses or appraises, the basis of the clients' claimed "entitlement."

In practice, few lawyers understand their advocacy responsibilities as narrowly or as unambiguously as Simon's dominant view describes. Most lawyers readily acknowledge that effective advocacy – which includes the ability to be convincingly firm by grounding the argument – also requires information gathering, appraisal and evaluation, and advice giving. Most regard counselling and weighing options as an important part of the service they offer their clients, rather than the blind adoption and pursuit of client goals. In particular, for small-town lawyers the "literalist" version of zealous advocacy has always been an inadequate description of the complexity of their role, which often encompasses counsellor and reality-tester, especially with clients with whom they have lifelong relationships.[11] For these lawyers, who often play a broader role in their community as a wise adviser, morally blind adherence to the clients' goals is not the way law has been traditionally practised or how they have historically understood their role.[12]

Nonetheless, the dominant view of legal advocacy – with its focus on assert, justify, demand – is highly influential, especially for law students and new entrants to the profession. This literalist version of zealous advocacy may seem divorced from the reality of most legal practice, but its clarity and simplicity are attractive. Because zealous advocacy equates advocacy with the pursuit of rights – other types of goals or strategies are generally not contemplated – it allows for uncontested control over strategy and decision making by counsel, who alone possesses the necessary expertise to succeed. The model is reinforced by the continued commitment of legal education to a model of lawyer dominance through substantive expertise. Acting as a zealous advocate is how most prospective lawyers first learn about and understand their professional identity. The zealous advocacy model is highly compatible with the three key beliefs that are first instilled in law school.

Another part of the appeal of a literal approach to zealous advocacy is the idea of strength and the power that it exemplifies.

> In the construction industry you have to be known to be tough ... All of the most successful construction firms have good lawyers who fight, and you know if you're going to fool around with these boys, you're going to have to fight.[13]

Students entering law school often picture themselves acting in this way on behalf of a deserving client, perhaps a vulnerable party facing a wealthy corporation or state authority.[14] They are highly susceptible to the position taking of competitive mooting as they focus, often intensely, on this rite-of-passage experience. The acceptance and adoption of some adversarial behaviours is also a part of the socialization of young lawyers working in large firms with competitive cultures. In these environments, commitment and dedication are associated with behaviours such as advancing positional arguments, disinterest in the issues raised by the other side, minimal communication, and the withholding or obstruction of any information that may be useful to the other side. Little or no attention is paid to interaction with clients or to considering giving advice or counselling or evaluating options. Zealous advocacy is all about dealing confidently and aggressively with the other side, rather than spending time with clients in a consultative role.

In this model of advocacy, the end goal – achieving the clients' legal goals – is disassociated from justice. Instead, it is all about winning.

> I'd come back from court and I'd say: "I'm a winner! I'm a winner!" Or, I'd come back from court saying: "Can you believe what that damn judge did?" It's about winning ... So what if the court agreed with your submission that was a little goofy and gives you $2,000 more per month that you shouldn't have gotten? You are a winner, and you did good for your client. So what if you took advantage of some other lawyer's stupidity? I don't care – I'm a winner![15]

Because zealous advocacy focuses on achieving client goals by winning, it is possible to justify almost any behaviour as a means to this end. Otherwise intolerable and unreasonable behaviour can be defended as perfectly rational and appropriate, and morally justified. Popular culture, and sometimes lawyers themselves, sometimes justify this behaviour as the result of the lawyer's search for "truth," but it is more accurate to understand the driving force as the dogged pursuit of client goals. As David Luban points out, a professional obligation to present facts selectively in accordance with advancing a client's position is unlikely to be an effective means of uncovering "truth."[16] "Winning advocacy" achieves victory by position taking, supplemented, if necessary, by intimidation and bluffing. In contrast, "winning outcomes," are enabled by skillful negotiation, creative problem solving, and the development of fair and reasonable solutions.

Many lawyers recognize that truth and its sister value, justice, are far less important as motivations for zealous advocacy than a total commitment to furthering client interests.

> Justice is too deep for me ... believe me, justice plays a little role. [T]he client just wants to know, will I win or will I lose? And I say you will win and the other lawyer says [to their own client] you will win.[17]

A Historical Perspective

How did the legal profession come to embrace a notion of advocacy that sees achieving justice as marginal and adversarial tactics as normative? The social history of the lawyering profession offers some insights into the evolution of zealous advocacy. Although extreme adversarialism among some lawyers may be a fairly recent phenomenon, some of the clues to its genesis lie in the historical development of law as a profession.

The expert status of lawyers is derived from eighteenth-century notions of "professionalism," which regarded law as a "gentlemanly" profession and a vocation or higher calling. The apparent selflessness with which lawyers devote themselves to their clients' cause legitimizes their unquestioned authority and expertise, and sets them apart from others who sell services with a lower social cachet. To claim this status, the lawyers' own gain or advantage must be secondary to furthering their clients' goals. In the words of Lord Brougham:

> An advocate, in the discharge of his duty, knows but one person in all the world, and that person is his client. To save that client by all means and expedients, and at all hazards and costs to other persons, *and amongst them to himself,* is his first and only duty.[18]

Historically, the tacit exchange between lawyer and client was that single-minded devotion to the service of the client's interests would be rewarded with unquestioned social status and professional autonomy. In this exchange, lawyers act as their clients' alter ego, free to reframe the facts of the conflict as suits the legal arguments. A techno-rationalist approach to professionalism – here the ability to predict legal outcomes – means that technical knowledge is prized above all other skills and aptitudes.[19] Lawyers will be unemotional and objective in reaching decisions about appropriate actions, and, in exchange, their clients will grant them complete or relative autonomy in the management of the case.

This exchange transaction was formulated at a time when lawyers were foreclosed, at least in principle, from a profit motive.[20] Eighteenth-century legal practice was a "gentleman's calling," and, as such, personal gain was seen as being antithetical to a principle of selfless professionalism. The clients of English barristers were expected to offer "honoraria" in "gratitude" rather than being formally charged fees.[21] Of course, there were some fairly clear social expectations, and a failure to remunerate would rarely be tolerated. Yet the principle was that lawyers served only at their clients' pleasure and should be rewarded in a way that reflected their success in achieving their clients' goals.

Of course, the business conditions of legal practice have changed fundamentally since the eighteenth century. No one would expect today that lawyers should be motivated by service in the absence of remuneration, and their eighteenth-century colleagues were likely not so disinterested in personal gain either. Zealous advocacy takes on a very different character when a profit motive is introduced. The populist conception is now more "hired gun" than alter ego. In the monetarized transaction of twentieth- and twenty-first-century lawyering, lawyers will "prove" their value to their clients by aggressively asserting their chosen legal strategy right up to the boundaries of the law, complete, in some cases, with dirty tricks aimed at the other side. Far from using dispassionate objectivity, lawyers may on occasion make an investment in winning the conflict that is as great as or greater than that of their clients.

In the eighteenth century, the notion of the lawyer as the (in theory) unpaid servant of the client afforded an honourable rationale for zealous advocacy – the selfless desire to achieve justice for the client. Late-twentieth and early-twenty-first-century economic competition and the pursuit of individual wealth maximization has changed the nature of the lawyer/client transaction. While the goal has always been to win, the contemporary model offers less autonomy and independent appraisal to the lawyer, who is paid by the client and is expected to adopt the client's goals. Building client loyalty is now less about demonstrating a personal commitment to justice and more about economic success – attracting and retaining clients is critical to the contemporary lawyer's personal advancement and economic well-being. In the cut and thrust of urban practice, it is, as Andrea Schneider reminds us, easier to err on the side of being too hard – aggressive, competitive, and overzealous – than too soft, and the culture of big firm practice expects this sort of behaviour.[22] As a result, contemporary zealous advocacy is more adversarial – perhaps more so than the original drafters of the *Model Rules of Professional Conduct* intended or anticipated – and less interested in "justice" than earlier models.

Tensions within Zealous Advocacy

Despite its functional efficiency and apparent clarity, the zealous advocacy model has a number of inherent tensions. In a time when so few cases go to trial, many of the goals and assumptions of traditional zealous advocacy are redundant. Moreover, the strategies and tactics associated with this approach to advocacy are far less useful in trying to settle lawsuits than in trying to win them. As the collaborative lawyer quoted in Chapter 4 pointed out, positional bargaining simply does not work when you are trying to persuade the other side to settle with you. Aggressively advanced positions, withholding of information, and an unwillingness to acknowledge any weakness or ambiguity in your case are seldom effective strategies in either negotiation or mediation. Many of the habits of positionality that characterize zealous advocacy impede problem solving. As one lawyer describes it:

> Less and less do I find that I have to take positions that are very black and white and simply advocate that position and put blinders on and go straight ahead and say there's an offer, take it or leave it – and maybe that's partly caused by repetitively being put in a room with a bunch of people and a mediator and sitting down to try and work out solutions to the problems.[23]

An increase in the use of settlement processes, many of them mandatory, means that lawyers are being asked to advocate in ways that are at odds with their formal training. As one explains:

> First and foremost our training is in rights-based advocacy, that's first and foremost and that creates the tension because you're saying settlement, they say why? You sort of feel like why do I have the right training, maybe ... I should just have the training in problem solving. We do have that training and it's there and you still have to use it and so the compromise is always cut against your training to a certain extent.[24]

Another tension comes from changes in the business conditions of legal practice. Part of the original exchange transaction between lawyers and clients was that in return for their commitment, lawyers were afforded significant professional autonomy to use their judgment in their clients' best interests – judgment based substantially on their knowledge and appraisal of the relevant law. This might include giving bad news when the lawyer's expert appraisal might point to a different course of action than the client originally desired and hoped for. In many contemporary lawyer/client relationships, especially those involving corporate and institutional clients, the notion that lawyers should use their independent judgment in pursuing the clients' goals by the best possible means is severely limited by an obligation to a client whose business is critical to the economic viability of a practice. As they charted the changes in firm size and structure that characterized the 1970s and 1980s, John Heinz and Edward Laumann noted that the prized notion of autonomy was significantly eroded for corporate-commercial lawyers working with large institutional clients (although less for personal services lawyers with a large and changing client base).[25] Similarly, Robert Nelson's research suggests that associates in larger firms perceive very little personal autonomy.[26] The central

importance of technical legal expertise and the assumption of lawyer autonomy in offering an expert opinion – the give and take of the original exchange
transaction between lawyer and client – fit uneasily with the blanket commitment to furthering client wishes that is the hallmark of the contemporary zealous advocacy model. What if the instructions the client gives are simply not in
his or her best interests, based on the lawyer's experience? Should the lawyer
assume that he or she knows best and persuade the client of this? How far
should counsel press the client to hold out for a better deal when the client is
ready to settle?

Unsurprisingly, many lawyers find the balance between client decision
making and lawyer expertise a difficult one to strike, especially within an
adversarial model that assumes fighting is *more* and settling is *less*. It is difficult
for lawyers to know how to manage a conflict between, for example, their
rights-based advice and a client's desire for resolution based on other factors.
Lawyers are not trained to recognize these tensions – other than intuitively –
much less to balance them. Resolving tension between what lawyers are trained
to do and what clients want to do is uncharted territory that most lawyers can
only approach instinctively. The zealous advocacy model offers little guidance
on how to conduct such lawyer/client negotiations. How does counsel raise
and discuss this with the client? And do a lawyer's responsibilities differ for a
first-time client, or for a regular client, or for a personal or a corporate client?
One lawyer describes this tension as follows:

> I've (sometimes) found it harder to take off the advocate hat and see clients com-
> ing in prepared to settle. I can think of one mediation with a number of different
> parties where once again, we were acting for a bank as a plaintiff in this case, and
> the bank's claim was $4,000,000. There were a number of parties including two
> insurers on the other side and the merits of the case I thought justified a pretty
> high settlement ... In this case a new account manager comes in and was about
> to retire and wanted to get a win on his docket before he retired. He just ended
> up settling for 20 or 30 cents on the dollar in order to avoid going to trial, and
> more importantly to wrap it all up before he retired. In that case I found myself
> in caucus saying to the client: "This is obviously your decision, this is a business
> decision and I will respect your decision but, I think the case is worth a lot more
> than 20 or 30 cents on the dollar." I have found it difficult at times to take off the
> advocate hat and to be sensitive to the client's business objectives.[27]

The zealous advocacy model assumes the "lawyer-in-charge" model,[28] in
which the client will always accede to the lawyer's advice. The example above

illustrates the difficulties that arise when this does not happen, not uncommon with sophisticated business clients (or highly emotionally invested personal clients). Both commercial and personal clients now want to see results that match their financial investment – which may often mean practical problem solving and compromise rather than the unyielding pursuit of a rights-based strategy. Most lawyers would agree that client goals and preferences must ultimately trump the lawyer's judgment, but how far does the zealous advocate press the rights-based case? Moreover, because the zealous advocacy model focuses lawyering on achieving the client's best legal outcome, the lawyer's relationship with other dimensions of conflict resolution – business goals, psychological interests – is ambiguous and undetermined. How much weight should a lawyer give to the client's non-legal goals? Central to the "hang tough" values of the adversarial model[29] is its rigidity and inflexibility, making it even more difficult to adjust to new conditions. There is little room in the traditional model for counsel to negotiate with the client, or internally with themselves – no built-in GPS for flexibility, detours, or innovations. Instead, there is certainty and resolution of purpose, which is seen as strength.

Zealous advocates also face a moral dilemma in relation to what types of behaviour are acceptable. The literalist model of zealous advocacy – especially in a competitive big-firm, big-city culture – encourages the idea that any means may be justified in relation to the (legal) end. Murray Schwartz has observed that some lawyers believe they operate under a principle of moral non-accountability so that they can be unrestrained in the zealous pursuit of their clients' goals.[30] This suggests that there is little or no need to maintain boundaries between zealous and immoral forms of advocacy. Significant economic rewards or losses may be at stake.[31]

For some lawyers, the principle of non-accountability only heightens the conflict they feel between their own values and those of their client or of the adversary system itself. One lawyer explains:

> My nature, my personality has always been much more collaborative. I struggled to get that adversarial model to begin with. It never felt right. I always felt that I wasn't giving as good service to my clients as I could be giving but I was forced into it because that is what the system required.[32]

These tensions within the zealous advocacy model, coupled with its inherent limitations in a legal culture that sees most cases settled rather than adjudicated, point to the need for a new and evolved model of legal advocacy. The zealous advocacy model fails to offer a complete or even adequate conceptualization of the lawyer's role in the twenty-first century.

A "new advocacy" designed to meet the changing conditions of practice and client expectations is increasingly imaginable. What would this look like?

Conflict Resolution Advocacy

The emergence of an alternative concept of advocacy is primarily the result of the cultural and institutional changes taking place in legal practice – the widespread introduction of court-connected and private mediation programs, case management, judicial mediation, and the "vanishing trial."[33] Another source of change are those members of the profession with an appetite for a more practical, problem-solving, civil approach to advocacy that advances their clients' interests more wisely and effectively. As or more important are changes in the expectations of clients. Both corporate and personal clients now pay increasing attention to how their money is spent – on settling, not fighting. More and more clients are looking for a nuanced and responsive advocacy that is custom-made for them rather than the result of traditional beliefs or habits.

In conflict resolution advocacy, the lawyer's responsibility for the best possible client outcome is not diminished. In fact, advocacy as conflict resolution places the constructive and creative promotion of partisan outcomes at the centre of the advocate's role and sees this goal as entirely compatible with working with the other side – in fact, this goal can be achieved *only* by working with the other side. But the New Lawyer will understand the advocacy role as more than fighting on his or her clients' behalf. Evaluating what outcomes are most durable, realistic, and cost-effective requires a deeper analysis than zealous advocacy offers. It requires discussion of client goals that goes beyond the information deemed necessary to formulate a rights-based approach in order to produce a more complex, multi-layered version – for example, considering business goals and priorities, weighing the needs of the client for closure, and re-emphasizing the needs and interests that lie behind the asserted positions.

Conflict resolution advocacy means a different relationship with the client – closer to a working partnership – and a different orientation towards conflict. New Lawyers must help their clients engage constructively with the conflict,[34] confronting the strategic and practical realities as well as making a game plan for success. They can offer their clients insight into how conflict develops and evolves over time, and its likely impact and consequences, drawing on the experience of working continually with others on (perhaps similar) disputes. Conflict engagement means working with clients to anticipate, strategize, assert claims, and negotiate over conflict, and, if possible, to implement jointly agreed outcomes. If jointly agreed outcomes are not possible or if they fall short of client goals, there are other, familiar, rights-based strategies available.

This alternative model of conflict resolution advocacy has much in common with Anthony Kronman's model of "deliberative wisdom," which he argues should temper or even supplant traditional zealous advocacy. Deliberative wisdom is more than simply a legal evaluation or the advice of a technical specialist. It also includes considering other, non-legal implications of the decision to act.[35] It might also include advice on the dilemmas inherent in bargaining described earlier, which are always present in the space between the lawyer's legal appraisal of the value of a case and the client's expectations or settlement goals. The practice of deliberative wisdom assumes that lawyers have something useful to say to clients about their moral and legal choices. Kronman urges contemporary lawyers to see offering deliberative wisdom as central to their advocacy role, and laments the lack of recognition of its importance.[36]

Reframing zealous advocacy as conflict resolution advocacy requires lawyers to modify two of their three key beliefs, and to extend the third. Conflict resolution advocacy challenges the primacy of rights-based dispute resolution, taking a multi-pronged (and continuously re-evaluated) approach to both fighting and settling. Rights-based strategies are seldom optimal tools for engaging with conflict and seeking solutions. Conflict resolution advocacy takes lawyers' historical commitment to an ideal of justice-as-process – integrity, fairness, and equality in legal processes and procedures – and challenges them to apply these same values to private and court-based systems that seek settlement. The New Lawyer will be deeply involved in and knowledgeable about the design of processes and standards that protect clients' interests and promote trust in the development of solutions. Finally, the traditional lawyer-in-charge needs to work much more closely with – and listen much more carefully to – his or her client in a conflict resolution advocacy model. Envisioning settlement outcomes and considering non-legal issues make the role of the client much more significant and challenges the assumption that the lawyer (as legal expert) must inevitably be in charge.

What Is Different about Conflict Resolution Advocacy?

The principal conceptual difference between zealous advocacy and conflict resolution advocacy is that the former is organized around a system of adjudication, whereas the latter is organized around a system of conflict resolution that includes, but is not limited to, adjudication. This sounds like a simple, realistic adjustment, but it has many implications for both the way lawyers understand their role and the way in which they carry it out. What types of professional commitments and practical skills does this conceptual shift translate into – what stays the same, recognizable as part of the zealous advocacy tradition, and what is different?

It is a common fallacy that in the pursuit of settlement, the commitment to one's client that lies at the heart of advocacy must somehow be compromised. New Lawyers remain just as dedicated as zealous advocates to achieving their clients' goals. What changes is how they get there. Their primary skills become their effectiveness and ability to achieve the best possible negotiated settlement, even as they remain prepared to litigate if necessary. There is no contradiction between a commitment to explore every possibility of facilitating an agreement with the other side and a strong primary loyalty to one's own client. One experienced lawyer describes this loyalty as follows:

> I think, to be honest, it's natural for an attorney ... that my best friend in the room is always going to be my client.[37]

Counsel's loyalty and focus should be on achieving the client's best possible outcomes. As a result, effective collaborative family lawyers can assure their clients: "I shall still get the best result for you."[38] Or, as a commercial litigator put it, "I see a completely different form of adversary process. You can call it a mediation because we're working together to come up with a deal, but we're still adversaries – I'm still trying to get the best possible deal I can."[39] A contradiction between client loyalty and creative consensus building exists only if counsel is convinced that the only effective way to advance the client's wishes is by aggressive position taking or by pressing rights-based processes to their final conclusion. Aside from these fairly exceptional cases, the goal of conflict resolution advocates is to persuade the other side to settle – on their clients' best possible terms.

In a model of conflict resolution advocacy, lawyers continue to encounter many of the same tensions and dilemmas that they do as zealous advocates – for example, when and how to settle, how to balance their judgment with the clients' aspirations, and how to balance what has been gained with what will be lost in settlement. However, zealous advocacy has no frameworks for resolving these dilemmas because admitting a need to compromise undermines the core of zealous advocacy. Conflict resolution advocacy both anticipates them and makes them resolvable on a principled basis. Whereas adversarial advocacy tends to see settlement as capitulation, conflict resolution advocacy is committed to evaluating the pros, cons, and alternatives of any settlement option throughout the case, which includes an evaluation of the legal, cognitive, and emotional dimensions because all of these are part of how clients appraise settlement.[40]

While standing ready and able to move to an adjudicated determination of their case, conflict resolution advocates plan their approach based on one simple and undisputed fact: that most cases settle. This recognition opens up the potential for bargaining, focusing counsel less on gamesmanship around the rules of engagement (the rules of civil procedure) and more on the management and tactics of negotiation.

A New Focus on Negotiation

Conflict resolution advocacy reverses the amount of time spent on procedural steps such as drafting and filing pleadings and preparing and bringing motions, and the time spent on developing negotiation strategy and on actual negotiation. Lawyers conventionally spend little time on negotiation compared with taking procedural steps,[41] so this reversal represents a significant shift of time and energy. Some lawyers may regard the time they spend on procedural matters as an aspect of negotiation – in effect, softening up and checking out the other side in preparation for bargaining – but this means treating negotiation as a mere subset of procedural manoeuvres rather than as an intentional and explicit tactic. In conflict resolution advocacy, development and implementation of effective negotiation strategies are central to what advocates offer their clients.

This shift transforms how we think about negotiation as a component of the skill set of the New Lawyer. It catapults the conscious development of negotiation skills up the hierarchy of lawyerly skills and capacities. Taking negotiation strategy seriously makes the routine dynamic of exchanging written offers before "sawing it off in the middle" seem inadequate and gauche. Conflict resolution advocacy demands instead that negotiation planning be addressed at the earliest stages of file development as lawyers discuss goals, priorities, and alternatives with their clients. An early focus on the potential for a fair and appropriate negotiated solution encourages both lawyer and client to frame the problem holistically, rather than focusing only on information that narrows the case to its generic legal issues. An early focus on negotiation may also shift planning away from procedural steps and deadlines, and towards the development of a complete strategy for the management (and resolution) of this file, perhaps worked out within a team or between those in a firm's litigation and corporate departments.[42] One lawyer whose practice was dramatically altered by the introduction of mandatory civil mediation reflected:

> My practice is more and more on the phone talking about *strategy.* Less and less do I ever mention the words *civil procedure.*[43]

Recognizing the central role of negotiation for the conflict resolution advocate means a new emphasis on skills that have often seemed peripheral to legal advocates, and a rejection of some of the negotiation tactics favoured by the most adversarial. Intimidation, aggressive positionality, and secrecy (withholding of information) are just not helpful in trying to build consensus. Summarized by one lawyer as "lose the bark, keep the bite,"[44] conflict resolution advocacy requires the development of intentional strategies to persuade the other side to first listen to you and then ultimately reach an agreement with you and your client.

Effective conflict resolution advocates ask questions that reveal critical information – information that they need to know about the other side in order to better persuade them to settle – rather than holding forth themselves. As an intentional negotiator, the conflict resolution advocate should be conscious of when to be accommodating and when to be tough in order to protect his or her client's interests. Every negotiation is a form of Prisoner's Dilemma,[45] with choices made in each round regarding cooperation or competition.

The New Lawyer should develop good instincts for when, and how, to use each strategy. Intentionality in negotiation is critical to working with the other side in legal negotiations to establish comfort, rapport, and eventually trust, through norms of reciprocity. This requires good interpersonal and communication skills, including the ability to put the other side at ease, demonstrate respect and perhaps even empathy, and, most challenging, foster trust. The development of trust is key to exploring enhanced mutual solutions, and it requires effective explanation, persuasion, and personal authenticity:

> I want to persuade and get the other party to understand what my client wants, so there's that part of the persuasion, but it's more based on building a foundation first, the more they understand, the more they trust then the more likely they are able to understand why we think we want a certain thing.[46]

Conflict resolution advocacy also requires new knowledge. For example, skillful negotiators understand the distinctive dynamics of both distributive (divide up the pie) and integrative (expand the pie, then divide it) negotiations as well as the need to move between these two modes depending on the type and stage of negotiation. Understanding the dynamics in negotiation of both value claiming (establishing and holding to a "bottom line" or core components of an acceptable solution) and value creating (exploring the additional benefits that the parties might jointly develop and share) creates balance and provides alternatives when one strategy gets "stuck." It allows for an expanded range of options to identify priorities and negotiate trade-offs.

If the New Lawyer understands and is comfortable with choosing different bargaining strategies to suit different contexts – whether distributive or integrative approaches, cooperative or competitive moves – he or she can be highly proactive in shaping negotiation outcomes. This means that legal negotiation is no longer "rote" – because there is no rote. Each situation requires a nuanced and, again, intentional approach. Experienced negotiators are also sensitive to the importance of identifying and allowing for cultural differences in framing and resolving conflict, recognizing that disputants often need to relate the process and the outcome to their cultural (familial, community, organizational, ethnic) expectations and preferences.

There are other new skills that enhance the effectiveness of the conflict resolution advocate. These include preparing an effective opening statement in negotiation or mediation, which adopts a firm yet not overly positional tone; matching the appropriate informal process to the case; displaying confidence and openness; and thinking outside the box of conventional, legal solutions in developing creative problem-solving skills. One observation made frequently by experienced counsel is the importance of being able to conceptualize and understand the dispute from the perspective of the other side. Critical to being able to persuade the other side to settle on your client's best terms – the goal of conflict resolution advocacy – is an understanding of what the other side needs in order to be able to settle. For example:

> You don't worry about the other side as much at a trial because *they're the other side*. When you're working towards a consensus – then it matters.[47]

Of course, this is not a new idea. Good negotiators have always operated with an awareness of the interests of the other side, and these lawyers already take the interests of the other side into consideration in order to enlarge the cooperative space in which negotiations can take place.[48] The belief that clients' best interests can be achieved only if the interests of the other side are taken into account is a central premise of the principled bargaining approach popularized by Roger Fisher and Bill Ury.[49] As an experienced litigator describes it:

Probably the biggest change I made was really thinking about ... the opposing party's profile and really making an effort to put myself in his/her shoes ... as I strategize the case.[50]

Constructive Conflict Engagement

When New Lawyers act as conflict resolution advocates, they are effectively encouraging their clients to constructively engage in the conflict – perhaps at a relatively early stage in the litigation process – in order to understand better what the strategic options might be. They are modelling an approach described by Bernie Mayer as "effective engagement" with the conflict, "accepting the challenges of a conflict ... with courage and wisdom."[51]

Conflict engagement does not necessarily mean resolution, as Mayer is at pains to point out. Instead, it is an attitude that allows for a realistic, hopeful, and ultimately value-affirming appraisal of conflict from both a cognitive and an emotional perspective. It does not mean filing legal papers and then consigning the file to the cabinet for the next six months. Instead of waiting for something to happen – a legal event, discoveries, perhaps an approach from the other side – conflict engagement means facing the realities and the impact of the conflict on the client, even at an early stage in litigation. Conflict resolution advocates are going to be more proactive, and a lot more curious, than traditional zealous advocates about what might be done to address the dispute from the very beginning of the lawyer/client relationship. They are going to get "engaged" in the conflict.

This means a constant conversation between lawyer and client that includes asking: What does this conflict mean to the client? What does the client understand as being at stake? What is the short- and long-term psychological impact on the client? What is the most realistic outcome of the case? This discussion might result in a decision to negotiate or, conversely, to wait it out. Whatever course is adopted, conflict engagement means taking every opportunity to reflect on possible strategies.

In order to develop a strategy – and perhaps to revisit and redefine this strategy on several occasions over the lifetime of a file – constructive conflict engagement requires the New Lawyer to ask the client what is essential – and what is less important – in this conflict. What is the historical context, and how does it animate the underlying dynamic between the parties? Does the client believe that there are important principles at stake here? Is the conflict escalating, or is there a stalemate? And is there an avenue for communication with the other side, if not full-blown negotiation? All of these are steps in conflict engagement.[52]

Information Exchange

Another important, and highly practical, difference between conflict resolution advocacy and zealous advocacy is the approach each takes to fact gathering and the use of information in legal negotiations.

The dominant epistemology of litigation described in Chapter 4 sees knowledge and information as solely for purpose of advancing the clients' legal case. This approach means that only information that fits the legal argument is either sought or used, leaving aside significant information that may be important to realizing the clients' goals. The zealous advocate's approach to information is highly competitive, with information routinely withheld even when it may be of little or no consequence, and often when it would be beneficial in clarifying the goals of each side.

The nature and uses of information in a conflict resolution model are quite different. First, the type of information that is potentially important is greatly expanded. Early client involvement in negotiation and mediation allows for the discussion of information – such as business or personal issues – that may have an important impact on how the client feels about resolving the conflict but might not ordinarily be a part of this conversation. The New Lawyer should seek out information that may be marginally relevant to the legal case but could be key to understanding how best to advance the client's interests and needs.

Second, conflict resolution advocates regard information as a shared resource that may advance all parties' interests. Effective conflict resolution advocates must also consider what information they believe the other side needs from them, in order to persuade them that they should settle on their best possible terms.

Lack of information exchange can be fatal to the possibility of early or even midway negotiation. As one federal lawyer explains:

> The parties have to have had enough information so that they can go into the process sort of with their eyes open ... [otherwise] ... Everybody's sort of ill-informed and it doesn't work. We've actually gone to them [the other side in the case] in the past where we just sit down and talk about something other than the case. Nobody has enough information.[53]

In order for a less aggressive and more collaborative approach towards information sharing to work, lawyers need to be able to build trusting relationships with other counsel. There is an obvious need for norms of reciprocity. Such norms tend to prevail in smaller communities, where lawyers are accustomed to providing information as requested without forcing their opponents to jump through procedural hoops. To do otherwise has social consequences. Larger urban centres still often see a dominant norm of secrecy and withholding of information.

The evolution of new informal practices over information sharing is apparent in some judicial centres with long-running mandatory mediation programs. For example, where mediation occurs before discoveries, and in the absence of formal requirements regarding documentary exchange, many counsel adopt the practice of exchanging affidavits of documents before mediation and agree to honour subsequent requests.[54] This is a sign of the growing recognition of the positive value of exchanging information, and a radical departure from the zealous advocacy norm.

Re-envisioning Outcomes

Another profound difference between conflict resolution advocacy and zealous advocacy lies in how counsel imagines and appraises the best outcome in any case. In zealous advocacy, the best outcome anticipated by counsel is always a victory on the legal arguments, which usually means a monetary judgment. Any negotiated outcome is measured by how close it comes to the "best-case" legal goals.

Of course, experienced counsel know that this is not the only measure of success, or even necessarily success as the client sees it. Even if a win is ultimately achieved, it may not be all that was hoped for. Emotional closure or business viability and recovery are often pushed further away in litigation. In civil trials, the process of resolution may be further prolonged by the need for enforcement steps after a favourable judgment has been secured. This may partly explain why in my 1995 Ontario study (matching a control group of litigants who went to trial with those who mediated their dispute), only 8.5 percent of trial group litigants described themselves as completely satisfied with the outcome of their case (either settled between the lawyers or adjudicated). The most frequently given reason for a negative or partly negative assessment of outcome in the remaining 91.5 percent (which obviously included some litigants who won their cases at trial) was the length of time and the emotional energy consumed.[55]

In evaluating potential outcomes, conflict resolution advocacy will certainly include a measures-based proximity to an ideal (i.e., successful) legal outcome, but many other factors will also be important. These may include legal costs, recognition and acknowledgment, business expansion or solvency, future relationships (both domestic and commercial), vindication and justice, emotional closure, and reputation. These interests have both short-term and long-term consequences, and they reflect not only outcomes but also procedural justice – feeling listened to, being taken seriously, and being fairly treated. Effective conflict resolution advocates understand that it is not just the nuts and bolts of the final deal that matter, but also how the client feels about the process.

In some disputes, it is important for the outcome to be responsive to systemic and underlying issues. This may come at the urging of one party – for example, the employee claiming discrimination who wants to see future procedures changed to avoid recurrence of the problem, or the manager who sees the need for a new set of procedures and protocols to enhance clarity and fairness in decision making. In some conflicts, it may also be important to set the stage for future re-engagements, which may be inevitable – for example, in disputes over land use between municipalities and communities, or between parents sharing custody of children. By stepping outside the limits of remedying the immediate problem, conflict resolution advocates take a proactive approach to averting future conflicts. Rather than thinking "solutionally" (a "rewind" approach), they think "preventively" (a "fast-forward" approach).[56]

Where there is the potential for repeated disputes, a systems approach may be important. The New Lawyer needs a basic understanding of how systems work, including the tendency for systems to create their own internal culture, and the risk that systems might function differently than intended (e.g., to suppress conflict). The New Lawyer also needs to be familiar with some basic system tools for planning, such as a spectrum of dispute resolution processes, process precedents, and effective tools for monitoring system processes and outcomes.

New Tensions in Conflict Resolution Advocacy

The Dilemma of the Two Hats

Lawyers who regularly participate in settlement processes such as negotiation and mediation experience changes in both their professional identity and their toolbox of professional skills. Unless they have eschewed litigation altogether, lawyers who practise conflict resolution advocacy need to constantly "switch hats" between a negotiation and a litigation mode. This creates a new set of tensions and challenges for the New Lawyer. Some lawyers describe this tension in an instrumental, matter-of-fact way:

> In drafting a mediation brief, for example, I'll often try and use plain language rather than inflammatory language simply because if you want to achieve the

The New Advocacy

settlement it may not be in your interest to get the other side going, and so you have to be a little cautious in terms of how you approach things. That's if you really do want to reach a resolution of the case that applies after the mediation – whereas if the case goes to trial, then I'll be as aggressive as I think necessary.[57]

I think in a mediation process I attempt as much as possible to be conciliatory and look for opportunities for resolution. Try to understand what might make the person on the other side of it tick. What would interest them in terms of a resolution. If I get in a courtroom I'm quite different. I think people all of a sudden see a different person, but that's just the nature of the business.[58]

Another lawyer described feeling less comfortable with this switch:

[The two roles] are completely separate. It feels kind of slimy doing it, from an ethical point of view. [I]t's a complete act and usually the clients on the other side are so naive as to buy into the act and from an ethical point of view that doesn't feel that great, but it's what we do.[59]

Two groups, in particular, experience a strong feeling of tension between their adversarial and settlement roles. One group is those lawyers who have extensive experience in mediation and other settlement-oriented processes and who enthusiastically support the use of mediation – the "True Believers."[60] Many lawyers in this group are working towards developing a settlement-only practice in order to avoid the role conflict described above. A second group especially sensitive to tension between settlement work and traditional advocacy comprises lawyers who are most negative towards mediation and other settlement processes. These lawyers see settlement advocacy as a "sell-out" of the lawyer's traditional adversarial role, and do not regard the two approaches as in any way complementary or commensurate. One lawyer articulated this view as follows: "Inevitably you have to stop one part of your role [the settlement-seeking part] in order to preserve the other part."[61] The preferred course of these so-called Oppositionists is the rejection of any developed role for lawyers in settlement advocacy.

Most lawyers, however, do not see this as a binary choice, although they may struggle at some level with the mismatch between their traditional advocacy identity and the role they must play in order to be effective in settlement processes. This is sometimes expressed as a sense that they are not doing what they were trained to do – and at the same time being expected to do something that they were not trained for. Moving between two different roles – for example, appearing in motions court in the morning and participating in mediation or in a settlement conference in the afternoon – can certainly be disorienting for both lawyers and clients. Can the roles of fighter and settler be reconciled? Does resolving the tension between the two require a commitment to one perspective or another, or can counsel prepare for war and peace at the same time?

New Lawyers must learn to wear the two hats of fighter and settlement negotiator, and understand when to take one off and put the other on. They must evaluate when one approach should be preferred over the other, when one approach should be entirely set aside or suspended, and even when both hats need to be worn at the same time (e.g., a last-ditch settlement meeting before initiating litigation or proceeding to trial). Lawyers who practise conflict resolution advocacy find themselves continuously assessing the balance between their private counselling role (offering the client Kronman's "deliberative wisdom"[62]) and public advocacy role (making the case for the client's position).

Historically, the separation of counselling and advocacy has enabled lawyers to adopt a confident and even aggressive attitude in public while adopting a more cautious tone in private consultations, to present certain information in private but not in public, and so on. Private counselling and public advocacy are no longer clearly separated in settlement processes that include the client as a direct participant. In collaborative law, client-attended mediation, and settlement conferences, New Lawyers must choose a place to stand on the fighter/settler continuum that takes account of the constant presence of the client and maintains consistency, both in public and in private.

Client Autonomy and Lawyer Direction

A related dilemma is how the conflict resolution advocate finds a balance between client autonomy and lawyer control of overall direction and strategy. Again, this is not a new challenge – it arises in zealous advocacy as well, of course – but the conflict resolution context adds additional complexity and nuance. Unlike adjudication, where the lawyer is the acknowledged expert, in settlement clients should make their own best, informed decision. A side negotiation inevitably takes place between lawyer and client as they develop strategy and tactics that are both procedural (do we negotiate? what do we offer? do we play hardball?) and substantive (what is a good outcome? what is a just outcome?).

It is difficult for lawyers to relinquish their traditional control over decision making. One lawyer comments:

> Lawyers often don't want clients settling unless there is a rationale (as defined by a lawyer) for the settlement. So some lawyers find it hard to understand

why [for example] their clients might be willing to pay more than they might.[63]

At a general level, this debate is often characterized as a contrast between client autonomy and lawyer paternalism. The premise of the autonomy approach is that the lawyer's primary responsibility as an advocate is to enable the client to assess his or her own situation in a manner that enables the client to determine his or her best possible course of action, including a negotiated settlement. The paternalistic approach, which is more closely associated with the norms of zealous advocacy and a rights-based approach, places a stronger emphasis on the expert judgment of the lawyer.

In practice, there is obvious overlap or blurring between the autonomy and paternalistic positions.[64] Some clients require significant input from their lawyers in order to reach an "independent" evaluation and decision. Given their power in the relationship, lawyers still heavily influence not only client decision making but also the appraisal of just how much clients need to know in order to function "autonomously." The lawyer often (and, with one-shot litigants such as divorce clients, usually) controls what information will or will not be presented for the client's consideration. It is also true that some clients invite their lawyers to decide for them, presenting New Lawyers with another challenge – how to ensure that their clients are fully informed and making an independent decision. Is this even possible in some cases (as when the client is emotionally distressed or cognitively impaired)?

With neither a "pure" paternalistic nor autonomous position likely in practice, the essence of this debate lies in finding the appropriate balance of power between counsel and client over the direction of the case and its eventual outcomes. Any amount of lawyer paternalism – whether or not it is presented as being for the client's own good – cannot exclude the influence of extra-legal considerations – including how the client feels about the proposed outcome, or their economic security or insecurity – that make it difficult for counsel to persuade the client to accept their advice. Key for the conflict resolution advocate is the importance of making these choices and dilemmas fully transparent to the client. This is a very different approach from the more traditional "I know best, trust me" approach, which is increasingly rejected by contemporary clients.

Personal Values and Professional Service

Even lawyers who regard client autonomy as being critical to conflict resolution advocacy still apply, perhaps unintentionally, their own values to choices over strategy, which may influence the client's decision-making process. Some conflict resolution advocates, such as the "True Believers" described above, bring a personal commitment to the pursuit of settlement through advocacy. In practice, with each client, counsel must negotiate the degree to which they will actively pursue settlement on the client's behalf.

A personal commitment to a particular approach may be difficult for counsel to set aside entirely. Clients whose instructions amount to "sue their lying lips off" may find themselves incompatible with settlement-oriented lawyers, and vice versa. A more common challenge, perhaps, is described as follows:

> Some clients come to a litigator and expect a bulldog who believes in their case, believes in their defence and isn't going to compromise and is going to go in there and fight for them – and what do they think if the second question out of the lawyer's mouth is, what are you prepared to pay or what are you prepared to settle for?[65]

Even when both lawyer and client have committed to a conflict resolution approach (e.g., by signing a collaborative retainer agreement), research shows that each adopts this strategy for different reasons. Lawyers are often motivated by deeply held values and beliefs about appropriate approaches to conflict resolution, while their clients are usually motivated by far more pragmatic considerations like minimizing the expenditure of time and money. Collaborative lawyers are sometimes taken aback when they find that their clients are less committed than they had hoped to consensus building; at this point, they may press them to accept their own values about "healthy family transitions" with minimal acrimony.[66]

The autonomy/paternalism debate highlights the ways in which lawyers' own values and beliefs inevitably influence their judgments regarding the best approach to client advocacy. Unlike the zealous advocacy model, which assumes that lawyers have no normative position of their own and no emotional attachment to the resolution of the issues in any particular way, conflict resolution advocacy recognizes that the reality is far more complex. While rights-based bargaining explicitly describes the normative basis for a position (in terms of an asserted legal principle), a negotiation over needs and interests also implies a set of underlying values and principles (e.g., if I want to return to school after my divorce to further my education, my normative assumption is that good parents can combine child rearing with furthering their own education). Interests-based bargaining is not neutral, and neither are conflict resolution advocates.

The challenge for New Lawyers – and the distinction between their approach and that of the traditional zealous advocate – is to be openly and willingly transparent about the values they bring to conflict resolution. This transparency includes where they stand on the fighter/settler continuum, whether they are committed to resolving matters by negotiation in every case or to trying to settle only to a certain point or for certain cases, and how comfortable they are in accepting and working with client values and priorities. Attitudes towards these and other issues that implicate personal values are an important part of the advocacy that lawyers offer their clients, and clients need to know what they are buying.

The Future of Advocacy

Reclaiming advocacy and changing the historical assumptions about what makes an effective legal advocate require new meta-principles that transcend the old. These include a new emphasis on the importance of negotiation in legal practice; a commitment to constructive conflict engagement, including appropriate information exchange; an ability to switch hats between fighting and settling; and a recognition of the value of non-legal, preventive, or systems-based solutions. A new model of conflict resolution advocacy should be alive to the many tensions that exist between lawyer's aspirations and clients' interests, between the long-term and short-term consequences of conflict resolution, between individual and community or systems interests, and between what disputants want and what they need. Into this fluidity and uncertainty we should also be willing to introduce an examination of the ways in which the advocate's own values and beliefs inevitably shape participation in the bargaining process.

The promotion of an alternative model of conflict resolution advocacy requires the thoughtful and skillful development of new behaviours, skills, and practices that reflect these meta-principles. Some of these skills are described in this book, but we have much more work to do on identifying and then teaching them. Some grow out of more traditional legal skills, whereas others are less familiar. As ever, the role of law schools in encouraging or neglecting the development of these skills will be critical. The most significant challenge, however, is a conceptual one. It requires us to be imaginative and flexible in contemplating the extent to which a partisan role can be effective in promoting problem solving. This is a major challenge for the New Lawyer – one that, if met, will profoundly change the goals and practice of legal advocacy.

6

The Lawyer/Client Relationship

Practising conflict resolution advocacy changes many aspects of the traditional lawyer/client relationship. The stable assumptions of the historical model, where clients "instruct" lawyers by accepting their expert advice, are challenged by a conflict resolution model that seeks to build consensus by drawing on the input of all parties. Conflict resolution processes require collaboration not only between the disputing parties but also between lawyer and clients. This collaboration offers clients the potential for a far more active role, one very different from that patterned on the traditional lawyer-in-charge model described in Chapter 3. At best, this is an authentic working partnership between lawyer and client.

The lawyer-in-charge model is not easily replaced by such a partnership. Many lawyers find it hard to cede power to their clients unless faced with explicit demands to do so (most likely from experienced parties and corporate clients). Even then, some lawyers struggle with the expectation of their experienced commercial clients that the clients should participate in all decision making, and with the growing expectation among personal clients that they need to be part of the action in order to protect the expenditure of their limited resources.

The roots of the word "client" can be traced back to a Latin verb that refers to the right of a Roman aristocrat to impose his own name on his slaves[1] – an unpromising start for a partnership. How did we get here?

Traditional Conceptions of the Lawyer/Client Relationship

In common with other aspects of the culture of legal practice, lawyers' expectations regarding "managing" both their client and the case are formed during law school. Real flesh-and-blood clients, with all their inconvenient idiosyncrasies and emotional needs, are virtually invisible in law school. They usually intrude only as names at the top of headnotes, rather than as real people with goals, needs, emotions, and challenges. Legal education does almost nothing to prepare prospective lawyers to relate to clients, as clients are sometimes painfully aware:

> Let's face it, what in law school teaches a lawyer how to read the needs of the client? Nothing.[2]

In law school, clients are presented as the object of a set of legal strategies directed by counsel. On the rare occasions that they are presented as real people, clients are often seen as minor irritants or, at worst, as obstacles to lawyers' pursuit of a rational legal strategy. In an adjudicative model of law, the characterization of clients as essentially passive is functionally efficient – in the same way that adversarial advocacy is functionally efficient – because clients are relevant only insofar as they provide the raw material for making legal arguments.

This idealization of lawyer/client relationships in a predictive, adjudicative frame implicates a model of lawyer/client relations that is focused on the technical knowledge required to achieve "best results" in adjudication. The relationship of lawyer to client is inevitably one of (substantive) expert to naïf, reflected in assumptions about decision making, judgment, and autonomy.[3] Traditional legal negotiations, which focus on legal rules and principles, "both grow from and reinforce the professional expertise of lawyers."[4] Since only lawyers have the skill and knowledge to engage in this type of negotiation, their clients have historically had little choice but to trust them to take control. In common with other elite professions whose expertise gives rise to a claim to autonomy, lawyers are accustomed to clients who give up their own judgment and hand the decision making over to their lawyers.[5]

Douglas Rosenthal's classic work on the dynamics of lawyer/client decision making proposes two models of lawyer/client relations: (1) the "traditional" model, in which the client is passive and the lawyer fairly autonomous, "assuming broad control over the solutions to the problems brought by the client";[6] and (2) the "participatory" approach, in which the client plays a more active role. Rosenthal's analysis suggests that the passive client, who follows the lawyer's advice and is detached from the problem-solving process, is the conventional model. Those who depart from this norm – that is, clients who want to actively participate in areas seen as the domain of lawyers – are seen as aberrant and even disruptive.[7] Despite the fact that Rosenthal's work is now almost fifty years old, its conclusions remain remarkably current, especially in relation to lawyers' expectations.

In the lawyer/client relationship, counsel demonstrate their professional effectiveness by behaving in a way that shows that they know exactly what to do and how to do it. "Taking instructions" from the client often amounts to telling the client what the lawyer will do, and perhaps asking if there are any questions. As one lawyer acknowledged to me:

> I think that ... as advocates ... we had a bad tendency – notwithstanding that we would say: "It's on instructions from my client" or "It's our client's wishes" – that we would really be telling the clients what they *should* do.[8]

Some lawyers are frank about the power and control they are accustomed to wielding in their client relationships, and the "rush" that this brings:

> You basically call the shots when ... client[s] entrust their case to you. A good litigator runs the show. The clients always say, do [what] you want to do ... It's kind of like a director of a play, and when you're in court the biggest CEO is a witness and he's in your world – and you ... direct this play to hopefully a good result at the end of the day in front of a judge.[9]

The traditional assumption of lawyer control and client passivity is strengthened by an underlying norm that has competent lawyers managing cases using routinized and "closed" systems of analysis and solution seeking. In order to advance their case, clients must allow their lawyer to transform their "story" into something that fits a legal frame of reference, which often means making it fit into a "stock story."[10] This influence includes reshaping the clients' expectations and objectives until they are in line with those of the lawyer – for example, moving from repairing a business relationship to obtaining a court order, from impoverishing an ex-spouse to proposing a settlement within the likely legal parameters, or from focusing on relationships to focusing on compensation. As Austin Sarat and William Felstiner remark in their study of divorce lawyers,

The Lawyer/Client Relationship

"time and again we observed lawyers attempting to focus their clients' attention on the issues the lawyers thought to be major while the clients often concentrated on matters that the lawyer considered secondary."[11] This professional reframing means that the lawyer assumes the client's permission to refashion the story in a way that makes it more likely to be successful in a legal-adjudicative framework, emphasizing certain details and overlooking others.[12] The default to a rights-based approach means that the client's narrative must be framed in a way that best advances rights-based arguments, and that this system or mode of analysis is self-contained, controlled by the lawyer, and closed to other perspectives, including that of the client naïf.

An important tenet of the traditional lawyer/client relationship is that only a professional can judge efficacy. If problems are solved by expert knowledge that only the lawyer is privy to, how can the client evaluate the lawyer's performance? Professionals, including not only lawyers but also doctors, engineers, architects, and others, have long assumed autonomy in their unique expertise. Historically, this expertise has been a hallmark of a profession. As one lawyer puts it:

> The way you treat your doctor, who says your child has a cold and you say: "Yes, thank you for helping me doctor." I assume people come to their lawyer, take their advice, and say thank you.[13]

Clients are expected to defer to their lawyer's expertise: "Since they are presumed to be the only judges of how good their work is, no layman or other outsider can make a judgment of what they can do."[14] Scrutiny by outside bodies and evaluation by clients themselves sit uneasily with these assumptions of power and control. While complaint procedures do exist (administered by law societies), these tend to focus on complaints about failure to communicate,[15] rather than on areas of judgment that are difficult for the client to second-guess.

Some law firms, serving primarily commercial clients, have begun to experiment with client evaluations of individual lawyers. Although the data remain in-house, this is an important development, as is the support of larger firms for the principle of client feedback.[16] Both complaints and evaluation occur only after the lawyer/client relationship has ended, and the questions only scratch the surface of the control exerted by lawyers in most client relationships. Nevertheless, this is an important step in awareness of the potential value of client feedback, which has historically been discounted as unimportant.

The bottom line is that there is a clear power imbalance in many lawyer/client relationships, especially those involving personal clients who are one-shotters.

The crux of the imbalance is the heavy reliance on technical legal expertise, which, absent egregious neglect or error, is virtually unassailable by lay persons.

Changing Conditions of a Changing Relationship

While the assumptions of Rosenthal's traditional "passive" model still resonate especially among some older lawyers, expectations of lawyer control today are often ameliorated by the power and status of the client. This is especially true of commercial clients, who have long assumed a larger role in decision making (described further below).[17]

Even outside this group, societal changes over the past fifteen years have significantly affected the extent to which personal clients, even "one-shotters," will accept a model that places them in an essentially passive role. The assumed deference of clients to professionals is eroding. There are more tools for self-help and access to knowledge, and ways for consumers to network, that support a stronger culture of self-empowerment among consumers. The World Wide Web facilitates access to information and opinion that was previously available only from professional sources. This information surplus has fed the public's appetite for consumer self-help, increased their desire to sit at the table for decision making, and fuels a demand for value for money.[18] In what William Ury calls "the age of knowledge," the Internet represents the potency of access to knowledge and global communication, which empowers consumers and revolutionaries alike.[19] Individuals who meet with lawyers in order to ask for "legal coaching" in order to represent *themselves* – typically the result of limited resources to pay for the cost of full representation – are far removed, conceptually and practically, from Rosenthal's "passive" client.[20]

There are many parallels between changes in client attitudes towards legal service providers and changes occurring in the practice of medicine. Just as in law, changing client expectations in medicine affect the relationship between medical doctors and their patients. Like lawyers, doctors are accustomed to using their expertise to identify and define the problems and to determine how these problems should be addressed. Earlier writing on doctor/patient relationships emphasized the role of the doctor in "fixing" the "problem" of sickness, which (somewhat like conflict) was considered a deviance.[21] In an echo of Rosenthal, passive patients who accept a doctor's advice without question and follow instructions are seen as compliant and easier to work with. In this traditional model, the doctor's expertise goes virtually unquestioned: "Professionalization grants physicians a monopoly on the definition of health and illness, and they use this power over diagnosis to extend their control."[22]

The pushback against presumptive professional control and expertise began in the 1950s with the work of Thomas Szasz and Marc Hollender, who argued that "a relationship of mutual participation" in medicine would produce better therapeutic outcomes.[23] In this model, patients should be encouraged to both raise and manage issues that relate to their care, including making informed choices about treatment. In law, pressure to rethink the traditional hierarchy of control within the lawyer/client relationship has come primarily from access-to-justice and poverty law advocates. Gerald Lopez has coined the expression "rebellious lawyering" – meaning to empower clients and collaborate with them.[24] These lawyers recognize that many people are excluded from legal processes because they have neither the skills nor the social power to participate in them in any meaningful way without counsel – but they cannot afford to pay for a lawyer. These constraints "undermine the capacity of many people in our society to use the procedural rituals that are formally available to them," and thereby undermine participation in a democratic society.[25] At the same time, there is growing recognition of the need for public participation in situations where decision making affects them.[26]

Whether or not the arguments of Szasz (in relation to medical practice) or Alfieri, White and Lopez, and others (in relation to legal practice) would have eventually succeeded in making inroads into the culture of client passivity in legal services, we shall never know – because the Internet has changed everything. Over the past two decades, the increasing availability of medical information through the World Wide Web has greatly accelerated patient empowerment. Patients are increasingly "literate" in medical developments, and by surfing the web may feel that they have access to an alternative viewpoint, if not a medical opinion. Medical malpractice litigation and the publicity that some cases attract have introduced a level of skepticism among patients. The important point here is that whether or not patients really do know and understand more about their healthcare options than they used to, they *believe* that they have the means to. This belief raises different consumer expectations and undermines the historical professional deference and status inequality between doctor and patient.

In law, too, the role of the Internet has been pivotal in changing client expectations. Websites offering legal information and even examples of correctly completed court forms proliferate, with more emerging every week.[27] Lawyers need to be conscious that this generation of consumers is likely to either have, or believe that they have, far more pre-existing knowledge than any previous generation. Two consequences are diminishing deference towards lawyers as the gatekeepers of professional knowledge, and greater demand among clients for what they see as value for money in legal services – what Richard Susskind dubs the "more-for-less" phenomenon.[28] As one self-represented litigant succinctly put it, "Google is my lawyer."[29] And Google is free.

Access to information on the web is also driving a self-help culture that routinely questions and even second-guesses the advice of experts.[30] Clients in all areas of legal practice are looking for greater involvement in decision making and empowerment regarding issues that are important to them, whether it is a business decision or the negotiation of a family conflict. Of course, some clients will always prefer to delegate decision making to their lawyer – these clients see the relief of responsibility for problem solving as the essence of what they are paying their lawyer for. But there is mounting evidence, both anecdotal and empirical,[31] that more and more clients prefer greater responsibility (especially when it saves them money) and the ability to exercise more control than simply handing over the matter to counsel for transformation into a legal dispute with its own mysterious narrative. They are less inclined to accept that their professional adviser always knows best and should function autonomously, without financial constraints.[32]

This development must be understood in the context of the costs of legal representation and its increasing unaffordability for most people. Few private individuals can afford a protracted legal struggle. Data from Canada, the United States, and the United Kingdom bear this out.[33] This is most succinctly expressed by the report of the Civil Justice Council of England and Wales to the Lord Chancellor:

> It is a reality that those who cannot afford legal services and those for whom the state will not provide legal aid comprise the larger part of the population of England and Wales. Thus for most members of the public who become involved in legal proceedings they will have to represent themselves. The thing that keeps that reality below the surface is simply the hope or belief on the part of most people that they will not have a civil dispute.[34]

The next sections consider changes in the traditional lawyer/client relationship in two distinct areas of practice: the service of corporate and institutional clients, and the service of personal clients.

Corporate and Institutional Clients

Signs of change in client expectations are most evident in corporate and institutional practice. Like personal clients, corporate and institutional clients have historically chosen to nominate their legal representatives as both managers

The Lawyer/Client Relationship

and agents in disputing[35] – the expertise of lawyers was seen as being sufficient and appropriate to resolve the problem, requiring minimal input from the business client – but a disruption has occurred in the last thirty years. The rising costs of legal action have motivated corporate clients to look for cost reductions and greater budgetary control over their legal portfolios, sometimes achieved by moving them in-house. At the same time, corporate clients have shed the deference traditionally afforded to counsel in favour of a more "businesslike" and hands-on approach to legal services.

One lawyer describes an incident early in his career when he realized that business clients saw themselves as "customers," rather than as subject to the authority and status of their lawyer:

> It was a very difficult realization for me when I watched a client walk all over a senior partner when I was a very junior associate. I was watching how a person I revered, as one of the smartest people I had ever seen in my life, was selling shoes, in effect, to a customer. This "customer" should have been holding the senior partner in reverence because he was such a brilliant, capable man but we're just shoe salesmen ... or dispute resolution salesmen. That's the basic underlying ... relationship with a client – I'm selling service and I want them to buy it ... It's not that I don't want to be a grand professional, or hold some 100 year old notion of a superior profession. But the reality is if the clients don't believe it, then it's not real anymore ... [M]y illusion in growing up and through law school was that you approach your professionals with a degree of respect and reverence ... I learned quickly that we are selling a service.[36]

A growing role for business clients is a natural consequence of exponentially rising legal costs and the increasing scrutiny of costs by clients. Maintaining business competitiveness means avoiding the absorption of corporate energy and monies in litigation potholes, and instead finding a smart route to settlement. The ballooning costs of litigation mean that experienced commercial clients are less willing to be passive and more inclined to assert expectations for efficient management of conflict. Business managers are showing an increased interest in participation and control, which has coincided with (or led to) the erosion of deferential barriers.

Many business clients feel that they can do better in moving towards a business solution if they participate actively and directly in discussions and can suggest opportunities for their input. Even though their role in planning and process may be limited (e.g., giving depositions, appearing at pre-trial conferences, or, more recently, participating in mediation), some corporate representatives build up considerable experience in litigation and some justifiably feel that they have more to contribute to the resolution of a business dispute than counsel might recognize. Some are forthright in bringing this to counsel's attention. There are of course many other variables, including how much an individual business client wishes to be closely involved with litigation, and the nature of the personal relationship that develops between the chief executive officer and counsel.

The same economic forces have led to demands for less costly and more efficient methods of dispute resolution – specifically, to a growing desire for early reporting, strategic settlement planning, and early dispute resolution.[37] In many cases, this is seen as more likely if legal work is done in-house, in keeping with the corporate culture.[38] Where outside counsel are still used, they find themselves subject to far more scrutiny. Commercial litigators sometimes rue this loss of control. The following quotations offer a few examples:

> When I started practising back in the mid 60s there was a terrible arrogance in our profession. We thought all clients were not necessarily idiots but didn't know what was best for them, and the client had no idea what was going on in the legal system. People are 100 percent more sophisticated now, know what goes on in the system generally, and are much more conscious of where their buck is going than they used to be.[39]

> The old "just fight-at-all-costs" and don't look at it [the legal bill], don't even think about an approach [opening negotiations], [that attitude] just doesn't seem to exist anymore.[40]

> Now more and more clients are asking for an assessment right at the top from a timing stand point, and asking you to analyze what's the best time to get a resolution of the thing and especially with in-house counsel involved. They are very conscious of the costs and they want to know up front where the thing is going.[41]

Many commercial lawyers now work directly with inside counsel. In many ways, corporate counsel inhabit a parallel universe to private practice. Unlike their private practice colleagues, inside counsel are obliged to account for and justify all litigation expenditure to a manager.[42] Unlike their peers in private practice, corporate counsel are generally valued and rewarded for their abilities to resolve disputes efficiently.

This approach to conflict resolution clashes with the adversarial culture of much private commercial practice. The extent of this divide is well captured in

John Lande's 1998 study comparing attitudes towards litigation between outside counsel, inside counsel, and executives. The faith of lawyers in litigation vastly outweighed that same sentiment in business executives. One business executive quoted by Lande comments:

> We are so anti-litigation that [someone in the company who would commence litigation] would get their hand slapped if they bring in the lawyers.[43]

Many executives find it hard to embrace a fixed and potentially constraining system of precedent or rules (such as the legal system). Another business executive interviewed for Lande's study remarks:

> As I look back at my business career, I have an antipathy for precedent at times because I find it constraining in terms of the ability to break new ground. So I don't necessarily always look for "Well, how was it done before? Or what did some previous court decide? Or what did some previous regulatory body conclude on this?" as opposed to "Give me the facts and circumstances today and where we want to go in the future. Try to define a problem or the opportunity in terms of the visions of the future as opposed to the precedent in the past."[44]

As their numbers rise, so do the status and clout of in-house counsel within their organizations.[45] The strong emergence of a new professional corporate counsel is just one of the ways in which traditional relationships between lawyers and their corporate and institutional clients are being widely renegotiated.

Personal Clients

Personal clients begin from a position that is generally far less powerful than that of commercial clients when attempting to renegotiate the lawyer/client relationship to reflect a new culture of affordability, value for money, and collaboration. They are often working with a lawyer for the first time, and their expectations may come from media or friends, rather than from direct experience. Despite this, there are many signs of change.

The factors driving these changes are broadly the same as those driving change in the relationships between lawyers and their more experienced corporate clients. Access to the World Wide Web enables prospective clients to feel that they enter with some pre-existing knowledge and have the alternative of representing themselves.[46] One respondent in the National Self-Represented Litigants Study described how she first "interviewed" prospective legal counsel (a new experience for some lawyers). She noted drily: "A lot of lawyers told me what they wanted to do as if it was *them* making the decision" (emphasis added).[47]

Self-representation (even partial) enables those who are otherwise or formerly personal clients[48] to experience the legal system directly, without an intermediary in the form of counsel. The results are striking. There is growing public criticism of archaic legal processes and procedures that protract disputes and drive costs up. There are growing complaints about legal representatives' being part of a "club" that works to marginalize those representing themselves, and even strategizes to disempower them.[49] These increasingly common experiences, along with the widespread problem of unaffordable legal services, supports calls for the expansion of para-professional legal services that are more affordable to many litigants,[50] and even for the deregulation of legal services. These are all clear signs that the public is rethinking legal services and is less willing than in the past to give the legal profession the benefit of the doubt.

At the same time, settlement processes allow for – or in some cases require – a greater role and involvement for personal clients. These include contracting with a lawyer to use procedures that give clients a clear role and set of responsibilities (such as collaborative family law) or procedural rules that require client attendance at mediation or case settlement.[51] And increasingly, third parties in these fora will expect to hear directly from the clients.

The idea that they will have more power and control in the negotiation process is an attractive one for contemporary personal clients. In their own words:

> I do need to have a sense of control ... This [collaborative law] is the process that is much more likely to give you that sense of control, the lawyers are much less likely just to say "we're doing this."[52]

> It gives you a sense of control. You are controlling your own destiny.[53]

> I like the idea of no fighting. Bypass the fighting and let's get to it. It's going to happen anyway, you know. It's not a nice process but it's happened, so let's get to the other side where I can heal.[54]

The traditional assumptions of control and hierarchy are challenged when counsel and client participate in both private and institutional settlement processes. For example, the "four-way" (two lawyers, two clients) negotiation structure used in collaborative law emphasizes "mutual participation" by lawyer and client. Collaborative law has raised new questions over the division of responsibility between lawyer and client, and how work is billed. One consequence is emergence of new complaints from clients that their lawyers now sit back and expect them to do all the work.[55] These comments – whether fair or not – point to the emergence of a more empowered, self-confident consumer who asks more questions than ever before and sets higher standards for competence and efficiency.[56] In the courts, mandatory and quasi-mandatory mediation and settlement conference programs are having a similar impact. Mandatory mediation means that clients who have no knowledge or experience of mediation are attending sessions with a mediator, along with their lawyers, early on in their file. Studies have consistently demonstrated that the vast majority welcome the chance for mediation and see it as a valuable opportunity, whether or not settlement follows.[57] There are also signs that personal clients sometimes grow impatient with their lawyer's hesitancy about opening negotiations with the other side, especially when the client is concerned about costs.[58] Interestingly, there is no significant difference in satisfaction levels, which remain consistently high, between clients mandated into mediation and those who chose the process voluntarily.[59] One client described the mediation experience as follows:

> [The process] gave me a chance to express my complaints ... I felt quite at ease and was able to express what I wanted to express, and the [other party] was able to express their concerns. We were both listening and talking. It had a good feeling in that respect.[60]

Some personal clients maintain that the mediation process is useful for them even in the face of their lawyer's discouragement and lack of session preparation. In such cases, clients sometimes suggest a reversal of the traditional hierarchy: that if their lawyers don't want to "get with the program," the clients might be better off without them. One client expressed this as follows:

> If I could have sat down with the other person, and no lawyer, we would have settled.[61]

Others criticize their counsel's approach to settlement, complaining that it made settlement more difficult.

> [My lawyer told me before mediation] you can't say this, this, and this. Because we're holding that as a secret weapon if we go to trial.[62]

Among former clients who are now self-representing, there is a consistent suspicion that their counsel intentionally "dragged things out," in order to make more in fees.[63]

Following Rosenthal's work, other writers have developed models of client-centred legal services that envisage greater equality and a working partnership between lawyers and their personal clients.[64] This approach requires the lawyer to adopt a holistic perspective on client issues, looking, for example, at how to transition a family through divorce rather than simply dealing with the legal issues of custody and property. Personal clients have expanding expectations of a more holistic service that provides them, for example, not just with a divorce decree (for which they may feel they could fill out the paperwork by themselves and save money on counsel) but also, for example, a parenting contract, financial planning and tax advice on post-divorce options, and referral to professional assistance to help with their children's special needs. One sign of this change is the emergence of websites that offer not only family law information but also assistance with negotiation, referral to counselling and mental health services, tax planning, and a range of other services.[65]

The New Lawyer should review legal needs within the context of a larger picture of the conflict and its consequences, and, where appropriate, refer clients to other professionals to address psychological, financial, and other needs outside the ambit of the lawyer's expertise. Therapeutic jurisprudence scholars describe this analysis as the identification of "psycho-legal soft spots," wherein lawyer and client identify sources of anxiety, depression, hurt feelings, and so on that may be the unintended consequences of a particular legal action or strategy.[66] The premise is that a cookie-cutter approach is both inappropriate and inadequate in addressing underlying client needs (especially where these flow from systemic inequities or disadvantages) or in ensuring that more harm is not done by formalistic legal interventions. Working from the client's own narrative rather than imposing an external framing of the issues enables the client to develop a closer working relationship with both legal counsel and the problem itself.

Across all sectors of legal practice, clients are signalling their changing expectations for shared responsibility and participation in legal problem solving. Participation and empowerment, rather than the unquestioning acceptance of professional advice on what to do and how to do it, are increasingly seen as important aspects of a democratic, participatory culture, in which "more-for-less"[67] and value for money are core consumer values. This calls for the development of a new model of a working partnership between lawyer and client. Four areas of lawyer/client relations both highlight these changes and illustrate some of the philosophical and practical terms of a new relationship.

The Lawyer/Client Relationship

These are: (1) how lawyers and clients plan and make decisions; (2) how lawyers respond to client demands for changing financial structures and greater transparency in legal costs; (3) how client participation in settlement processes impacts the dynamics of such processes; and (4) the personal or affective[68] dimensions of a new working partnership between lawyer and client.

Planning and Decision Making

Reframing the lawyer/client relationship as a working partnership has profound implications for the balance of power in decision making. A partnership gives the client power not only to review and critique decisions but also to participate in making those decisions. This shift of power also requires clients to take greater responsibility for choices and outcomes. Whereas clients once told their lawyers, "I trust you; you go ahead and decide," now more and more want in on the process of decision making. As one client put it, "[I want to be] in the mix at all times."[69]

The contrast with the "old style" is made clear in this interview with a younger lawyer:

INTERVIEWEE: Counsel who practised for many years under the old style ... I think that they had a stronger sense of their lead role ... of their role in making all decisions on how a case should be managed.
INTERVIEWER: Rather than sharing those decisions with the client?
INTERVIEWEE: Rather than getting the client involved [as they are involved under mandatory mediation].[70]

Mandatory settlement processes that require the participation of clients change the extent and type of information that counsel need from their clients. Instead of filing the pleadings and waiting for the legal process to grind along, mandatory settlement meetings force lawyers to ready their case for negotiation at an early stage. Practically speaking, they need significant input from their clients in order to do this effectively. In anticipation of early mediation, there are many questions that lawyers now need to ask at the planning stage, questions that only clients can answer and that are not necessarily related to making the legal case. Gathering and analyzing this information may even enable counsel to make an early offer to the other side to settle the case; where cases are referred to mandatory mediation, studies show that they tend to settle before mediation.[71] If decision making is to be undertaken jointly, there should be no surprises for the lawyer in a future meeting, collaborative negotiation, or mediation:

I ask them [the client], "what's *really* going on in the dispute?" If they're the defendant, what they really think the reason for the dispute is? If they're the plaintiff, what they think the reason is that the defendant isn't doing what they want them to do? What's the real reason behind it – do they have financial difficulties, that type of thing.[72]

For instance, in commercial areas you want to know about the business relationship between the two parties – how long it's been going on, what future opportunities there are together, whether there is an interest in keeping the relationship together for long-term purposes or other business opportunities and so you want to know a lot more about that than you would if you were strictly looking at that case at hand and the legal rights in the dispute issue.[73]

The different types and volume of information shared between lawyers and clients are a natural consequence of engaging the latter more completely in the development of a dispute resolution strategy. For example, business clients who are directly involved in planning for mediation can provide additional information on business needs and goals, both long-term and short-term, which can be effectively incorporated into planning a strategy for negotiation. Issues that would not otherwise surface may do so; for example, a manager may introduce a discussion of systemic issues relating to workforce management that will affect his or her willingness to settle. Instead of removing emotional and psychological issues from the negotiation, the inclusion of clients in planning may mean that important and otherwise unspoken barriers to settlement can be raised and discussed. One writer neatly encapsulates this shift in the agenda for lawyer/client discussions as enabling "more space for human agency within [the] lawyering project."[74]

The bottom line: for counsel to make effective use of early settlement processes, they will need to plan carefully with their clients. If this takes place before discoveries, counsel will probably find themselves relying to a substantial degree on what their clients tells them, without the opportunity to verify what they have been told and still gather appropriate supporting evidence for a claim. A joint decision to try to settle early might be a simple matter of math:

If there is a possibility of settlement before discovery then it's a good thing to ... try and do that because of the cost associated upfront with legal expenses.[75]

On a small claim, sometimes it's just better to go ahead with less information because it's not cost effective to actually get all the records or do all the interviews, if you're only talking about a claim that might only be worth $15,000, $20,000 or something like that.[76]

The sharing of planning and strategic decisions between lawyer and client means that some of the weight of both moral and practical responsibility shifts from the lawyer to the client.

> The overall responsibility has shifted to the clients. We tell the clients they are responsible for the problem. We are going to help you to fix it. We will give you the mechanism, the procedure for resolving it. But it's not our problem. Before, I think too many lawyers would make their clients' problems their own.[77]

Depending on the extent to which counsel embraces a working partnership with their clients, this shift may be significant or marginal, but it will occur. This rebalancing relieves a significant source of stress for many lawyers, who testify to the toll exacted by litigation:

> I hated taking these things home with me. I really worried about the outcomes. I would be up to 2 a.m. preparing.[78]

Not all lawyers welcome this opportunity to relinquish some control. Some find it an unsettling and disconcerting experience. Relying on the client for information prior to an early negotiation or mediation may be nerve-racking, and it is certainly counterintuitive for lawyers accustomed to the lawyer-in-charge model. Even lawyers committed to a client partnership and a settlement-oriented strategy find some of the consequences of client empowerment uncomfortable. Some collaborative lawyers have described to me their discomfort when their clients become sufficiently self-confident that they meet without their lawyers and make a "kitchen-table agreement."[79] Others note that it is now more common for clients to question their final bill.[80] Collaborative lawyers who offer their family clients additional choices such as working with a therapist or financial specialist may then feel excluded and strangely powerless if clients like this approach so much that they spend more time with the other professional than with their lawyer.

A similar ambivalence over the reality of sharing control is sometimes expressed by clients. Some clients resist participating in the planning or implementation of joint strategies, preferring to hand over their dispute to their lawyer in a more traditional fashion, describing this as "what I pay him/her for." Others may embrace a partnership approach in principle, yet express resentment that they are paying a lawyer as well as being asked to carry out many of the functions themselves (e.g., gathering documents and preparing plans before meetings).

Some commentators have pointed out that not all clients want to work as partners, nor are all capable. A good example is the degree to which previously financially inexperienced partners in divorce (often the wife) are asked to consider the data and make their own decisions about financial support. One collaborative client described a conversation in which her lawyer explained a financial issue and then asked her if she understood:

I said no, [I don't], but I trust you.

Her lawyer was not willing to accept this role and pressed her further:

He replied "No, K., you need to understand this issue to make a decision about it." So he explained it again and asked me what I thought.[81]

Even when both lawyers and clients are committed to shared decision making, we are still learning about the prerequisites for such a partnership to work well in practice. One is ensuring that the client can give informed consent. This does not preclude the lawyer from making a recommendation or stating a preference – for example, about a preferred approach to dispute resolution, or a strategic choice. But, for example, offering clients a single option or course of action and asking them to "decide" is not authentic shared decision making.[82] Whether a lawyer is positive or negative about a particular procedure is extremely influential in determining the clients' own views.[83] The New Lawyer should be transparent about process preferences, but avoid advocating for a single course and placing perhaps unintended yet significant pressure on the client. In a working partnership, each party may have preferences and they should be mindful of this. At this point, the lawyer needs to be able to step back and let the client decide.

This interaction of information and choice goes to the heart of the adjustment that is taking place in the lawyer/client relationship. It can be a difficult transition for both lawyers and clients habituated to the "old" approach. From law school on, lawyers are trained to take responsibility for directing their clients towards what they believe is best for them – in this way, the lawyer-in-charge belief is first planted and encouraged. Engaging in an authentic and open-ended dialogue, both at the planning stage and throughout the implementation of a dispute resolution strategy, runs contrary to many of these instincts. But finding the balance between continuing to offer expertise and respecting the autonomy of clients in setting their goals is key to successful lawyer/client relationships for the New Lawyer. It is what modern-day clients expect.

Financial Choices and Alternatives

An increasingly prominent aspect of changing client expectations is access to more affordable and collaborative services, for example, the use of limited-scope retainers,[84] fixed-fee services, and legal coaching.[85] A renegotiated relationship over strategy and decision making is part of this demand. Growing numbers of self-represented litigants are seeking legal assistance via limited-scope retainers to ensure that they keep control over costs, while carrying out themselves many of the tasks traditionally undertaken by a lawyer. The parameters of the retainer may be the subject of bargaining between lawyer and client. Limited-scope retainer agreements commonly list a number of possible legal services that lawyer and client can tick off or not.[86] The traditional assumptions regarding an open-ended retainer agreement are challenged by clients seeking value for money and questioning whether they need or can afford a full-representation model.

Many lawyers express understandable anxiety about an arrangement where they do not have a complete picture of the case or control over next steps, and are instead only consulted from time to time – for example, to review documentation or to prepare the (primarily) self-represented litigant for a particular event. They worry that clients may not fully understand the limits of their responsibilities, and that they may not be fulfilling their fiduciary duties.[87] Lawyers who are starting to offer limited-scope services to the self-represented sometimes express anxiety about their loss of control and professional liability issues,[88] while others welcome the shifting of responsibility to their sometime client.[89] Some clients who choose the unbundled option begin with high hopes of working autonomously without the assistance of counsel, but as they become increasingly overwhelmed by the complexity of the legal process, they may choose to hand over more and more work to their lawyer.[90]

The New Lawyer, especially one working in personal legal services, has little choice but to embrace these challenges. They flow from the shifting nexus of power and control in lawyer/client relationships, and are a response to changing consumer demands. While many practitioners will continue to work on a largely or wholly retainer/billable-hours arrangement, more and more lawyers will be asked by their clients to consider either coaching, unbundled services, fixed-fee services, or a combination of these approaches. Law societies across Canada permit limited-scope retainers, and the legal insurers indemnify lawyers offering such services.[91] Despite widespread and often fearful speculation on this point, there is no evidence that there is a higher rate of complaints (or lawsuits) when lawyers offer limited-scope retainers. In the United States, insurers have not reported higher levels of malpractice claims arising from unbundling.[92] Similarly, there is no reported rise in complaints to professional bodies as a result of limited-scope retainers.[93] There are no Canadian data because no provincial law society yet tracks this information, although in an informal file "audit," two provincial law societies reported that they had no complaints at all from clients about limited-scope retainers.[94]

Personal services clients want lawyers to offer limited-scope services because this is more affordable and because it enables clients to feel that they remain in control of both the overall direction of the file and its associated costs. In a sample of 253 self-represented litigants, virtually all described searching for some type of limited legal assistance. Only thirteen found a lawyer wiling to "unbundle," usually their former counsel.[95] Respondents described seeking assistance with completing forms, reviewing completed forms and other documents, writing a letter to the other side, answering questions of law, preparing for a hearing, and representation in court for one hearing only. There was widespread public bafflement at this – why would a lawyer not accept their money for a few hours of assistance? While the reasons may be clearer to lawyers, the public does not understand this inflexibility: "A mechanic will tell you how long and about how much it will cost – a lawyer won't do that."[96] The legal profession is on notice to become more open to offering different types of financial arrangements, or at minimum, adequately explaining to clients why they do not.

A similar groundswell of dissatisfaction exists in relation to the lack of transparency in a traditional retainer/billable-hours model. The stories of shocking bills appearing after relatively short periods of time are legend.

> Martha [not her real name] was shocked to receive court papers seeking joint custody of her young daughter, from the putative father with whom she had had a short-term relationship. "Once those papers were served, it was like a runaway train. There was no opportunity for us to talk reason." Her ex was a lawyer and knew what to do and had the money to do it. He wouldn't mediate.
>
> Alarmed, Martha retained a lawyer right away and paid her a $5,000 retainer. Six weeks after the retainer agreement was signed, Martha received a bill for a further $24,000 on top of the retainer. By this time she had had one court date. She cashed in her RRSPs to pay this bill.

"It seemed to be the only option because it was so close to the beginning of the process – and I desperately needed a lawyer to represent me. She told me 'if you represent yourself you will be eaten alive.' But I was scared about what more it was going to cost."

Shortly after this, Martha decided she would have to represent herself because she had no funds left to pay for legal representation.[97]

Complaints about the lack of transparency in legal service costs – including a failure in some cases to provide itemized statements of account – has led some jurisdictions to require lawyers to provide more upfront, detailed information to clients.[98]

The New Lawyer should anticipate that clients will expect transparency about likely costs and should receive regular updates. The assumption that clients should delegate to their lawyer the stewardship of their funds is no longer acceptable for many clients who, while they may come to trust their lawyer, still want to know what their choices are, and exactly how their money is being spent.

Client Participation in Settlement Processes

I described earlier how client participation affects lawyer/client planning for a dispute resolution event like a mediation or a settlement conference. Another consequence of client participation in settlement processes is the need to prepare for the client's actual contribution to the negotiation – how extensive will it be, when will the lawyer speak for the client, and when will the client speak for himself or herself, and how will lawyer and client stay on the same page as partners throughout the process? However minimal the client's role may be in practice,[99] the willing or reluctant inclusion of the client as a player in negotiations constrains lawyers' autonomy to play out the conflict relying solely on their own strategies. The New Lawyer needs to be able to maximize the benefits of the client's presence and participation, and anticipate and minimize any possible negative consequences.

One lawyer describes his early experiences with bringing clients to mediation thus:

It completely caught me off guard at first. The first few mediations, I hadn't had any mediation training. My only training was the general attitude in the profession that this is a lot of horse crap and I had settlements hit me between the eyes and I couldn't believe my clients sold out on me the way they did. I was concerned that I had a serious client-control problem.[100]

Having clients present redirected the locus of control in a way this lawyer did not expect and had not planned for. In informal settlement procedures, lawyers have far less control over the proceedings and need to understand how their clients will behave and how to relate to them throughout the process. The presence of clients changes the practical dynamics of decision making – instead of lawyers bringing back the other side's proposal to their client and presenting it with their own overlay of analysis and recommendations, decisions in mediation may be made on the spot as new offers emerge or solutions develop.

The past thirty years have seen the introduction of a range of dispute resolution processes that either mandate or strongly encourage client participation. Jacquie Nolan-Haley suggests that the strong trend towards client participation changes the client-involvement question from "whether" to "how": "The critical decision-making questions in mediation are concerned not with the extent to which clients should be allowed to participate, but rather the manner in which lawyers should be involved."[101] Some might see such an assessment as premature, but it presages the significance of a change in practice that has fundamental implications for the balance of power between lawyers and clients. Attitudes towards considering client participation in dispute processes are a litmus test of how far lawyers are willing to share control and decision making in a partnership, or whether the old hierarchy will reassert itself. This is at least partly a matter to be resolved by experience. Effective power sharing requires more than a brief conversation outside the settlement conference room or mediation venue (which is still typical).[102] Counsel experienced in mediation and other convened settlement processes know that bringing in an unprepared client who has not agreed in advance on how to present the issues (e.g., how much and what information to disclose, or what options to canvass) may be a recipe for disaster. As one lawyer reflected:

> I am much more involved with the client in terms of what we're going to say and what we're not going to say in a mediation case as opposed to a standard litigation, because you just have to micro-manage what your client's saying in a mediation because if it doesn't settle, you've let time bombs loose.[103]

The unease inexperienced lawyers feel about the participation of clients in settlement processes speaks volumes about how much it challenges conventional lawyer/client norms. Inexperienced lawyers sometimes use their control to ensure that their client's participation is minimal and that the discussion remains dominated by the lawyers, leaving the clients to simply be "wallflowers."

Some are candid about this strategy. In the following examples, "them" refers to clients in general:

> I'll warn them – I say if you're saying stuff and I can't tell you in a quiet way I will kick you – so they know it's coming.[104]

> I teach them to "shut-up."[105]

Nancy Welsh has argued that there is significant evidence of the silencing of clients in court-connected mediation (which lawyers are customarily required to attend with their clients).[106] Although clients increasingly accompany lawyers to settlement discussions (either because they are required to under the rules of civil procedure, or have voluntarily agreed to protocols such as collaborative law), many clients complain that their lawyers often fail to fully prepare them or to consult with them about how to effectively use the process. In reflecting on the disparity between advocates for mediation (who emphasize "decision control" by clients) and disputants themselves (who present mixed assessments of their actual control), Welsh points out that while lawyers assume their clients understand that their consent is required to any agreement, clients themselves may not experience a lawyer-dominated negotiation as being under their own "control."[107] This underscores the fact that unless both lawyer and client embrace a new partnership model, new inclusive processes may function in a very similar manner to more traditional ones (such as motions hearings), where clients are entirely, or almost entirely, passive.

The efforts made by some lawyers to maintain complete control in mediation has not gone unnoticed by their clients. Some clients report extreme dissatisfaction with being excluded or silenced by their lawyers in mediation:

> In the first few mediations, our lawyer told me to speak only when I was asked a question, and the mediation was mostly an exchange between the lawyers. Then the city solicitor changed. He told me that mediation was really for the clients to talk, not the lawyers – that we can use it to do the [public relations] thing and if it's a legitimate case say sorry – and that he would take care of the legal issues. Now my feeling about mediation has totally changed.[108]

In some instances, exposure to mediation leaves clients feeling frustrated by their lawyers' unhelpful attitudes. Clients sometimes say that they are more solution-focused and less emotional and rigid than their lawyers. For example:

The lawyers' egos got in the way of the discussions ... it may have worked better without the lawyers being there.

It seemed like the lawyers came in with more of a chip on their shoulders than the parties.[109]

Once counsel have recovered from the culture shock of sharing space in a negotiation setting with their clients, the results can be very positive. One lawyer described the contribution of the client as

the intangibles that a lawyer can't bring. Like what was said at a particular meeting when the deal was done or what everybody's perceptions were of what was going to transpire. So that you can sort of retrace the chain of events that lead to the dispute and see where everybody's expectations have fallen short, not just the claimants' expectations.[110]

Another lawyer told the following story to illustrate the way in which these clients reframed the conflict through their own prism in mediation:

In this particular case we were done by noon. I thought we were going to go all day because this particular person was ready for blood. She hated everybody ... then we get into the room and somebody just magically says something along these lines ...

CLIENT 1: "Well, why didn't you say that before? And why didn't anybody call me? And why didn't anybody come to see my basement?"
CLIENT 2: "Well, we did come to see it."
CLIENT 1: "Well sure you did, you came a year afterwards, after I already sent a nasty letter to you" ...

He went on to reflect:

We're lawyers, not psychologists, and we don't always know what's going on. The interesting part is, it comes up in commercial litigation and yet you think these are all rough, tough people, business people. You know, that's where it comes up because that's where the feelings get hurt, that's where it's personal, it's about an ability to run or operate a business, and that's personal. It may be about money but it's personal.[111]

It appears that the more experience counsel gain with settlement processes that include the client, the more open they become to accepting client participation. The importance of the plaintiff's having a "voice" via mediation or negotiation is sometimes described as decisive in settlement. One counsel described a file in which the plaintiff was able to put his/her point of view across and speak directly to the person understood as responsible for the alleged injury.

> [This] mediation settled for a very minimal amount. What was most compelling was ... X appearing and speaking to [the plaintiff] and listening to [the plaintiff] and really trying to understand the grievance against X ... then also explaining to [the plaintiff] just how her understanding was absolutely wrong and X would never have ever intended to hurt [the plaintiff] and apologized at the mediation, not for having hurt [the plaintiff] but for ... this misconception out there.[112]

Counsel may even become sanguine about the potential risks of the client "speaking out of turn":

> I don't see the harm in it, if my client says off the record: "So you think those things we delivered didn't work?" I don't really see that as really hurting me because probably my client's going to have to say that on discovery, or it's going to be proven out one way or another. So if my client says that in those circumstances, I don't think you're giving much away. It's going to come out anyway and, quite frankly, sometimes showing that bit of weakness is worthwhile if the object is to settle this. Somebody's got to give something.[113]

These lawyers see the potential for the client to play a practical role in proposing and testing possible solutions. A working partnership between lawyer and client aims to produce superior solutions – that is, better than those negotiated privately by lawyers or imposed by a judge. Involving clients in negotiation and mediation processes can significantly advance this goal.[114] Face-to-face interaction enables parties in both domestic and commercial disputes to explore their understanding of what feels fair and realistic and to refine details that might be neglected in a discussion only between counsel. There is the potential for value-added outcomes that include creative substantive dimensions not forthcoming in other fora, as well as secondary benefits such as enhanced communication and relationships.

In addition, when clients participate in negotiation or mediation, the role of their lawyers in filtering and framing information is diminished – and this alone may open up new pathways to an agreement. A settlement proposal can be presented directly to a client, instead of the agent presenting it to the client following the meeting. The client can consider the proposal on the spot, ask questions, or press for further enhancements rather than managing this follow-up through counsel. Face-to-face communication between the parties is often critical to enabling an interim, or "trial," solution. Clients may be less trusting about such an experiment if they have not been a part of the dialogue.

Simply bringing the clients into the room to haggle over a proposal appears to have a significant impact on deal making – on its scope, its procedure, its timing, and its overall viability. This growing realization means that New Lawyers need to take client participation in dispute resolution processes seriously, and work constructively to enhance the consequences of this change – as well as deal with their anxiety about it.

Affective Lawyering

Many emotions, both positive and negative, are generated in the lawyer/client relationship. Yet the traditional paradigm assumes that the affective or psychological dimension of lawyering – what lawyers feel about their clients – has no place in a professional relationship. Lawyers who act "professionally" should not experience a personal emotional response, and any emotions manifested by their clients should be controlled and suppressed lest they derail the lawyers' legal strategy.

Regardless, numerous emotions come to the surface when a professional adviser – whether a lawyer, a doctor, a therapist, or other – relates to a client at a time of crisis. These are what Marjorie Silver calls "intense, non-reciprocal relationships involving power imbalances."[115] Lawyers and their clients often work together at times of great stress in the client's life, and, for short periods, they may spend many hours together. This proximity produces an emotional intensity. In practice, many lawyers become emotionally invested in their cases, whether in the position taken by their own clients, in clients personally, or in opposing the position of the other side.[116]

Over the past thirty years, scholars have studied the usefulness of the psychological dimensions of the lawyer/client relationship (e.g., the work of the late Andrew Watson and, more recently, David Wexler and Bruce Winick).[117] This work has received little attention in legal education. From law school onward, young lawyers have been taught to devalue emotional responses – both their own and those of their clients. As Gerry Spence writes:

What we really experienced at law school was a lobotomy of sorts, one that anesthetizes the law student against his emotions and attempts to reduce law to some sort of science.[118]

In the traditional paradigm, lawyers keep their interactions with their clients focused on law and legal solutions, conveying the message that emotional reactions to conflict are at best irrelevant and at worst an indication of embarrassing weakness. An imaginary but rigid boundary between a technical-rational analysis and an analysis influenced by emotions or intuition is maintained by the lawyer-in-charge. Lawyers who subscribe to this belief will resist being drawn into discussions that appear to have little legal relevance but that offer the client psychological support or encouragement. Instead, they model for the client the importance of separating emotional from legal considerations and not letting emotions direct legal strategy.[119]

The New Lawyer's working partnership with clients cannot function effectively within such rigid parameters. A partnership requires a degree of mutuality – of goals, power, and action. New Lawyers must seek to reconcile their goals with those of their client and to make decisions jointly. Each must have some measure of power in the relationship – lawyers will have superior knowledge; clients will have ownership of the conflict – and each must understand how they will share this power in developing and implementing a strategy for problem solving. When lawyer and client "meet" in the space between their different worlds, there will be a mutuality between them. Both will experience some emotion, and this emotion will be another aspect of their mutuality.

A critical aspect of this mutuality is the importance of empathy in the lawyer's recognition of the client's problem. Empathy has traditionally been seen as incompatible with professional, objective detachment, sometimes provoking complaints that "we are not social workers" from lawyers. However, a new generation of clients is dissatisfied with technical legal advice – "weather forecasting," as Anthony Kronman calls it[120] – and looks for more holistic problem solving that requires contextual understanding and empathy for the client's situation. In their book *The Good Lawyer,* Doug Linder and Nancy Levit argue that empathy is the number one quality of a good lawyer:

Clients place a higher value on the "soft skills" of lawyers than lawyers generally imagine. What clients want most from their lawyers is a sense that they really *care* about them and their problem.[121]

Practicing empathy has practical consequences inside the lawyer/client relationship that are highly compatible with the demands of working directly with clients in dispute resolution. Linder and Levit offer an "Empathy Checklist" for lawyers that reflects the principles of holistic lawyering ("be curious about your client's entire story"), interests-based strategies ("ask your client open-ended questions"), and a working partnership ("think of yourself as a coach as well as a provider of legal services").[122] They also note that lack of empathy – leading clients to feeling undervalued and misunderstood – is significant and pervasive in client complaints.[123]

Many lawyers describe their first encounters with clients, either in a law school clinic or in a law firm, as something of a seismic shock. They are meeting with real human beings who bring emotion, either under control or not, and who raise an emotional response in them. Naturally, there will be some type of human connection, good or bad, weak or strong, with each client. The meaning and impact of what happens in the affective dimension between lawyer and client is important to recognize and understand. As Linda Mills explains, "this [the affective] method acknowledges that clients demand an emotional response, explicitly or implicitly, and that lawyers must have the skills to address the anger, frustration, despair or even indifference that legal interactions evoke."[124] Rather than denying the reality of human connection, New Lawyers need to be highly conscious of their emotional response to each client and to identify their personal biases.

Having let emotions out of the box, what should the lawyer do with them? Just how far should the personal connection go? The client relationships sought by some lawyers who embrace consensus building and settlement work may be unrecognizable to more traditional practitioners. Consider the following descriptions:

> I open a dialogue with the client on a more interpersonal level – the connection is different.[125]

> I am becoming much less of a traditional lawyer and much more of a coach. So the language that I'm using with you is language of connection, it's the language of support.[126]

Charles Fried developed a notion of "lawyer as friend" that emphasized the role of a friend as a positional ally who fights ruthlessly for the advancement of the "friend's" legal position.[127] Many have pointed out the problem with this understanding of "friendship" in a commercial relationship – arguing, for example, that it is more accurately described as an "advantage-friendship," one in which clients pay lawyers to adopt their goals and lawyers adopt them because they are getting paid.[128] Anthony Kronman offers a more nuanced idea of the lawyer as friend:

A lawyer needs to place himself in the client's position by provisionally accepting his ends and then imaginatively considering the consequences of pursuing them, with the same combination of sympathy and detachment the lawyer would employ if he were deliberating on his own account.[129]

This is reminiscent of earlier work by Thomas Shaffer and Robert Cochran, who suggest a "lawyer as friend" who represents the Aristotelian "moral virtues" of friendship. This assumes that friends take responsibility for raising questions of morality, integrity, and fairness with one another, motivated by both respect for the friendship and respect for the values of the wider community.[130] This may include giving clients advice they do not agree with or like. Perhaps none of these earlier writers imagined the scope and focus of the therapeutic relationship that some collaborative lawyers and others now see as a natural evolution of their new intimacy with their clients, which in turn reflects different assumptions for clients who are uncomfortable with the old lawyer-in-charge notion. More lawyers now consider at least a part of their role to be providing a supportive and healing environment for their clients, and more clients appear to expect this.

At the same time, claiming the intimacy of a quasi-therapeutic relationship raises dangers, especially if one accepts that lawyers inevitably bring their own values and beliefs to the client relationship. Jack Sammons has warned of the dangers of "moral imperialism" by lawyers acting as know-it-all friends and assuming shared moral values with the client.[131] Does an overly "zealous friend" risk overwhelming the client with "the moral paternalism of the guru lawyer"?[132] The imposition of moral values is suggested in the language used by some collaborative lawyers, who present divorce as a journey of personal growth. For example:

A part of my goal for them is to try to leave their dysfunctional communications systems behind and replace them, basically from the ground up, starting with baby steps, medium steps, and then larger steps, with the goal being that they replace the old system with a new communicative system [and do not] lapse back into the old dysfunctionality.[133]

Lawyers are generally neither authorized nor qualified to undertake a therapeutic role. Some collaborative law clients (whose own lawyers described their role in interviews as a therapeutic one) point to a lack of training to properly equip lawyers to offer this type of support, noting that mental health professionals are not only more competent than lawyers in this capacity but usually much less expensive.[134] Some mental health professionals who work with collaborative lawyers express a similar skepticism, expressing concerns about the blurring of boundaries between their role – for which they are professionally trained and qualified – and that of a lawyer:

> When lawyers begin to cross into the therapy role, there is a wobble there. Lawyers are not accountable about how they understand family systems theory, they can just wing it any way they want it.[135]

Collaborative family practice may be something of a special case. In the development of an authentic working partnership with their client – whether in negotiation, in mediation, or as a dimension of offering unbundled or limited legal services – the core question for most lawyers is how to establish appropriate boundaries in a personal relationship with the client. Their challenge is to act as their clients' "friend" without creating emotional or psychological attachments and/or dependence, and to avoid their own unintentional transference onto clients' issues.

It is almost always easier to advocate for someone one likes and trusts, and correspondingly more difficult to do the same for someone one finds less attractive and credible. Within the affective dimension of the lawyer/client relationship, there are many examples of transference (when clients projects onto counsel their emotions of rage, fear, or bitterness) and countertransference (when lawyers assume some of these emotions as their own).[136] Some clients may want their lawyers to act as their alter ego, acting out their anxieties and concerns for them or bolstering them to act tough. In the frank words of one client:

> [In litigation] the lawyer becomes your surrogate angry person.[137]

Removing the traditional assumption of emotional distance and detachment on both sides casts the New Lawyer into new and unfamiliar territory. Acknowledging the existence of personal connection means giving up the comfort of the (albeit artificial) boundaries between the lawyer's professional and personal reactions to a file, and obliges counsel to consider how to handle this aspect of the relationship with the client. It is important for New Lawyers to accept that their personal values and feelings will become a part of their practice. They need to be able to recognize cases when this may interfere with their ability to provide effective service – for example, when they have overidentified with a client's goals or, conversely, when they cannot offer loyalty and commitment to a client because of conflicted personal feelings. It may sometimes mean that they cannot work comfortably with a particular client on a particular file.

As we begin to learn more about this and other aspects of a new working partnership between lawyer and client – in which "no one person is in control"[138] – there is no rule book and, as yet, little in the way of role models for lawyers to follow. We need to begin teaching these ideas to future lawyers, and allow them to think about how the dynamics of a partnership might be managed.

The Challenges of a Working Partnership

The re-envisaged partnership between lawyer and client described in this chapter does not resolve all of the challenges that were part of the traditional paradigm; in fact, it creates some new ones. The continuity between the old and the new is exemplified by a classic dilemma that is common to both. When should counsel advise a client to accept terms offered in settlement, and when should the advice be for the client to resist and continue to fight? The impact of adopting the partnership model I am proposing is less on the substantive outcome of reviewing a settlement offer and more on the process of reaching a joint decision. How do counsel and client together analyze, reason, debate, and ultimately choose an outcome?

This is a dilemma that may be made more acute by a converse reaction between lawyer and client – that is, when the lawyer thinks the client should settle and the client does not want to, or when the client wants to settle and the lawyer thinks that he or she should hold out for more. The conditions and circumstances will vary widely, from a lawyer advising a commercial client who wants to settle as a result of internal operational pressures, not for top dollar, to a lawyer working with an Aboriginal band whose values and norms about fairness may be different from those of the Western legal system.[139] However, the moral and practice dilemma comes down to the same question: in an authentic partnership, how much and what type of persuasive pressure should the New Lawyer put on the client to settle?

This dilemma illustrates many of the choices and actions this chapter has discussed: Who participates in settlement discussions, and in what capacity? Who controls the choice of strategy and outcome?[140] Who ultimately makes a decision, and on what basis? And what feelings does this process generate on both sides? Oddly, it remains rare for this all too common practice dilemma to be openly identified and discussed, and it may never be raised in three years of law school.

When asked about how they resolve this dilemma, most lawyers – regardless of whether they work in collaborative law or mediation, as a traditional litigator, or in non-contentious work for corporate clients – will quickly acknowledge that the ultimate decision maker is the client. Their focus will likely be to ensure that they have satisfied due diligence in warning the client about the consequences of the client's decision, in order to avoid a future malpractice suit. Reframing the decision-making process as a partnership, how would the New Lawyer work through this situation? What new challenges are raised, aside from "cover my ass"?

Moving beyond the Three Key Beliefs

Lawyers who are heavily committed to rights-based dispute resolution will often feel that their advocacy role is compromised when clients say that they are ready to stop fighting. If they are committed to the lawyer-in-charge model, they are also likely to feel that clients are "wrong" (and being troublesome) not to accept their advice, which is likely to be superior to the clients' own knowledge of the legal probabilities. They may also feel that an early settlement offer should naturally be resisted because clients have not yet had "their day in court." Finally, lawyers who do not acknowledge the affective dimensions of the relationship, and their own and their clients' emotional reaction to a settlement offer, may be confounded by a response from a client that appears to be a capitulation or, equally puzzling, stubborn resistance. Lawyers may be simply unaware of the emotional or psychological reasons that make it difficult for clients to accept an offer or that make it impossible for them to refuse one. They may also be unaware of any (perhaps unintentional) pressure that they place on their clients, fuelled by their belief that cases are best resolved by rights-based outcomes (e.g., how close is the offer to an adjudicated outcome?).

In contrast, New Lawyers will not let the three beliefs dictate how they process each serious settlement offer with the client. The New Lawyer's assessment of the offer will not be exclusively about its proximity to an adjudicated outcome but also about how far the offer meets the client's prioritized needs. The timing of a good offer to settle – however close to the beginning of the litigation process – should not be an impediment to settlement *if* the offer meets the client's needs. Lawyers who believe that their client could do better by pursuing further rights-based processes must assist in evaluating the costs of continuing the litigation. Recognizing that there are emotional dimensions to the question of whether to fight or to settle, they must also accept and incorporate the client's own sentiments about the emotional and other non-legal consequences of either course. And as conflict resolution advocates, New Lawyers should aim to protect their client from exploitation where an offer appears unreasonable, premature, unfair, or unlikely to achieve the client's goal.

All much easier said than done, but New Lawyers come to this classic dilemma with some new tools, skills, and attitudes from working with the client over earlier choices, such as clarifying and prioritizing goals and interests, decisions about dispute resolution process choices, and the joint development of a strategic approach.

The following two stories are based on real-life accounts by lawyers and their clients. Both cases involve full representation, but it is instructive to also anticipate that they might raise further nuances were the lawyers retained on a limited-scope basis. Issues that might be anticipated include what work the clients have done independently of their lawyers to improve their position, and how far they have shared this information with their lawyers; what, if any, agreement the lawyers and clients have come to over settlement decision making and the involvement of the lawyers; and how the lawyers might wish to qualify their advice on settlement in the context of a limited retainer arrangement.

The first story describes a settlement negotiation in a commercial case, described in the words of the litigator for the defendant. The second is my summary of a story told to me in separate interviews by a client and her lawyer on a collaborative family case. The two cases turn on similar issues of decisions over settlement offers but in very different contexts. The additional contrast is that the first involves a fairly traditional commercial litigator, whereas the second involves a committed (and trained) collaborative lawyer.

A Business Settlement

I acted for the defendant. We had a huge case in dollars and cents of sure business. I had what I considered to be a 100 percent case. You don't often get those. I know people have accused me of being a little bit opinionated sometimes in the worth of my case, but this was a good one.

My client did not want to litigate [earlier in the interview, this lawyer had said that he was aware that his client was approaching retirement and that he was very motivated to clear up this dispute before he left the company, and to leave without any "blemish" on his record]. I had $250,000 in my pocket to settle. This case wasn't worth $25,000 and wouldn't have cost more than $70,000, worst case scenario to litigate, but they wanted to settle. For the other side, it was a stab for some easy money.

I knew they would back off, but my instructions from my client were to settle this thing and do not leave that mediation without a settlement. I've got $250,000 of the clients' money in my pocket and every instinct in my body says: "This is stupid."

My client was sophisticated. My client was giving me instructions, obviously I have to follow my client's instructions. There's nothing immoral about them, nothing unlawful about them. So I have to follow them.

We went down there and we settled it for $165,000. $165,000 more than I thought the case was worth, so justice was not done. These people who sued picked up $165,000 that they weren't entitled to.

Was it a good settlement? My client was delighted. They had $250,000 in their pocket and they got out of there with $165,000 and one of the two people I was getting the instructions from thought we had won because he was able to go back and say I still have $85,000.

My job was to save as much of the $250,000 as I could. If I had to pay the whole $250,000, then I would have been really browned off. I was disappointed – but the client is as happy as hell and they're sending me something else. They're delighted with my handling of it. I'm not, I think I lost. I don't think we won, we lost. Justice was not done there.[141]

A Divorce Negotiation

A and B are negotiating their divorce using the collaborative law process. They have been married for twenty years and have three children, aged nineteen, sixteen, and ten. A, the wife, graduated high school but has not completed college – she has taken courses part-time on and off for years but finds it is always too much to juggle with child care and her job as a telemarketer. Her husband, B, has a college education and is a member of the Canadian Armed Forces. He has been offered a promotion and relocation to another city, which he intends to take once the divorce is finalized.

The main issue here is money – there is not a lot to go around. A and B want to sell their house and believe they will realize about $10,000 after the mortgage is paid off. A will remain in the town with the children and rent a home. The rental housing market is presently very expensive, and she is concerned about making ends meet. She makes $1,000 a month at her job.

Early on in the negotiations, before the first four-way, B begins to press for A to give up her share of his pension. A feels that this is unfair – and she is worried *about money – but also wants to get the matter resolved. She wants B out of the matrimonial home and is afraid he will not leave until the deal is done.*

A is worried that B will tell different stories to different people to satisfy them but ultimately will not be straight in the negotiations. She is beginning to feel that she needs to do the best she can and get it over with. She muses, "I could walk away with just nothing, I could say, 'Fine, you want it, take it.'"[142]

The two lawyers on the file agree that B needs a reality check on the question of the pension, and he is told that his wife has a legal right to share his pension. At first, B seems to accept this, but the issue comes up again once the four-way meetings begin. This becomes an impediment to a final settlement.

Between the four-way meetings, A discloses to her lawyer that her middle son – aged sixteen – is skipping school, and the school principal has called her expressing concern. She has not shared this information with B because she is worried that he may become very angry with his son. A's lawyer puts some pressure on her to put this information on the table in a four-way meeting. With some misgivings, A does so. At the meeting, B responds calmly enough. However, when he gets home after the meeting, he is very angry with their son, and A regrets revealing this information.

At the end of the collaborative process, A agrees to take 30 percent of B's pension. They make an agreement for monthly support. A remains in the matrimonial home paying the mortgage and the equity is to be shared once it is sold. A feels mostly positive about this agreement. She is relieved that she kept some of her pension entitlement and attributes this to the combined pressure of the two lawyers on her ex-spouse: "With both lawyers showing him what was fair it was not like me and my lawyer against him and his lawyer."[143] *However, there is no doubt that A concluded the agreement partly because of a need for closure and partly because of a fear of emotional abuse from B, who was still residing in the home up to the point of the agreement. Her own lawyer was aware of these fears, but the other lawyer was not.*

Analysis: What Would the New Lawyer Do?

In the business law story, the lawyer felt that he had not seen "justice" done. Nonetheless, his client was telling him that he was perfectly happy with the outcome. While the lawyer was aware of a likely motivation for settlement – the client's impending retirement – he did not directly discuss this motivation with the client. Had this issue been raised and discussed between them, without judgment, the lawyer may have been better able to understand and evaluate the decision to settle. The client was a sophisticated individual who had presumably made a sound business decision. If the client had shared with his counsel more of his reasoning and calculations regarding the settlement – which may have required the lawyer to ask him directly, or at least to indicate that this would be important information for him to have – the lawyer may have been better placed to offer an appraisal of the complete picture.

The lawyer's reaction to the settlement also suggests that he may have had an unconscious personal investment in a particular outcome. Despite his client's needs being met, the lawyer was dissatisfied. Counsel's goals and his client's goals are not necessarily synonymous – and cannot be expected to be.[144] The New Lawyer needs to be aware of any personal feelings that are affecting his professional response. Why did he feel so strongly that the client should not settle? How much of this was due to the influence of the key beliefs in his training and practice, and how much a well-founded fear of the client "selling himself short" in the settlement stakes?

The family case turns on similar issues, but in this case the client is a vulnerable woman who is negotiating a divorce and who has continuing responsibility for her three children. Her decisions will have significant repercussions for her own future and that of her children. It was vital that A's lawyer feel comfortable that she had explored all of her options, including holding out for a better deal. Interviewed after the settlement was finalized, A's lawyer justified the outcome in relation to the pension division, stating that "her focus was on the present, not the future [the pension], and she needed a good deal for the present." She went on to say, "I suspect that so much will happen in the next twenty years that this will probably not be important to her by then."[145] Trained as a collaborative lawyer, she was careful not to insist on a conventional legal distribution of the assets when her client preferred another approach. She also wanted to enable her client, who on the face of it was very vulnerable and relatively powerless, to act as powerfully as possible based on her own judgment.

However, this lawyer may have underestimated the extent or source of the various pressures being placed on her client. It is unclear whether A and her lawyer fully examined all the relevant information – including the behaviour of B, the husband, who for economic reasons was still living in the matrimonial home at the time of the negotiations, an arrangement that created daily stress for A. While she said that she did not feel physically afraid of him, in my interview with her she made it clear that she experienced his constant presence as an additional source of pressure.

Both A and her lawyer recognized the practical reality that the settlement had to be concluded before B would be able to leave the matrimonial home. A did not have the resources to conduct protracted negotiation or litigation. These circumstances put a great deal of pressure on A to accept the offer.

There may have been space for A's lawyer to sit down with her client and discuss how they could enhance her "best alternative to a negotiated agreement" (BATNA) in a way that would enable her to reach a decision under less pressure. For example, perhaps there could have been a short interim agreement for B to move out of the house at their shared expense. This would have relieved A from the intense pressure she faced to accept B's offer. Within the realities of their clients' situation, New Lawyers should work hard to maximize advantages where possible. This requires identifying where pressure is coming from, and why.

This story also suggests the potential for having both lawyers work together on a single issue. For example, A said she felt that having both lawyers talk to her husband on the topic of her pension rights was helpful. A similar discussion between all parties might also have been helpful in helping the husband's lawyer recognize the problem of A making decisions under pressure. A's lawyer did not reveal to the other side what she knew about the stress of the shared living arrangement. In hindsight, this may have been a misjudgment.

Each of these stories illustrates the need for lawyer and client to fully understand each other's assessments and motivations in making a settlement decision. In different ways, the stories demonstrate the capacity of clients, both business and personal, to make decisions that diverge from traditional notions of justice and fairness. This reality was part of the experience of the last generation of legal practitioners, whether as commercial litigators or family practitioners.

While the dilemmas are often same, what is different in an authentic lawyer/client partnership is the constancy and scope of the conversation. The New Lawyer brings together both legal and non-legal considerations in an appraisal of a settlement offer. Fighting is not the only advocacy role. In bridging the gap between formal rights-based justice and informal, client-chosen "justice," the New Lawyer must ensure that clients are fully informed and aware of all possible options, and understand their choices. Best practice norms for an authentic working partnership with the client would see the New Lawyer offering sound advice and strong advocacy that reflects what the client wants and needs, rather than imposing what the lawyer determines is "best" for the client.

7

The Shadow of the Law

When you practise long enough, you'll understand there are
some brilliant legal arguments that are not worth making.[1]

The successful use of consensus-building processes to resolve disputes depends on more than polished legal arguments. It also requires the New Lawyer to be an effective negotiator, a good communicator, an assertive advocate, and a partner with his or her client in the business of conflict resolution. What then is the role of law and legal advice in consensus building, and how do lawyers apply their specialist knowledge in their new professional role?

The role of law and legal advice in a model of conflict resolution advocacy is one of the most contentious and challenging dimensions of the practice of the New Lawyer. There are no simple answers here. Suggesting that lawyers eschew the use of legal argument in a negotiation or not offer their clients specialist legal advice conflates the symptoms of overzealous legal advice – for example, case inflation and positional bargaining – with the application of legal expertise. Neglecting the use and application of legal knowledge to dispute resolution is a disincentive for some lawyers who might otherwise take the practice of conflict resolution advocacy more seriously. And it is an inaccurate characterization of the integration of law and legal principles into the practice of the New Lawyer.

Some advocates for mediation and collaborative processes appear to suggest that there is no longer a real role for legal expertise. Occasionally this discussion even goes so far as to suggest that lawyers must commit to "paradigm change" by forswearing habitual use of the law to resolve conflicts, in a manner similar to the recovering alcoholic's predicament. In this chapter, I shall argue that this is a mischaracterization and oversimplification of the New Lawyer's role. Thomas Kuhn's original concept of "paradigm shift" means the actual replacement or substitution of the old with a new paradigm, rendering the old obsolete.[2] But the specialist legal expertise – and the requisite skills such as legal research and analysis – of lawyers is not being replaced or made obsolete with the increase of settlement work.

Instead, what is needed to complement the changes in legal disputing processes is a careful reformulation of the place and role of traditional legal advice. This is a shift in emphasis, rather than a rejection of traditional legal knowledge and analysis. This shift requires the New Lawyer to harness the predictive power of law, which casts its long shadow on every legal negotiation.[3] But it also requires a deeper understanding of the relationship between informal norms and recognized rules and standards in conflict resolution.

The Role of Legal Expertise in Legal Negotiation and Consensus Building

Negotiation skills occupy an explicit and central role within the skill set of the New Lawyer, and effective negotiators must be able to do more than state and restate a positional legal argument. Nonetheless, the use of the law to predict alternatives to settlement remains a critical dimension of negotiation.

First, the law provides an important benchmark against which to appraise options and measure outcomes. Used in this way, legal analysis is more than a threat to go to trial – a threat that is rarely carried out and therefore has limited impact. Instead, law offers one means (as we shall see below, just one means) of agreeing on an external standard or norm.

Second, in order to be most effective in a conflict resolution advocacy model, the New Lawyer must integrate legal intelligence into the discussion between the parties in a way that can be heard and has credibility. The way in which this intelligence is offered affects the way it is heard and understood. This means abandoning the fiction of presenting legal opinion as neutral, or "just the way it is," without recognizing that any legal analysis includes a measure of interpretative subjectivity. Instead of being presented as an immutable position, a threat, or an "unfortunate reality," predictive legal opinions in negotiation should be presented with as much sensitivity for the communication frame as any other negotiating tactic.

Communication theorists point out that the continuous use of unequivocal arguments that attack the goals of the other side often leads to impasse, whereas an analysis that explores underlying problems opens up the possibility of problem-solving discussions. This scholarship suggests that the most credible messages are those that are direct and clearly outline consequences, rather than those characterized by overstatements, ambiguity, or vagueness, which are likely to be less believable and have far less impact.[4] This means that while legal arguments remain an important part of legal negotiations, their delivery should be tactical – that is, they must recognize the context of consensus building – rather than presented as unassailable and given.

Third, New Lawyers owe their clients a number of important professional obligations.

> I don't want to pay my lawyer to do therapy. I want my lawyer to give legal advice, [so that I] know my rights.[5]

The New Lawyer should have no less commitment to legal research and advice giving than in the traditional model. However, the enhanced mutuality of purpose and action between lawyer and client – the goal of a working partnership – requires a different type of exchange over legal intelligence. Recognizing that legal advice is rarely unassailable, it is critical for New Lawyers to be transparent about the uncertainty involved in predicting legal outcomes while still offering their best appraisal. Lawyers are sometimes guilty of overselling legal outcomes and minimizing their uncertainty.[6] As well, the costs involved in pursuing a legal remedy must be set out clearly and in detail. This is an area in which there is growing client dissatisfaction. The growing unaffordability of legal services is compounded by poor or vague information about actual legal costs.

The correlation of desired outcomes to legal remedies should also be clarified; clients sometimes imagine that remedies are available to them that are simply beyond the court's jurisdiction.[7] Not every legal solution meets each disputant's particular moral, cultural, and economic needs.[8] New Lawyers must ensure that their clients understand that law is just one way of approaching a principled basis for resolution.

Legal Norms and Social Norms

In order to settle a dispute on a basis that the parties can accept as just, reference to norms and principles – including but not limited to legal norms and principles – is always important. Mediation theory suggests that parties determine what norms to adopt in order to resolve their conflict, whether these are "given" (by reference to societal standards or legal obligations) or created by the parties themselves.[9] Where the possibility for appeal to an adjudicator lies in the background, we should expect the role of formal norms – their shadow – to be more pronounced. This evaluation will doubtlessly affect the disputants' appraisals of the offers on the table. At the same time, counsel should ensure that their clients understand the infrequency of adjudication and the likelihood that settlement will occur at some point short of trial – a difficult balance to strike. The so-called shadow of the law[10] is an important predictive tool when resort to law or a continuation to trial is a possible consequence of failure to settle.

What Is the Significance of Legal Norms?

The relationship between legal rules and social norms is much debated. Legal rules and social norms are clearly not perfectly commensurate. But given the multicultural nature of modern Western societies, there is relatively little public debate over the appropriateness of laws, with notable exceptions at any one point in history (current North American examples include gun control, the legalization of marijuana, and abortion rights). Certainly not all laws have universal support, but in the West, formal legal systems are a remarkably stable and consistent source of public values. Even when there is evidence of alienation or dissent from particular laws, law as an entity continues to have meaning for conflict resolution as a source of norms and values. In some cases, it may be the most important source on which disputants can agree.

The explanation for the remarkable support enjoyed by the legal system from large sectors of the community may lie less in its substantive content and more in its symbolic significance as a source of social and moral stability. The use of law by disputants as a source of norms may represent an acceptance of its authority as much or more than actual agreement with its substantive content. This dynamic is evident when, for example, disputants seem willing to accept the authority of the law in the absence of personal knowledge (and therefore assessment) of the precise nature of these rules. Susan Silbey and Patricia Ewick have explored how "ordinary people" caught up in legal conflicts relate to the rules they assume or believe exist.[11] They find a widespread need to believe in a system of authoritative norms that frames credible, acceptable outcomes. Appeal to law sometimes seems to endow a claim with an extra level of moral authority. "People turn to legality to assert values, rights (their own or others), or even some conception of justice."[12]

Law is understood as being both remote from everyday problems and yet crucially authoritative.[13] A belief in law may take on a value that is independent of a particular code, and is, instead, a belief in a system of law. A similar phenomenon may be observed when faith communities subscribe to an internal informal system of dispute resolution; their investment in that system is less about the content of the rules (which they may have differing understandings of) and more about a belief in the importance and legitimacy of the community's system.[14]

In a similar way, belief in the formal legal system and in the idea that its rules are synonymous with just outcomes appears to be highly normative among those untrained in law. Law is regarded as an impartial, objective, external norm that is separate and removed from everyday life (and therefore not subject to picky objections or trifling criticisms). As a result, the law can "get away with" making demands that might not otherwise be acceptable. For example, Silbey and Ewick point out that despite the fact that references to waiting and time wasted in experiences of the legal system "defies reproduction," this inefficiency is widely accepted without serious complaint.[15] As a result of its normative status, law influences behaviour and outcomes among disputing parties both within and outside the system. In so doing, law plays a crucial role in dispute resolution that goes beyond its use by lawyers to predict adjudicative outcomes.

The Significance of Social Norms

It is important to remember that the use of the legal system lies on the margins of real-life disputing, with just 10–20 percent of disputes involving over $1,000 using a lawyer.[16] Informal systems of norms besides law – for example, established social norms or widely practised customs – are extremely important in conflict resolution. The influence of informal norms is especially significant in a culture where "lumping it" or using self-help for a remedy outside the formal legal system to resolve conflicts is highly normative.

Informal and shared systems of social norms are evident in many communities that may be isolated or alienated from the "actual" legal system.[17] These informal systems may be crucial to practicalities of coexistence and cooperation. Norms and values, often unarticulated, surround every dispute. Conflicts become framed as an appeal to what the disputants would argue are the dominant (most reasonable, widely recognized, and longest established) norms and the subsequent behavioural expectations (of response or redress). The resolution of marital conflict inside North American Muslim communities provides an excellent example of this dynamic, as husbands and wives appeal to what they believe to be the most "Islamic" approach to resolving their conflict, often accusing one another of "un-Islamic" behaviour around the same set of contested norms.[18]

Robert Ellickson's study of cattle ranchers in Shasta County, California, provides another example of the influence of social norms in dispute resolution.[19] The ranchers have their own sophisticated system of values and beliefs about justice and due process, which they use as an almost complete substitute for the legal system but which shares many of its features. Ellickson provides an example of one widely followed convention that establishes just how much evidence a person must have about another's alleged wrongdoing before it is acceptable for them to make a public accusation against the other person.[20] He describes another norm that allows for a "freighted warning" (usually including the expression "or else"), after which an extraordinary remedy beyond damages would be necessary.[21]

The New Lawyer should expect to see a claim to an authority and a rule in every negotiation, whether this is formalized as law or as a family, community, or industry value.

The Role of Law and Legal Advice in Consensus Building

Law and legal principles are a part of the normative framing lawyers bring to a negotiation. Legal norms are a legitimate source of power for clients that they pay for when retaining a lawyer. How can and should the New Lawyer use legal intelligence in the effort to develop consensus between disputing parties?

Legal Frameworks Can Protect Vulnerable and Less Powerful Parties

Many of the concerns articulated about informal consensus building using negotiation and mediation relate to the fear that such processes will not protect basic rights and that the development of private agreements will undermine formal protections for those individuals otherwise disadvantaged in terms of resources, social status, and political power. Coercion behind closed doors might persuade less powerful parties to give up entitlements that are meant to level the playing field between their lack of power and the advantage of institutional actors and those privileged by gender, race, or class. There are additional fears that the agenda of the mediator may skew the process and the outcome.[22] Feminists point to a well-founded concern that mediators may adopt ideological agendas and impose them on the parties.[23] Another theme in this critique is the risk that emphasizing the "emotional" and "personal" elements of a conflict delegitimizes the role of the law and rights entitlements and may distance the outcomes from these basic norms.[24]

But negotiation and collaboration do not require parties to give up their rights. In fact, there is no reason why the New Lawyer cannot insist that any consensus building must uphold basic rights concepts, particularly where these protect a vulnerable client. While dominant interests often seek to use the law to their advantage – and sometimes succeed – lawyers can and do also use the law to protect the fundamental equality rights of less powerful parties. They can do this in consensus building as well as in adjudication. As Gemma Smyth puts it, consensus building "does not have to involve a trade-off between negotiation and human rights."[25]

Rights precedents as well as widely accepted social norms of fairness can and should be referenced when one party proposes an unfair, oppressive, or coercive outcome. Individuals buying legal services should expect the basic protection of the law. Racial, gender, and socio-economic characteristics do not need to disadvantage a party if their lawyers ensure that any emerging consensus in negotiation or mediation upholds basic standards of equality and fairness, in relation to both fair procedures and just outcomes. These need not be identical to legal protections, but should not violate principles of equality, anti-discrimination, or non-oppression.[26]

An explicit commitment to these principles may be an important first step for lawyers in setting the parameters and reference points of a consensus-building process. Ellen Waldman proposes a model of "norm-advocating" mediation in which either counsel or a third party may insist that relevant legal (and perhaps ethical) norms are incorporated into any possible agreement.[27] For example, it is commonplace for jurisdictional regulations or guidelines on child support payments to be used as a general guideline in family mediation. A norm-advocating approach will not be appropriate for all clients since it may constrict the range of possible outcomes, but when counsel believes there is a risk that a client may be pressured to accept an unfair or oppressive agreement, and/or when significant long-term rights and entitlements are at stake, it should be planned for and proposed at the outset.

New Lawyers have an important responsibility to ensure that their clients are not bullied or intimidated into accepting a prejudicial agreement that compromises rights entitlements and that may have a long-term impact on either the client or other third parties (such as dependents). There may be a useful parallel here with the approach taken by many codes of conduct developed for mediators, which commonly require their members to withdraw rather than abet an oppressive agreement. For example, the *Code of Professional Conduct* of Family Mediation Canada includes a provision that mediators should withdraw if they believe an agreement that is being reached is "unconscionable."[28] Similarly, lawyers should ensure that any emerging consensus in negotiation or mediation upholds basic standards of equality and fairness.

New Lawyers should be open and able to use rights arguments to defend important entitlements in negotiation and mediation, especially when their client is vulnerable or susceptible to undue pressure from the other side. They must work with their client to find the appropriate balance between party self-determination and rights protections. As we have seen, this dilemma is not a new one for lawyers, and already arises every time legal agents are involved in private ordering and settlement.

New Lawyers have some new conceptual frameworks and tools with which to manage this dilemma within the lawyer/client partnership.[29] They accept that, in practice, parties will sometimes agree to outcomes that in some way diverge from their formal legal entitlements. Commercial lawyers can supply numerous examples of this, and divorce negotiations also offer many practical illustrations. Diverging from or modifying the relevant legal rule may amount to a restructuring of benefits; for example, an undertaking to pay the costs of returning to school in exchange for a lump-sum payment, or an agreement to delay sale of the matrimonial home or another asset where continued joint management benefits all parties. Alternatively, one party may decide in the course of negotiations to leave benefits to which they are entitled "on the table" – for example, a share of a particular asset legally classified as "joint," or entitlement to an unlimited period of spousal support.

Any divergence from what appears to be a legal entitlement should be carefully evaluated to ensure informed consent and the absence of coercion. The New Lawyer should be especially careful to ensure that the client does not waive rights as a result of oppression, intimidation, lack of knowledge, or lack of power. The two case studies at the end of in Chapter 6 suggest some of the challenges and complexities of this evaluation.

It is also important that research continue, as far as possible, to monitor the outcomes of informal processes for signs of abusive or oppressive use against less powerful parties. To what extent do parties in consensus-building processes who are represented by lawyers waive or diminish their legal entitlements? Are waivers of rights mostly balanced (for instance, in the example above of exchanging a lump-sum payment for college tuition) or are they obviously one-sided (such as in the divorce negotiation at the end of Chapter 6)? Some data presently available (on financial outcomes in family support negotiations) suggest that informal agreements may in fact achieve outcomes that are somewhat better than legal entitlements (in the sense of higher monetary settlements).[30]

The answers to this question may also depend on the issue and forum. Within the small sample of the Collaborative Lawyering Research Project,[31] there appeared to be little difference between the actual outcomes and the likely legal outcomes. When asked at the end of the case to compare the negotiated outcome with the likely legal outcome, collaborative lawyers said that the substance of the outcome in collaborative family lawyering was no different or had very little difference from what they might have expected in a traditional litigation-negotiation process, especially in relation to financial support. As one put it:

> How different is this outcome from a litigated one? Not much at all. What is different is how they got there and what they are feeling about it.[32]

Going forward, access to confidential processes and agreements is a formidable obstacle for empirical research here. It is also difficult to empirically value non-monetary benefits that might be received in exchange for a reduction of a legal demand. Nonetheless, where possible, legal standards can and should be used as a means of monitoring privately negotiated outcomes.

For the New Lawyer, formal legal standards can offer an authoritative means of negotiating and perhaps adjusting privately agreed outcomes. The moral strength and authority of legal standards should be used to protect those who might otherwise be unfairly treated by more powerful parties or institutions, no less in consensus building than in adjudication.

Predictive Legal Assessment

Legal advice that accurately and realistically predicts legal outcomes is a crucial aspect of client advocacy in negotiation and mediation. Reference to a likely legal outcome may also be what brings the other side to the table in the first place – and perhaps keeps them there when bargaining bogs down.

The legal advice that clients receive from their lawyers as the negotiation proceeds enables an appraisal of the risks and rewards of the options on the table at any one time. It will be key to the development of a realistic and complete scenario for what will happen if settlement cannot be reached.

The appraisal of risks and rewards inherent in potential resolutions is often described in conflict resolution literature as the best alternative to a negotiated agreement (BATNA).[33] The concept of BATNA has been popularized by Roger Fisher, Bill Ury, and Bruce Patton as a tool to assess the risk of continuing with a dispute. BATNA suggests the identification of a hypothetical best-case scenario if negotiation does not result in settlement before adjudication.[34] Examining a hypothetical "best alternative" to a negotiated solution, which usually implies, at minimum, increased costs, mounting levels of stress, and continuing personal and/or commercial uncertainty, provides disputants with both a benchmark and a reality check against which to assess the benefits and downsides of a proposed settlement. General legal knowledge among one-shot litigants is very low, making the realistic development of both BATNA and WATNA ("worst alternative to a negotiated agreement") crucial for clients who may otherwise overestimate the certainty and likelihood of their chances of success.[35]

Counsel's use of law in the development of an alternative to negotiation should not overstate the case to be made, however tempting. Ideally, counsel should be able to stand back and review all contested legal arguments objectively. Lawyers sometimes chide their clients for holding on to unrealistic ideas about what they might achieve by using the legal system. However, just as often, it seems, lawyers are themselves the source of those overblown expectations.[36] Sometimes clients are initially painted an overly optimistic picture by their lawyer, only to be told to "face reality" further down the line when they are given a settlement offer. In developing an alternative to negotiation, counsel should be careful to be consistent and to carefully note the potential variables (which include the growing pressure the client may feel to settle the matter as time goes by).

The careful and thorough development of BATNA (and WATNA) also provides the client with important information about the legal consequences of negotiated outcomes that they may not otherwise anticipate, including, for example, advice on the tax consequences of particular settlement options, advice on any other regulatory framework that may impact the potential agreement, or simply information about realistic timing or enforcement of a proposed outcome (e.g., a monetary judgment).

The New Lawyer should understand that the concept of BATNA is incomplete if it is understood only as an assessment of likely legal outcome. Predictive legal advice should be woven into other considerations, including information about legal costs, timing, business consequences, and possible non-legal solutions. The most complete and useful sense of "best alternative" is one that integrates anticipated legal outcomes with other consequences of not settling the dispute at that time.

In these ways, the New Lawyer uses legal intelligence in combination with knowledge of negotiation strategy and awareness of the context of the dispute to create a clear and strong BATNA for the client. Done well – that is, realistic, not inflated, complete, not partisan – and integrated into what is important for this client, predictive legal advice is an important strategic tool for the New Lawyer in negotiation.

The Limits of the Law in Consensus Building

Recognizing the importance of law in creating lasting agreements through negotiation does not mean that its value and application are limitless. Private ordering using informal negotiation processes is sometimes referenced to legal norms, and sometimes not. People cannot be forced to contract into rights; they can only be offered them. We know that the vast majority of conflicts are resolved privately rather than in court.

It is important for New Lawyers to recognize that law will often be peripheral to dispute resolution, and consider how they may nonetheless serve their clients by substituting alternate norms for formal legal rules. This may be especially significant where the outcomes sought cannot be fully addressed by a formal legal remedy.

The Limits of Legal Remedies

The remedies made available to disputants through the legal system are behavioural – that is, they generally require certain actions to be done or ended (on pain of punishment, although such punishment is usually minimally effective). By far the most common remedy is an award of damages, which monetizes the harm done or the value of the right infringed. The only time legal remedies go beyond monetary outcomes is when they occasionally require certain acts to cease (injunctive relief) or, in rare circumstances, the specific performance of an obligation.[37]

A focus on monetary remedies in law means that the options in play in a negotiation where legal argument dominates conform to these same monetary models. This limits the potential creativity of both lawyers and clients, and means that any other or additional proposed solution is inevitably compared to a strictly monetary outcome. The distance between judgment and enforcement also means that sometimes – for example, when a judgment cannot be collected – legal remedies do not provide for behavioural resolution either.

The direct impact of legal sanctions is therefore that (at best) they affect behaviour, whether by requiring a payment in compensation or proscribing certain actions. Yet resolving a conflict often requires closure in a number of ways that go beyond the performance or cessation of certain behaviours. Bernard Mayer suggests that people have conflict resolution needs along three dimensions, of which behaviour is just one. The other two dimensions are cognitive and emotional resolution.[38]

Emotional resolution allows disputants to feel less intensely about a conflict, stop emotionally depleting themselves by brooding over the conflict, and consign it to the past. While divorce has a legal endpoint (the final decree), many people who go through the procedure say that there is a moment at which they finally "feel" divorced, regardless of the stage of legal (behavioural) resolution.

Cognitive resolution occurs when people's beliefs and perceptions about a conflict alter – perhaps when they recognize a range of reasons for an injury they have suffered, rather than holding fast to the belief that the other side deliberately and maliciously harmed them. Cognitive change may, of course, never occur; at best, it may take place gradually, long after behavioural and emotional resolution.

Legal remedies generally do not provide for cognitive and emotional resolution, and few lawyers or clients would suggest that they do. To be fair, most lawyers would not encourage their clients to believe that they could expect to obtain emotional or cognitive resolution using legal procedures for dispute resolution. Clients may have a sense of satisfaction of being "done" when legal proceedings or negotiations are completed, but there may also be a pervasive sense that a focus on purely legal arguments and remedies somehow misses the "real" problem. Some clients continue to feel a lack of closure, even when they have won their case.[39]

Changing one's cognitive perceptions of the other side probably requires setting aside a positional rights-based argument, and emotional closure is also less likely when the parties remain at arm's length and deal exclusively through agents. In contrast, mediation and other dialogue processes open up these possibilities, with or without achieving legal (behavioural) resolution. Achieving a measure of cognitive or emotional resolution often requires an intentionally constructed dialogue process, perhaps including face-to-face discussion between the disputants, and making space for the discussion of issues beyond the securing of legal remedies.

Clients in mediation speak about the satisfaction of talking face to face, whether or not they achieve a legal resolution.

"David," a corporate client involved in a contract dispute, said that he was able to gain more information than he would have in any other process, because the discussion was not constrained by the law. Mediation helped the parties reach an agreement, although the resolution was not finalized for two or three months after the session. He assigned importance to being able to speak honestly, without fear of legal repercussions: "It helped me to offload where I couldn't before"; "I felt I had something to say and to contribute to the process."[40]

For some clients, this chance to talk face to face leaves them feeling better about the dispute. An individual involved in a debt collection with a large organizational plaintiff described his experience as follows:

[The process] gave me a chance to express my complaints ... I felt quite at ease and was able to express what I wanted to express, and the [other party] was able to express their concerns. We were both listening and talking. It had a good feeling in that respect.[41]

The limitations of a behavioural approach to outcomes can be seen in mediations where despite the willingness of one party to provide a remedy similar or even identical to what is demanded, the other side is still not willing to agree. I have encountered this situation a number of times as a mediator.[42] This can be extremely disorienting for counsel, who may be unable to understand rejection of a substantively satisfactory offer as anything other than stubbornness on the part of the client. However, the underlying reason for settlement resistance is almost always the existence of an unmet need that is beyond the scope of what a legal remedy may offer. It may be that – in addition to the behavioural resolution, such as an agreement to compensate – an apology or an acknowledgment is needed, or that a gesture of taking responsibility needs to be made by the other side. Or it may be that a procedural adjustment is required so that the party to whom the "reasonable offer" is being made can feel fairly treated and really listened to.

Securing a legal remedy, virtually always financial compensation, is by no means always the answer to a hard-to-settle case. In most cases, clients will settle only when they feel that their reasonable expectations (from their perspective) have been met. For sophisticated and one-shot clients alike, these expectations sometimes require both a process and an outcome that recognizes the need for cognitive and/or emotional resolution *as well as* a behavioural outcome. The sources of individual expectations are both complex and highly diverse. They reflect our past experiences and the values that we have formed as a result. Since expectations are highly personal, they are often implicit rather than explicit and are felt rather than known, and they may or may not be capable of rational articulation.

The Limits of Legal Analysis

Individual expectations for the outcome of the dispute are often a critical element in the internal dynamic of disputing,[43] but they may be obscured by generic legal definitions of injury and redress (the "stock stories" of legal pleadings).[44] This may be a symptom of a wider issue: that the problem itself has been misidentified or misunderstood.

Framing a negotiation issue only in terms of legal principles will often exclude practical options that may be acceptable to the parties – whether business parties seeking a practical commercial solution, family members trying to resolve conflict among themselves, or larger organizations dealing with their own employees or third parties. Moreover, relying on an exclusively legal framework to resolve a conflict is unlikely to address long-term relational problems, such as acrimony between trading or investment partners, co-parenting between disputing ex-spouses, or workplace culture or productivity inside a corporation. This is in part because a legal remedy is often incomplete – as we saw above, it is behavioural and not emotional or cognitive. But it is also because a purely legal analysis obscures or overlooks other issues that are not suitable for legal arguments and redress.

A legalistic approach to the problem is unlikely to deal with deeper underlying issues, such as different parenting styles, poor workplace morale leading to high absenteeism, systemic discrimination or harassment issues, or ineffective or inadequate communication systems. A purely legal approach to understanding the issues may suppress some of the most important elements of the conflict, such as articulating differences in parenting styles and values, poor leadership within the corporation or a dysfunctional management culture, or inadequate conflict monitoring and early resolution systems.[45]

I once worked with two parties disputing a monetary holdback on a private residential property sale. The reason given for the holdback by the new owners of the property was that they had found water leaking into the basement after they took possession. At the time of the mediation, an offer had been made by the new owners to the vendors (a couple) that represented most, although not all, of the holdback. The vendors would not even consider this (apparently reasonable) offer, however. In private caucus, the female vendor revealed a key event in the development of the dispute that had not been mentioned in the pleadings for either side or in the earlier joint session.

Evidently, it had been agreed between the parties at the time of the sale that the vendors would return to pick up a child's playhouse located in the backyard of the property a few days after the transfer of ownership. The playhouse had great historical and sentimental value for the female vendor. When the purchasers moved in, and after they discovered the water in the basement, they trashed the playhouse before the vendors could return to collect it.

The female vendor expected that the purchasers would appreciate the importance of the playhouse to her and would allow her to return to collect it, despite their disappointment with the state of the basement. When they did not follow through with their agreement and instead trashed the playhouse, this became a significant part of her grievance against them. She felt unable to discuss settlement of the holdback issue without first raising this issue.

Once the issue of the playhouse was formally added to the agenda, the substantive matter of the holdback settled quickly. The female vendor explained what the playhouse had meant to her, and her great disappointment. She immediately received a simple but genuine apology. The purchasers – a childless couple – were also able to explain that they were unaware of the full significance of the playhouse.

The vendors had not told their lawyer about this issue, believing it had no legal relevance (it probably did not). As a result, the legal pleadings obscured what was for the female vendor a central part of her experience, and a key issue in the conflict.[46]

Limits on Law's Cultural Responsiveness

Legal principles reflect dominant cultural values, but these may not be the cultural norms of the parties to the negotiation. Regardless, legal norms claim legitimacy partially through an assertion of universality. Legal norms must claim to be equally applicable to all persons of all cultures: in effect, that they are "culture-blind." In fact, they mirror the cultural values and beliefs of the most powerful groups in that society. For example, when American Muslims look at the family law system in Canada and the United States, they see a system of "legal rules about the relative roles, rights and responsibilities of spouses and their children (that) reflect innate (Judeo-Christian) values about the appropriate way to structure and run a family."[47]

The cultural background of the disputants is often a significant factor in preferring certain processes, setting particular goals for conflict resolution, and finding "justice" in a process and an outcome.[48] Generalizable conflict orientations and bargaining styles have been described for certain groups, primarily distinguishable in terms of ethnicity and gender.[49] Some work has also attempted to relate conflict style to socio-economic status.[50] How people make sense of their experiences needs to be understood as both more individual – and pervasive – than such broadly drawn distinctions. "Personal culture" in the disputing world includes all of the values and beliefs that inform how each individual understands his or her experiences of conflict, whether these are derived from family upbringing, religious affiliation, industry or sector experience, and so on.[51] Our cultural norms direct us towards certain behaviours, and guide our expectations of others. They represent the beginning of our theory of any conflict we find ourselves in, and the assumptions that will guide our future responses and behaviours. Understood at this granular level, cultural variables are present in every conflict. As one writer describes it, culture is not a variable but rather "the law of variation" in conflict analysis.[52]

The legal model's claim to universalism ignores the pervasive and significant impact of cultural variables on disputing and dispute resolution. The misapprehension that the law is culturally neutral – in its language, procedures, and rules – obscures the significance of cultural expectations and assumptions in disputing, and limits the potential of the law to consensually resolve conflicts in a number of ways. Disputants may become disillusioned when they find their expectations disappointed. They may feel that the law can neither help them nor address their problems, and so they become a part of the silent majority who simply "lump it" when they find themselves in conflict. And law's claim to universalism means that it has no mechanisms for identifying personal cultural norms or cultural misunderstandings between disputants.

I once worked with a First Nations community where two lawsuits had been brought by band members against the Band Council, one involving an employment matter and the other a construction dispute. Each plaintiff had hired a (non-Aboriginal) lawyer from outside the community, and the Band Council had gone to their lawyers (also non-Aboriginal) for advice.

Each case followed the same pattern. A settlement had been proposed by the plaintiffs' lawyers and then considered by the lawyers for the Band Council. In each, the defence lawyers recommended that the chief and council reject the settlement offer, advising them that the plaintiffs were unlikely to do as well in court. I was asked to co-mediate both disputes along with a band member.

The parties in each lawsuit decided in advance of mediation that they did not want their legal representatives present, nor did they wish to review any settlement proposals that emerged from mediation with their counsel before making a decision. Since my own cultural norms suggested that for a party to entirely dispense with legal advice might be prejudicial to their interests, I spent some time checking with each side that this was indeed their wish, and going over the implications with them of making a binding agreement in mediation. My co-mediator, a respected band member and a lawyer herself, assured me that the parties were comfortable with this arrangement – in fact, they would not agree to mediation on any other basis. Everyone was clear that an agreement reached in mediation would be a matter of honour, agreed fairness, and a decision for the community, and that they would not seek legal advice on any such agreement.

Both disputes settled in mediation. In each case, the amount agreed in settlement, plus a series of non-monetary undertakings, was considerably higher than the sum that the Band Council's lawyers had advised it to reject in the earlier settlement offer. Each settlement was taken to the full Band Council for review. No member of council suggested that the council should turn down the settlements because the settlement sums were higher than the earlier offers that the council had been advised by its lawyers to reject. Instead, discussions were limited to the perceived fairness, appropriateness, and practicality of the settlement in each case. Once satisfied, the Band Council members ratified the settlements and the suits were discontinued.[53]

These cases and their outcomes (extraordinary to the mediator and to counsel but perfectly normative for the disputants and their Band Council) illustrate the limits of legal principles in resolving disputes within cultures that do not "own" or recognize these same principles. The law is only minimally relevant to resolving disputes that have a significant cultural (personal, institutional, ethnic) element, and at best provides a touchstone for how one particular culture (often not that of the disputants themselves) would deal with this dispute. Addressing cultural variations is an important part of the work of negotiators and mediators – and hence also of lawyers – in developing processes and outcomes that are responsive to these types of differences.

The limits of legal remedies, legal analysis, and "culturally neutral" legal norms in facilitating consensus building that I have described here should alert the New Lawyer to an important reality. Client decision making regarding settlement is not always based on a rational and (internally) objective appraisal of the proper application of the law.

For some disputants, predictive data regarding legal consequences may be sufficient to decide whether or not they should continue with a dispute, or accept an emerging settlement. These are probably clients who are distanced from the conflict, and who feel little or no personal investment in the outcome. This is a limited group, even in the corporate context – it is unusual to find a corporate decision maker who regards the dispute as both someone else's fight and of no personal consequence. Rational decision making in disputing that is based solely on predictive legal advice is, in my experience, somewhat rare.

Instead, the New Lawyer should assume that predictive legal advice represents just one – although sometimes a very significant – factor in the client's decision on how to manage the dispute. Legal risk appraisal alone, especially when offered at an early stage in the file, may feel remote from the disputant's understanding and actual experience of the conflict.[54] On other occasions, expert legal advice will be accepted because of its authoritative source, but the disputant's continuing ambiguity will resurface in other ways (commonly in last-minute roadblocks to settlement or in non-compliance with the terms of settlement). Such dynamics are symptomatic of an overreliance on legal models of analysis and redress, without appreciating the other influences that affect individual judgment over resolution and sometimes relegate law to the sidelines.

How Clients Manage Legal Advice and Consensus Building

> I give as little legal advice as possible, because there is so much contamination and you are trying to get them focused back on life issues.[55]

This quote from a collaborative lawyer illustrates an attitude expressed by some lawyers whose commitment to collaborative processes appears to amount to a rejection of law as a tool in these negotiations. Some collaborative lawyers feel that giving legal advice is no longer appropriate in their new role. For example, as one lawyer explains, "I don't give any legal advice and am very careful not to even be too directed towards idea suggestion."[56] Another says, "I don't give clients [specific] legal advice in the briefing or in the initial interview – I macro it."[57]

There is a whiff of paternalism in the way some lawyers describe the need to keep the law "away" from their clients.[58] These lawyers appear to believe that providing their clients with legal advice will only harden their positions, or prematurely close down the consideration of a range of options for resolving the dispute. But the rejection of law as a tool to resolve conflict is both an overreaction (the notion that any mention of law will doom consensus building) and an oversimplification of the relationship between law and conflict resolution. Failure or refusal to provide specific legal advice is a breach of the professional responsibilities that lawyers owe their clients, absent an explicit waiver. Second, ignoring or minimizing the role of law in litigation fails to recognize the usefulness and power of law as a social system of norms. Adjudication on the basis of legal principles is the context within which legal negotiations take place, however unlikely it is that a trial will result. Third, what disputants think about the law – and how they believe it applies to their dispute – is a critical aspect of almost every matter handled by a lawyer.

In the partnership between New Lawyers and clients, legal advice is an important tool offered to deal with the conflict. How this information is used in bargaining is for lawyer and client to determine, but first it has to be provided. Lawyers should point out to their clients that legal outcomes are always uncertain, and may be affected by factors beyond their control (e.g., which judge sits on the case). They should acknowledge the importance of other factors in reaching the best solution for their client, including timing, the stress of legal proceedings, and the preservation of relationships. They can also, if they wish, advise clients that a better and more lasting solution would invoke the shared norms of the parties (whether or not these have a strictly formal legal basis). New Lawyers should assume that their clients are capable (with their coaching) of discriminating between legal principles that can be used to influence an outcome and those that risk escalating the conflict. They should trust their clients to manage this information, and should not withhold legal advice because of fears that it will destroy the possibility for consensus.

How Conflict Resolution Advocates Can Use the Law

Participating in settlement processes does not negate the application of legal knowledge, any more than it negates advocacy on the clients' behalf. Conflict resolution advocacy requires a thorough appraisal of the impact the law may have on the outcome, as well as what other means may be available for determining an outcome that is acceptable to the parties. It challenges counsel to understand when law can be effective in moving towards just resolution, and when it may impede, constrain, or obscure possibilities.

The process of consensus building requires the New Lawyer to pay attention to the usefulness and appropriateness of legal norms in each particular negotiation, rather than promoting the law as a general approach to dispute resolution (the first core belief from Chapter 3). Raising legal issues in consensus building is one way – just one way – of framing the dialogue. As this chapter has argued, it may be especially important where there is a danger of an unfair agreement between unequal parties.

The relationship between law and legal negotiation is a reflection of the relationship between rights and interests, and distributive and integrative models of bargaining. Appeals to rights, alongside discussion of interests, can be integrated into a dialogue that emphasizes persuasion over compulsion. Neither substitutes for or overrides the other, and ideally each complements the other in producing the best possible outcome for the client. Each is less the opposite or a contradiction of the other, and more the other face of the same coin, reflected in a difference in "depth of analysis and style of presentation."[59] Interests are not the antithesis of positions, but rather the uncovering of the motivations behind the purpose stated in the position (e.g., the playhouse story described above). Similarly, the legal principles involved in any one dispute do not oppose or contradict other possible solutions the parties may agree on, but offer another choice for the parties (e.g., the Band Council story described above). Some aspects of the dispute may be best resolved using legal principles (perhaps the distributive elements), whereas others require creative problem solving and integrative bargaining. Understanding the relationship between law and informal dispute resolution in this more complex way avoids the simplistic characterization of consensus building as necessitating "paradigm change" that rejects the use of predictive legal advice.

New Lawyers should use their legal intelligence to further their clients' chances of an outcome that meets their needs, and is feasible and durable. Their legal knowledge can be used to convince another party to take a conflict seriously, to develop a fair and realistic agreed solution, and sometimes to reality-test entrenched or inflated expectations. Lawyers can offer clients as clear a picture as possible of their rights entitlements and, where appropriate, either promote these explicitly or ensure that any bargain does not fall below this standard. What New Lawyers should not expect from the law is that its standards will always be the best fit for the needs and values of the parties; instead, they should always explore the type of tailor-made, nuanced solution that often appeals to both domestic and commercial clients. Counsel should also be cautious about the potential for legal theories to frame the conflict in a way that does not represent the real core of the struggle, and may impede a whole problem analysis that is the key to settlement.

Legal advice isolated from problem solving has never been an effective strategy for legal counsel. The creative and practical use of legal intelligence is a critical skill and a strategic tool, and remains a central professional responsibility for the New Lawyer.

8

Ethical Challenges for the New Lawyer

Legal ethics is the applied philosophy of lawyering;
it goes to the heart of what it means to be a lawyer.[1]

The evolving nature of legal practice continuously creates new ethical and conduct challenges for the legal profession. Some of these are contemporary versions of old dilemmas; for example, where do appropriate professional boundaries lie in a digital world where communication is faster and more frequent? Others emerge from new practices such as conflict resolution advocacy. One that has been discussed throughout this book is how New Lawyers should balance getting the best outcome for their clients with a serious commitment to settlement. Other, more recent conduct dilemmas are the consequence of the growing numbers of self-represented litigants whom lawyers encounter in the courts, and the necessity of dealing with those without counsel with respect, patience, and professionalism.

At the heart of these and other ethical issues is the rapidly changing relationship between lawyer and client in the modern era, which is creating a host of new and so far mostly unsettled questions. We have seen that client expectations of the role they will play – whether in dispute resolution processes, the development of strategy, the expenditure of their funds, or other decision making – have changed significantly in the last twenty-five years. Clients want more say in case management.

Client participation in processes such as mediation, collaborative law, and settlement conferences moves counsel from the traditional arm's-length agency into a direct working relationship with their clients. Where those processes are private and informal, taking place behind closed doors, there is the additional problem of how to create and sustain norms of professional behaviour. Where dispute resolution processes are overseen by courts – for example, judicial conferencing and court-connected mediation – conduct guidelines are starting to emerge but monitoring and enforcement (should this be the responsibility of the mediator? a court committee?) remains a challenge. Finally, where lawyers find themselves facing a self-represented litigant on the other side, there are few if any recognized practice rules to follow, and lawyers are left largely to formulate their own norms. The following comments made by self-represented litigants (SRLs) are unfortunately typical:

> As soon as he (opposing counsel) knew I was representing myself, he went in for the kill.[2]

> The lawyers strategize to marginalize you because you are an SRL ... painting the angry stereotype SRL. I am shocked at the success of this stereotyping and how negative it is.[3]

This chapter considers how the ethical and conduct framework of the New Lawyer can and should adjust to these changing conditions. But first, let's consider the ongoing discussions within the profession at a time of widespread public cynicism towards lawyers. It is no coincidence that a debate over professionalism is occurring at the same time that the work lawyers do for their clients is changing rapidly.

Ethics and Professional Identity

A debate over professionalism taking place in bar associations all over North America reveals that while law continues to prosper as a business in some sectors, the public image of lawyers is increasingly negative. The chosen expression, "professionalism," suggests a constellation of values such as high ethical standards, competence, civility, collegiality, and commitment to public service. Professionalism seems to represent the wider goals of the profession to improve standards and its image in the eyes of the public, in a way that reasserts its value.

The precise relationship between professionalism and ethical conduct is often unclear. The notion of professionalism seems to transcend the rule-bound sense of ethical conduct widely taught in law school classes on professional responsibility. Anthony Kronman aptly describes the relationship between ethical behaviours and professionalism as the difference between learning the grammatical rules of a language and being able to actually converse in this language.[4]

The notion of professionalism incorporates not only the profession's regulatory ethical frameworks – the codes of conduct – but also its culture and mores. According to Andrew Abbott, professional identity includes not only substantive knowledge but also a highly developed abstract knowledge system that guides social practices.[5] It is within this abstract knowledge system that professions develop models of "appropriate" professional and ethical behaviours, which are less explicit but just as or even more important than formal, substantive rules of conduct contained in codes. This includes professional mores where there are no rules – for example, behaviour towards the other side in negotiations, interactions with opposite counsel in social and professional settings, the tone of professional correspondence, relationships with members of the bench, and, most recently, working opposite self-represented litigants.

A Decline in Professionalism?

A decline in professionalism and ethical standards – often described as a loss of vocation or calling among practising lawyers, and manifest in complaints about lawyer incivility and "sharp" behaviour – has been a constant theme in the legal literature for the last quarter of a century. Many writers argue that over that period there has been a general deterioration in professional civility and habits of professional courtesies.[6] This is an issue, evidently, on which many practising lawyers hold an opinion, with numerous articles on this topic appearing in bar journals and professional publications.[7]

Despite these alarms, the formal teaching of professional and ethical conduct for lawyers has remained the "orphan" of legal education. Whereas in the United States professional responsibility is a required course for American Bar Association schools, in Canada it is an optional course taken by a minority of law students.[8] More significantly, professional ethical issues are rarely raised and are addressed at best tangentially in the rush to cover material in substantive law courses. Writers in Canada and the United States have sharply criticized both professional bodies and the law schools for their neglect of the teaching of professional responsibility.[9]

In the last ten years, many professional associations and regulators have started to look for ways to revitalize a debate over professionalism and ethics by instituting task forces and think tanks, commissioning research, and holding conferences and other fora. The growing realization that the legal profession is in a state of change brings with it a fear that it is no longer tethered to the fundamental ideals of a shared vocation encompassing a range of social roles and purposes, including access to justice, and that it has lost its way in the increasing focus on law as a business. In *The Lost Lawyer: Failing Ideals of the Legal Profession,* Kronman describes how a narrow focus on lawyers as specialist technicians (often the servants of corporate interests) has overwhelmed the moral purpose of lawyering in which the lawyers saw themselves as engaged in a lifelong endeavour to work for the public good.[10]

In *The Lawyer's Myth: Reviving the Ideals of the Legal Profession,* Walter Bennett describes the moral impotence he sees assumed by his law students, in which they believe themselves powerless in a world of practice that dismisses idealism and high moral purpose as irrelevant.[11] Bennett's assertion that law students often give up on the goals and visions with which they came to law school is supported by numerous studies of the impact of law school on idealism and goals.[12] Both Kronman and Bennett argue that the diminution of the purposive moral aspects of lawyering results in a void of professional identity, too often filled by crude adversarialism and a general decline in the norms of civility and ethical practice. Both scholars see this not only as a crisis that implicates the work, profitability, and reputation of the profession but also as a loss of professional ideals and dignity. As Kronman starkly puts it, the legal profession is "in danger of losing its soul."[13]

The lament for the decline in professionalism is often permeated with nostalgia for older, disappearing forms of practice. This is problematic given the gendered, racial, ethnic, religious, and economic exclusions that allowed for a complacent collegiality of traditional legal professionalism. The broadened demographic of the profession inevitably presents new challenges to old practices, and loss of core ideals may be explained by the welcome inclusion of a wider and more diverse population of lawyers. In some quarters, one suspects that the yearning for the ideals of traditional practice may be less about turning away from adversarialism and commercialism and more about returning to the "good old days" of a homogeneous and exclusionary bar. As Fred Zacarias wryly notes: "No term in the legal lexicon has been more abused than 'professionalism.'"[14]

More concretely, Kronman argues that professional role identities are tied to hierarchies of skills and values, and thus to the skills and motivations of individuals who are drawn to and remain in the legal profession. As we change the role identity of the lawyer, we also change what we value about lawyers. The attributes appropriate to a profession constantly "on its feet" in court making legal arguments have become less relevant to a profession that specializes in conflict resolution advocacy and deal making, whether in big-firm commercial practice or small-town general practice. Perhaps eventually I shall no longer read applications to law school that constantly assert that the applicant is suited to legal practice because he or she is good at arguing with people.

In *The Lost Lawyer*, Kronman looks back at a "nostalgic" model of small-town legal practice and compares it with contemporary, urban, "mega-firm" practice. There are differences in skills and abilities associated with the different models. Kronman's small-town lawyer-statesman needed excellent personal judgment in advising and dealing with clients – his personal judgment was a critical aspect of what clients valued. In contrast, today's big-firm lawyers rarely question, contradict, or refuse to follow their clients' wishes.[15]

The changes taking place within legal practice mean that the heart of what it means to be a legal professional is changing. One result of this uncertainty is a sense of vocational "drift." Of course, law is not the only profession experiencing this phenomenon. A similar state of flux can be observed in the medical profession, for example, in the shift in some types of general practice responsibility from doctors to nurses, who are now qualified as nurse practitioners. This change has unsettled the role identity and status of doctors as they adjust to the inclusion of other professionals within hospitals and general practices who share some, but not all, of their skills and qualifications. In common with law, the medical profession has been greatly affected by the growth of accessible information via the World Wide Web and the empowerment of its users, who may no longer see their physician as an unassailable expert. The redrawing of professional roles and identities leads to uncertainty, stress, and sometimes conflict.

The changes described throughout this book suggest that instead of a choate core of professional values, the legal profession is fragmenting into different modes of service and profit making. Different sectors of the bar – large urban firms, small country practices, local bar associations, and courts – appear to be developing internal professional norms and values, and none is as cohesive as when the profession was less diverse. One example of this is the response of the bar to demands from personal clients for more affordable and flexible models of service, including unbundled legal services using limited-scope retainers and fixed-fee products. While some lawyers are stepping forward to innovate and adjust their service menu, others remain convinced that only a full-representation, billable-hours model is for them.

I'm just the kind who wants to act for the person all the way through.

I'm busy enough, why "recreate the wheel"?[16]

Without a clear consensus within the profession, and uncertainty over everything from client service models to the nature of professionalism, the New Lawyer must find a way to recognize and respond professionally to new ethical and conduct dilemmas as these arise.

A Rule-Based Approach to Legal Ethics

In times of change, the New Lawyer needs a broad conception of what "ethical" and "professional" behaviours and values are that goes well beyond the existing formal rules of conduct, and that emphasizes the importance of personal judgment that is value-based, intentional, and responsive.

This is not how lawyers have historically been trained to think about legal ethics. When I asked one senior litigator, widely respected by his peers for his professionalism and integrity, what he did when faced with an ethical dilemma, he told me, "I reach for the Code of Conduct and look it up." I was taken aback. I had expected a more reflective answer. But of course his answer made perfect sense. Like the rest of his generation, this lawyer had been taught that "ethics" is synonymous with the rules of professional conduct. When I pressed him on what he did if the code did not provide an answer, he laughed. "I can usually figure something out." Since this lawyer had led a highly principled professional life, this had clearly worked out for him. Others, one suspects, may be less successful.

There is logic to the legal profession's reliance on formal rules to bring lawyers to conclusions about ethical practice. The focus of the codes – broadly consistent among multiple jurisdictions – is generally on behaviour and choices that arise in the process of adjudication. For example, the lawyer's duty to the court, the limiting of services to one's competencies, the duty to avoid conflicts of interest (in an actual or potentially adversarial process), the responsibility to protect client confidentiality – historically these issues arose in relation to an adjudicative process of dispute resolution, and they are addressed using rules and rights-based thinking.[17]

The resulting focus on rules neglects or ignores ambiguity, novel situations, or the use of personal discretion and contextual judgment. For example, in the literature on lying, a central concern is whether a lie is later discoverable, rather than, for example, with the risk of building an agreement on deception or the effect of truth telling or lying on the future of the bargaining relationship.[18]

A rule-based approach also entrenches dominant norms rather than reflecting practice changes, and thus offers no solutions to new questions. An example is the tendency to regard negotiation as a corollary to litigation and adjudication, perhaps to be used for advantage – for example, to press a position or as a tactical ploy. By contrast, in a model of conflict resolution advocacy, negotiation, mediation, and other collaborative settlement processes represent a commitment to use negotiation to genuinely explore settlement, and to advocate for a good solution. If the rules of conduct guided negotiation in this way – assuming an openness towards a range of possible outcomes and a closer working partnership with the client – it would enable the New Lawyer to better anticipate potential ethical dilemmas in settlement-oriented processes. This is a far cry from "how much lying/evasion/aggression can I get away with under the rules?"

A Practice-Based Approach to Legal Ethics

To properly understand and analyze the conduct issues that the New Lawyer faces in private dispute resolution processes, court-run settlement processes, and new practice challenges, we must first broaden our understanding of ethics for the purposes of this discussion. If we limit what we mean by ethics to situations in which there is an existing rule of professional conduct – such as conflict of interest or privilege and confidentiality – we shall miss the heart of the New Lawyer's professional challenge.

Instead, I propose a wider definition of ethical issues for legal practice. Rather than understanding ethical decision making as arising only in the context of the rules of conduct – essentially asking, "Am I allowed to do this?" – I suggest that every time a *value-based* choice is presented between alternate courses of action, an ethical decision is being made. This may be a conscious choice or one that is intuitive and unconscious. In general parlance, ethics is understood as the choice between two or more competing courses of action, where one choice (made on the basis of a particular principle or value) will be morally superior to the other.[19]

This broad definition means that many decisions taken by counsel – in the moment, perhaps intuitively – are potentially "ethical" in their ramifications. Of course, many decisions over choosing one or another course of action concern minor details that do not have an impact on ethics and professionalism. For instance, deciding on which end of the negotiation table your client will sit, whether a negotiation should take place in your offices or the offices of the other side, or even, perhaps, whether you and your client are sufficiently prepared for a settlement discussion are rarely questions that raise serious ethical dilemmas. But many other aspects of planning and participating in dispute resolution processes sometimes raise questions about appropriate professional behaviours – for example, the decision over whether to engage in negotiation at all,[20] or refusing to cooperate with information exchange, or coming to mediation with no intention of discussing settlement.[21] What about refusing to communicate with an SRL on the other side? Or "snowing" him or her with paperwork that counsel is aware will intimidate and confuse? To say that because the codes of conduct are vague, or even silent, on such matters there is no ethical issue is a wholly inadequate response.

Framing ethics as value-based choices recognizes the highly contextual nature of many choices made by counsel, admitting no one right answer. In the absence of applicable rules and principles, personal judgment is often critical. The concept of "discursive ethics" is useful here.[22] Discursive ethics attempts to understand the moral reasoning behind any decision or action by examining the assumptions within the situation – for example, what language is used, how powerful (or not) the participants believe themselves to be, their preferred outcomes, and so on. In this analysis, our effort is directed not towards the rightness or wrongness of the decision or action itself, but rather towards first uncovering and then evaluating the basis for the choice that was made. This approach to ethical decision making reflects feminist theories of knowledge that understand truth as contextual and therefore forever fluid – "situated and provisional rather than absolute and final."[23]

The discursive approach seems particularly appropriate in situations for which there are no rules or even, as yet, conventions of fair process. It points to the need for a frank discussion between lawyer and client over such issues, with the goal of developing a shared understanding of ethical behaviours and responses. The decisions and strategies that emerge may be individual and experiential "truths," but they will be underpinned by a moral reasoning that both lawyer and client feel comfortable with, and are able to articulate and defend.

The remainder of this chapter explores five ethical issues relevant to the practice of the New Lawyer. While these are not intended as a comprehensive review of the difficult ethical choices raised by the changing conditions of legal practice, these issues raise many important and unresolved questions about ethical and professional conduct. The first three issues – furthering client interests in consensus building, bargaining in good faith, and applying pressure to settle – present regular challenges in dispute resolution processes. A fourth, the importance of securing informed client consent, appears in multiple guises now that clients play an increasingly active role in settlement processes. The fifth and final issue is relatively new: how counsel communicates with and relates to an SRL on the other side.

Before beginning this discussion, it is important to note that the first three ethical issues examined here arise most often in private negotiations. This is not to say that they do not also arise in court-supervised settings (e.g., court-connected mediation, judicial settlement conferencing), sometimes as a continuation of a private negotiation, but characteristically these are private processes. This adds an additional layer of complexity to the discussion, since practitioners rarely share their experiences or openly discuss the ethical and conduct dilemmas they encounter behind closed doors.

Furthering Client Interests in Consensus Building

Managing the tension between securing the best possible outcome for one's client, while acknowledging what the other side is willing and able to agree to, is perhaps the single most complex ethical dilemma for the New Lawyer. Finding this balance is a recurring challenge at many stages of consensus building, from an initial decision to exchange information, to the conduct of the negotiation itself, to the evaluation of a settlement proposal. The tension flows directly from a commitment to problem solving in a system that has historically prized a "win" over a good solution. Carrie Menkel-Meadow asks:

If lawyers were to see their social and legal role less as "zealously representing" clients' interests and more as solving clients' ... problems, what legal ethics would follow?[24]

A problem-solving approach to conflict resolution in negotiation, collaboration, or mediation blurs the sharp battle lines adversarial advocacy draws between one's own client and the other parties to the dispute. Adversarial advocacy offers the seductive clarity of remaining inside a "bubble" of positional argument and justification. Consensus building bursts this bubble since the other side takes on far greater strategic and practical significance in attempting to resolve conflict rather than in fighting.

The suspicion lingers that if lawyers care – practically speaking – about the other side's interests, they might be unable to protect and stand up for their own clients' rights. But this presupposes that the only "true" advocacy is advancing a positional argument. In fact, advocacy means advancing one's clients' best and most important interests. As one collaborative lawyer put it, "This is not litigation-lite."[25]

Nonetheless, a commitment to advancing client interests while remaining responsive to what the other side needs and wants is a challenging balance to find. This is the classic Prisoner's Dilemma[26] – how to protect one's own (or the client's) interests while recognizing that, short of a pre-emptive and decisive strike, achieving this goal is largely dependent upon satisfying the interests of the other party. As one lawyer put it, "[My] success ... is based on the strength of my relationships with colleagues."[27] How can counsel claim value for their own clients while maximizing mutual gains? Isn't some element of loyalty and commitment to one's clients lost in the process?

Working with an explicit agenda of collaboration and accommodation makes these tensions obvious, but this is a familiar challenge in many fields of legal practice. Commercial lawyers must balance the best rights-based out-come for their client with what makes business sense, especially if there are continuing relationships and perhaps other (time, resource, market) con-straints on profit making. Family lawyers often understand their professional responsibility to include whole family considerations, especially in divorce cases when young children are involved. For example:

As an advocate, I am looking more at the family as a unit.[28]

[I make a] contract with the client to find a solution which is in the interests of the whole family.[29]

Nonetheless, the relationship with one's own client is different, and special. The best description of this that I ever heard was from a collaborative lawyer who said:

I think, to be honest, it's natural for an attorney ... that *my best friend in the room* is always going to be my client.[30]

Another family lawyer put it this way:

I absolutely think I have a special responsibility to my client. I mean I am their attorney. I am her attorney or his attorney and there is no question in my mind that that is my primary duty. I mean, that's what my job is, that's what I'm being retained for.[31]

An ethical approach to managing the tension between consensus building and client advocacy in family law requires that counsel acknowledge their primary attachment to the client, while recognizing the interrelationship of all family members in achieving the best all-round outcome. A practical challenge for the New Lawyer seeking this balance is how to relate to opposing counsel. Typically in (public) lawyer-to-lawyer interaction, it is normative to be assertive, even aggressive, with counsel for the other side. Clients rarely feel that their lawyer is more committed to counsel for the other side than to their interests. In fact, clients are far more likely to complain that the level of animosity between opposing lawyers may further escalate the conflict.

However, when lawyers regularly work together in settlement processes – especially in smaller communities, or in specialty networks within larger organizations – they often develop relationships that are personal as well as professional. These relationships may generate their own internal incentives for successful outcomes, independent of the clients' interests. The lawyers like working together, feel like they are a "team," and want to continue to maintain this close working relationship. They may feel accountable to one another, as well as to their individual clients.

It is revealing that while most collaborative lawyers see only a positive impact of a better relationship between counsel, their clients see more downsides. The hurt and dissatisfaction that an overtly amicable approach may create, especially when this has not been discussed as an intentional strategy with the client in advance, is exemplified by one collaborative client who commented that her lawyer "wanted to chat up my husband and bond with him ... I felt abandoned."[32] Once again, open discussion with the client that anticipates the issue emerges as key to professional behaviour. One lawyer described telling her clients in advance, "Even if I am nice to the other side, I am *your* lawyer."[33]

New Lawyers should be aware of the consequences of close professional ties with opposing counsel– for example, membership in the same professional network or formal practice group – as well as of the importance of being transparent in discussions about these relationships with their clients. This rapport will be important to developing good outcomes, but some practice scenarios may alarm a client. New Lawyers should be able to set boundaries within professional relationships that are comfortable for their practice as well as for their clients.

Another challenge that may arise over balancing client loyalty with commitment to consensus building is the choice of dispute resolution process. The Collaborative Lawyering Research Project found that a small number of collaborative lawyers felt that their commitment to the process of collaboration actually superseded their loyalty to their client. These lawyers felt that building the field of collaborative law is a higher professional responsibility than the outcomes of their individual cases – a view, unsurprisingly, not shared by their clients. These lawyers express complete faith that the collaborative law process (negotiation without litigation) will always produce an acceptable outcome and expect the same measure of faith from clients. Failed cases that do not reach settlement are explained as failures to use the process properly. At its most extreme, this attitude can be articulated in the following way:

> I don't really care about whether the outcome is optimal in terms of dollars and cents, but that [my client] and I live up to our collaborative principles.[34]

Similar attitudes towards mediation were expressed by a small number of lawyers in the Culture Change Project. The so-called True Believer[35] has made a strong personal commitment to using mediation, using quasi-religious metaphors such as "converted" (e.g., "I'm a person who has now converted and I admit to being a believer in mediation"[36] and "I got religion"[37]) to describe a process of personal and professional change.

Whatever the strength of their commitment to a particular dispute resolution process, New Lawyers should not allow their faith in a particular process to supersede their loyalty to their client. The client's interest should always come first – which means that each case and every client require an assessment of suitable dispute resolution processes, rather than an assumption that one particular approach will always work. Lawyers have an obligation to ensure their client's informed consent (see below). The unbiased presentation of information about dispute resolution choices has a special significance because counsel's opinion is very influential.[38] New Lawyers should always offer a broad spectrum of dispute resolution options rather than simply directing the client to their preferred process. Overzealous commitment to one particular dispute resolution model raises a danger that commitment to the process itself overrides this particular client's interests.

The primary loyalty of New Lawyers, just as in times past, is to their clients. This does not mean that dispute resolution process preferences and good working relationships with other counsel are inappropriate – in fact clarity and conviction on these elements often enhance client service. But the key is responsiveness to the clients' particular needs and interests. As I have often described this in training workshops, the primary task of conflict resolution advocates is to persuade the other side to agree to their clients' best terms. This framing encompasses both client loyalty and mutual collaboration.

Bargaining in "Good Faith"

Complaints that the other side came to a settlement meeting unprepared to participate in a serious discussion of an agreed outcome, intending to use the process instrumentally, or lacking "good faith" in some other way are common.[39] Naturally, the cause of the problem is always laid at the feet of the other side. Blaming the other side is always a useful way of explaining why settlement was not achieved, but to be fair, there is plenty of evidence (especially in court-connected mediation) to show that some counsel deploy tactics deliberately intended to undermine the purpose and possible outcomes of such a meeting. These include using a face-to-face meeting to intimidate the other side into reducing its expectations, and using such a session as a "fishing expedition" for information without any serious intent of settling.[40] The following statement, made by a commercial litigator speaking about mandatory mediation, is a frank example of the potential for abuse of the mediation process, and of disregard for any notion of good faith, however defined:

> If I act for the Big Bad Wolf against Little Red Riding Hood and I don't want this dispute resolved, I want to tie it up as long as I possibly can, and mandatory mediation is custom made. I can waste more time, I can string it along, I can make sure this thing never gets resolved because you've already figured out that I know the language. I know how to make it look like I'm heading in that direction. I make it look like I can make all the right noises in the world, like this is a wonderful thing to be involved in when I have no intention of ever resolving this. I have the intention of making this the most expensive, longest process but is it going to feel good. It's going to feel so nice, we're going to be here and we're going to talk the talk but we're not going to walk the walk.[41]

The strategy described in this quotation appears to be an unambiguous example of "bad faith." There is also a range of well-documented and widely observed practices in mediation that are more accurately described as "lacking in good faith." These include failing to prepare adequately, failing to bring the necessary personnel to the mediation session, failing to exchange relevant information in advance or to bring it to the mediation, and so on. These lapses may have more to do with a lack of familiarity with the mediation process than with intentional bad faith, but the cumulative effect is much the same – mediation is generally frustrated by these types of behaviours. In an evaluation of the Saskatchewan Queen's Bench mediation program in 2003, a number of lawyers expressed high levels of frustration about the likelihood that they would prepare conscientiously for mediation and bring their client, only to be confronted by a lawyer on the other side who was not willing to bargain openly or in good faith. The following comments are typical:

> Some lawyers make only pathetic efforts to prepare in [sic] mediation. Some lawyers – they are living in the dark ages – tell their clients not to say anything, and this makes mediation a waste of time for myself and my client. It can be embarrassing where you prep and bring your client, and then the other side walks [out] after ten minutes.[42]

Some jurisdictions in North America have adopted a rule that enables mediators to impose sanctions if they believe that one party or the other has not come in good faith, adequately prepared, and ready to bargain seriously.[43] There is enormous difficulty in defining bad faith, and it is even more difficult to pin down an "absence of good faith." For example, is the refusal to disclose a particular piece of information prior to mediation justifiable client advocacy, or is it a breach of good faith? If one side asks for an adjournment of mediation, what makes this good faith and what makes it bad faith? Is the delivery of a patently insincere apology, such as the one described by a client as being a statement that "only a moron would think [that] was coming from the heart,"[44] a matter of bad faith, or simply poor stage management? And, most controversial of all, is a failure to deliver a "reasonable" offer in mediation a sign of bad faith or simply a carefully considered conclusion not to offer settlement at this time?

The difficulty of drawing these lines has produced an extended debate in the United States over the feasibility of the mediator's defining and policing good faith.[45] Concerns centre on the definitional questions and the need to involve the court in making these decisions (and perhaps intruding on process confidentiality). Some commentators have suggested that legislating a good faith rule encourages bad faith conduct because it provides a benchmark that some lawyers will then find a way to get around – for example, by giving untruthful responses to questions about settlement authority and readiness to negotiate.[46] There are also concerns that a good faith rule with strict sanctions may be used to intimidate weaker parties.[47] In Canada, these concerns appear to have stalled – for the time being, at least – any further debate over good faith regulations in mandatory mediation programs.

With or without regulation, the question remains: what standards of behaviour should New Lawyers adopt to demonstrate good faith, and what can they reasonably expect of other lawyers? Some local legal cultures are developing their own norms of good faith bargaining behaviours before and during settlement meetings, in much the same way that they have developed informal protocols in other areas, such as plea bargaining with the local Crown counsels or in-chambers discussions with a particular judge or master. Smaller and more cohesive communities are often successful in setting and largely maintaining widely accepted standards and conventions. In mediation, these usually include conventions for adequate preparation for mediation (sometimes including a style of mediation brief), documentary exchange (e.g., beginning with the voluntary exchange of the affidavit of documents), and sometimes a frank discussion between lawyers to avoid the unnecessary expenditure of energy if one side believes mediation to be inappropriate or premature. One lawyer in the community of Prince Albert, Saskatchewan (population forty thousand), explained:

> Prince Albert has a collegial culture, and negotiation and collaboration is part of that culture. This is as easy a place to talk rationally about a file as anywhere, and this program [mandatory mediation] has worked well here because that was already the mindset.[48]

This helps to explain the positive reactions to mediation expressed by lawyers working in smaller communities in the course of a review of mandatory mediation programs in Ontario (1999–2000) and Saskatchewan (2002–03). Lawyers in these jurisdictions asserted that even if the program were to be discontinued, they would continue to use mediation because it is widely accepted within their communities of practice.[49] For these lawyers, and inside their legal communities, good faith bargaining had become an established norm, complete with social sanctions for breach. Once accepted, these changed norms represent both community values and a personal commitment, demonstrated by the investment that many lawyers in smaller communities put into maintaining mediation programs either formally or informally. Under these circumstances, a good faith rule may be unnecessary – peer pressure does the job much more effectively.

In other legal communities – often larger, more competitive, and sometimes (by dint of numbers) more anonymous environments – it is still normative and even assumed that counsel will often use mediation and other collaborative processes instrumentally and sometimes in bad faith.[50] This difference is so well established that some lawyers practising in smaller communities anticipate that they should expect a different attitude from lawyers from larger and less collegial communities. The following comment is typical:

Ethical Challenges for the New Lawyer

I see a real difference of attitude in Toronto lawyers compared to Ottawa lawyers about mediation. They have not accepted it and they still hold back. They don't go in there with the intention of disclosing, baring your soul ... it's not working in Toronto the way it should work ... there's a really different attitude ... I've tried to persuade some Toronto counsel to go to mediation or to even just sit down and talk when the case is not one of the ones in the [mandatory mediation] system, and you just don't get that type of cooperation. In Toronto ... there's still the ambush mentality ... There's always been a difference in how they practice law in Toronto – just read a discovery transcript.[51]

Faced with what feels like "bad faith" in negotiation, mediation, or collaboration, how should the New Lawyer respond? Some lawyers take on the task of "educating" their peers on this question with almost missionary zeal.[52] This may make a difference over the long term, but rarely answers an immediate problem in a current negotiation. In such situations, lawyers sometimes heed the advice of social scientist Robert Axelrod[53] and react to perceived bad faith by responding in kind – the so-called tit-for-tat strategy. For example, if the other side fails to disclose requested information, your side does the same; if the other side refuses to put an offer on the table, you do too.

But the tit-for-tat strategy also carries some dangers. Mimicking bad faith behaviour undermines the integrity of the process and, quite possibly, the lawyer's own reputation. It also inevitably escalates the process and may result in an impasse. There is a difficult balance to be struck between withdrawing from a process that seems to have limited usefulness in advancing the client's goals, and directly addressing bad faith behaviour in an effort to salvage the negotiation.

New Lawyers should talk directly and explicitly to the other side about issues of bad faith and, based on those discussions, advise their client whether or not to continue in efforts to settle. New Lawyers and their client must jointly determine whether to continue to negotiate when there are signs of bad faith. There are differences of degrees here: for example, whether the problematic behaviour is simply unhelpful or downright obstructive; whether there is a failure to disclose information or intentional obfuscation or deception. In deciding how to respond, counsel must responsibly evaluate what interests their client has in continuing to bargain, whether the process is salvageable or whether trust has been irreparably damaged, and what alternatives there are to continuing in negotiation.

In mediation, there is a possibility that counsel can expect the mediator to take some responsibility for confronting bad faith tactics. Data from clients suggest that some would like to see the mediator play a more proactive role in managing recalcitrant and obstructive behaviour on the part of counsel.[54] Some lawyers agree: "[In this case], the mediator made all the difference despite the lawyer telling the client not to speak. The mediators should be willing to get their hands dirty" – that is, by being interventionist when counsel is being obstructive to the process.[55] Not all mediators are willing to play such a proactive role, whether because of concerns over alienating future customers if they lean too heavily on individual counsel or because of a lack of personal confidence and experience. How they might handle such an issue may be an important question for counsel to raise with potential mediators before retaining them, especially if counsel is concerned about the possibility of bad faith bargaining.

Another issue is what New Lawyers should do when faced with bad faith behaviour by their own clients. Many clients who are repeat users of mediation and other settlement processes recognize the potential benefits of using these processes to gather information about the other side, and regard them as a serious attempt at resolution. However, clients may sometimes suggest elements of an agreement that they cannot deliver, or present information in a way that obfuscates its real meaning or omits important details.

Counsel should discourage this type of bad faith on the part of their clients just as strongly as they would if it emanated from the other side. However powerful the client, counsel should point out the practical risks of a purely instrumental use of opportunities for negotiation and mediation, such as impeding any possibility of early settlement and/or risking the durability of any agreement reached. Counsel should also be willing to point out the ethical implications of exploiting the good faith of the other side without reciprocation. As they develop a stronger sense of their own professional ethical responsibilities in good faith bargaining, New Lawyers will be able to more confidently tackle this conversation with their clients.

Applying Pressure to Settle

The focus on bad faith and the potential for some lawyers to use settlement processes for instrumental reasons has often overshadowed another important ethical issue that arises for New Lawyers – what is legitimate pressure on a client to accept a settlement offer that counsel considers fair and reasonable? And how might counsel discourage a client from accepting an offer that they consider to be less than fair, or lower than might be possible?

Between 1999 and 2004, a small but growing number of cases were brought to US federal and state courts requesting that mediated settlements be overturned on the basis of duress by either the mediator (seventeen cases in total) or the lawyer (eighty-two cases).[56] These cases used traditional contract arguments, such as duress, mistake, and undue influence. In response to rising levels of litigation seeking to overturn mediated agreements, a debate has begun over the use of "cooling-off periods" in mediated agreements to ensure that parties and counsel are fully comfortable with their shared understandings, and to avoid litigation over enforceability.[57]

What are the sources of pressure to settle, and how should the New Lawyer respond?

Process Pressures

When lawyers negotiate with one another, they exchange proposals and ultimately convey a recommendation to their clients for the clients' instructions. This often amounts to lawyers' simply telling their clients what they should do. When clients accompany their lawyers to meetings designed to explore resolution, this immediately changes the dynamics of decision making around settlement.[58] When clients participate in negotiation, they hear for themselves what is being offered (or denied). There is no sugarcoating of the offer by their lawyer – equally, there may be something that the client hears in the offer that counsel would not have recognized the importance of. The possibility of settlement becomes at once concrete and immediate.

A potential downside is that clients may sometimes feel pressured to agree to a settlement without adequate time to reflect and consider. The incentive to get the matter "done today" affects both counsel and client. There may be a rush to a solution that is later regretted. When clients attend negotiation, decisions may be reached more rapidly and in an intense climate. The following comment about the dynamics of mediation could apply equally to collaborative four-way meetings or settlement conferencing:

> There becomes an intense pressure to settle because you want to be successful at the mediation. So the mediation creates an expectation. And I think some people try to use that to force the other side to give up more than they should because everyone wants so desperately for it to work. So there does become this quite intense pressure by the end of the day to get to yes.[59]

It is important for New Lawyers to understand this intrinsic desire to "get it done." They may be able to do little to restrain the natural tendency to want closure, but they should pay close attention to the possibility that something is driving the client towards an agreement that may later give rise to "buyer's remorse"; for example, a fear of holding out for more in the face of a hostile spouse who still shares living space, the need to placate a third party, or a time-limited opportunity (e.g., a new job prospect) that depends on the other side's goodwill.

Counsel should anticipate the possibility of a momentum towards settlement that might "railroad" their client into an agreement in much the same way that they would anticipate other internal pressures to settle, such as a financial crisis or the expiration of an offer. Such considerations may mean that the client is right to settle – but the New Lawyer should be aware of psychological pressures and incentives that impact the client, and be able to discuss these openly. This includes ensuring that a client fully understands and provides informed consent to any agreed outcome, even when the mooted solution appears to be "obviously" in the client's interests.[60]

Pressure from Lawyers

The case law analysis described above shows that lawyers, and not third parties, are the most common focus of client complaints about pressure in settlement processes. It is relatively rare for such pressure to be manifestly coercive. It is more commonly subtle yet persistent. When counsel feels that a proposal offers a good outcome, how much pressure should be placed on the client to accept it? When does such pressure become inappropriate and coercive?

Clients will often invite counsel to advise them on a settlement proposal, and are usually highly susceptible to counsel's opinion. It is important to check that clients understand the offer and its consequences, as well as what they may be giving up, before acceptance. In other instances, counsel may feel frustrated that despite the emergence of a reasonable offer, a client remains unwilling to accept it. This is a good moment for the New Lawyer to remember the many dimensions that can impact the client's readiness to settle – psychological (emotional readiness), cognitive (e.g., accepting a new personal status such as "divorced" or "single," or no longer employed in a particular position), and behavioural (accepting what is offered as a consequence of settlement).[61] Many factors contribute to the "ripeness" of a dispute for settlement,[62] and rational risk assessment (is this the best possible offer?) plays a relatively small part next to expectations, cultural loyalties and assumptions, and a need to feel fairly treated.[63] Any such factors should be part of what the New Lawyer knows about the client, and is able to discuss frankly and weigh openly in order to remove any feeling of a rush to a solution.

The collaborative law process sets up some unique pressures to settle that need to be carefully anticipated and managed by collaborative lawyers to avoid the potential for pressure to settle. The collaborative law retainer agreement, which requires that counsel withdraw if the client commences litigation (the so-called disqualification clause), is inevitably a source of some process pressure. The personal investment of some collaborative lawyers in the collaborative process (discussed earlier in this chapter) may exacerbate this problem. One collaborative client commented that given the investment of the lawyers, the rhetoric ("you may choose to withdraw at any time") and the reality are not always lined up:

> I think the lawyers can't be objective because they want this process to work. [My lawyer] said I could step out of the process anytime I wanted to. In fact, that wasn't very helpful![64]

The disqualification clause is justified as a mutual incentive to work at settlement. However, it also means that the greater the client's investment – in the form of time, money, and emotional energy already expended, as well as the working relationship developed with the collaborative attorney – the greater the loss if he or she withdraws and has to begin again with a different lawyer. As one client put it:

> Now that we're this far, it's hard to leave. I have already spent around [dollar amount] and all of this time.[65]

Some collaborative lawyers take steps to address this feeling of entrapment by scheduling regular discussions with their clients about whether or not to continue in the collaborative process. This is an excellent ethical practice, and one that should be widely adopted by the New Lawyer, whatever the particular settlement mechanism. Sometimes, counsel may encourage the client to hang in just a little longer in order to see results, as every negotiation meets roadblocks on the way to settlement. However, commitment to exploring settlement is rarely open-ended or, outside collaborative law, exclusive – the parties may need to proceed with litigation and then return to bargaining at a later stage. The New Lawyer has an ethical responsibility to continuously reappraise the situation and be genuinely open to a change of strategy.

Another ethical question: what should New Lawyers do if they believe that the lawyer on the other side is placing undue pressure on his or her own client? Aside from the ethical ramifications, there is no practical advantage in obtaining an agreement for one's own client that has been extracted under duress from the other side. There is the risk that an agreement will be invalidated in the future for duress – or simply fall apart because the other party did not fully understand the consequences. However, counsel's professional responsibility for informed consent extends only to his or her own client, and not the client on the other side.

Often such pressure is implicit – for example, a common behaviour in mediation is for the lawyers to dominate the discussion, and when one makes a new proposal across the table, the other will not consult or even make eye contact with his or her client before rejecting the offer. While this behaviour is inconsistent with the commitment of the New Lawyer to joint decision making, there is no direct responsibility for similar respect to be shown to the other side.

I would argue, however, that in order to maintain the integrity of informal bargaining processes, the exclusion of any client from active decision making or, conversely, pressure to agree should be treated very seriously. Any concerns about this should be raised privately with opposing counsel, and the nature of those concerns – both practical and procedural – clearly articulated. One would hope that over time, any behaviour by counsel that presses for a particular client decision on settlement without appropriate consultation will be widely regarded as unprofessional and unethical.

Pressure from Third Parties

In third-party-led settlement processes such as mediation and judicial settlement conferencing, counsel is not the only source of client pressure – there is also the possibility that such pressure may come from the mediator, judge, or other third-party actor. Third parties, especially authoritative ones, have many ways of pressuring disputants. The three highly coercive mediator styles memorably named "hashers, bashers, and trashers" by James Alfini over twenty-five years ago are still prevalent today.[66] There is a sense among some mediators that part of the value-added service they offer is their ability to twist the arms of parties in order to push them towards settlement. Lawyers themselves sometimes seek out "hashers, bashers, and trashers" (or "muscle mediators") for clients who they feel need some strong "reality checking." While it may be appropriate to sometimes use an authoritative third party to convince a client that he or she faces a poor outcome at trial, the New Lawyer must be careful not to encourage undue pressure, especially by a third party who has no decision-making role.

The use of strong-arm tactics may be the consequence of the fact that mediators' reputations are often tied to their volume of settlements. In one notorious

Ethical Challenges for the New Lawyer

case, a mediator told the parties that he would lose his 100 percent settlement record if they refused to sign the agreement.[67] Research suggests that lawyers prefer mediators who settle, and often pick mediators based on this record alone.[68] Other widespread strategies, especially common in aggressive bargaining cultures such as labour/management negotiations but also seen in court-connected mediation programs, include using fatigue and hunger as levers to persuade the parties to agree. In Ontario's 1995 pilot civil mediation program, as many as 30 percent of clients interviewed said they experienced some pressure to settle.[69] Comments from one client group included "I agreed just to get it over with" and "I felt bulldozed by the mediator," as well as the following reference to the physical conditions:

> I felt that we settled under duress. No food, no restaurants in the area, the coffee was awful, no one had change for the machine. I felt hurried and pressured at times.[70]

New Lawyers have a clear ethical responsibility to ensure that clients are protected from mediator strategies to pressure them into agreement and to make it clear to their clients that, if necessary, the mediation can be suspended or even terminated. This is one of the many important ways in which strong client advocacy within mediation is critical to maintaining the procedural fairness of the process.

Another source of pressure to settle may be an established relationship between particular mediators and the lawyers who work with them on a regular basis. Mediators have an incentive to develop positive relationships with "repeat-player" lawyers (and, less often, "repeat-player" clients) since their livelihood usually depends on the market's assessment of their work. From the perspective of counsel, a special relationship with a particular mediator could encroach on client loyalty. As John Lande points out, "mediators and lawyers may find that they share an interest in pressuring principals to settle."[71] While resorting to a "muscle mediator" may be an appropriate strategy in some cases, it is important for lawyers to be clear that their primary relationship and commitment is to their client, and not to the mediator.

A final source of potential pressure to settle in the process is the increasing use of judges as third parties in public dispute resolution. Civil and family court judges play an increasingly activist role in settlement. The degree of pressure a judge places on a disputant in, for example, a judicial settlement hearing may result in the conflation of voluntary settlement with adjudication in the disputant's mind.[72] Judges possess unique social power to persuade a party to settle. Similarly, judicial referral to private mediation may amount to pressure, where the client believes that participating in mediation is a way of buying favour with this judge in a future hearing before him or her.[73]

Whatever the source of pressure to settle, the key ethical and professional issue for the New Lawyer is the line between acknowledged and legitimate sources of pressure, and coercion. Pressure is inherent in any lawsuit. There is a natural desire in most cases to close the conflict and move on, and this may be heightened in the moment and by the negotiation process itself. To manage these pressures, New Lawyers need to have a constant and fully transparent conversation with their client about the factors that go towards, and against, settlement. They should also see it as their responsibility to protect the client from undue pressure from other sources, such as opposing counsel, mediators, or judges, and should step in to neutralize that pressure, enabling a calm lawyer/client appraisal that focuses on the best interests of the client. New Lawyers and their clients are building a space where they can work together on the resolution of the conflict, with all of the information available to them, which includes a recognition of all the sources, both appropriate and less so, of pressure to settle.

It would be naïve to suggest that the line between legitimate and inappropriate pressure is always clear. An excellent example of this quandary is costs, often the most significant factor in producing pressure to settle in litigation. The goal of cost reduction frequently influences reluctant parties to at least consider settlement. The ethical dilemma is this: in seeking a cost-efficient solution, how often should this information be pressed on the parties? For example, how often is it appropriate for counsel (or a third party) to remind the parties of the costs associated with continuing their conflict? How far should a collaborative lawyer go in persuading disillusioned parties to stay with the process a little longer in order to (perhaps) see some return on their investment in negotiations? And when is the use of pressure – perhaps pressure from a third party selected by counsel for this purpose – appropriate to check the unrealistic expectations of a client?

These questions are only now beginning to be raised and will take time and experience to answer. The bottom line for New Lawyers is that they commit to a decision-making process with their client that ensures that all settlement decisions are made with informed consent.

Informed Consent by Clients

Informed consent – ensuring that a client understands the consequences of a decision or action and has been adequately advised of both the potential risks

Ethical Challenges for the New Lawyer

and rewards – is a perennial ethical challenge for lawyers. Obtaining informed consent to a litigation strategy, to a legal document such as a contract or a will, or to a settlement offer is a delicate negotiation and may be especially difficult when the client is distressed, stubborn, or simply confused. Counsel must decide with how much force to present their advice, and how much room to give to client autonomy. There must be space for clients to reject the lawyer's advice and yet clients must, at the same time, be "informed" – meaning that they have reached a different conclusion from their lawyer's. In practice, this difference of opinion may be difficult for the lawyer to accommodate.

The more choices and decisions faced by clients, the more professional advice they require. Clients using lawyers as advisers in both contentious and non-contentious matters have many more choices available to them today than thirty years ago. In non-contentious matters, where the primary focus of the lawyer's work is likely to be the drafting of documents, expanding legal and technological frameworks for the planning and regulation of commercial and personal relationships offer more complex options and choices. In litigation, the single-track litigation model has been replaced by numerous alternatives, some mandatory and some voluntary, and all potentially ethically problematic in the absence of informed consent. Before the advent of extensive case management and court-initiated settlement processes, clients were asked to formally consent to filing or defending a suit, but after this occurred there was little call for lengthy client consultations over procedure. In the absence of procedural interventions such as case management or mediation, there is relatively little for lawyer and client to debate outside of how much money to spend, and over how long a period. The initiation of legal action, or even the retaining of a lawyer, has traditionally been understood as a handing over of authority by the client to the lawyer, and a general consent to accepting the lawyer's best judgment in pursuing a winning strategy.

In today's dispute resolution environment, all but the most routine matters require thoughtful discussion. Ontario has recognized this reality in a rule of professional conduct requiring lawyers to discuss process options with their clients, and other jurisdictions have similar provisions.[74] In order to comply with this rule, lawyers need to inform themselves about the available options, and need to dedicate time to this conversation with their clients. When lawyers propose new and unfamiliar dispute resolution processes to their clients, they are obligated to ensure that clients provide informed consent to whatever strategy or combination of strategies is adopted.

Obtaining informed consent to a process choice means more than simply describing a single option and asking the client to agree to this approach.

Promoting a single process – collaborative law, mediation, or litigation – risks unreasonably limiting the client's options. Informed consent requires that clients understand that they are choosing this process as an *alternative* to other possibilities. An informed decision includes understanding the particular characteristics of this process, and what its potential advantages and drawbacks might be.

A crucial aspect of informed consent is the accurate setting of client expectations. Where lawyers are relatively inexperienced – for example, where counsel has just started a collaborative practice, or when a new judicial settlement program starts in the local court – it may be challenging for counsel to anticipate how to manage client expectations. Even for experienced lawyers, some important expectations are always difficult to explain to a new client. Simply going through the necessary information – for example, the impact of a clause disqualifying a collaborative lawyer from representing the client in the event that the client decides to litigate, or the limited scope of an "unbundled-services" retainer, may not really "connect" with the client, who will probably be stressed and prefer to assume that neither event would prove to be a problem. The challenge in each example is how to create a real understanding for a naïve, possibly first-time client of the practical meaning and substance of the formal language of the retainer agreement. Sometimes the problem is less what the lawyer does and says and more the unbridled optimism of the client, but in every case the lawyer has a professional responsibility to ensure that the client is provided with as complete, accurate, and realistic a picture of what he or she is contracting into as possible.

Some basic best practices can help. It is important for New Lawyers to caution clients at the outset to be prepared for unpredictability. Clients who contract for specific unbundled services – for example, assistance that is limited to document review, or preparation for a specific event – may reach a point at which they wish to extend the services provided by the lawyer. And in any settlement effort, there are likely to be delays – the process will move at the speed of the slowest party, who may not be your own client – and the parties may reach impasse. While these are worst-case scenarios, an experienced lawyer knows that this type of background information is important to setting realistic client expectations and ensuring informed consent at the contracting stage.

In mandatory court-connected processes such as case management, court-connected mediation, and settlement conferences, research suggests that a common complaint is that clients are poorly prepared for these sessions and sometimes attend with little or no idea of what to expect. The fact that these processes are mandatory does not relieve or reduce counsel's obligation to ensure sufficient client understanding of the process. The efforts of court programs to convey explanatory literature to parties is often frustrated by the failure of lawyers to pass on this information to their clients.[75] In the Ontario court-connected pilot, an evaluation in 1995 found that 79 percent of clients said they had been briefed by the lawyer "just before" the mediation session. Fifty-eight percent described themselves as being "not at all familiar" with mediation before the session.[76] The following quote is typical of the general confusion and lack of clarity that seemed to surround the mediation process for clients at that time:

> I didn't find out [about the mediation session] until my lawyer informed me on the way down to Toronto [for the session]. Until then I thought that we were going to trial.[77]

The obligation to ensure informed consent to mediation or collaboration should be especially strictly adhered to when there is a potential for harm to a vulnerable client. The necessity of carefully screening potential mediation and collaborative law clients for a history of domestic violence and intimidation is now widely recognized, but complaints continue that some counsel (and mediators) do not take these issues seriously enough and sometimes inadvertently place their clients at risk.[78] In working with at-risk clients, the New Lawyer should appreciate that clients may avoid answering questions about family violence, or give only partial answers. Clients may feel embarrassed and ill at ease or even unsafe being asked such questions by their lawyer. Screening is more than a matter of putting questions to the client – they must be asked clearly and sensitively. Counsel should be trained to recognize signs and cues that suggest a history of domestic violence or intimidation.

Decisions about services (full representation, limited scope) and decisions about processes (collaborative law, mediation, private negotiation) must always ultimately be the client's, no matter what the lawyer advises. When New Lawyers feel that their client is making a wrong, prejudicial, or even dangerous choice, what should they do? Some lawyers may prefer not to work with clients when they feel "out of their depth" – for example, in high-conflict cases in which there is a history of intimidation. A lawyer who continues with a potentially vulnerable client into collaboration or mediation should understand the potential impact of this vulnerability on the quality of communication in the bargaining process, and the additional risks and stresses for the client. The lawyer must help the client prepare for what will usually be face-to-face communication. This discussion between lawyer and client – which should touch on comfort, safety, and assertiveness – should continue throughout the process. Informed consent lasts only as long as each meeting, and needs to be regularly revisited when there are special concerns.

Working Opposite a Self-Represented Litigant

Since the publication of the first edition of this book, the likelihood that a lawyer will face a self-represented litigant (SRL) on the other side of a case has increased substantially.[79] Formal ethical guidance on how to relate to a layperson on the other side is still limited, but a debate over how counsel should deal with and relate to an SRL is now in full swing.

Unfortunately, some of this discussion appears to accept now widely discredited myths about SRLs and their motivations. For example, some lawyers continue to believe that SRLs are "lawyer-haters" set on causing chaos in the courts. This stereotype – perhaps a holdover from an earlier time when self-representation was very rare[80] – does not accord with research that now consistently shows that the primary reason for self-representation is financial. Most SRLs work very hard to try to do the best they can in a complex and sometimes hostile legal system.[81] Nonetheless, some lawyers continue to believe that SRLs are representing themselves because they think that they can do at least as good a job as a lawyer. For example, in a 2012 study, 7 percent of lawyers reported that the most likely reason that family litigants have no lawyer is that these people think they can do as good a job as a lawyer. The same study reported that 19 percent of lawyers believe that an important factor in self-representation is that SRLs want to directly confront a former partner in court.[82]

In contrast, studies in both Canada and the United States report that the majority of SRLs continue to seek legal assistance and would much rather have a lawyer – but they simply cannot afford one.[83] Few SRLs actually want to be representing themselves:

> I have no choice – I am unrepresented not self-represented. It's not that I think I can do this better than a lawyer, I have no choice. I don't have $350 an hour to pay a lawyer.[84]

> I was scared out of my mind. But I had a hard choice – either learning to do this for myself, or letting my daughter go, forever.[85]

With the increasing incidence of judicial impatience with SRLs, there are signs that some lawyers are taking advantage of this by encouraging the simple stereotype that SRLs are vexatious and troublesome and should be discouraged. Data collected by the National Self-Represented Litigants Project from the Canadian Legal Information Institute (CanLII) (and confirmed by independent data analysts[86]) show a very large increase (800 percent even after filtering out cases that involved allegations of "vexatiousness" on the part of the SRL) in the use of summary judgment applications in the ten years from 2004 to 2014. Ninety-six percent of these applications were brought by represented parties against unrepresented parties. Ninety-five percent of them were successful.[87]

This raises the question of whether application for summary judgment is emerging as an intentional strategy used by represented parties against SRLs. Of course, it is logical that a rise in summary judgment procedures would follow a rise in the numbers of untrained members of the public using the courts. Growing numbers of SRLs in civil and family courts raise considerable challenges for the efficient use of available justice system resources, but this concern must be balanced with a commitment to access to justice, as described by the Supreme Court of Canada in *Hryniak v Mauldin*.[88]

It is also unremarkable that lawyers would be more successful against SRLs than against other professionals. However, when the success rate of summary judgment procedures brought against SRLs reaches the high 90 percentiles, there is at minimum a public perception of unfairness, which reinforces a frequent complaint voiced by SRLs that "the deck is stacked" against them. Motions involving lawyers on both sides reflects a more even contest. There are also access-to-justice concerns about whether it is appropriate to ask for summary judgment when an SRL is struggling with procedure – for example, pleading improperly or not understanding what evidence he or she needs to bring forward in order to plead successfully. Is it ethically fair and reasonable to hold SRLs to the same standards as expert agents?

How Lawyers and SRLs Experience One Another

There appears to be a chasm of mistrust and misunderstanding between many lawyers and SRLs. While some SRLs in the National Canadian Study[89] spoke of the helpfulness and civility of the lawyer on the other side, others described their vulnerability in an obviously uneven contest.

I'm scared because I doubt myself and there is a lawyer sitting on the other side.

It is not surprising that an SRL might experience this imbalance very nega-tively. Some SRLs believed that opposing counsel deliberately exploited their advantage by using tactics designed to exploit a courtroom novice. Specific complaints consistently voiced by SRLs about opposing counsel included extremely adversarial behaviour and tactics, and unwillingness to discuss and seriously explore settlement.[90]

SRLs often feel that the behaviour of opposing counsel is unprofessional and inappropriate. Some, although by no means all, of these criticisms may arise from a lack of information about exactly what a lawyer's professional responsibilities are towards his or her client. For example, many lawyers are concerned about the possibility of a complaint from their own client if they appear to be too attentive to the SRL on the other side.

Thrown into working opposite SRLs, especially in family court, where more than half of all litigants are now without counsel,[91] many lawyers take a very cautious and conservative view of their professional responsibilities. There is a tendency to neglect to establish a relationship when the other side is self-representing, which probably reflects the many uncertainties of how to conduct that relationship in an appropriate and professional way.

To date, regulators in North America have provided little guidance. A major difficulty for lawyers working opposite SRLs is the ambiguity and uncer-tainty that they feel surrounding how they play their role in relation to their own client, while dealing with someone without legal training on the other side. These doubts are exacerbated in some legal quarters by a suspicion that SRLs will be treated more favourably than they: some lawyers point out that some judges will take more time and are more patient with SRLs and may even "bend the rules" for them[92] – the opposite of what most SRLs believe.

Current Professional Guidance for Lawyers

Professional regulators have begun to outline guidance to lawyers when they are representing a client against an SRL, but much of what can presently be gleaned from the codes is by inference. A notable exception is the Law Society of England and Wales, which has already produced guidelines to deal specific-ally with the challenges of working with an SRL.[93]

As we await more specific written guidance, there are a number of existing ethical principles in professional codes that can be applied by extension to the new SRL challenges. The first is that lawyers have a professional responsibility – as well as a broader ethical duty – to treat everyone with whom they deal in the legal system with courtesy and respect, including SRLs. Because SRLs frequently complain that they are not afforded such basic respect, this is an important admonition.[94]

In Ontario, the Law Society of Upper Canada's *Rules of Professional Conduct* states: "A lawyer shall be courteous, civil, and act in good faith with all persons with whom the lawyer has dealings."[95] This means that lawyers must maintain a level of collegiality and civility not only with other lawyers but also with others in the justice system, including SRLs. There is also a reverse obligation not to be rude: lawyers have an obligation *not* to communicate to a client, other legal practitioner, or any other person, including SRLs, "in a manner that is abusive, offensive, or otherwise inconsistent with the proper tone of a professional communication from a lawyer."[96]

This does not, of course, prevent lawyers from showing an appropriate professional detachment in interactions with an SRL on the other side, and a clear commitment to their own client – that is the nature of the adversarial system. When New Lawyers finds themselves working across from an SRL, it is vital to ensure that the SRL is not "under the impression that their interests will be protected by the lawyer,"[97] and to ensure the SRL understands that they are acting exclusively in the interests of their own client. John-Paul Boyd makes this point clearly in his "Rights and Responsibilities of Self-Represented Litigants":

> These codes of conduct require lawyers to treat opposing parties who are not represented by counsel politely and in the same courteous manner as they would treat a fellow lawyer. Of course, litigation can be difficult and emotional at times, and you must remember that the lawyer's job is to represent his or her client, not you, and to advocate for his or her client's interests, not your interests.[98]

For example, opposing lawyers may present a vigorous argument that their interpretation of the law is correct, and that the SRL's interpretation is not.[99] It is important when working with laypersons who may not be familiar with the modus operandi of the adversarial system that this tactic does not come across as bullying or high-handed, and that New Lawyers remain aware of how much power they hold as a professional vis-à-vis an SRL novice.

Communication with an SRL on the other side is obviously necessary if New Lawyers are to discharge their ethical duty to resolve a case as quickly and effectively as possible.[100] Communication in such cases may include providing basic information that enables the matter to move forward. This is an area in which counsel is understandably nervous about divided loyalties. In some ways, these tensions resemble those between working for one's client's best outcome and working towards an agreed settlement. The Ontario Advocates' Society describes this balance as follows:

> Counsel should try to communicate with and be fair with self-represented litigants. This is consistent with a lawyer's duty to the administration of justice. If assisting a self-represented litigant does not prejudice counsel's client, will move the case forward and will not result in significant costs, counsel should strongly suggest providing assistance.[101]

For example, it may be necessary to offer a basic explanation or clarification to an SRL on the other side of a case in order to ensure that the matter moves forward in a timely and appropriate fashion (e.g., how to respond to a filing). If this seems necessary, it is important for New Lawyers to explain to their client why such assistance should be provided to the SRL. Where New Lawyers face an SRL on the other side, there is an argument for anticipating some of these difficult decisions through a pre-emptive discussion with the client.

Another pertinent rule found in many codes of conduct is the obligation not to take advantage of the other side's errors – the "sharp practice" rule.[102] While this has historically been understood as behaviour between lawyers, commentators increasingly assume that the "sharp practice" rule should also apply to lawyer's dealings with an SRL. For example, "Counsel should advise a self-represented party if she or he has made a procedural error, and advise his or her client that s/he cannot rely on that error. Taking advantage of a SRL's error is reportable."[103]

Working opposite an SRL is an excellent example of an emerging area of practice that the codes of conduct have not yet caught up with. It is an area that requires a broader conversation about best practices. Some degree of uncertainty and ambiguity over ethical responsibilities is inevitable as lawyers become incrementally more accustomed to the challenges that arise when the other side is self-represented, and more confident and experienced in discussing these dynamics with their own client. The diversity and variety of individuals who are representing themselves in the legal process also make for many variables – for example, how competent and sophisticated is the SRL? What is the nature of the SRL's relationship with opposing side? Is it an ongoing relationship? What type of working relationship is possible between counsel and the SRL? How adversarial is the matter and what stage is it at? This is an example of an area of ethical practice that would benefit from a discursive approach to best practices as the New Lawyer learns to adjust to very high volumes of self-representation as "the new normal."

Conclusions

New Lawyers takes on all the traditional professional responsibilities of counsel as well as some additional, emerging ones. These new responsibilities include educating the client on a range of alternate process options; establishing a constructive relationship with the other side that does not undermine their loyalty to their client; committing to the good faith use of appropriate conflict resolution processes; anticipating pressures to settle; establishing informed consent throughout the process, and advocating strongly for a consensus solution that meets, above all, the needs of their client. New Lawyers may also face the uncertainty and challenges of interacting with an SRL, whose cooperation and functionality are critical to the progress or their own client's case.

At a time of flux and change in legal practice, ethical issues often arise, especially in informal dispute resolution. Frequently, the appropriate professional and ethical response is unclear or absent. In the absence of rules or even clear guidance on behaviours and best practices, counsel must identify pathways that are, first, acceptable within their own ethical framework, and, second, acceptable within their community of practice.

Where codes of conduct do not offer answers, many lawyers turn to their colleagues, mentors, and personal advisers for assistance.[104] Ideally, a sense of what is and what is not appropriate behaviour emerges from a combination of experience, dialogue, and reflection, a "discursive ethics" that explores the assumptions behind choices. Raising and discussing with a client the issues highlighted in this chapter requires a commitment to a more transparent culture and a more open and inclusive debate, incorporating the experiences and perspectives of clients as well as lawyers. This is the first step towards the New Lawyer's development of best practices in new and unfamiliar settings, where the "right" answers are elusive.

9

Where the Action Is
Sites of Change

In the first edition of this book, I talked in this final chapter about three critical sources of influence and leadership in developing a new professional identity for lawyers in the twenty-first century. Described as "sites of change" because of their potential to promote both debate and initiatives that support evolution of the New Lawyer, the three "sites" were legal education, the role of the judiciary, and the relationship of law to a growing constellation of related professional disciplines and innovations in inter-professional collaboration.

The end of the twentieth century and the beginning of the twenty-first have witnessed tremendous changes for the legal profession. A complete picture of the many ways in which legal practice is changing must include structural, economic, demographic, procedural, and cultural elements. These do not fit seamlessly together to form a single, consistent theory of change. Nor do they provide us with a clear prediction of what the legal profession will look like another ten, twenty, or thirty years from now. This is not surprising, since each elements of change has evolved piecemeal, without a relationship to the other elements and largely in response to market conditions. There has been no intentional "grand strategy" to modernize legal services, but rather pressure from multiple sources for a different business structure and a recrafted professional service model ushering in a new professional identity for lawyers. This book is an effort to solidify and to advance this debate.

In this second edition, I am adding two new sites of change: (1) self-represented litigants (SRLs) and the Access to Justice movement; and (2) "disruptive" technologies.[1] First, let us consider the impact and importance of the original three sites, and what, if anything, has changed in the past decade.

Legal Education

In Chapter 2, legal education was recognized as critical to both the creation and reinforcement of the dominant norms and values of the legal profession. I argued that legal education remains in thrall to the traditional models of lawyering that are beginning to lose their place in the delivery of legal services – for instance, the image of the lawyer as trial lawyer; the values of adversarial advocacy; the assumption that technical expertise translates into authority in client relationships; the belief that clients can and will pay for an opaque legal costs model that they cannot afford or understand; and, more generally, the social and economic elitism that characterized an overwhelmingly white, male legal profession until recently.

When I became a law professor more than thirty years ago, I was convinced that legal education could be an effective vehicle for bringing about change in these and other flawed aspects of traditional legal practice. I have remained convinced that the very best thing about legal education is our students, who come to us bright, motivated, challenging, resilient, and determined to do good. I shall confess here, however, that my conviction that the law schools can and will step up to the responsibility of doing what they can to understand, respond to, and support changes in legal practice burns less strongly after three decades of disappointment.

Change within the core of legal education continues to be glacial in pace. Some of my colleagues in the academy would argue that it is not the place of legal education to confront the deficiencies of legal practice. There is a feeling that law school should somehow rise above debates over the nitty-gritty of practice and client service. I cannot agree. We still seem stuck in these old tired debates, even as the evidence for the disconnect between legal education and legal practice mounts ever higher, and graduating law students face longer and longer odds on a return on the investment of their tuition fees, especially in the United States.[2]

Law school education focuses on conflict resolution exclusively via adjudication using the study of appellate judgments. It presents a picture of legal practice as litigation and especially as trial work that is outdated and unrealistic. It virtually ignores transactions and non-contentious work. It neglects to integrate clients – presented only as plaintiffs or defendants who represent a vehicle for making a legal argument – into this picture. The existence of clients as real people, with motivations and interests, is rarely, if ever, alluded to in law school classrooms, let alone their stories, their needs and goals, or their expectations for effective dispute resolution services. Practical skills and the conceptual frameworks for developing and modifying such skills are taught in limited elective courses or sometimes in legal clinics. These courses and programs are often considered intellectually "soft" options and are often taught by practitioners outside the elite circle of full-time faculty. They and the students they teach occupy a subculture within the law school.

As I have written elsewhere,[3] the dominant epistemology of law school assumes that all disputing is normative, with a "right" and a "wrong" (or technically less strong) position. In this model, the function of knowledge is to enhance the power to win, hence the highly competitive culture of law school and the obsession with the "magic bullet," which is the appellate decision that will clinch the argument in the hypothetical trial. The law curriculum seems to unself-consciously reinforce a model of conflict that has been largely unchanged for decades and is increasingly out of step with process innovations and an emerging culture of practical conflict resolution. As this litigator looks back on his legal education:

They never talked about settling in law school.[4]

By focusing almost exclusively on a single, rights-based approach to conflict resolution, so removed from the reality of most legal disputing, legal education does worse than simply not educate future lawyers about how to use new dispute resolution processes effectively in their clients' interests. It fails to foster the capacity for creative problem solving and reflexivity that is widely recognized as critical to twenty-first-century legal practice.[5] In this narrow and rigid culture of learning, even promising elective courses that highlight critical theory or legal skills often fail to challenge the central assumptions of what success in legal practice looks like, who are the clients that lawyers serve, or what are the most important skills of the lawyer. Instead, these courses tend to focus on developing a more critical theoretical perspective on law and lawyering, rather than questioning the practice assumptions and mores of the profession.

Depressingly, I have to conclude that legal education – some bright and hopeful bubbles of innovation aside[6] – continues to offer students and faculty an alternative reality to legal practice that they are, for the most part, comfortable accepting. The actual work and changing tasks of lawyers are either not discussed at all or are presented as constant trial work and heroic fights against oppression and wrongdoers. Few, if any, law school classes allude to the realities of the changes in legal practice described in this book, such as less courtroom advocacy, fewer trials, increasingly dissatisfied and often demanding clients, growing volumes of self-represented litigants, and sometimes routine, mundane, and boring work with marginal professional autonomy. Beyond the intrusion of job fairs and career days, law school exists in a zone that is both conceptually and practically isolated from legal practice. This isolation is despite the fact that the most important topic on the minds of upper-year law students is obtaining a position in a reputable firm. Lawyers in practice tend to look back on their days at law school with wry hindsight that amounts to "that was fun, and sometimes interesting, but completely removed from what I do now." It is little wonder that some law graduates are disappointed by what they find in practice, as well being ill prepared.

The reasons for this lack of progress towards a more realistic and grounded curriculum and set of teaching pedagogies appear to be the very same ones that I first encountered when I began teaching law in 1981. For the most part, law schools do not see themselves as teaching students about how to be a lawyer, what that might be like, and what choices and challenges they might face in practice, but rather how to "think like a lawyer." This bifurcation between "thinking" and "doing" is reflected in an apparently interminable and seemingly inconclusive debate over the extent to which the law curriculum should be driven by the exigencies of legal practice – that is, how far law school should teach practical professional skills along with conceptual tools for analysis and reflection. The problem with this debate – and perhaps the reason it never seems to advance – is the tendency to assume that a choice must be made between two dichotomous goals for legal education: vocational training and intellectual development.[7] The fallacy of this dichotomy is immediately obvious if one recognizes that the law always draws its meaning from the context in which it is applied.[8] Any level of legal studies, whether it is basic or advanced, theoretical or applied, jurisprudential or interdisciplinary, must reflect the ways in which law is understood, used, and practised in the real world, notwithstanding the program's focus on academic analysis or vocational applications.[9] The intellectual understanding of law is embedded in its practical applications, and practical applications require legal knowledge and comprehension. In this way, the conceptual and practical dimensions of learning about the law are inextricably linked. As one lawyer comments, "Law schools teach law as stripes – but legal practice is really plaid."[10]

If the debate over learning about law is reframed within the recognition of the inevitable and essential interconnectedness of theory and practice, it becomes obvious that we have been asking, or understanding, the wrong question all along. The real issue is not whether legal education should take a special place for itself in developing the intellectual capacities of future legal practitioners – the answer to this is obviously yes. At no other point in their careers are lawyers going to be afforded the opportunity to study (for example) feminist legal theory, critical race theory, or legal history, all of which have the potential to significantly deepen and enrich their understanding of the role of law and lawyers. No one disputes the fact that law school is the place where future lawyers must learn to read, analyze, and dissect appellate cases for arguments that they can apply to their own files. The real question is the extent to which legal education understands its intellectual mission to include an appreciation of the realities of legal practice and the choices (ethical and practical) that exist, the skills that are required, and the centrality of human conflict and dispute resolution in all of their many forms to the mission of legal services. A simple dichotomy between practical and abstract knowledge is misleading and unhelpful, and the fact that we are still having this simplistic bifurcated debate and allowing it to impede meaningful curriculum change in law school is nothing short of horrifying.

Every law school exercises choices over just how far to intentionally integrate practice into theory (and vice versa), and how. For example, almost every North American law school has a mooting program. Why do the law schools continue to invest in skills training in appellate advocacy – far less relevant now than when mooting programs were first introduced into many law schools in the 1970s – to the extent that they do and to the exclusion of other, perhaps more relevant and useful professional skills? This question becomes more urgent in light of the changes occurring within the profession and the persistence in law school of outdated and inaccurate stereotypes about legal practice. The virtual disappearance of trial advocacy from many sectors of practice seems to have no impact on continuing investment in mooting programs, which continue to dominate extracurricular activities, fundraising, and school prestige.

Concerns about the relevance of legal education and the subsequent competence of those individuals admitted to practice have been voiced for as long as I have been a law professor (three decades and counting). During the late 1980s, there was vocal criticism of law school and professional education as being too remote from the realities and practicalities of legal practice (particularly in the United Kingdom, the United States, Australia, and New Zealand).[11] This was followed by the development of skills-based professional courses in some jurisdictions (e.g., in British Columbia, Canada, and at the Institute of Professional Legal Studies in New Zealand), which taught and assessed the basics of client interviewing, negotiation, legal drafting, and trial advocacy. A report by the Canadian Bar Association in 1999 recognizes this crossroads, arguing that law schools should start taking seriously the training of students in a more multidisciplinary body of skills and knowledge, including communication, psychology, and human relations skills.[12] In the United States, the 1992 MacCrate Report[13] urged American law schools to "narrow the gap" between their mission and the profession's work by ramping up the teaching of professional competencies such as problem solving, negotiation, communication, and counselling.[14] Almost twenty-five years after MacCrate, the American Bar Association recognized that little progress had been made and that the same questions were still being asked.[15]

Creating a meaningful relationship between legal practice and legal education requires us to think about how to move the teaching of law from "stripes" to "plaid." We need to develop courses that look at the actual, rather than the glamourized, business of legal practice: dealing with clients, resolving matters by negotiation, using written advocacy. This includes ensuring that no law student graduates without the knowledge – along with some developed analysis and evaluation of the consequences for legal practice – of the reality that almost every civil and family case will settle before trial and that up to 80 percent of litigants in family court are now self-representing. The fact that most law students continue to graduate without even encountering these most central facts in the revolution of legal services is disgraceful. Students also need to learn about practical ways to structure their assistance to clients in models other than the full-representation retainer that is now out of the reach of the vast majority of personal clients. If they do not know and understand these realities, their brilliant and in-depth knowledge of individual legal specialisms will allow them neither to serve clients nor to repay their student loans.

We also need pedagogies that enable the integration of theory and practice in a simple yet meaningful way. "Reflective practice,"[16] used widely in medical and nursing education,[17] focuses on teaching future professionals to analyze and learn from their experiences, emphasizing self-awareness, self-critique, and constant analysis and review. The next generation of lawyers will not learn by rote the ever-changing and expanding substance of legal regulation and precedent. Instead, they require effective problem-solving skills and the ability to learn from their experiences. The emphasis on information transmission and knowledge testing in law school does little or nothing to teach and promote reflective practice and the related capacity for problem solving. This does not mean that students in (for example) Torts should not be taught the leading cases, but they should also be taught about dispute resolution, client service, and professional attitudes that promote problem solving. Problem solving and reflective practice require adaptability, flexibility, and an openness to change; law school teaches adherence to rules, regulations, and existing legal, pedagogic, and cultural norms. If we are serious about accepting responsibility for relating legal education to legal practice, we must be ready to challenge the entrenched values and pedagogic assumptions of legal education and consider radical redesign.

So far, this discussion has concentrated on how legal education might be brought into closer alignment with legal practice to ensure that it teaches the qualities needed for effective lawyering in the twenty-first century. A further question that we should be asking – on behalf of our students as they rack up debt, on behalf of the public who increasingly cannot afford lawyers, as well as for the sake of the profession we love – is whether legal education can and should go further in playing a proactive role in change. What changes in legal education have taken place since the 1980s – for example, the development of an expanded skills-based and clinical curriculum in a handful of schools in the United Kingdom and Australia in the 1980s – have been the result of innovations trickling down from the profession to academe.[18] While it may seem natural for changes in the profession to (eventually) trickle down to the law schools, accepting this one-way movement of ideas means that the law schools further limit their relevance and influence. Imagine, instead, a scenario in which the law schools take on a leadership role in response to changes in legal practices and curriculum change, a pre-emptive strike by the academy?

This would include both anticipating change and critically responding to it. Legal educators could anticipate the ways in which the curriculum needs to adjust to better prepare students for the realities of legal practice in the twenty-first century. Such preparation would include envisioning many different types of legal practice for law graduates, including commercial/corporate work with a preventive law dimension, partnerships with other professionals, in-house counsel to corporations and government departments, settlement specialists, the development of limited but affordable legal representation models, "coaching" the primarily self-represented, and so on. Despite their diversity, all of these avenues share common needs for education and training, including the importance of problem solving using a wide range of conflict resolution skills, and, for some sectors, client relations and communication skills.

Being proactive about change does not mean that it should be reflected uncritically in the law school curriculum. On the contrary, if the law schools step up to the challenge of preparing students to be New Lawyers, this is an important opportunity for faculty, practitioners, and students to work together on emerging issues of professional identity in a critical environment. Individual law schools could choose to go further still by making their own individual determination of what norms and values will be important to the lawyers of the future, including professional attitudes and approaches to managing client relations, and then teaching these explicitly and transparently in their curriculum. The significance of the years spent in law school in the moral and professional development of the law student is well established. Legal education has a critical role to play in the regeneration of professional attitudes and mores.

A proactive effort to face these challenges will take more than simply the introduction of a few more courses teaching the formal rules of professional conduct, or a week of "skills-intensive" classes. Law students need to be confronted with practical dilemmas to negotiate and evaluate in an environment that is open, questioning, and constantly aware of the real human stories behind the face of legal practice. Far from demeaning themselves to the level of "trade schools," this would allow the law schools to extend, rather than squander, the vast intellectual capital embedded in their expertise in teaching and learning about law.

If legal education is to remain relevant to the delivery of legal services in the twenty-first century, the law curriculum needs to be reoriented and refocused. If law school is to maintain its power and prestige in the development and training of young lawyers, it must realign legal education with the realities of legal practice, yet not uncritically. Academics and practitioners alike[19] agree that process pluralism – characterized by "the availability and acceptability of a wide range of goals, norms, procedures, results, professional roles, skills and styles in handling disputes involving legal issues"[20] – is the "new normal." This fact is beginning to be recognized in individual law school initiatives. More, much more, must follow.

The New Judge

The role of the judge in the civil courts is changing as the institutionalization of case management and settlement processes place judges in an increasingly supervisory and managerial role.[21] Processes facilitated by judges now include early case management (agreeing on a schedule for the production of documents, a timetable for discoveries, and the resolution of threshold issues), judicial mediation (when the judge is charged with bringing the parties to settlement), as well as more traditional pre-trial processes (where judges play an evaluative role). In some jurisdictions, judges play a crucial role in deciding whether or not to require parties to attend mediation (e.g., with an outside mediator); in such cases judicial support and understanding of the process being offered is key to the effectiveness of the program.[22] The timing of such interventions is diverse, as are the requirements (if any) for briefs or documents filed in advance, the attendance of clients, and so on. Styles and philosophies also vary widely. In some courts, judges understand their role as purely facilitative, while in others they assume a more evaluative stance, whatever the formal process. In some, judges encourage or even demand the participation of clients; in others, they deal only with counsel. All settlement programs, including pre-trials, are careful to ensure that the same judge never presides over both a settlement and a trial of the same matter.

This still leaves other important policy questions unanswered. For example, to what extent should those appointed as authoritative decision makers within a system of justice be involved in facilitating resolution that may draw on principles chosen by the disputants themselves (in an agreed outcome) rather than the rules for which judges are responsible? And since a judge is the ultimate "knower of rules" within an adjudicative model, what does this mean for the facilitation of an agreement by an authoritative decision maker either before or outside this adjudicative system? Can judges ever be perceived as neutral settlers of cases? What about their innate authority and ability to "persuade"? How are courts monitoring the outcomes of judicial settlement programs? Will such evaluations consider the impact on using judges in settlement on public perceptions of the legitimacy and fairness of the justice system?[23]

In the criminal courts, the introduction of juvenile diversion and alternative measures regimes is impacting the role of the criminal court judge. In some matters, criminal court judges are required to consider alternative measures to incarceration,[24] and sometimes they become involved in aspects of diversion into community processes such as victim/offender mediation and community panels. There is also a growing interest among judges working in criminal justice and mental health areas in the ideas of therapeutic jurisprudence, which cast the judge in a dynamic, interactive dialogue with the offender or patient rather than as a remote figure passing down judgment from the bench.[25] Judges who have been instrumental in establishing alternative forms of criminal courts – for example, Judge Alex Calabrese of the Red Hook Community Justice Center in New York – are motivated by a sense that these alternative approaches to crime are changing the ability of the community to police and take care of itself. As Judge Calabrese comments in an interview:

> I feel that I can accomplish much more at the Justice Center. The options that I had at the Criminal Court were basically jail and no jail, with very limited drug treatment. At the Justice Center, I have a full range of services where I can

release a defendant on the condition that he or she take advantage of all these services. So you have a real chance at getting to the problem and preventing the defendant from coming back to the justice system.[26]

In the United States there has been a significant growth, supported by the federal government, in the establishment of "drug courts" that approach drug addiction as an integral part of the criminal law problem when an offender comes to court.[27]

There is also some progress in parts of Canada and the United States towards specialist family courts staffed by specialist judges, and the integration of a range of supportive family services into these courts, such as parent education programs, mediation, and counselling, is also changing the way these judges understand their role. Working in tandem with other professionals, including social workers, mental health workers, and child welfare specialists, judges in the most innovative family service centres see themselves as members of a team and their own intervention as just one element in managing family conflict. Referral to complementary services both enlarges judges' sense of what is available and possible and gives them an insight into the impact of such programming on the lives of those with whom they are dealing in family court.

These and other procedural innovations are having a significant impact on the way some judges understand their role in the criminal, civil, and family courts. Other important factors have also contributed to this evolving sense of identity for our judiciary. One is the widespread recognition that faith in justice systems is declining, along with access, as many who would use the courts cannot afford a lawyer to represent them, or begin with a lawyer but run out of funds. This means that judges are seeing a very significant increase in numbers of self-represented litigants, which is profoundly changing the way they do their work, especially in civil and family court, where judges are left to assess the individual litigant's ability to make appropriate decisions in the absence of legal advice. The concept of "active adjudication," where the hearings officer or judge will play a role in assessing the fairness of a procedure in which one or more parties may not fully comprehend their options and advance their interests, is beginning to develop some currency, especially in the tribunal sector.[28] One consequence is that more judges regard communication and conflict management skills as critical for their day-to-day courtroom hearings. They are now dealing not only with lawyers but also directly with members of the public, many of whom are distressed, confused, and sometimes frustrated and angry.

Subtle but significant changes in the judicial role, and the new skills that these changes imply, were already evident in a survey I conducted for the

Canadian National Judicial Institute in 2002.[29] When judges were asked, "What abilities and skills do you personally consider to be most important for a judge?" what they said and what they did not say was noteworthy. The most consistent characterizations of pre-eminent abilities and skills concerned communication skills (including listening, explaining in clear language, managing people, and managing difficult courtroom interaction) and personal attributes (e.g., open-mindedness, empathy, patience, and respect for litigants). Formal legal knowledge was usually mentioned as an aside or as an assumed basis of the judicial function. Furthermore, when respondents did allude to legal knowledge, it was almost always in combination or integrated with communication skills and/or personal attributes. Typical is the comment of one respondent, who, after listing communication and people management qualities, ended by stating: "And if [a judge] knows the law, so much the better."

When asked to identify areas of new skills and practice in which they felt the need for more skills development, 45 percent of judicial respondents stated that enhancing settlement conferencing skills was a personal priority for them.[30] This result seems to reflect a real appetite among some sectors of the bench for casting themselves as settlement specialists. It seems likely that, just as we are seeing within the profession, the judiciary will divide into those who enthusiastically embrace dispute settlement as a new and exciting aspect of their role and others who feel less comfortable with this extension of their professional function and responsibilities.

Members of the bench continue to wield significant influence in pressing for and then supporting professional and procedural changes, especially within the legal profession. Judges have demonstrated time and again that they can play a significant role in changing local legal culture.[31] A critical element of changing attitudes towards any innovation or change is the credibility bestowed by the support of professional leaders, and none are more significant than members of the judiciary in any one jurisdiction or region. During the collection of data for the Culture Change Project (1999–2000), every one of the lawyers in the Ottawa sample made unprompted remarks about the exceptional leadership role played by Justice James Chadwick and Master Robert Beaudoin in building support for mandatory mediation in Ottawa. In Toronto, some professional leaders are committed to mediation, but these are fewer and less powerful than their compatriots in Ottawa. These differences were clearly reflected in different peer group norms regarding recourse to mandatory mediation between Ottawa and Toronto.[32] As the urgency and contentiousness of the debate over the use of limited-scope retainers to offer services to the primarily self-represented shows, the judiciary are once again recognized as thought-leaders.[33] Some judges are making efforts to directly encourage local lawyers to consider offering these services, which have the potential to can make their own interaction with the self-represented more efficient and functional.

The changes summarized in this section, as well as signs of failing faith in the legal system among those members of the public whose financial resources make them unable to afford legal representation, represent a seismic shift in the way that judges work, and the types of skills and sensitivities that they require. This begs the question: Do we need new judges to work with New Lawyers?

The Institute for the Advancement of the American Legal System has published a series of papers under the aegis of its Quality Judges Initiative that propose not only different nomination and selection methods but also a different skill set for nominees (including "patience" and "an ability to convey to the parties that they have been heard"[34]), as well as processes for regular judicial evaluation once in office.[35] We should expect to see and hear a great deal more of this, especially in light of the number of unrepresented private citizens who now interact directly with judges.

Inter-professional Collaboration

No book on the future of the legal profession is complete without considering the challenges to the traditionally solitary nature of professional legal advice and representation from related professions, and the possibilities of inter-professional collaboration. Some clients are looking for a comprehensive and integrated professional service, whether it is in relation to a business matter (law, accountancy, tax advice, or financial planning) or a family conflict (law, child welfare specialists, counselling, or social work). Others ask why a less expensive professional – a paralegal, or a limited-licence legal technician in the Washington state model,[36] for example, rather than a lawyer – cannot assist them with all or part of a straightforward matter.

Unchallenged in their dominance in legal services for centuries, lawyers have faced over the past thirty years the growing incursion of paralegals into areas that were once considered the "bread and butter" of small-town lawyers (real estate, wills, small claims, and family). The legal profession has invested significant energy into countering this challenge – described by Richard Abel as "repelling the barbarians"[37] – using various strategies, including price fixing, lobbying for restrictions on representation, and even imposing insurance penalties on lawyers who break ranks and work with the "barbarians."[38] The profession has also relied heavily on the classic arguments advanced by specialists resisting competition: that only lawyers can meet the highest professional practice and ethical standards. Inevitably, the paralegal community has responded with efforts to regulate themselves and present themselves as professionals. The contemporary reality is that the legal profession is forced to accept paralegals on terms they hope will be of their choosing, including agreements on restrictions on the unauthorized practice of law that define the area of work that can be conducted only by a licensed practitioner.[39] This continues to be highly controversial, with growing pressure to allow paralegals to expand the scope of their services, especially into family cases where there appears to be the greatest need.[40]

A related but different challenge has come from other professionals offering advice to individuals (often the primarily self-represented) and businesses in times of stability (in the form of planning) and crisis (in the form of interventions). There are many examples of this "incursion" in both corporate and personal sectors of legal services. Business clients obviously benefit from and increasingly demand the combined services of lawyers, accountants, financial planners, investment advisers, merger and acquisition specialists, tax specialists, human resource and organizational development specialists, and labour relations specialists. In the family area, family clients can benefit from the combined expertise of lawyers, therapists, child and family counsellors, child welfare specialists, and financial planners. Those who cannot afford legal services at all may seek the assistance of a former self-represented litigant or a professional editor, or speaking coach.

Where lawyers participate in business arrangements with other professionals, concerns have centred on business structures and fee arrangements. Currently, most Canadian provinces and US states do not allow fee sharing among lawyers and professionals from other disciplines, although many have initiated a process of review and debate over so-called alternative business structures, or ABS, which would allow co-ownership of firms offering legal services by both lawyers and non-lawyers.[41] In other common law countries, law societies and bar associations are beginning to develop regulations permitting multidisciplinary practices (MDPs), but there are continuing battles over the form these associations will take and the business models they will adopt. In some jurisdictions, MDPs are permitted only if lawyers remain in overall control of the enterprise. In these models, lawyers are allowed to associate with other regulated professionals only, and MDPs can offer only services that either qualify as legal services or support the practice of law.[42]

The regulation of ABS and MDPs raises many other practice issues, including the proper protection of lawyer/client privilege when lawyers work alongside other professionals who do not have similar obligations, and the potential

Where the Action Is

for an increased volume of conflicts of interest that could result when a multi-disciplinary firm "shares" clients. These new structures pose a number of "unresolved ethical, regulatory and disciplinary questions, in respect of which legal norms provide little guidance."[43] The potential of new business models to enhance Access to Justice is unclear; most MDPs pair law firms with accountancy firms and house a range of business services. In most debates to date, the profession has focused on the business arguments for shared ownership and intra-professional practice – demonstrating the nervousness of lawyers about forming professional associations with other professions, as well as concerns about losing business to comprehensive financial services firms – rather than the client service side.[44]

Some intra-professional developments are occurring within family law, such as the inclusion of on-site counselling and specialist child welfare or mediation services. One format that has emerged is the "collaborative divorce team," where lawyers committed to the collaborative law model partner with other professionals, including mental health practitioners, therapists, child welfare specialists, and financial advisers, who are likely to be involved in the management and resolution of a divorce file.[45] The emergence of the team model provides an interesting example of what inter-professional collaboration might look like, as well as its special challenges. Despite an apparent difference in motivation between the formation of MDPs, which are generally regarded by commercial lawyers as a sound business move rather than an ideological choice, and the development of collaborative divorce teams, which are usually inspired by a belief that combining professional expertise brings better results to family clients, many of the same issues and dilemmas arise in each context.

The themes – and the practice challenges – are power and control within a multidisciplinary team. Some of this relates to fee disparities and who is paid to do what. Lawyers are generally paid more than mental health professionals, and paralegals are paid at a fraction of the hourly cost of a lawyer. In a collaborative partnership, what fee differentials are justified and how is the client assured the best value for money? Are there tasks that could be competently completed by a paralegal, or even a legal secretary, for a fraction of the cost of a lawyer? Then there is the dilemma of who makes these decisions for the team. Who directs the traffic and brings professionals "on board" in a multidisciplinary office team is just one of a raft of issues that arise in relation to control and hierarchy within the team.

There is also the question of staying within one's professional competencies, which may be highlighted by the composition of a multidisciplinary team.

Some mental health professionals who have worked in collaborative processes with lawyers are critical of their encroachment on the therapist's role:

> I question the fact that they [lawyers] are charging huge lawyer's fees for doing a process that is not legal. Their legal expertise does not come into this very much, and the clients are being charged as if they are getting legal expertise.[46]

> Lawyers are not accountable about how they understand family systems theory, they can just wing it any way they want it. Therapists are supervised and tested in student papers and practica.[47]

Some therapists raise concerns that lawyers may be encouraging their clients to deal with emotional issues in four-way sessions without being able to really understand and manage the ensuing dynamics. The reflections of some collaborative clients bear out this concern.[48]

A different but equally hard to manage strain may be placed on interprofessional collaboration when a collaborative client finds that she prefers working with her therapist over her lawyer, because legal expertise and the skills offered by her lawyer are not the real focus of what she needs and wants. When clients prefer to use therapists to resolve their conflicts and work out a basic agreement, which is then presented to the lawyers to be formally memorialized, the lawyers may feel excluded and unsure of what their real function is in relation to the clients.[49] They are uncomfortable that so much of the bargaining and decision making has gone before them without their input. Similar struggles over "shares" of the client, and resulting issues of overall control and direction of the file, can be envisaged in MDPs and business partnerships.

Aside from issues of control and role parameters, there are also obvious differences in practice methodology and underlying philosophy between different professions. For example, each profession has its own distinctive approach to questions of client confidentiality. Whereas lawyers can ask their clients to voluntarily waive their entitlement to solicitor/client privilege, leaving them free to share information with the other side, many therapists feel uncomfortable even broaching this topic with their clients. The need to maintain the commitment to protect client confidences is a core value for therapists that comes with a strong sense of moral as well as practical obligation. There are also ingrained differences in how lawyers and mental health professionals approach problem solving, reflecting different training and traditions of analysis. For example, lawyers often find open brainstorming – putting any and all ideas on the table without evaluation or censorship – extremely difficult. Lawyers are unaccustomed to this type of creative problem solving, and are trained to assume that even the most tentative proposal means letting information "out of the bag." As well, lawyers find it difficult to problem-solve without almost immediately coming up with a suggestion as to how to solve the problem. Therapists embrace creative option generation much more naturally, since it does not contradict any innate principles of their training. There are also differences between lawyers and therapists in relation to conceptions of advocacy. One lawyer described the way that different approaches to client advocacy might cause confusion within a collaborative divorce team:

> Coaches are more inclined to look at this as problem solving for the family – they are less aware of how something they might say might shift the whole negotiation in the room. Lawyers are more aware of what might affect their own client – and lawyers and coaches are sometimes on different wavelengths about this.[50]

Similar problems are seen in in multi-professional healthcare settings where doctors, nurses, nurse practitioners, social workers, public health workers, and others often clash over appropriate forms of treatment for a patient and just whose expertise should prevail in case of conflict. Inter-professional collaboration may be especially problematic for lawyers, who have historically had so little experience in working with other professionals, and then only at arm's length.

The resolution of these challenges will come only with experience, and the current constraints on ABS and MDP suggest that development of collaborative partnerships will be slow. In this area, as in other aspects of service provision, we are most likely to see momentum coming from client demands for integrated services and service "hubs" that offer value for money – where the price tag accurately and fairly respects the level and scope of professional competence rather than a traditional hierarchy comprising lawyers and "others."

Conflict resolution advocacy means that client problems are framed more broadly and holistically, and draw the lawyer into other approaches to problem solving. These approaches may require or suggest new professional partners for the New Lawyer. But in seeking new partners, lawyers must identify a clear (and indispensable) role for themselves. The absence of a clear and choate professional identity may be slowing the pace at which lawyers are presently exploring and developing the potential for inter-professional collaboration. In order to work collaboratively and constructively with other professionals, lawyers must ask themselves a number of searching questions, including:

- What do I bring to my clients as their lawyer that other professionals do not?
- What are the core functions of the lawyer's role?
- Where do the boundaries lie between my work and the work of other professionals?
- What is my work worth to the individual client, compared with the input of other professionals?
- Is there a less costly way for this client to obtain a good result?
- When does my client need the advice and input of another professional?
- How well am I able to recognize client needs that I cannot meet, and refer the client to an appropriate specialist?
- Are there cases I cannot begin to assist in unless and until other types of professional assistance are first provided?

As well as the voices of consumers, this is a debate that will include individuals other than lawyers who are themselves well-educated professionals with strong opinions. It is not simply a matter of lawyers deciding, as they are accustomed to doing, what the rules of the new game of inter-professional collaboration should be. Lawyers may find themselves having to adjust their expectations of control and autonomy in relation not only to their own clients but also to other professionals. The bottom line is whether lawyers can sufficiently expand both their imaginations and their collegial instincts in order to work effectively and productively in collaboration with other professionals. If they can do so, both promising new business models and a greatly enhanced client service model will be available to them.

"Disruptive" Legal Technologies

"Disruptive" technologies are those that disrupt the usual form and management of legal services and offer new possibilities for both clients and practitioners. It is obvious that this is a very significant site of change for the New Lawyer.

The massive increase in free online information about the law and the legal system is changing not only the way that prospective clients think about working with counsel but also how counsel work with clients. Richard Susskind describes access to information technology as transforming legal practice from a "bespoke" industry (providing individually customized professional advice and counselling) to one in which "commodification" is possible for many services. Initially standardized standard form contracts, template systems for making or defending claims, procedural checklists that are generated internally to law firms, these products to enable routinized and repetitive transactions can be ultimately turned into accessible online products for which there is a competitive market.[51]

Commodification in turn supports the outsourcing of some legal work, whereby low-level tasks that do not require client or case-specific insights – form completion, document review, and even some legal research tasks – are assigned to lower-cost providers. Files can be easily transferred electronically, and systems for both task completion and quality control built in. It is estimated that outsourcing to countries where salaries are significantly lower – India and the Philippines are often given as examples[52] – can reduce the costs of a North American law firm to one-fifth to one-quarter of their usual level.[53] Businesses that exist for the sole purpose of connecting law firms with outsourced workers are emerging.[54] Outsourcing can also operate inside North America, where work is transferred to paralegals, or to local lawyers who can make a physical appearance at a motion or a settlement conference more inexpensively than flying a lawyer hundreds of miles.

There are numerous questions and concerns about outsourcing, just as there are with other aspects of commodification, including just what type of quality a commodified product can provide compared with a bespoke one and how clients are guided to such decisions. Outsourcing raises additional issues regarding lawyer/client privilege and confidentiality, as well as questions about ethical standards in other countries and for paralegals. It is clear that New Lawyers will be working in a global marketplace of legal services, but just how those products will be harnessed to serve the best interests of their clients is so far very unclear. How decisions and evaluations are made about quality and cost in the lawyer/client relationship, and who makes those decisions, will be critical here. Efforts to impose and even to limit choices – for example, by outsourcing document review to India but refusing to use local paralegals – are likely to encounter the same resistance and questions from clients that can be seen in relation to so many other aspects of the new lawyer/client dialogue.

The availability of information on the web is driving a range of forms of online legal guidance. Some of these private products are developed for existing clients (e.g., case summaries and articles), whereas others (the most disruptive by far for legal services) offer free open-source information and advice. Beginning with access to basic legal information and rules of procedure – often difficult to use without some legal knowledge[55] – legal aid boards and public legal education agencies are beginning to offer increasingly ambitious resources designed for public users to enable some individual case analysis and even instruction on "next steps." The sophistication of such projects is growing in leaps and bounds as some take advantage of tested models for public access and application, such as the "guided pathways" approach piloted in British Columbia by the Legal Services Society of British Columbia.[56]

In addition to efforts by third parties to provide this level of assistance to those unable to afford access to a lawyer, there is the potential for legal "wikis" developed by a wider collaborative community. While these would lack the authority and reliability of resources created by legal aid boards, courts, and other public agencies they could include other resources that many self-represented litigants would find useful and important, including the experiential accounts of other SRLs, court briefs from earlier cases, and even legal advice memos provided by lawyers that are then posted by individuals who have already paid for this service. Aside from text-based resources, other types of interactive resources, such as videos and even instructional games,[57] are beginning to appear. The input of SRLs and members of the public – as "testers" and in focus groups – will be crucial to the effectiveness and impact of online legal guidance, as well as the inclusion of access to a live lawyer for some individuals and some types of assistance.

The creation of online dispute resolution systems that allow for participation without legal representation is yet another disruptive technology faced by the legal profession. In British Columbia, the launch of the Civil Resolutions Tribunal (initially offering online access without legal representation for strata [condominium] disputes[58]) has been met with resistance from the bar[59] but was still moving ahead with a gradually expanding mandate from 2016. Similar online tribunals designed for public access without counsel are proposed in England and Wales.[60]

As a site of change, disruptive technologies seem limitless, unstoppable, and inevitable. The same could be said of the impact of the next and final site I shall address: the huge increase in the number of self-represented litigants, particularly in family and civil courts.[61]

The Self-Represented Litigant Phenomenon

Since the first edition of this book was published in 2008, the significance of the large and still rising volume of those coming to court without counsel has burst into prominence. This phenomenon is being experienced across the common law world, especially in family and civil courts. Essentially a crisis caused by the unaffordability of lawyers for the vast majority of the population,[62] the SRL phenomenon converges with disruptive legal technologies to create the potential for change in everything from the regulation and delivery of personal legal services, the role of judges, and the focus of public assistance to process (both fora and rules) reform and innovations.

There is also a social and political impact of the SRL phenomenon. Widespread public dissatisfaction with barriers to accessing legal services and the growing numbers of individuals who have either directly experienced, or know someone who has directly experienced, the often bruising, disappointing, and traumatic effort of self-representation, is creating an Access to Justice movement demanding change. There is a clear impact on the legitimacy, credibility, and reputation of the legal system and everyone who works within it that reflects a dramatic loss of faith in our legal institutions. The following statement is typical:

> No matter how right your cause is, you do not get the justice you deserve because it is about your resources.[63]

The SRL phenomenon also places significant burdens on many of those working inside the justice system. In particular, front-line court services staff are bearing the brunt of a high volume of stressed and often confused and emotional self-represented litigants.[64] Many judges and masters now see individuals presenting their own cases every day in their courtrooms; some judges feel overwhelmed and impatient, but others find themselves caught between their desire to offer assistance and their awareness of the need to maintain impartiality, and sometimes trying to manage the discontent of counsel on the other side if they spend more time with or offer the SRL basic information. The task of judges in relation to SRLs is discussed briefly above, and is likely to become a consuming topic in the coming years.

The New Lawyer should anticipate being part of major changes that are the consequence of the SRL phenomenon. These include changes in the structure of the delivery of legal services (the growth of alternative billing arrangements and "legal coaching" or partial representation); an expansion in the roles of para-professionals (including paralegals but also "McKenzie Friends"[65]) who can assist SRLs at a lower cost than lawyers; increasing pressure on restrictive regulatory regimes that aggressively defend against the "unauthorized practice of law";[66] more pressure than ever for rule simplification; and the potential expansion of online, lawyer-less dispute resolution processes. Over the next decade, the SRL phenomenon may become the most dynamic, destabilizing, and transformative site of change of all.

Epilogue

This book has attempted to describe what has changed about the practice of law over the past thirty years. Given the scale and pace of change, it is an ambitious task. I have tried to identify the most significant developments that have affected the way in which law is practised as well as the resulting changes in models of client service and advocacy, and, in particular, to integrate into this analysis some understanding of how client needs and expectations are also changing.

I believe that the work of integrating client expectations and needs into new models of legal services – and ultimately a new professional identity, described in this book as the New Lawyer – is not a philanthropic mission reserved for a few committed to Access to Justice and *pro bono* service. It is the urgent and unavoidable responsibility of every member of the legal profession and its related institutions (the judiciary, the courts, the law schools, and the regulators, among others). Neglecting the profound and increasingly vocal dissatisfaction of many past and prospective consumers of legal services is not an option if the legal profession is to continue to be a force for social stability, justice, and the rule of law. The voices of clients that resonate in the pages of this book need to be listened to carefully, respectfully, and seriously. That listening needs to begin right away.

In the course of conducting research with lawyers and their clients over the past twenty years, I have often had the impression that some in the profession and the academy have their eyes tightly closed, and are hoping that when they open them again everything will have gone back to "normal." This resistance to change is natural and is likely to be especially prevalent where the stakes are high

– and law is an elite profession. Most recently I have had that strong feeling again in talking to lawyers about the self-represented litigants phenomenon. What has changed already will not change back. And there is much more change on the horizon as the basis for resistance is increasingly eroded. As William Felstiner points out: "Change and resistance are inextricably tied together in an oppositional tension where the weight shifts gradually from one to the other, even shifts backwards at times, but in the long run runs in the direction of change."[1]

In the last five years, I have also seen evidence of generational change that has been far more noticeable than earlier in my research career. Younger lawyers, and especially those who are trying to figure out how to pay off their tuition debt, are more naturally open to change and do not cling to the core beliefs or to assumptions about how services should be structured in the same way as their elders. They are accustomed to a world in which information is at everyone's fingertips, just a smartphone away. They belong to a generation that accepts the need for adjustment of market services to meet changing consumer expectations, and they embrace the democratization of knowledge that the World Wide Web represents. As well, some veteran lawyers are stepping forward as thought-leaders as they encourage others less experienced to listen to their clients and to rethink how they practise.

The most successful lawyers of the next generation will be those who commit their professional expertise to developing authentic partnerships with their clients – both domestic and corporate – by truly understanding how best to achieve what they need and want. This means that these lawyers will be practical problem solvers, creative and strategic thinkers, excellent communicators, and conflict engagement specialists who understand the toll that conflict takes on individuals and institutions. They will be persuasive and skillful negotiators and thoroughly prepared advocates for good settlements, willing to work in a new type of professional partnership with their clients and aware of the need to develop financial structures that offer choice, value for money, and accessibility as well as competence. This is the lawyer as conflict resolution advocate – the New Lawyer.

There will not be just one type of New Lawyer. In fact, diversity and responsiveness rather than conformity and traditionalism are embedded in the very concept of the New Lawyer. There is a need for a diversity of lawyers and lawyer styles to meet different client needs. No one process of dispute resolution is appropriate for all conflicts. There will continue to be many different arenas of professional practice for lawyers, but each practice setting will need a plan for the future that embraces change and anticipates more to come. While some lawyers may choose, for example, collaborative family law practice on Main

Street over corporate commercial work on Bay Street (and vice versa), neither of these worlds can escape the impact of the other, and both are a part of the future of legal practice. Both Bay Street and Main Street firms need a business model that enables them to stay competitive in an era of paralegals, in-house counsel, and other specialists. Every member of the legal profession is affected by negative public attitudes towards lawyers and justice systems, and must be ready to meet this challenge by listening to clients, making changes, and promoting the values of professionalism and integrity.

A coherent professional identity for lawyers requires an integration of these changes into their values, behaviours, and goals for their future careers. Satisfied and fulfilled professionals are those who possess a clear sense of professional identity and purpose. This is a worthy goal for both new and older members of the profession in these times of change. The emerging model of the New Lawyer offers present and future members of the profession the philosophical and practical framework for a renewed sense of focus, commitment, and satisfaction.

Notes

Chapter 1: Changes in the Legal Profession and the Emergence of the New Lawyer

1 J. Macfarlane, *The National Self-Represented Litigants Project: Identifying and Meeting the Needs of Self-Represented Litigants: Final Report* (May 2013) at 45, online: <https://representingyourselfcanada.files.wordpress.com/2014/02/reportm15-2.pdf> [hereafter *National SRL Study*].

2 Ontario Civil Legal Needs Project Steering Committee, *Listening to Ontarians: Report of the Ontario Civil Legal Needs Project* (Toronto: The Committee, May 2010) at 39, online: Law Society of Upper Canada <http://www.lsuc.on.ca/media/may3110_oclnreport_final.pdf>.

3 John Lande points out the contrast between the values of business, which are often reflected by in-house counsel, and those of traditional legal practice (for example, an emphasis on precedent and a lack of creativity). See J. Lande, "Failing Faith in Litigation? A Survey of Business Lawyers' and Executives' Opinions" (1998) 3:1 Harv Negot L Rev 1.

4 Macfarlane, *National SRL Study*, see note 1 above at 35.

5 M. McKiernan, "The Going Rate," *Canadian Lawyer* (June 2015), online: *Canadian Lawyer* <http://www.canadianlawyermag.com/images/stories/pdfs/Surveys/2015/CL_June_15_GoingRate.pdf>. The average cost of a two-day trial leaped 43 percent from 2014 to $31,330 in 2015. Ten-year calls bill on average $360 an hour, while first-year calls bill on average $230 an hour.

6 Macfarlane, *National SRL Study*, see note 1 above at 33–34.

7 Around one in five SRL respondents expressed a personal determination to take their matter forward themselves, as well as acknowledging financial reasons to self-represent. Approximately one in ten expressed confidence from the outset that they

could handle their case themselves and saw retaining legal counsel as a poor use of resources when relatively little money was at stake: ibid. at 7 and 9. Note that these findings are consistent with a study conducted by the Institute for the Advancement of the American Legal System <http://www.iaals.org> in five US states: *Cases without Counsel: Research on Experiences of Self-Representation in US Family Court* (Denver: IAALS, June 2016), online: IAALS <http://iaals.du.edu/sites/default/files/documents/publications/cases_without_counsel_research_report.pdf>.

8 R.L. Kiser, M.A. Asher, and B.B. McShane, "Let's Not Make a Deal: An Empirical Study of Decision Making in Unsuccessful Settlement Negotiations" (2008) 5 Journal of Empirical Legal Studies 551, online: <http://www.blakemcshane.com/Papers/jels_settlement.pdf>.

9 See Macfarlane, *National SRL Study,* note 1 above at 63–67. Examples include: CanLII <http://www.canlii.org/en/index.html>; Justice Education Society of British Columbia collection of online videos <http://www.justiceeducation.ca>; Legal Services Society of British Columbia, MyLawBC <http://www.mylawbc.com/>; J.P. Boyd on Family Law (a privately maintained website) <http://bcfamilylawresource.blogspot.ca/>; Alberta Court Services <http://www.albertacourts.ca>; Ontario Ministry of the Attorney General <https://www.attorneygeneral.jus.gov.on.ca/english/>.

10 Examples of practice areas open to paralegals in Ontario include small claims, traffic and tribunal work, and some provincial offences. In British Columbia, all paralegal activity is to be done under the supervision of a lawyer. "Paralegals – Part of the Access to Justice Solution," *Benchers' Bulletin* (Fall 2012), online: Law Society of British Columbia <http://www.lawsociety.bc.ca/page.cfm?cid=2570>.

11 See F.S. Mosten, *Unbundling Legal Services: A Guide to Delivering Legal Services a la Carte* (Chicago: American Bar Association, 2000); and F.S. Mosten, "Unbundling Legal Services Today – and Predictions for the Future" (2013) 35 Family Advocate 14.

12 Initiatives to increase access to justice include British Columbia's *Civil Resolution Tribunal Act,* SBC 2012, c. 25, which will create North America's first online tribunal to deal with small claims and strata property disputes without legal representatives; unbundled legal services (see Mosten, *Unbundling Legal Services,* note 11 above); and the web-based examples at note 9 above.

13 B. Curran and C. Carson, *The Lawyer Statistical Report: The US Legal Profession in the 1990s* (Chicago: American Bar Foundation, 1994).

14 *Crystal Clear: New Perspectives for the Canadian Bar Association* (report of the Canadian Bar Association Future Committee) (Ottawa: Canadian Bar Association, 2006) at 13.

15 Canadian Bar Association, *The Future of Legal Services in Canada: Trends and Issues* (Ottawa: Canadian Bar Association, 2013), online: Canadian Bar Association <http://www.cba.org/CBAMediaLibrary/cba_na/PDFs/CBA%20Legal%20Futures%20PDFS/trends-isssues-eng.pdf>.

16 Heenan Blaikie is an example of the collapse of a mega-firm. J. Middlemiss, "Frankenstorm Brings Down Heenan Blaikie," *Canadian Lawyer* (July 7, 2014), online:

Canadian Lawyer <http://www.canadianlawyermag.com/5194/Frankenstorm-brings-down-Heenan-Blaikie.html>.

17 D. Gruber, "Lakehead Law Launches," *Canadian Lawyer* (August 26, 2013), online: *Canadian Lawyer* <http://www.canadianlawyermag.com/4773/Lakehead-law-launches.html>; G. Kauth, "TWU Decision Unreasonable, Federal Government Argues," *Canadian Lawyer* (May 4, 2015), online: *Canadian Lawyer* <http://www.canadianlawyermag.com/legalfeeds/2675/twu-decision-unreasonable-federal-government-argues.html>.

18 M. Neil, "Law School Applications Down 37 Percent since 2010; First-Year Class Could Be Smallest in 40 Years," *ABA Journal* (July 22, 2014), online: *ABA Journal* <http://www.abajournal.com/news/article/law_school_applications_down_8_percent_new_lsac_survey_shows_theyve_dropped/>.

19 D. Olofsson, "Legal Farm Teams," *Canadian Lawyer* (October 7, 2013), online: *Canadian Lawyer* <http://www.canadianlawyermag.com/4842/Legal-farm-teams.html>.

20 Craigslist.com. Craigslist is a website of local classifieds and forums, community-moderated and largely free.

21 J. Heinz et al., "Diversity, Representation and Leadership in an Urban Bar: A First Report on a Survey of the Chicago Bar" (1976) 1 American Bar Foundation Research Journal 717.

22 See J. Heinz, R. Nelson, and E. Laumann, *Summary of Chicago Lawyers II* (Chicago: American Bar Foundation, 1995).

23 J. Hagan and F. Kay, "Social Mobility and Hierarchical Structure in Canadian Law Practice" in W. Felstiner, ed., *Reorganisation and Resistance* (Oxford: Hart Publishing, 2005) 281 at 282.

24 R. Daniels, "The Law Firm as an Efficient Community" (1992) 37 McGill LJ 807; and J. Hagan and F. Kay, *Gender in Practice: A Study of Lawyers' Lives* (New York: Oxford University Press, 1995), which draws on a 1990 survey of Ontario lawyers.

25 William G. Ross has estimated that while associate salaries have risen by 1,000 percent in the preceding thirty years, billing rates have risen by "only" 400 percent. W.G. Ross, *The Honest Hour: The Ethics of Time-Based Billing by Attorneys* (Durham, NC: Carolina Academic Press, 1996).

26 Patrick Schiltz, formerly a partner in a large law firm, argues persuasively that this gap can be bridged only by requiring ever-increasing numbers of billable hours from associates and then selling those hours to clients at a far higher rate than the associates are paid. See P. Schiltz, "On Being a Happy, Healthy and Ethical Member of an Unhappy, Unhealthy and Unethical Profession" (1991) 52 Vand L Rev 872.

27 Hagan and Kay, "Social Mobility and Hierarchical Structure," see note 23 above at 282.

28 See R. Nelson and R. Sandefur, "From Professional Dominance to Organisational Dominance" in Felstiner, *Reorganisation and Resistance,* see note 23 above at 313.

29 *General Counsel with Power? The Implications for Legal Practice, Law Firms and the Global Value Chain in Law,* Novak Druce Centre Insights No. 7, online: Said Business

School, Oxford University <http://www.sbs.ox.ac.uk/sites/default/files/Novak_Druce/Doc/General%20counsel%20with%20power.pdf>.

30 R. Stock, "The Future for In-House Counsel," *Legal Tech Insider*, June 2008, at 1.

31 M.C. Daly, "The Cultural, Ethical, and Legal Challenges in Lawyering for a Global Organization: The Role of the General Counsel" (1997) 46 Emory LJ 1057.

32 R. Nelson, "The Futures of American Lawyers: A Demographic Profile of a Changing Profession in a Changing Society" in R. Abel, ed., *Lawyers: A Critical Reader* (New York: New Press, 1997) 20 at 21.

33 Association of Corporate Counsel <http://www.acca.com>; Rees Morrison, "Wish We Had Clarity on the Number of Lawyers per U.S. Company with a Law Department," online: General Counsel Metrics <http://www.lawdepartmentmanagementblog.com/law_department_management/2011/08/wish-we-had-clarity-on-the-number-of-lawyers-per-us-company-with-a-law-department.html>. The *2015 ACC Global Census: A Profile of In-House Counsel,* online at <http://www.acc.com/vl/public/Surveys/loader.cfm?csModule=security/getfile&pageid=1411922&page=/legalresources/resource.cfm&qstring=show=1411922&title=2015%20ACC%20Global%20Census%20Executive%20Summary&recorded=1>, shows the numbers of corporate counsel continuing to rise across all specializations and organizations (at 27–30).

34 Canadian Corporate Counsel Association <http://www.cancorpcounsel.org>.

35 Hagan and Kay, "Social Mobility and Hierarchical Structure," see note 23 above.

36 Nelson, "The Futures of American Lawyers," see note 32 above at 26.

37 Hagan and Kay, "Social Mobility and Hierarchical Structure," see note 23 above at 281.

38 B. Wilson, Chair, *Touchstones for Change: Equality, Diversity and Accountability* (Ottawa: Canadian Bar Association, 1995).

39 F. Kay, "Flight from Law: A Competing Risks Model of Departures from Law Firms" (1997) 31 Law & Soc'y Rev 301.

40 F. Kay, C. Masuch, and P. Curry, *Diversity and Change: The Contemporary Legal Profession in Ontario* (Toronto: Law Society of Upper Canada, 2004) at 27.

41 F.N. Weekes and A.E. Spears, *Survey of Black Lawyers, Black Articling Students and Recently Called Black Lawyers* (Toronto: Law Society of Upper Canada, 1992). See also M.B. St. Patrick, "Black Bay Street Lawyers and Other Oxymora" (1998) 30 Can Bus LJ 267.

42 Kay, Masuch, and Curry, *Diversity and Change,* see note 40 above at 41.

43 Chapter 11 of *Ontario Civil Justice Review: First Report* (March 1995), online: Ontario Ministry of the Attorney General <http://www.attorneygeneral.jus.gov.on.ca/english/about/pubs/cjr/firstreport/cost.asp>. Today, this figure would be closer to $50,000 (all figures in Canadian dollars).

44 The most recent (2002) study shows that just 1.8 percent of filings in the US Federal Court go to a full trial, down from 11.5 percent in 1962. See M. Galanter, "The Vanishing Trial: An Examination of Trials and Related Matters in Federal and State Courts" (2004) 1 Journal of Empirical Legal Studies 459.

45 Ibid.

46 J. Twohig, C. Baar, A. Meyers, and A.M. Predko, "Empirical Analyses of Civil Cases Commenced and Cases Tried in Toronto 1973–94" in Ontario Law Reform Commission, ed., *Rethinking Civil Justice: Research Studies for the Civil Justice Review,* vol. 1 (Toronto: Ontario Law Reform Commission, 1996) at 77.

47 Note that pre-trial activity over the same period has increased. See, for example, G. Hadfield, "Where Have All the Trials Gone? Settlements, Nontrial Adjudications and Statistical Artifacts in the Changing Disposition of Federal Civil Cases" (2004) 1 Journal of Empirical Legal Studies 705. Similarly, in Ontario, courtroom time attributed to motions and to pre-trials rose by 69 percent and 140 percent, respectively, between 1989–90 and 1993–94. Chapter 4 of *Ontario Civil Justice Review,* see note 43 above, online: Ontario Ministry of the Attorney General <http://www.attorneygeneral.jus.gov.on.ca/english/about/pubs/cjr/firstreport/courts.asp>.

48 See J. Macfarlane, "What Does the Changing Culture of Legal Practice Mean for Legal Education?" (2001) 20 Windsor YB Access Just 191; and J. Macfarlane and J. Manwaring, "Reconciling Professional Legal Education with the Evolving (Trial-less) Reality of Legal Practice" (2006) 1 J Disp Resol 253.

49 See note 11 above.

50 Macfarlane, *National SRL Study,* see note 1 above at 109–10.

51 Ibid. at 95–104.

52 The Law Society of Upper Canada Paralegal Rules of Conduct, effective May 1, 2007. Amendments current to October 1, 2014. As of May 1, 2007, paralegals were not permitted by the Law Society of Upper Canada to appear in Family Court, pursuant to By-law 4 of the LSUC Rules of Professional Conduct.

53 Twohig et al., "Empirical Analyses of Civil Cases," see note 46 above.

54 The Canadian Minister of Justice, Allan Rock, speaking to the House of Commons Standing Committee on Justice and Legal Affairs. *Minutes of Proceedings and Evidence,* Issue No. 62, November 17, 1994.

55 See "Incarcerated America," Human Rights Watch Backgrounder (April 2003), online: Human Rights Watch <http://www.hrw.org/backgrounder/usa/incarceration/>.

56 *Criminal Code,* RSC 1985, c. C-46 s. 718 (e) states that "all available sanctions other than imprisonment that are reasonable in the circumstances should be considered for all offenders, with particular attention to the circumstances of aboriginal offenders."

57 *Youth Criminal Justice Act,* SC 2002, c. 1.

58 The relationship between criminal and civil matters and appropriate processes to deal with each is examined at length in Law Commission of Canada, *Transforming Relationships through Participatory Justice* (Ottawa: Law Commission of Canada, 2004).

59 Especially in relation to case flow and settlement timelines and in terms of client satisfaction. See R.L. Wissler, "The Effectiveness of Court-Connected Dispute Resolution in Civil Cases" (2004) 22 Conflict Resolution Quarterly 55.

60 See the assessment offered in Law Commission of Canada, *Transforming Relationships,* note 58 above at 15–87.

61 These terms occur frequently in the data collected for the Culture Change Project; see J. Macfarlane, "Culture Change? A Tale of Two Cities and Mandatory Court-Connected Mediation" (2002) 2 J Disp Resol 241. For other studies that suggest a relationship between experience with mediation and positive attitudes towards its use, see R.L. Wissler, "When Does Familiarity Breed Content? A Study of the Role of Different Forms of ADR Education and Experience in Attorneys' ADR Recommendations" (2002) 2 Pepp Disp Resol LJ 199; C. McEwen, N.H. Rogers, and R.J. Maiman, "Bring in the Lawyers: Challenging the Dominant Approaches to Ensuring Fairness in Divorce Mediation" (1995) 33 Me L Rev 237; J. Lande, "Getting the Faith: Why Business Lawyers and Executives Believe in Mediation" (2000) 5 Harv Negot L Rev 137 at 199; M. Medley and J. Schellenberg, "Attitudes of Attorneys toward Mediation" (1994) 12 Mediation Quarterly 185 at 195–96; and Macfarlane, *National SRL Study,* see note 1 above at 299–301.

62 Unpublished data from a 2002–03 evaluation of the court-connected mediation program in the Saskatchewan Court of Queen's Bench. The evaluators (J. Macfarlane and M. Keet) conducted interviews and focus groups with both lawyers and their clients.

63 J. Macfarlane, "Culture Change? A Tale of Two Cities and Mandatory Court-Connected Mediation" (2002) 2 J Disp Resol 241 at 262, 317.

64 Unpublished data from J. Macfarlane and M. Keet, *Learning from Experience: An Evaluation of the Saskatchewan Queen's Bench Mediation Program* (Regina: Saskatchewan Justice, April 2003).

65 J. Macfarlane, *Analysis Project of the Federal Experience with the Use of Mediation and Other Dispute Resolution Processes* (Ottawa: Department of Justice Canada, 2009) at 60.

66 *Rules of Civil Procedure,* RRO 1990, Reg. 194, r. 24.1. See also Ministry of the Attorney General, "Fact Sheet: Mandatory Mediation under Rules 24.1 and 75.1 of the Rules of Civil Procedure" (January 2010), online: Ontario Ministry of the Attorney General <http://www.attorneygeneral.jus.gov.on.ca/english/courts/civil/fact_sheet_mandatory_mediation.pdf>.

67 See, for example, N. Welsh, "Making Deals in Court-Connected Mediation: What's Justice Got to Do with It?" (2001) 79 Wash ULQ 788 at 795–804; K. Kovach and L. Love, "Mapping Mediation: The Risks of Riskin's Grid" (1998) 3 Harv Negot L Rev 71 at 96; and Macfarlane, *National SRL Study,* see note 1 above at 268–77.

68 *Rules of Civil Procedure,* see note 66 above.

69 See B. McAdoo, "A Report to the Minnesota Supreme Court: The Impact of Rule 114 on Civil Litigation Practice in Minnesota" (2002) 25 Hamline L Rev 401 at 417–19; and see the description of the "Dismissers" in Macfarlane, "Culture Change?" see note 63 above at 257–58.

70 Macfarlane, ibid. at 302.

71 Unpublished data from the Culture Change Project. See Macfarlane, "Culture Change?" note 63 above, for project details.

72 See A. Schneider, "Shattering Negotiation Myths: Empirical Evidence on the Effectiveness of Negotiation Style" (2002) 7 Harv Negot L Rev 143 at 187–90. Schneider finds that the adversarial negotiators have become more extreme and "nastier" over the past

twenty-five years (the original Williams study was undertaken in 1976). See G. Williams, *Legal Negotiation and Settlement* (St. Paul, MN: West Publishing, 1983); and Macfarlane, "Culture Change?" see note 63 above at 302 and 306.

73 R.J. Gilson and R.H. Mnookin, "Disputing through Agents: Cooperation and Conflict between Lawyers in Litigation" (1994) 94 Colum L Rev 509 at 535; and J.L. Barkai and G. Kassebaum, "Using Court-Annexed Arbitration to Reduce Litigant Costs and to Increase the Pace of Litigation" (1989) 16 Pepp L Rev 43 at 47.

74 While much ink has been spilled on this topic recently, it has been a pervasive concern for over a decade. For substantive rather than nostalgic approaches, see, for example, F. Zacharias, "Reconciling Professionalism and Client Interests" (1995) 36 Wm & Mary L Rev 1303; and J. Sammons, "The Professionalism Movement: The Problems Defined" (1993) 29 Ga L Rev 1035.

75 See, for example, in the United States, American Bar Association, Section of Legal Education and Admissions to the Bar, *Legal Education and Professional Development – An Educational Continuum: The Report of the Task Force on Law Schools and the Profession: Narrowing the Gap* (Chicago: American Bar Association, 1992), online: American Bar Association <http://www.americanbar.org/content/dam/aba/publications/misc/legal_education/2013_legal_education_and_professional_development_maccrate_report). authcheckdam.pdf>.

76 L. Riskin, "Mediation and Lawyers" (1982) 42 Ohio St LJ 41 at 43–48.

77 American Bar Association, *Legal Education and Professional Development*, see note 75 above.

78 Canadian Bar Association, *Futures: Transforming the Delivery of Legal Services in Canada* (Ottawa: Canadian Bar Association, 2014), online: Canadian Bar Association <http://www.cbafutures.org/CBA/media/mediafiles/PDF/Reports/Futures-Final-eng.pdf?ext=.pdf>; Canadian Bar Association, *The Future of Legal Services in Canada*, see note 15 above.

79 See, for example, Institute for the Advancement of the American Legal System, *Cases without Counsel*, see note 7 above; Dewar et al., *Litigants in Person in the Family Court of Australia* (2000); Civil Justice Council, *Access to Justice for Litigants in Person (or Self-Represented Litigants): A Report and Recommendations to the Lord Chancellor and to the Lord Chief Justice* (November 2011), online: Courts and Tribunals Judiciary <https://www.judiciary.gov.uk/wp-content/uploads/2014/05/report-on-access-to-justice-for-litigants-in-person-nov2011.pdf>.

80 R.C. Post, "On the Popular Image of the Lawyer: Reflections in a Dark Glass" (1987) 75 Cal L Rev 379 at 380; and B. Ong Hing, "In the Interest of Racial Harmony: Revisiting the Lawyer's Duty to Work for the Common Good" (1994–95) 47 Stan L Rev 901 at 927.

81 J. Nolan-Haley, "Lawyers, Clients and Mediation" (1998) 73 Notre Dame L Rev 1369 at 1372.

82 Macfarlane, *National SRL Study*, see note 1 above at 46.

83 J. Macfarlane, "Don't Leave Me, Please Help Me, but Do It Differently: A Plea to the Bar" (2016), online: The National Self-Represented Litigants Project Blog <http://

representingyourselfcanada.com/dont-leave-me-please-help-me-but-do-it-differently
-a-plea-to-the-bar/>.

84 M. Heumann and J. Hyman, "Negotiation Methods and Litigation Settlement Methods in New Jersey: You Can't Always Get What You Want" (1997) 12 Ohio St J Disp Resol 253 at 295–305.

85 Thomas Kuhn's concept of "paradigm shift" means the actual replacement or substitution of the old with a new paradigm. T. Kuhn, *The Structure of Scientific Revolution* (Chicago: University of Chicago Press, 1962).

86 Macfarlane, "Culture Change?" see note 63 above at 306 [emphasis added].

87 For example, J. Cooley, *Mediation Advocacy* (Louisville, CO: National Institute for Trial Advocacy, 1996); and C. Noble, L. Dizgun, and P. Emond, *Mediation Advocacy* (Toronto: Emond Montgomery, 1998).

88 Abel, *Lawyers*, see note 32 above.

89 Macfarlane, "Culture Change?" see note 63 above at 316.

90 This point may also apply to the development of voluntary networks. For example, in Medicine Hat, Alberta (population 51,000) the two most prominent members of the Family Bar (totalling eighteen lawyers) attended training for collaborative law in the late 1990s. They returned inspired and began a collaborative lawyering group for family lawyers. Within a year, all but one of the members of the Family Bar had joined up. Not practising collaboratively was considered countercultural in Medicine Hat.

91 On members of the judiciary, see R. Wissler, "Barriers to Attorneys' Discussion and Use of ADR" (2004) 19 Ohio St J Disp Resol 459 at 488–89. On seasoned litigators, see M.W. Isenhart and M.L. Spangle, *Collaborative Approaches to Resolving Conflict* (Thousand Oaks, CA: Sage Publications, 2000) at 156. Australian example: J. Wakefield, "Judges Make the Case for Arbitration," *Lawyers Weekly* (May 11, 2015), online: *Lawyers Weekly* <http://www.lawyersweekly.com.au/opinion/16496-judges-make-the-case-for-arbitration>.

92 Dean Beeby, "Canadians' Lack of Faith in Courts Can Be Overcome with Education, Report Urges," *Globe and Mail* (February 17, 2014), online: <http://www.theglobeand mail.com/news/politics/canadians-lack-of-faith-in-courts-can-be-overcome-with-education-report-urges/article16926079/>; Dean Beeby, "Study Finds Canadians Have Little Confidence in Justice System," *CTV News Online* (February 17, 2014), online: <http://www.ctvnews.ca/canada/study-finds-canadians-have-little-confidence-in-justice-system-1.1689727>; Paul Russell, "Today's Letters: No Faith in Our Justice System," *National Post* (May 22, 2012), online: <http://news.nationalpost.com/full-comment/todays-letters-no-faith-in-our-justice-system>.

93 Macfarlane, "Culture Change?" see note 63 above.

94 Ontario Family Legal Services Review (forthcoming).

95 D. Goldman, *Emotional Intelligence: Why It Can Matter More Than IQ* (New York: Bantam Books, 1994); D. Linder and N. Levit, *The Good Lawyer: Seeking Quality in the Practice of Law* (New York: Oxford University Press, 2014) at 12–35.

96 Unpublished data from the Culture Change Project.

Chapter 2: The Making of a Lawyer

1 Dedicated websites include Lawyer Jokes and Cartoons <http://www.lawyer-jokes. us/> and Lawyer Joke of the Day <http://www.ahajokes.com/lawyer_joke_of_the_day. shtml>; texts include A. McMeel, *Lawyers Quotes, Jokes and Anecdotes* (Kansas City: Andrew McMeel Publishing, 2001); and B. Tripmacher, *The Best Lawyer Jokes Ever* (New York: Metrobooks, 2002).

2 Respectively: *To Kill a Mockingbird,* starring Gregory Peck, directed by Robert Mulligan (Universal Studios, 1962); *Clarence Darrow,* starring Henry Fonda, directed by John Rich (Kultur Video, 1974), based on the life and trials of the real-life lawyer; *Inherit the Wind,* starring Spencer Tracy, directed by Stanley Kramer (United Artists, 1960), based on the 1925 Scopes trial. The Spencer Tracy character was based on Clarence Darrow.

3 L.E. Gross, "The Public Hates Lawyers: Why Should We Care?" (2000) 29 Seton Hall L Rev 1405; M. Galanter, *Lowering the Bar: Lawyer Jokes and Legal Culture* (Madison: University of Wisconsin Press, 2005); and W.K. Olsen, *The Rule of Lawyers: How the New Litigation Elite Threatens America's Rule of Law* (New York: St. Martin's Press, 2003).

4 R.C. Post, "On the Popular Image of the Lawyer: Reflections in a Dark Glass" (1987) 75 Cal L Rev 379 at 380.

5 See, for example, J. Macfarlane, *The National Self-Represented Litigants Project: Iden-tifying and Meeting the Needs of Self-Represented Litigants: Final Report* (May 2013) at 44, online: <https://representingyourselfcanada.files.wordpress.com/2014/02/report m15-2.pdf> [hereafter *National SRL Study*]. For a somewhat less critical study but one expressing unease about levels of lawyer competence and trustworthiness and the ability of the regulator to properly discipline misconduct, see Law Society of British Columbia, *2010 Law Society Commissioned Public Opinion Poll on Lawyers and Effectiveness of Law Society* (Vancouver: Law Society of British Columbia, 2010).

6 J. Elkins, "Reading/Teaching Lawyer Films" (2004) 28 Vt L Rev 813 at 830.

7 See, for example, D. Kellner, *Media Culture: Cultural Studies, Identity and Politics be-tween the Modern and the Post Modern* (London: Routledge, 1995).

8 Known as the "cultivation theory." See, for example, G. Gerbner et al., "Growing Up with Television: The Cultivation Perspective" in J. Byrant and D. Zillman, eds., *Media Effects: Advances in Theory and Research* (Hillsdale, NJ: Lawrence Erlbaum Associates, 1994) at 17.

9 Ibid. at 23–25.

10 A. Chase, "Lawyers and Popular Culture: A Review of Mass Media Portrayals of American Attorneys" (1986) 11 American Bar Foundation Research Journal 281; Christopher Snead, *The Downward Spiral: A Look at the Depiction of Lawyers in Mov-ies* (Senior Project, Knoxville Trace: Tennessee Research and Creative Exchange, University of Tennessee, 2002), online: <http://trace.tennessee.edu/cgi/viewcontent. cgi?article=1104&context=utk_interstp2>.

11 On Gareth Pierce: *In the Name of the Father,* starring Emma Thompson, directed by Jim Sheridan (Universal Pictures, 1993); on Erin Brockovich: *Erin Brockovich,* starring Julia Roberts, directed by Steven Soderbergh (Universal Pictures, 2000).

12 See the discussion in J. Grant, "Lawyers as Superheroes: *The Firm, The Client,* and *The Pelican Brief*" (1996) 30 USF L Rev 1111.

13 For a meta-analysis of the qualities associated with prelaw students, success at law school, and professional practice, see S. Daicoff, "Lawyer, Know Thyself: A Review of Empirical Research on Attorney Attributes Bearing on Professionalism" (1997) 46 Am U L Rev 1337.

14 J. Macfarlane, "Mediating Ethically: The Limits of Codes of Conduct and the Potential of a Reflective Practice Model (2002) 39 Osgoode Hall LJ 49 at 51–54.

15 For an extended discussion of the challenges of teaching ethics to prospective lawyers and the extent to which the law schools fall short, see, for example, B. Balos, "The Bounds of Professionalism: Challenging Our Students; Challenging Ourselves" (1997) 4 Clinical L Rev 129; P. Brest, "The Responsibility of Law Schools: Educating Lawyers as Counselors and Problem Solvers" (1995) 58 Law and Contemp Probs 5; J. Sammons, "Rank Strangers to Me: Shaffer and Cochran's Friendship Model of Moral Counselling in the Law Office" (1995) 18 U Ark Little Rock L Rev 1; and D.B. Wilkins, "Redefining the 'Professional' in Professional Ethics: An Interdisciplinary Approach to Teaching Professionalism" (1995) 58 Law and Contemp Probs 241.

16 D. Rhode, "Ethics by the Pervasive Method" (1992) 42 J Legal Educ 31 at 41.

17 The bell curve is an example of a "competitive" grading policy, in contrast with an "individualistic" or a "cooperative" model.

18 A. Hochschild, "Inside the Clockwork of Male Careers" in F. Howe, ed., *Women and the Power to Change* (New York: McGraw-Hill, 1975) 47 at 64. In law school, this is often manifested by one's ability to assimilate and converse in the "special language" of law.

19 See J. Macfarlane, "Teacher Power in the Law School Classroom" (1996) 19 Dal LJ 71 at 82.

20 See, for example, the critique of "relevancy" made by Mary Jane Mossman in "Feminism and Legal Method: The Difference It Makes" (1986) 30 Australian Journal of Law and Society 30 especially at 44–45.

21 J. Moulton, "A Paradigm of Philosophy: The Adversary Method," cited in L. Code, *What Can She Know? Feminist Theory and the Construction of Knowledge* (Ithaca, NY: Cornell University Press, 1991) at 23–24. "The adversary method is most effective," Moulton claims, "in structuring isolated disagreements about specific theses and arguments. Hence it depends for its success on the artificial isolation of such claims and arguments from the contexts that occasion their articulations" (at 23).

22 L. Riskin, "Mediation and Lawyers" (1982) 42 Ohio St LJ 29 at 41–43.

23 Macfarlane, "Teacher Power," see note 19 above at 81–84.

24 W. Conklin, "Teaching Critically within a Modern Legal Genre" (1993) 8 CJLS 33 at 41.

25 See, for example, L. Silver, "Anxiety and the First Semester of Law School" (1968) 4 Wis L Rev 1201; and S.C. Segerstrom, "Perceptions of Stress and Control in the First Semester of Law School" (1996) 32 Willamette L Rev 593.

26 *Placement Report 2003/2004 of Students Enrolled in the 46th BAC 2003* (July 2004), online: Law Society of Upper Canada <http://bit.ly/2h0I0qj>. In the 2003–04 year, 66.4

percent of students indicated that they had secured employment at the time of their call to the bar. This is an increase from 62.5 percent the previous year. The hire-back rate of students returning to the firm they articled with remained steady at 49.7 percent.

27 See, for example, H.S. Erlanger and D.A. Klegon, "Socialization Effects of Professional School: The Law School Experience and Student Orientation to Public Interest Concerns" (1978) 13 Law & Soc'y Rev 11.

28 See, for example, Daicoff, "Lawyer, Know Thyself," note 13 above.

29 L. Mather, C. McEwen, and R. Maiman, *Divorce Lawyers at Work: Varieties of Professionalism in Practice* (Oxford: Oxford University Press, 2001) at 41–63.

30 Ibid.

31 Ibid. at 61.

32 See, for example, H. Kritzer and F. Zemans, "Local Legal Culture and the Control of Litigation" (1993) 27 Law & Soc'y Rev 535 (where a change in the rules of civil procedure that made lawyers more accountable for frivolous actions was differentially applied across several jurisdictions); T. Church, "Examining Local Legal Culture" (1985) 3 American Bar Foundation Research Journal 449; and, most recently, "Toward an Understanding of 'Local Legal Culture'" (1981) 6 Justice System Journal 200 (arguing that local legal culture can be used to explain differences in case processing timelines and delays and backlogs between different courts).

33 See the established conventions described in the smaller community of Prince Albert, Saskatchewan, in J. Macfarlane and M. Keet, *Learning from Experience: An Evaluation of the Saskatchewan Queen's Bench Mediation Program* (Regina: Saskatchewan Justice, April 2003) at 18.

34 Even in larger legal communities, norms can be established among lawyers who work regularly with one another, although these may be more difficult to establish and more subject to change. For example, in Toronto, some litigators now routinely exchange affidavits of documents in advance of mediation. See J. Macfarlane, "Culture Change? A Tale of Two Cities and Mandatory Court-Connected Mediation" (2002) 2 J Disp Resol 241 at 262.

35 Macfarlane, *National SRL Study*, see note 5 above at 42 and 81.

36 J. Macfarlane, "Unbundling 'Unbundling': Separating the Myths from the Realities" (April 11, 2016), online: The National Self-Represented Litigants Project Blog <http://representingyourselfcanada.com/unbundling-unbundling-separating-the-myths-from-the-realities/>.

37 Unpublished data from the Culture Change Project.

38 Mather et al., *Divorce Lawyers at Work*, see note 29 above at 91.

39 An example given by several lawyers participating in the Culture Change Project was the Canadian Medical Association, which is evidently highly resistant to any form of mediated compromise. Insurance carriers were also identified as taking a similar approach, and some were more open to settlement discussion.

40 Unpublished data from the Culture Change Project.

41 Macfarlane, "Culture Change," see note 34 above at 279.

42 I am indebted to Lidia Imbrogno for her assistance with the development and writing of this section.

43 "Nearly 1 in 2 Employers Has Researched a Job Candidate on Social Media, Finds Career-builder.ca Survey" (2015), online: Careerbuilder.ca <http://www.careerbuilder.ca/ca/share/aboutus/pressreleasesdetail.aspx?sd=5/14/2015&id=pr82&ed=12/31/2015>.

44 M.E. Lackey Jr. and J.P. Minta, "Lawyers and Social Media: The Legal Ethics of Tweeting, Facebooking and Blogging" (2012) 28 Touro L Rev 149 at 153.

45 Sometimes described as a social constructionist perspective. See, for example, P. Berger and T. Luckmann, *The Social Construction of Reality: A Treatise in the Sociology of Knowledge* (New York: Doubleday, 1966).

46 J. Macfarlane, *The Emerging Phenomenon of Collaborative Family Law (CFL): A Qualitative Study of CFL Cases* (Ottawa: Department of Justice, 2005) at 26, online: Department of Justice Canada <http://www.justice.gc.ca/eng/rp-pr/fl-lf/famil/2005_1/pdf/2005_1.pdf>.

47 That is, behaviour is not determinative of attitudes and vice versa. See, for example, M.J. Saks and E. Krupat, *Social Psychology and Its Applications* (New York: Harper and Row, 1988) at 197–98. However, dissonance theory also suggests that we try to reduce the dissonance between our behaviour and our attitudes in order to avoid the discomfort this produces.

48 For a policy proposal on the appropriate use of mandatory processes to encourage consensus building and settlement, see Law Commission of Canada, *Transforming Relationships through Participatory Justice* (Ottawa: Law Commission of Canada, 2004).

49 In Ontario, *Rules of Civil Procedure*, RRO 1990, Reg. 194, amended to O. Reg. 260/05, Rule 24.1. In Saskatchewan, *Queen's Bench Rules,* Rule 641. In Florida, *Florida Statutes,* c. 44. In California, *California Code of Civil Procedure,* tit. 11.6, ss. 1775–1775.15.

50 For relevant research on this point, see, for example, R.L. Wissler, "When Does Familiarity Breed Content? A Study of the Role of Different Forms of ADR Education and Experience in Attorneys' ADR Recommendations" (2002) 2 Pepp Disp Resol LJ 199; and C. McEwen, N.H. Rogers, and R.J. Maiman, "Bring in the Lawyers: Challenging the Dominant Approaches to Ensuring Fairness in Divorce Mediation" (1995) 33 Me L Rev 237.

51 Unpublished data from Macfarlane and Keet, *Learning from Experience,* see note 33 above.

52 Unpublished data from the Culture Change Project.

53 W. Bennett, *The Lawyer's Myth: Reviving the Ideals of the Legal Profession* (Chicago: University of Chicago Press, 2001) at 28–50.

54 A. Dershowitz, *Letter to a Young Lawyer* (New York: Basic Books, 2001).

55 In a class exercise, most of the students were unable to identify a satisfactory role model from inside the legal profession. Of those chosen from outside the profession, Oprah Winfrey and Wayne Gretzky topped the list.

56 See, for example, the story told by Mona Harrington in *Women Lawyers: Rewriting the Rules* (New York: Penguin, 1985) at 82–86.

57 See the concerns articulated in B. Wilson, Chair, *Touchstones for Change: Equality, Diversity and Accountability* (Ottawa: Canadian Bar Association, 1995).

58 Since alcohol consumption is a prevalent part of many social professional settings, observant Muslims and others who do not drink alcohol may feel excluded or feel that they must exclude themselves.

59 D. Wilkins and Gulati G. Mitu, "Why Are There So Few Black Lawyers in Corporate Law Firms? An Institutional Analysis" in R. Abel, ed., *Lawyers: A Critical Reader* (New York: New Press, 1997) 101 at 102.

60 See, for example, the *Solicitors' Practice Rules* (1990); and the Law Society of Upper Canada's *Code of Advocacy* (last amended January 13, 2003), both available at <http://www.lsuc.on.ca/lawyer-conduct-rules/>.

61 Law Society of Upper Canada, *Rules of Professional Conduct* (2000), Rule 4.01, online: Law Society of Upper Canada <http://www.lsuc.on.ca/lawyer-conduct-rules/>.

62 American Bar Association, *Canons of Professional Ethics* (first adopted August 27, 1908), Canon 7, online: American Bar Association <http://www.abanet.org/cpr/mrpc/Canons_Ethics.pdfModel>.

63 Law Society of Upper Canada, *Rules of Professional Conduct*, see note 61 above, Commentary on Rule 4.01.

64 American Bar Association, *Model Rules of Professional Conduct* (2007 version), Rule 3.1, online: American Bar Association <http://www.abanet.org/cpr/mrpc/model_rules.html>.

65 Law Society of British Colombia, *Canon of Legal Ethics* (1992), Rule 3(5), online: <https://www.lawsociety.bc.ca/page.cfm?cid=1027>.

66 This distinction is discussed in A. Zariski, "Disputing Culture: Lawyers and ADR" (2000) 7 Murdoch UEJL 1 at 2; and, on the relationship between material and immaterial elements of culture generally, see C. Geertz, "Thick Description: Toward an Interpretive Theory of Culture" in C. Geertz, ed., *The Interpretation of Cultures* (New York: Basic Books, 1973) 3 at 3–30.

67 In contrast, see *Ethical Principles of Psychologists and Code of Conduct* of the American Psychological Association (1992) at <http://www.apa.org/ethics/code/code-1992.aspx>. The preamble ends with these words: "Each psychologist supplements, but does not violate, the Ethics Code's values and rules on the basis of guidance drawn from personal values, culture and experience."

68 This is the distinction between "espoused theory" and "theory-in-action" drawn by Donald Schon. See, for example, D. Schon, "Educating the Reflective Practitioner" (1995) 2:1 Clinical L Rev 231; and D. Schon, *The Reflective Practitioner* (San Francisco: Jossey-Bass, 1983).

69 See M.A. Wilkinson, C. Walker, and P. Mercer, "Do Codes of Ethics Actually Shape Legal Practice?" (2000) 45 McGill LJ 645.

70 A number of lawyers have described this to me as their "go-to" resource when they face an ethical dilemma. They also acknowledge that they rarely find the answer in the code.

Chapter 3: What Lawyers Believe

1 R. Nelson and D. Trubek, "Arenas of Professionalism: The Professional Ideologies of Lawyers in Context" in R. Nelson, D. Trubek, and R. Solomon, eds., *Lawyers' Ideals/ Lawyers' Practices* (Ithaca, NY: Cornell University Press, 1992) 177 at 177.

2 The Royal Charter establishing the Law Society of England and Wales was issued in 1845.

3 R. Kidder, "The End of the Road? Problems in the Analysis of Disputes" (1980–81) 15 Law & Soc'y Rev 717 at 719 and 723.

4 Ibid.

5 R. Bell, *Understanding African Philosophy: A Cross-Cultural Approach to Classical and Contemporary Issues* (New York: Routledge, 2002) at 77.

6 Unpublished data from the Culture Change Project.

7 See, for example, Boston Bar Association Task Force on the Right to Civil Counsel, *The Importance of Representation in Eviction Cases and Homelessness Prevention* (Boston: Boston Bar Association, 2012), online: Boston Bar Association <http://www.boston-bar.org/docs/default-document-library/bba-crtc-final-3-1-12.pdf> (showing that unrepresented tenants in landlord and tenant cases fared worse in adjudicated cases than those with representation, although those who negotiated an outcome did not show the same differences); R.E. Kaufman, M. Davis, and H.Wegleitner, "The Interdependence of Rights: Protecting the Human Right to Housing by Promoting the Right to Counsel" (2013–14) 45 Colum HRL Rev 772 at 782.

8 C. Simmel, *Conflict* (New York: Free Press, 1955).

9 V. Aubert, "Competition and Dissensus: Two Types of Conflict and Conflict Resolution" (1963) 7 J Confl Resolution 26.

10 Kidder, "The End of the Road?" see note 3 above at 723.

11 From advertisements and billboards across the United States.

12 Unpublished data from the Culture Change Project.

13 J. Macfarlane, "Culture Change? A Tale of Two Cities and Mandatory Court-Connected Mediation" (2002) 2 J Disp Resol 241 at 282.

14 Andrea Schneider's "redo" of Gerald Williams's original study of the effectiveness of different negotiation styles (G. Williams, *Legal Negotiation and Settlement* [St. Paul, MN: West Publishing, 1983]) shows continuing pressure on young lawyers to demonstrate their "toughness" in negotiation, despite the reality that this may be an ineffectual approach. See A. Schneider, "Shattering Negotiation Myths: Empirical Evidence on the Effectiveness of Negotiation Style" (2002) 7 Harv Negot L Rev 143.

15 R.L. Kiser, M.A. Asher, and B.B. McShane, "Let's Not Make a Deal: An Empirical Study of Decision Making in Unsuccessful Settlement Negotiations" (2008) 5 Journal of Empirical Legal Studies 551, online: <http://www.blakemcshane.com/Papers/jels_settlement.pdf>.

16 Ibid.

17 See, for example, D. Lax and J. Sebenius, *The Manager as Negotiator: Bargaining for Competitive Gain* (New York: Free Press, 1986); and C. Menkel-Meadow, "Towards An-

other View of Legal Negotiations: The Structure of Problem-Solving" (1984) 31 UCLA L Rev 754.

18 J. Macfarlane, *Court-Based Mediation in Civil Cases: An Evaluation of the Toronto General Division ADR Centre* (Ottawa: Queen's Printer, 1995) at 22.

19 See, for example, J. Macfarlane, K. Trask, and E. Chesney, *The Use of Summary Judgment Procedures against Self-Represented Litigants: Effective Case Management or Denial of Access to Justice?* (Windsor, ON: Windsor Law, 2015), online: National Self-Represented Litigants Project <https://representingyourselfcanada.files.wordpress.com/2015/11/nsrlp-the-use-of-summary-judgment-procedures-against-srls1.pdf>; and Kaufman et al., "The Interdependence of Rights," see note 7 above.

20 From a video by former self-represented litigant Kelly Anne Christian, online: National Self-Represented Litigants Project <https://representingyourselfcanada.com/2015/01/15/kellys-experiences-as-a-self-represented-litigant/>.

21 J. Macfarlane, *The National Self-Represented Litigants Project: Identifying and Meeting the Needs of Self-Represented Litigants: Final Report* (May 2013) at 11, online: <https://representingyourselfcanada.files.wordpress.com/2014/02/reportm15-2.pdf> [hereafter *National SRL Study*].

22 Ibid. at 13.

23 See R. Susskind, *The End of Lawyers? Rethinking the Nature of Legal Services* (Oxford: Oxford University Press, 2008) at 121–30.

24 In other words, those conflicts are the appropriate subject of public discourse because of their wide implications for standards of fairness and justice throughout society. See, for example, O.M. Fiss, "Against Settlement" (1984) 93 Yale LJ 1073; and D. Luban, "Settlements and the Erosion of the Public Realm" (1995) 83 Geo LJ 2619.

25 See T. Church, "Examining Local Legal Culture" (1985) 3 American Bar Foundation Research Journal 449; and M. Heumann, *Plea Bargaining: The Experience of Prosecutors, Judges and Defense Attorneys* (Chicago: University of Chicago Press, 1978).

26 Church, ibid. at 506.

27 For example, British Columbia undertook an extensive examination of potential rule simplifications in 2006 (Civil Justice Reform Working Group, *Effective and Affordable Civil Justice: Report of the Civil Justice Reform Working Group to the Justice Review Task Force* (BC Justice Review Task Force, 2006), online: BC Ministry of Attorney General <http://www.ag.gov.bc.ca/public/bcjusticereview/cjrwg_report_11_06.pdf>. The report was "the result of two years' work, including consultation with the legal profession, review of 35 written submissions, a conference on restructuring justice, a Supreme Court file review and extensive analysis of research in Canada, the United Kingdom, the United States and Australia." The proposals were vigorously opposed by the Trial Lawyers Association of British Columbia, who campaigned against virtually all the recommendations and set up a dedicated website to oppose them (http://www.protectingjusticeforbc.org).

28 See, for example, P.V. Niemeyer, "Is Now the Time for Simplified Rules of Civil Procedure?" (2013) 46 U Mich JL Ref 673 at 678–79, online: University of Michigan <http://

repository.law.umich.edu/mjlr/vol46/iss2/15> (describing efforts over thirty years to limit the scope of discovery processes in US federal cases).

29 Unpublished data from the Culture Change Project.

30 The Trial Lawyers Association of British Columbia drew extensively on this image of the system as inherently fair and balanced in its opposition to the BC reforms (see note 27 above). For example, it described the existing BC civil process as "a system that is the envy of the world for its commitment to individual rights, the rule of law and impartial justice" (from its June 14, 2007, letter to the Civil Justice Reform Task Force).

31 Unpublished data from the Culture Change Project.

32 A. Sarat and W. Felstiner, "Law and Strategy in the Divorce Lawyer's Office" in R. Abel, ed., *Lawyers: A Critical Reader* (New York: New Press, 1997) 44.

33 Ibid. at 48.

34 Ibid.

35 Unpublished data from the Culture Change Project.

36 See, for example, T. Tyler, "Achieving Peaceful Regime Change: Why Do Losers Consent?" (2013), online: Yale Law School <https://www.law.yale.edu/system/files/documents/pdf/sela/SELA13_Tyler_CV_Eng_20130321.pdf>.

37 J. Thibaut, L. Walker, S. LaTour, and S. Houlden, "Procedural Justice as Fairness" (1974) 26 Stan L Rev 1271; and J. Thibaut and L. Walker, *Procedural Justice: A Psychological Analysis* (New York: Erlbaum, 1975).

38 Similar results are reported from a study asking citizens for their appraisal of (1) the fairness of government policy, and (2) their personal benefits (specifically regarding taxation and benefits). See T. Tyler, K. Rasinski, and K. McGraw, "The Influence of Perceived Injustices on Support for Political Authority" (1985) 15 Journal of Applied Psychology 700. It has been further suggested that preference for procedural fairness, as well as the identification of the factors that make up procedural fairness, is fairly consistent across a range of cultural contexts. See, for example, K. Leung and E.A. Lind, "Procedural Justice and Culture: Effects of Culture, Gender and Investigator Status on Procedural Preferences" (1986) 50 Journal of Personality and Social Psychology 1134; E.A. Lind, Y.J. Huo, and T. Tyler, "And Justice for All: Ethnicity, Gender and Preferences for Dispute Resolution Procedures" (1994) 18 Law and Human Behavior 269; and E.A. Lind and T. Tyler, *The Social Psychology of Procedural Justice* (London: Plenum Press, 1998) at 107–11.

39 T. Tyler, "The Role of Perceived Injustice in Defendants' Evaluations of their Courtroom Experience" (1984) 18 Law & Soc'y Rev 51.

40 Macfarlane, *National SRL Study,* see note 21 above at 10.

41 For example, Law Society of Upper Canada Professional Code of Conduct, Rule 6(03)3: "[A lawyer] shall not take advantage of or act without fair warning upon slips, irregularities, or mistakes on the part of other licensees not going to the merits or involving the sacrifice of a client's rights."

42 Macfarlane, "Culture Change?" see note 13 above at 22.

43 See T. Tyler, "Conditions Leading to Value Expressive Judgments of Procedural Justice: A Test of Four Models" (1987) 52 Journal of Personality and Social Psychology 333. See generally Lind and Tyler, *The Social Psychology of Procedural Justice,* see note 38 above at 104–6.

44 See Thibaut et al., "Procedural Justice as Fairness," see note 37 above; and G.S. Leventhal, "What Should Be Done with Equity Theory? New Approaches to the Study of Fairness in Social Relationships" in K. Gergen, M. Greenberg, and R. Willis, eds., *Social Exchange: Advances in Theory and Research* (New York: Plenum, 1980) at 27–55.

45 J. Resnik, A. Lind, R. MacCoun, P. Ebener, and W. Felstiner, "In the Eye of the Beholder: Tort Litigants' Evaluations of Their Experiences in the Civil Justice System" (1990) 24 Law & Soc'y Rev 981 (studying tort litigants).

46 Macfarlane, *National SRL Study,* see note 21 at 46–48.

47 See, for example, H. Genn, *Paths to Justice: What People Do and Think about Going to Law* (Oxford: Hart Publishing, 1999) at 228–30.

48 Macfarlane, *National SRL Study,* see note 21 above at 110–11.

49 J. Macfarlane, B. Mayer, and M. Keet, *An Evaluation of the Saskatchewan Access Facilitation/High Conflict Custody and Access Mediation Projects: Final Report* (Saskatchewan Ministry of Justice, January 2010) at 19.

50 N. Welsh, "Disputants Decision Control in Court-Connected Mediation: A Hollow Promise without Procedural Justice" (2002) 1 J Disp Resol 179 at 179–80. See also N. Welsh, "Making Deals in Court-Connected Mediation: What's Justice Got to Do with It?" (2001) 79 Wash ULQ 788.

51 See A. Lind, "Procedural Justice, Disputing and Reactions to Legal Authorities" in A. Sarat, ed., *Everyday Practices and Trouble Cases* (Evanston, IL: Northwestern University Press, 1998) 177, especially the discussion of litigants' reactions to settlement conferences at 188.

52 Ibid.

53 Macfarlane, *National SRL Study,* see note 21 above at 110.

54 Unpublished data from the Culture Change Project.

55 D. Rosenthal, *Lawyer and Client: Who's in Charge?* (New York: Russell Sage Foundation, 1974). See also C. Hosticka, "We Don't Care about What Happened, We Only Care about What Is Going to Happen: Lawyer-Client Negotiations of Reality" (1979) 26 Social Problems 559 (examining relationships between legal clinic lawyers and their clients). However, see the doubts cast on this unproblematized view of power by W. Felstiner and A. Sarat in "Enactments of Power: Negotiating Reality and Responsibility in Lawyer/Client Interactions" (1992) 77 Cornell L Rev 1447.

56 Macfarlane, *National SRL Study,* see note 21 above at 46.

57 See R. Gilson and R. Mnookin, "Disputing through Agents: Cooperation and Conflict between Lawyers in Litigation" (1994) 94 Colum L Rev 509.

58 M. Galanter, "Why the 'Haves' Come Out Ahead: Speculations on the Limits of Legal Change" (1974) 9 Law & Soc'y Rev 95.

59 See D. Schon, *The Reflective Practitioner* (San Francisco: Jossey-Bass, 1983). See the further discussion in J. Macfarlane, "Look before You Leap: Knowledge and Learning in Legal Skills Education" (1992) 19 JL & Soc'y 291.

60 See L. Riskin, "Mediation and Lawyers" (1982) 43 Ohio St LJ 29 at 43–48. This is what Anthony Kronman describes as "thin advice." A. Kronman, *The Lost Lawyer: Failing Ideals of the Legal Profession* (Cambridge, MA: Harvard University Press, 1993).

61 J. Macfarlane, *The Emerging Phenomenon of Collaborative Family Law (CFL): A Qualitative Study of CFL Cases* (Ottawa: Department of Justice, 2005) at 51–55, online: Department of Justice Canada <http://www.justice.gc.ca/eng/rp-pr/fl-lf/famil/2005_1/pdf/2005_1.pdf>.

62 *The CanLII Primer: Legal Research Principles and CanLII Navigation for Self-Represented Litigants* (Windsor, ON: Windsor Law, 2015), online: National Self-Represented Litigants Project <https://representingyourselfcanada.files.wordpress.com/2015/03/nsrlp-canlii-primer-v11.pdf>.

63 "We're just salesmen, in our case, brain salesmen" (Kidder, "The End of the Road," see note 3 above); unpublished data from the Culture Change Project.

64 Kronman, *The Lost Lawyer,* see note 60 above at 121–28.

65 Riskin, "Mediation and Lawyers," see note 60 above at 43–48.

66 W. Simon, "The Ideology of Advocacy: Procedural Justice and Professional Ethics" (1978) 29 Wis L Rev. 29 at 96.

67 Macfarlane, *National SRL Study,* see note 21 above at 46.

68 The concept of legal coaching, where lawyers assist or "coach" clients to undertake some tasks themselves, is set out in J. Macfarlane, "Seriously? Lawyers Coaching SRLs in Self-Advocacy?" (December 14, 2013), online: National Self-Represented Litigants Project <https://representingyourselfcanada.com/2013/12/14/seriously-lawyers-coaching-srls-in-self-advocacy/>, and "Providing Legal Services in a Coaching Model: The What, Why and How" (December 18, 2013), online: National Self-Represented Litigants Project <https://representingyourselfcanada.com/2013/12/18/providing-legal-services-in-a-coaching-model-the-what-why-and-how/>. See also the Legal Coaching Project described <http://representingyourselfcanada.com/legal-coaching/>.

69 Macfarlane, *The Emerging Phenomenon of Collaborative Family Law,* see note 61 above at 62 and 79.

70 R. Gellman, "Disintermediation and the Internet" (1996) 13 Government Information Quarterly 1.

71 R. Susskind, *Tomorrow's Lawyers: An Introduction to Your Future* (Oxford: Oxford University Press, 2013) at 15–19.

72 K.B. Gerdy, "Clients, Empathy and Compassion: Introducing First-Year Students to the "Heart" of Lawyering" (2008) 87 Neb L Rev 1 at 8–11; L.J. Shapiro, *Public Perceptions of Lawyers: Consumer Research Findings* (Chicago: ABA Litigation Section, 2002) at 4.

73 Macfarlane, *National SRL Study,* see note 21 above at 46.

74 L. Mather and B. Yngvesson, "Language, Audience, and the Transformation of Disputes" (1980–81) 15 Law and Soc'y Rev 775. On further aspects of this problem, see

J. Macfarlane, "The Mediation Alternative" in J. Macfarlane, ed., *Rethinking Disputes: The Mediation Alternative* (Toronto: Emond Montgomery and Cavendish Publishing, 1997) 1 at 4–7.

75   Macfarlane, *National SRL Study,* see note 21 above at 47.

76   J. Macfarlane, "The Empathy Deficit: Why So Many Lawyers Believe Their Job Is to Be a Jerk" (February 10, 2015), online: National Self-Represented Litigants Project <https://representingyourselfcanada.com/2015/02/10/the-empathy-deficit-why-so-many-lawyers-think-their-job-is-to-be-a-jerk/>.

77   Gerdy, "Clients, Empathy and Compassion," see note 72 above at 8; Gary A. Hengstler, "Vox Populi: The Public Perception of Lawyers: ABA Poll" (1993) 79 ABA J 60 at 60. The study was conducted by Peter D. Hart Research Associates Inc.

78   D. Linder and N. Levit, *The Good Lawyer: Seeking Quality in the Practice of Law* (Oxford: Oxford University Press, 2015) at 7.

79   See, for example, "Top Complaint against Lawyers Is Rude or Uncivil Behaviour," *Law Society of British Columbia Benchers' Bulletin* (Summer 2011); D. Pinnington, "The Biggest Malpractice Claim Risks," *LawPRO Magazine* (Summer 2008), online: practicePRO <http://www.practicepro.ca/LawPROmag/Pinnington_Biggest_Malpractice.pdf.>

80   J. Heinz, E. Laumann, C. Cappell, and M. Schaalman, "Diversity, Representation and Leadership in an Urban Bar: A First Report on a Survey of the Chicago Bar" (2006) 1:3 Law & Soc Inquiry 717.

81   R. Nelson, "Ideology, Practice and Professional Autonomy: Social Values and Client Relationships in the Large Law Firm," in Abel, ed., *Lawyers,* see note 32 above at 73. Robert Nelson and Rebecca Sandefur's later study bears out this phenomenon, tying it directly to organizational structure (lawyers working in large corporate firms and government departments) as well as to client groups. See R. Nelson and R. Sandefur, "From Professional Dominance to Organisational Dominance" in W. Felstiner, ed., *Reorganisation and Resistance: Legal Professions Confront a Changing World* (London: Hart Publishing, 2006) 313.

82   Arguably inconsistent with absorbing and practising an ethos of ethical professionalism. See Schon, *The Reflective Practitioner,* note 59 above, and the further discussion in Chapter 8.

83   What David Luban describes as the principle of moral non-accountability. See D. Luban, "The Adversary System Excuse" in D. Luban, ed., *The Good Lawyer: Lawyers' Roles and Lawyers' Ethics* (Totowa, NJ: Rowman and Allenheld, 1983) 83; see also M. Schwartz, "The Professionalism and Accountability of Lawyers" (1978) 66 Cal L Rev 669. See also the further discussion in Chapter 5 of this book.

84   Macfarlane, "The Mediation Alternative," see note 74 at 17–19.

85   Unpublished data from the Collaborative Lawyering Research Project.

86   Macfarlane, "The Mediation Alternative," see note 74 above at 18.

87   There are growing signs of an effort to take the highly theoretical ideas developed by therapeutic jurisprudence and turn them into a practical theory of lawyering (and

judging). See, for example, D. Stolle, D. Wexler, B. Winick, and E. Dauer, "Integrating Preventive Law and Therapeutic Jurisprudence: A Law and Psychology-Based Approach to Lawyering" (1997) 34 Cal WL Rev 15; and B. Winick, "Therapeutic Jurisprudence and the Role of Counsel in Litigation" (2000-01) 37:1 Cal WL Rev. 105. See also the work of Cutting Edge Law <http://www.cuttingedgelaw.com> and the Integrative Law Institute <http://integrativelawinstitute.org> in promoting an integrative practice of law that integrates personal values into professional work. See also the discussion in Chapter 9.

88 See, for example, E. Martin, P. Seligman, Paul R. Verkuil, and Terry H. Kang, "Why Lawyers Are Unhappy" (2005) 10 Deakin L Rev 49 at 50; and John P. Heinz, Kathleen E. Hull, and Ava A. Harter, "Lawyers and Their Discontents: Findings from a Survey of the Chicago Bar" (1999) 74 Ind LJ 735. This article cites statistics from a number of surveys, each of which reveals that a majority of the lawyers questioned would not, if they could start over again, join the legal profession.

89 See P. Schiltz, "On Being a Happy, Healthy and Ethical Member of an Unhappy, Unhealthy and Unethical Profession" (1991) 52 Vand L Rev 871 esp. at 874–87. Schiltz cites a number of studies suggesting that lawyers suffer from low career satisfaction. Note, however, that others contest just how widespread this discontent is. See Nelson and Sandefur, "From Professional Dominance to Organisational Dominance," note 81 above at 336.

90 See, for example, F. Zacharias, "Reconciling Professionalism and Client Interests" (1995) 36 Wm & Mary L Rev 1303; Kronman, *The Lost Lawyer*, see note 60 above; and A. Kronman, "Professionalism" (1999) 2 JISLE 89; Gerdy, "Clients, Empathy and Compassion," see note 72 above at 33.

Chapter 4: Legal Negotiations

1 For more on the relationship between beliefs and behavioural norms, see T. Parsons, *The Structure of Social Action* (New York: McGraw Hill, 1937). Parsons's original view of the universality of values and norms has been substantially refined by the literature of social constructivism and interpretivism; for example, see E. Durkheim, *Suicide: A Study in Religion* (London: Routledge and Kegan Paul, 1970; first published in French), and H. Garfinkel, *Studies in Ethno-Methodology* (Englewood Cliffs, NJ: Prentice Hall, 1967), to recognize cultural and other contextual factors; and D.M. Schneider, "Notes toward a Theory of Culture" in K.H. Basso and H.A. Selby, eds., *Meaning in Anthropology* (Albuquerque: University of New Mexico Press, 1976) 197 at 203. See also the discussion in Chapter 2.

2 M. Galanter, "The Vanishing Trial: An Examination of Trials and Related Matters in Federal and State Courts" (2004) 1 Journal of Empirical Legal Studies 459.

3 J. Macfarlane, "Culture Change? A Tale of Two Cities and Mandatory Court-Connected Mediation" (2002) 2 J Disp Resol 241 at 292.

4 Ibid. at 291.

5   M. Heumann and J. Hyman, "Negotiation Methods and Litigation Settlement Methods in New Jersey: You Can't Always Get What You Want" (1997) 12 Ohio St J Disp Resol 253.

6   See, for example, C. Argyris and D.A. Schon, *Theory in Practice: Increasing Professional Effectiveness* (San Francisco: Jossey-Bass, 1974); D.A. Schon, *Educating the Reflective Practitioner* (San Francisco: Jossey-Bass, 1987); C. Argyris, *Knowledge for Action: A Guide to Overcoming Barriers to Organizational Change* (San Francisco: Jossey-Bass, 1993).

7   H. Genn, *Paths to Justice: What People Do and Think about Going to Law* (Oxford: Hart Publishing, 1999).

8   J. Baldwin and M. McConville, *Negotiated Justice* (London: Martin Robertson, 1977).

9   See L. Mather, C. McEwen, and R. Maiman, *Divorce Lawyers at Work: Varieties of Professionalism in Practice* (Oxford: Oxford University Press, 2001) at 113–14.

10 See A. Schneider and N. Mills, "What Family Lawyers Are Really Doing When They Negotiate" (2006) 44 Fam Ct Rev 612 at 616–19. Schneider and Mills explain their finding by pointing to the emotional and vengeful context of family law.

11 See, for example, G. Goodpaster, "Lawsuits as Negotiations" (1992) 8 Negotiation Journal 221; H. Kritzer, *Let's Make a Deal: Understanding the Negotiation Process in Ordinary Litigation* (Madison: University of Wisconsin Press, 1991); and C. Honeyman and A. Schneider, *The Negotiator's Fieldbook* (Chicago: American Bar Association, 2006).

12 Unpublished data from the Collaborative Lawyering Research Project.

13 See, for example, C. Menkel-Meadow, "Lawyer Negotiations: Theories and Realities – What We Learn from Mediation" (1993) 56 Mod L Rev 361; S.H. Clarke, E.D. Ellen, and K. McCormick, *Court-Ordered Civil Case Mediation in North Carolina: Court Efficiency and Litigant Satisfaction* (Chapel Hill: Institute of Government, University of North Carolina, 1995); and Genn, *Paths to Justice,* see note 7 above.

14 Seeking a "good" rather than a "best possible" outcome is, John Lande argues, common for litigators. His "ordinary legal negotiation" model suggests that much legal negotiation is neither intentionally positional nor planned explicitly around client interests – in other words, it is unconscious and habitual. See J. Lande, "Teaching Students to Negotiate Like a Lawyer" (2012) 39 Wash UJL & Pol'y 109 at 120.

15 Ibid.

16 See B. Mayer, *The Dynamics of Conflict Resolution: A Practitioner's Guide* (San Francisco: Jossey-Bass, 2000) at 151–55.

17 "Pareto optimality" refers to the point at which all possible benefits to each side have been examined, and no additional benefit can be added at the expense of one side over the other. Ibid. at 158–60.

18 J. Macfarlane, *The Emerging Phenomenon of Collaborative Family Law (CFL): A Qualitative Study of CFL Cases* (Ottawa: Department of Justice, 2005) at 43, online: Department of Justice Canada <http://www.justice.gc.ca/eng/rp-pr/fl-lf/famil/2005_1/pdf/2005_1.pdf>.

19 Unpublished data from the Culture Change Project.

20 A.K. Schneider, "Shattering Negotiation Myths: Empirical Evidence on the Effectiveness of Negotiation Style" (2002) 7 Harv Negot L Rev 143 at 172–75 and 180–84.

21 Macfarlane, *The Emerging Phenomenon of Collaborative Family Law,* see note 18 above at 30.

22 Unpublished data from the Collaborative Lawyering Research Project.

23 Unpublished data from the Culture Change Project.

24 Macfarlane, "Culture Change?" see note 3 above at 306.

25 Ibid.

26 N.A. Welsh, "The Reputational Advantages of Demonstrating Trustworthiness: Using the Reputation Index with Law Students" (2012) 28 Negotiation Journal 117 at 126–39.

27 Macfarlane, "Culture Change?" see note 3 above at 302.

28 D. Litowitz, *The Destruction of Young Lawyers: Beyond One L* (Akron, OH: University of Akron Press, 2005).

29 J. Macfarlane, "The Empathy Deficit: Why So Many Lawyers Believe Their Job Is to Be a Jerk" (February 10, 2015), online: National Self-Represented Litigants Project <https://representingyourselfcanada.com/2015/02/10/the-empathy-deficit-why-so-many-lawyers-think-their-job-is-to-be-a-jerk/>.

30 Ibid. Gerald Williams's original survey is reported in G. Williams, *Legal Negotiation and Settlement* (St. Paul, MN: West Publishing, 1983). The qualities associated with adversarial bargaining in Schneider's study include some fairly extreme characteristics, such as arrogance, manipulation, and evasion. See A. Schneider, "Shattering Negotiation Myths," note 20 above, Appendix A at 210.

31 Schneider, ibid. at 146.

32 R. Axelrod, *The Evolution of Co-operation* (New York: Basic Books, 1984).

33 See R. Gilson and R. Mnookin, "Disputing through Agents: Cooperation and Conflict between Lawyers in Litigation" (1994) 94 Colum L Rev 509.

34 This can be contrasted with information exchange as a means of sharing "power with" the other side to achieve a good settlement, rather than one side's exclusive access to knowledge as an assertion of "power over" the other side. G. Chornenki, "Mediating Commercial Disputes: Exchanging 'Power Over' for 'Power With'" in J. Macfarlane, ed., *Rethinking Disputes: The Mediation Alternative* (Toronto: Emond Montgomery and Cavendish Publishing, 1997) 159 esp. at 162–65.

35 W. Simon, *The Practice of Justice* (Cambridge, MA: Harvard University Press, 1998) at 64–65; and see J. Macfarlane, "The New Advocacy: Implications for Legal Education and Teaching Practice" in R. Burridge et al., ed., *Effective Teaching and Learning in Law* (London: Kogan Page, 2002) 164 at 173–77; and J. Macfarlane, "What Does the Changing Culture of Legal Practice Mean for Legal Education?" (2001) 20 Windsor YB Access Just 191 at 200–5.

36 Genn, *Paths to Justice,* see note 7 above.

37 See, for example, Heumann and Hyman, "Negotiation Methods and Litigation Settlement Methods in New Jersey," note 5 above; and C. Menkel-Meadow, "The

Transformation of Disputes by Lawyers: What the Dispute Paradigm Does and Does Not Tell Us" (1985) 2 Mo J Disp Resol 25.

38 Galanter, "The Vanishing Trial," see note 2 above.

39 For example, T. Eisenberg and C. Lanvers, "What Is the Settlement Rate and Why Should We Care?" (Cornell Law Faculty Publications, Paper 203, 2009).

40 To give just one example: there were a total of just seventeen civil trials in the Saskatchewan Court of Queen's Bench in 2015.

41 Galanter, "The Vanishing Trial," see note 2 above.

42 G.K. Hadfield, "Where Have All the Trials Gone? Settlements, Nontrial Adjudications, and Statistical Artifacts in the Changing Disposition of Federal Civil Cases" (2004) 1 Journal of Empirical Legal Studies 705 at 706.

43 See Kritzer, *Let's Make a Deal,* note 11 above at 130–34; H. Genn, *Hard Bargaining* (Oxford: Oxford University Press, 1987) at 30–36.

44 Kritzer, ibid. at 130–34.

45 See the classic description in S.H. Clarke, E.D. Ellen, and K. McCormick, *Court-Ordered Civil Case Mediation in North Carolina: Court Efficiency and Litigant Satisfaction* (Chapel Hill: Institute of Government, University of North Carolina, 1995).

46 R. Susskind, *The End of Lawyers? Rethinking the Nature of Legal Services* (Oxford: Oxford University Press, 2010).

47 Unpublished data from the Culture Change Project.

48 J. Macfarlane, *Analysis Project of the Federal Experience with the Use of Mediation and Other Dispute Resolution Processes* (Ottawa: Department of Justice Canada, 2009) at 60.

49 Ibid.

50 Ibid. at 43.

51 Ibid. at 39.

52 Kritzer, *Let's Make a Deal,* see note 11 above at 130–34; and Genn, *Paths to Justice,* see note 7 above at 30–36.

53 Unpublished data from the Culture Change Project.

54 Macfarlane, "Culture Change?" see note 3 above.

55 For example, R.L. Wissler, "Court-Connected Mediation in General Civil Cases: What We Know from Empirical Research" (2002) 17 Ohio St J Disp Resol 641 at 650–51.

56 A similar conclusion is observed in J.L. Barkai and G. Kassebaum, "Using Court-Annexed Arbitration to Reduce Litigant Costs and to Increase the Pace of Litigation" (1989) 16 Pepp L Rev 43.

57 Macfarlane, "Culture Change?" see note 3 above at 292.

58 Ibid. at 246.

59 "Day's Lawsuit Cost Taxpayers Close to $800,000," CBC News (January 17, 2001), online: <http://www.cbc.ca/news/canada/critics-demand-judicial-review-of-day-settlement-1.275295>.

60 See R.L. Kiser, M.A. Asher, and B.B. McShane, "Let's Not Make a Deal: An Empirical Study of Decision Making in Unsuccessful Settlement Negotiations" (2008) 5 Journal

of Empirical Legal Studies 551, online: <http://www.blakemcshane.com/Papers/jels_settlement.pdf>.

61 See also S. Gross and K. Syverud, "Getting to No: A Study of Settlement Negotiations and the Selection of Cases for Trial" (1991) 90 Mich L Rev 319.

62 J. Macfarlane and M. Keet, "Civil Justice Reform and Mandatory Civil Mediation in Saskatchewan: Lessons from a Maturing Program" (2004) 42 Alta L Rev 677 at 686.

63 The original Rule 24.1 (January 1999) required mediation within 90 days of the filing of the first statement of defence. A revision (Rule 78, from May 2005), which applied case management to all mandatory mediation cases, bowing to pressure from the bar, allowed mediation to take place whenever counsel believed that "mediation is most likely to be effective." Further revision of Rule 24.1 (effective January 1, 2010) now requires mediation to take place within 180 days of the filing of the statement of defence.

64 J. Macfarlane, *Court-Based Mediation in Civil Cases: An Evaluation of the Toronto General Division ADR Centre* (Ottawa: Queen's Printer, 1995).

65 See R. Hann, C. Barr, and Associates, *Evaluation of the Ontario Mandatory Mediation Program (Rule 24.1) Final Report: The First 23 Months* (Ottawa: Queen's Printer, 2001).

66 See, for example, Macfarlane and Keet, "Civil Justice Reform," see note 62 above at 688–90.

67 In Saskatchewan, experience led to growing calls for flexibility in timing but a greater openness to early mediation. For a description of the stages of experience with a maturing mandatory mediation program, see Macfarlane and Keet, ibid. at 700–2.

68 Ibid. at 291–92; and B. McAdoo, "A Report to the Minnesota Supreme Court: The Impact of Rule 114 on Civil Litigation Practice in Minnesota" (2002) 25 Hamline L Rev 401 at 432–37.

69 *General Rules of Practice* (1994), Rule 114, online: Minnesota Office of the Revisor of Statutes <https://www.revisor.mn.gov/court_rules/rule.php?type=gp&id=114>.

70 See McAdoo, "A Report to the Minnesota Supreme Court," note 68 above at 35–37.

71 Macfarlane, *Analysis Project,* see note 48 above at 42.

72 Ibid. at 40.

73 Ibid. at 43.

74 Macfarlane, "Culture Change?" see note 3 above at 303.

75 W. Felstiner and A. Sarat, "Enactments of Power: Negotiating Reality and Responsibility in Lawyer/Client Interactions" (1992) 77 Cornell L Rev 1447.

76 D. Binder and S. Price, *Legal Interviewing and Counseling: A Client-Centered Approach* (St. Paul, MN: West Publishing, 1977).

77 Gilson and Mnookin, "Disputing through Agents," see note 33 above at 537–41.

78 J.Z. Rubin and F.E.A. Sander, "When Should We Use Agents? Direct versus Representative Negotiation" (1998) 4 Negotiation Journal 395 at 398.

79 Although some argue that we still have a long way to go before clients routinely participate fully and actively. See N. Welsh, "The Thinning Vision of Self-Determination

in Court-Connected Mediation: The Inevitable Price of Institutionalization?" (2001) 6 Harv Negot L Rev 101. For some alternative perspectives and for a deeper examination of this topic, see the discussion in Chapter 6.

80 Macfarlane, "Culture Change?" see note 3 above at 268–70.

81 Ibid. at 269.

82 Ibid. at 270.

83 Judges themselves are identifying the development of new skills in order to manage these fora as a new priority for judicial education. See B. McAdoo, "All Rise, the Court Is in Session: What Judges Say about Court-Connected Mediation" (2007) 22 Ohio St J Disp Resol 377 esp. at 397–402; and see the discussion of the "New Judge" in Chapter 9.

84 J. Macfarlane, "ADR and the Courts: Renewing Our Commitment to Innovation" (2012) 95 Marq L Rev 927 at 937.

85 J. Macfarlane, *The National Self-Represented Litigants Project: Identifying and Meeting the Needs of Self-Represented Litigants: Final Report* (May 2013) at 53, online: <https://representingyourselfcanada.files.wordpress.com/2014/02/reportm15-2.pdf> [hereafter *National SRL Study*].

86 Ibid. at 122.

87 Ibid. at 91.

88 Ibid. at 92. There is emerging case law that shows some high – even punitive – levels of costs being imposed on SRLs; see for example *Pintea v Johns* (2016) ABCA 99 and *Dorey v Dorey* (2016) ONSC 2746.

89 For example, in one study, 7 percent of lawyers reported that the most important reason for family litigants to have no lawyer is that they think they can do as good a job as a lawyer. In addition, the same study reported that 19 percent of lawyers believe that SRLs desire to directly confront one's former partner in court. J.-P. Boyd, "The Self-Represented Litigant's Bill of Rights ... and Responsibilities" (September 30, 2012), online: JP Boyd on Family Law <http://bcfamilylawresource.blogspot.ca/2012/09/the-self-represented-litigants-bill-of.html>.

90 Macfarlane, *National SRL Study*, see note 85 above at 40.

91 Law Society of Upper Canada, "Dealing with Self-Represented Litigants" (n.d.), online: Law Society of Upper Canada <http://www.lsuc.on.ca/with.aspx?id=2147499412>.

92 For example, counsel is obliged to treat an SRL with respect and courtesy, and avoid "sharp practices." See the further discussion in Chapter 8.

93 See F.S. Mosten, *Unbundling Legal Services: A Guide to Delivering Legal Services a la Carte* (Chicago: American Bar Association, 2000); and F.S. Mosten, "Unbundling Legal Services Today – and Predictions for the Future" (2013) 35 Family Advocate 14.

94 See, for example, J.L. Barkai and G. Kassebaum, "Using Court-Annexed Arbitration to Reduce Litigant Costs and to Increase the Pace of Litigation" (1989) 16 Pepp L Rev 43 at 47; and Weinstock, Osborne and Company Students at Law, "Let's Play Twister, Let's Play Risk, Yeah Yeah Yeah: An Analysis of Discovery Abuse in Civil Litigation"

(March 2001) Weinstock, Osborne and Company, online: <http://www.cfcj-fcjc.org/sites/default/files/docs/hosted/17425-twister.pdf>.

95 Macfarlane, "Culture Change?" see note 3 above at 282.

96 Ibid.

97 Ibid. at 311.

98 R. Fisher, "What about Negotiation as a Specialty?" (1983) 69 ABA J 1220.

99 W. Coyne, "The Case for Settlement Counsel" (1999) 14 Ohio St J Disp Resol 367.

100 For a description of the work that would need to be done in order to create a broader alternative dispute resolution culture within a law firm, see the materials produced by the International Institute for Conflict Prevention and Resolution (CPR) at http://www.cpradr.org.

101 The CPR offers members a corporate pledge that undertakes to "seriously explore negotiation, mediation or other ADR processes in conflicts arising with other signatories before pursuing full-scale litigation." The CPR claims 4,000 corporate signatories and 1,500 law firm signatories (http://www.cpradr.org). A similar scheme exists in the United Kingdom, sponsored by the Centre for Effective Dispute Resolution <http://www.cedr.co.uk>, which also provides model alternative dispute resolution contract clauses drafted by lawyers from leading commercial law firms.

102 Axelrod, *The Evolution of Co-operation*, see note 32 above.

103 Some lawyers who practise cooperative law also practise "collaborative law" when their clients are willing to sign a formal retainer agreement to this effect. For a description of the rationale and possible mechanisms of cooperative lawyering, see J. Lande, "Negotiation: Evading Evasion – How Protocols Can Improve Civil Case Results" (2003) 21 Alternatives to the High Cost of Litigation 149. See also J. Lande, *Lawyering with Planned Early Negotiation: How You Can Get Good Results for Clients and Make Money* (Chicago: American Bar Association Dispute Resolution Section, 2011).

104 The so-called disqualification clause.

105 T. Sholar, "Collaborative Law: A Method for the Madness" (1993) 23 Memphis State University Law Review 667.

106 The need for a disqualification agreement is still hotly debated. See, for example, Lande, "Negotiation," note 103 above at 149.

107 See, for example, the discussion in J. Lande and G. Herman, "Fitting the Forum to the Family Fuss: Choosing Mediation, Collaborative Law, or Cooperative Law for Negotiating Divorce Cases" (2004) 42 Fam Ct Rev 280.

108 J. Macfarlane, "Experiences of Collaborative Law: Preliminary Results from the Collaborative Lawyering Research Project" (2004) 1 J Disp Resol 179.

109 In their study of divorce lawyers, Mather, McEwen, and Maiman describe the communities of practice – geographic, client-based, and substantive – that anchor individual divorce lawyers to a set of informal norms and etiquettes. See Mather, McEwen, and Maiman, *Divorce Lawyers at Work*, note 9 above at 41–48.

110 Macfarlane, "Experiences of Collaborative Law," see note 108 above at 198.

111 R. Abel, *American Lawyers* (Oxford: Oxford University Press, 1989).

112 Macfarlane, "Culture Change?" see note 3 above at 292.

113 The relationship between rights- and interests-based approaches to the resolution of conflicts is considered further in Chapter 7, which analyzes the impact of the shadow of the law (rights-based evaluation) on consensus building. For an excellent discussion of the relationship between rights and interests and distributive and integrative bargaining, see Mayer, *The Dynamics of Conflict Resolution,* note 16 above at 145–60.

114 Unpublished data from the Collaborative Lawyering Research Project.

115 For a detailed discussion of this issue, see J. Macfarlane, "Will Changing the Process Change the Outcome? The Relationship between Procedural and Systemic Change" (2005) 65 La L Rev 1487.

116 See, for example, R.L. Wissler, "When Does Familiarity Breed Content? A Study of the Role of Different Forms of ADR Education and Experience in Attorneys' ADR Recommendations" (2002) 2 Pepp Disp Resol LJ 199; J. Lande, "Getting the Faith: Why Business Lawyers and Executives Believe in Mediation" (2000) 5 Harv Negot L Rev 137 at 199; and M.L. Medley and J.A. Schellenberg, "Attitudes of Attorneys toward Mediation" (1994) 12 Mediation Quarterly 185 at 195–96.

Chapter 5: The New Advocacy

1 All seen in advertisements for lawyers on billboards on I-94 in Michigan.

2 The slogan for a lawyer advertising in Michigan.

3 J. Macfarlane, *The National Self-Represented Litigants Project: Identifying and Meeting the Needs of Self-Represented Litigants: Final Report* (May 2013) at 45, online: <https://representingyourselfcanada.files.wordpress.com/2014/02/reportm15-2.pdf> [hereafter *National SRL Study*].

4 B. Mayer, *Beyond Neutrality* (San Francisco: Jossey-Bass, 2004).

5 J. Coleman, *Community Conflict* (New York: Free Press, 1957); J. Laue, "Third Men in New Arenas of Conflict: An Assessment of the Work of the National Center for Dispute Settlement" (1970) [unpublished paper on file with the author]; and J. Laue and G. Cormick, "The Ethics of Intervention in Community Disputes" in G. Bermant, H. Kelman, and D. Warwick, eds., *The Ethics of Social Intervention* (Washington, DC: Halstead Press, 1978) at 205–32.

6 See, for example, the work of Donald Landon on country lawyers. D. Landon, *Country Lawyers: The Impact of Context on Professional Practice* (New York: Praeger, 1990).

7 See, for example, A. Kronman, *The Lost Lawyer: Failing Ideals of the Legal Profession* (Cambridge, MA: Harvard University Press, 1993); W.H. Simon, "The Ideology of Advocacy: Procedural Justice and Professional Ethics" (1978) 29 Wis L Rev 34; and W. Simon, *The Practice of Justice* (Cambridge, MA: Harvard University Press, 1998).

8 See the American Bar Association's *ABA Model Code of Professional Responsibility* (1969), Canon 7, online: American Bar Association <http://www.abanet.org/cpr/mrpc/mcpr.pdf>, and the "Model Rules of Professional Conduct: Preamble & Scope"

(1983; revised 2002), online: American Bar Association <http://www.americanbar.org/groups/professional_responsibility/publications/model_rules_of_professional_conduct/model_rules_of_professional_conduct_preamble_scope.html>.

9 Simon, *The Practice of Justice,* see note 7 above at 8. Simon also describes the "public interest view," which measures appropriate advocacy according to its contribution to the public good, and the "contextual view," which assumes that each situation must be judged on its special circumstances rather than assuming any one dominant approach.

10 See also Kronman, *The Lost Lawyer,* note 7 above at 146–48. On the problem of "cognitive dissonance," see Simon, "The Ideology of Advocacy," note 7 above at 68–69.

11 See Landon, *Country Lawyers,* note 6 above.

12 Ibid.

13 Unpublished data from the Culture Change Project.

14 In practice, of course, the zealous advocacy principle and the adversarial spirit that is associated with it demand this type of unquestioning commitment to all clients, not only to those who appear "deserving."

15 J. Macfarlane, "Experiences of Collaborative Law: Preliminary Results from the Collaborative Lawyering Research Project" (2004) 1 J Disp Resol 179 at 203.

16 D. Luban, "The Fundamental Dilemma of Lawyering: The Ethics of the Hired Gun" in R. Abel, *Lawyers: A Critical Reader* (New York: New Press, 1997) 3 at 6.

17 Unpublished data from the Culture Change Project. Instead, those who tried to articulate some type of justice concept substituted justice-as-process for substantive justice. See the further discussion in Chapter 3.

18 Lord Henry Brougham, quoted in Luban, "The Fundamental Dilemma of Lawyering," see note 16 above at 4 [emphasis added].

19 For a critique of the impact of the elevation of technical rationality on professional education, see D. Schon, *The Reflective Practitioner* (San Francisco: Jossey-Bass, 1983).

20 Note that Lord Henry Brougham is also famously quoted as saying, "A lawyer is a gentlemen that rescues your estate from your enemies and then keeps it to himself." Lord Henry Brougham, quoted in Luban, "The Fundamental Dilemma of Lawyering," see note 16 above at 3.

21 See B. Abel-Smith and R. Stevens, *In Search of Justice: Society and the Legal System* (London: Allen Lane, 1968); and see the discussion in H. Kritzer, *The Justice Broker* (Oxford: Oxford University Press, 1990) at 7–8.

22 A. Schneider, "Shattering Negotiation Myths: Empirical Evidence on the Effectiveness of Negotiation Style" (2002) 7 Harv Negot L Rev 143 at 146.

23 J. Macfarlane, "Culture Change? A Tale of Two Cities and Mandatory Court-Connected Mediation" (2002) 2 J Disp Resol 241 at 297.

24 Ibid. at 302.

25 J. Heinz and E. Laumann, *Chicago Lawyers: The Social Structure of the Bar* (New York: Russell Sage, 1982).

26 R. Nelson, "Ideology, Practice and Professional Autonomy: Social Values and Client Relations in the Large Law Firm" in Abel, *Lawyers,* note 16 above, 70 at 73. See also the discussion in Chapter 3 of this book.

27 Macfarlane, "Culture Change?" see note 23 above at 304.

28 See the discussion in Chapter 3.

29 J. Macfarlane, "The Empathy Deficit: Why So Many Lawyers Believe Their Job Is to Be a Jerk" (February 10, 2015), online: National Self-Represented Litigants Project <https://representingyourselfcanada.com/2015/02/10/the-empathy-deficit-why-so-many-lawyers-think-their-job-is-to-be-a-jerk/>.

30 M. Schwartz, "The Professionalism and Accountability of Lawyers" (1978) 66 Cal L Rev 669.

31 Patrick Schiltz notes that it is "common for the top partners in the biggest firms to earn upwards of $2 million per year." P. Schiltz, "On Being a Happy, Healthy and Ethical Member of an Unhappy, Unhealthy and Unethical Profession" (1991) 52 Vand L Rev 871 at 900.

32 Unpublished data from the Collaborative Lawyering Research Project.

33 M. Galanter, "The Vanishing Trial: An Examination of Trials and Related Matters in Federal and State Courts" (2004) 1 Journal of Empirical Legal Studies 459.

34 See B. Mayer, *Staying with Conflict* (San Francisco: Jossey-Bass, 2009), and the further discussion below.

35 Kronman, *The Lost Lawyer,* see note 7 above.

36 Ibid. at 41–43 and 128–34.

37 Macfarlane, "Culture Change?" see note 23 above at 204.

38 Ibid.

39 Ibid. at 256.

40 See the detailed discussion in J. Macfarlane, "Why Do People Settle?" (2001) 45 McGill LJ 663.

41 See H. Kritzer, *Let's Make a Deal: Understanding the Negotiation Process in Ordinary Litigation* (Madison: University of Wisconsin Press, 1991) at 130–34. See also the discussion in Chapter 3 of this book.

42 Macfarlane, "Culture Change?" see note 23 above at 298.

43 Ibid. [emphasis added].

44 C. Guittard, "Preparing for Mediation and Negotiation" (1991) 37 Practical Lawyer 65.

45 The Prisoner's Dilemma analogy comes from the work of Robert Axelrod, *The Evolution of Co-operation* (New York: Basic Books, 1984). Axelrod posits that effective negotiation requires the self-conscious and intentional choice of a cooperative, a competitive, or a "mixed" strategy in each round of negotiation, and that the "best" (in game simulations, most successful) approach is a "tit-for-tat" strategy that begins cooperatively but is provokable in the face of competitive moves by the other side.

46 Unpublished data from the Collaborative Lawyering Research Project.

47 Macfarlane, "Culture Change?" see note 23 above at 297 [emphasis added].

48 For example, the strategic importance of considering the interests of the other side is identified by Mather, McEwen, and Maiman as a convention in divorce advocacy. L. Mather, C. McEwen, and R. Maiman, *Divorce Lawyers at Work: Varieties of Professionalism in Practice* (Oxford: Oxford University Press, 2001) at 115.

49 W. Ury, R. Fisher, and B. Patton, *Getting to Yes,* 2nd ed. (New York: Penguin, 1991).

50 Macfarlane, "Culture Change?" see note 23 above at 298.

51 Mayer, *Beyond Neutrality,* see note 4 above at 14.

52 Mayer, *Staying with Conflict,* see note 34 above at 38–53.

53 J. Macfarlane, *Analysis Project of the Federal Experience with the Use of Mediation and Other Dispute Resolution Processes* (Ottawa: Department of Justice Canada, 2009) at 41.

54 Macfarlane, "Culture Change?" see note 23 above at 262; and J. Macfarlane and M. Keet, "Civil Justice Reform and Mandatory Civil Mediation in Saskatchewan: Lessons from a Maturing Program" (2005) 42 Alta L Rev 677 at 689–90.

55 J. Macfarlane, *Court-Based Mediation in Civil Cases: An Evaluation of the Toronto General Division ADR Centre* (Ottawa: Queen's Printer, 1995) at 22.

56 On preventive law and its relationship with therapeutic jurisprudence, see, for example, D.P. Stolle, D.B. Wexler, B.J. Winick, and E.A. Dauer, "Integrating Preventive Law and Therapeutic Jurisprudence: A Law and Psychology Based Approach to Lawyering" in D.P. Stolle, D.B. Wexler, and B.J. Winick, eds., *Practicing Therapeutic Jurisprudence: Law as a Helping Profession* (Durham, NC: Carolina Academic Press, 2000).

57 Unpublished data from the Culture Change Project.

58 Ibid.

59 Ibid.

60 Macfarlane, "Culture Change?" see note 23 above at 302.

61 Unpublished data from the Culture Change Project.

62 Kronman, *The Lost Lawyer,* see note 7 above at 62–74.

63 Unpublished data from the Collaborative Lawyering Research Project.

64 Simon, *The Practice of Justice,* see note 7 above at 165.

65 Ibid.

66 J. Macfarlane, *The Emerging Phenomenon of Collaborative Family Law (CFL): A Qualitative Study of CFL Cases* (Ottawa: Department of Justice, 2005) at 25–28, online: Department of Justice Canada <http://www.justice.gc.ca/eng/rp-pr/fl-lf/famil/2005_1/pdf/2005_1.pdf>.

Chapter 6: The Lawyer/Client Relationship

1 Lucie White makes this point in "The Transformative Potential of Clinical Legal Education" (1997) 35 Osgoode Hall LJ 603 at 610, and cites the definition in the *Oxford English Dictionary,* 2nd ed., vol. 3 (Oxford: Clarendon, 1989) at 320.

2 Unpublished data from the Collaborative Lawyering Research Project.

3 The classic model of lawyer dominance is described in Z. Bankowski and G. Mungham, *Images of Law* (London: Routledge and Kegan Paul, 1976).

4   C. McEwen, "Pursuing Problem-Solving or Predictive Settlement" (1991) 19 Fla St UL
    Rev 77 at 81.

5   See H. Becker, *Education for the Professions* (Chicago: University of Chicago Press,
    1962), on the traditional conceptions of professionalism that have dominated profes-
    sional/client relationships for most of the twentieth century. See also the discussion of
    the historical origins of the lawyers' professional norms in Chapter 2.

6   D. Rosenthal, *Lawyer and Client: Who's in Charge?* (New York: Russell Sage Founda-
    tion, 1974) at 7.

7   Ibid. See also C. Hosticka, "'We Don't Care about What Happened, We Only Care
    about What Is Going to Happen': Lawyer-Client Negotiations of Reality" (1979) 26
    Social Problems 559 (examining relationships between legal clinic lawyers and their
    clients). However, see the doubts cast on this unproblematized view of power by W.
    Felstiner and A. Sarat, "Enactments of Power: Negotiating Reality and Responsibility
    in Lawyer/Client Interactions" (1992) 77 Cornell L Rev 1447.

8   J. Macfarlane, *The Emerging Phenomenon of Collaborative Family Law (CFL): A Quali-
    tative Study of CFL Cases* (Ottawa: Department of Justice, 2005) at 30, online: <http://
    www.justice.gc.ca/eng/rp-pr/fl-lf/famil/2005_1/pdf/2005_1.pdf>.

9   J. Macfarlane, "Culture Change? A Tale of Two Cities and Mandatory Court-Connected
    Mediation" (2002) 2 J Disp Resol 241 at 293.

10 C. Menkel-Meadow, "The Transformation of Disputes by Lawyers: What the Dispute
    Paradigm Does and Does Not Tell Us" (1985) Mo J Disp Resol 25 at 31.

11 A. Sarat and W. Felstiner, "Law and Strategy in the Divorce Lawyer's Office" in R. Abel,
    ed., *Lawyers: A Critical Reader* (New York: New Press, 1997) 44 at 49.

12 L. Mather and B. Yngvesson, "Language, Audience, and the Transformation of Disputes"
    (1980–81) 15 Law & Soc'y Rev 775.

13 Unpublished data from the Culture Change Project.

14 H.S. Becker, *Education for the Professions* (Chicago: National Society for the Study of
    Education, 1962) at 38. In this book, Becker is writing about professions in general, but
    the point is highly pertinent to the legal profession.

15 Fifty-six percent of complaints in 2013 concerned failure to communicate, which falls
    within the service issue category. Z. One, *Analysis of Complaints Received by Profes-
    sional Regulation in 2013* (Toronto: Law Society of Upper Canada, June 12, 2014) at 8;
    and see, for example, *Law Society of Upper Canada Annual Report of Complaints and
    Investigations 2013,* online: Law Society of Upper Canada <http://www.annualreport.
    lsuc.on.ca/2013/en/operational-trends/complaints.html>.

16 "Client Communication Feedback Survey," online: National Self-Represented Liti-
    gants Project <http://representingyourselfcanada.com/client-communication-feedback
    -survey/>.

17 See R. Nelson and R. Sandefur, "From Professional Dominance to Organisational Dom-
    inance" in W. Felstiner, ed., *Reorganisation and Resistance: Legal Professions Confront
    a Changing World* (London: Hart Publishing, 2006). At the same time, it is important

to recognize that conflicts between lawyers and their clients are relatively rare and that many lawyers adopt a highly influential and even controlling role, but without explicit conflict or challenge. See R. Nelson, "Ideology, Practice and Professional Autonomy: Social Values and Client Relationships in the Large Law Firm" in Abel, *Lawyers,* see note 11 above, 70.

18 See, for example, S. Henshall, "The COMsumer Manifesto: Empowering Communities of Consumers through the Internet" (2000) First Monday 5, online: <http://www.first monday.org/ojs/index.php/fm/article/view/747/656>.

19 W. Ury, *The Third Side* (New York: Penguin 2000) at 95 and 97.

20 A preliminary concept of legal coaching, where lawyers assist or "coach" clients to undertake at least some tasks themselves, is set out in J. Macfarlane, "Seriously? Lawyers Coaching SRLs in Self-Advocacy?" (December 14, 2013), online: National Self-Represented Litigants Project <https://representingyourselfcanada.com/2013/12/14/seriously-lawyers-coaching-srls-in-self-advocacy/>, and "Providing Legal Services in a Coaching Model: The What, Why and How" (December 18, 2013), online: National Self-Represented Litigants Project <https://representingyourselfcanada.com/2013/12/18/providing-legal-services-in-a-coaching-model-the-what-why-and-how/>.

21 For the origins of a functionalist theory of the doctor/patient relationship, see T. Parsons, *The Social System* (Glencoe, IL: Free Press, 1951).

22 J. Hughes, *Organization and Information at the Bed-Side: The Experience of the Medical Division of Labor by University Hospitals' Inpatients* (PhD dissertation, University of Chicago, 1994), c. 1, online: <http://www.changesurfer.com/Hlth/DPReview.html>.

23 T. Szasz and M. Hollender, "A Contribution to the Philosophy of Medicine: The Basic Models of the Doctor-Patient Relationship" (1956) 97 Archives of Internal Medicine 585.

24 For example, G. Lopez, "Reconceiving Civil Rights Practice: Seven Weeks in the Life of a Rebellious Collaboration" (1989) 77 Geo LJ 1603; and G. Lopez, "Training Future Lawyers to Work with the Politically and Socially Disadvantaged: Anti-Generic Legal Education" (1989) 91 W Va L Rev 305, online: <https://rebelliouslawyeringinstitute.org>.

25 L. White, "Subordination, Rhetorical Survival Skills: Notes on the Hearing of Mrs G." in Abel, *Lawyers,* see note 11 above, 300 at 300–1. See also L. White, "Mobilization on the Margins of the Lawsuit: Making Space for Clients to Speak" (1987–88) 16 NYU Rev L & Soc Change 535; and A. Alfieri, "Reconstructing Poverty Law Practice: Learning Lessons of Client Narrative" (1991) 100 Yale LJ 2105.

26 Illustrated by the increasing use of "public involvement projects" in resource management and environmental decision making; see, for example, Lawrence Susskind and Denise Madigan, "New Approaches to Resolving Disputes in the Public Sector" (1984) 9 Justice System Journal 179; and F. Dukes, "Public Conflict Resolution: A Transformative Approach" (1993) 9 Negotiation Journal 45.

27 See, for example, MyLawBC, developed by the Legal Services Society of British Columbia <http://mylawbc.com/>; the Legal Information Society of Nova Scotia <http://www.legalinfo.org/i-have-a-legal-question/all/>; Steps to Justice (Community Legal

Education Ontario) <http://yourlegalrights.on.ca/steps-to-justice>; and Swift Action <https://swiftaction.ca/>.

28 R. Susskind, *Tomorrow's Lawyers: An Introduction to Your Future* (Oxford: Oxford University Press, 2013) at 68–70.

29 J. Macfarlane, *The National Self-Represented Litigants Project: Identifying and Meeting the Needs of Self-Represented Litigants: Final Report* (May 2013) at 35, online: <https://representingyourselfcanada.files.wordpress.com/2014/02/reportm15-2.pdf> [hereafter *National SRL Study*].

30 Described by sociologists as "disintermediation." See E. Katz, "Disintermediation: Cutting Out the Middle Man" (1988) 16 Intermedia 30.

31 Macfarlane, *National SRL Study*, see note 29 above at 46.

32 Leading growing numbers of clients to ask for alternative fee arrangements. See A. George, "The Future of Legal Services: It's All about Client Empowerment" (n.d.), online: LawKick <http://blog.lawkick.com/the-future-of-legal-services/>, and S. Lingos, "The Empowerment Model: An Innovative Approach to AFA's [alternative fee arrangements]," (June 2013) online: Law Practice Today <http://www.americanbar.org/content/newsletter/publications/law_practice_today_home/lpt-archives/june13/the-empowerment-model-an-innovative-approach-to-afas.html>.

33 Macfarlane, *National SRL Study*, see note 29 above; *Cases without Counsel: Research on Experiences of Self-Representation in US Family Court* (Denver: IAALS, June 2016), online: IAALS <http://iaals.du.edu/sites/default/files/documents/publications/cases_without_counsel_research_report.pdf>; Civil Justice Council, *Access to Justice for Litigants in Person (or Self-Represented Litigants): A Report and Recommendations to the Lord Chancellor and to the Lord Chief Justice* (November 2011), online: Courts and Tribunals Judiciary <https://www.judiciary.gov.uk/wp-content/uploads/2014/05/report-on-access-to-justice-for-litigants-in-person-nov2011.pdf>.

34 Civil Justice Council, ibid. at 8.

35 See R. Gibson and R. Mnookin, "Disputing through Agents: Cooperation and Conflict between Lawyers in Litigation" (1994) 94 Colum L Rev 509.

36 Unpublished data from the Culture Change Project.

37 Macfarlane, "Culture Change?" see note 9 above at 293–95.

38 See the discussion in Chapter 1.

39 Macfarlane, "Culture Change?" see note 9 above at 295.

40 Unpublished data from the Culture Change Project.

41 Macfarlane, "Culture Change?" see note 9 above at 255.

42 C. McEwen, "Managing Corporate Disputing: Overcoming Barriers to the Effective Use of Mediation for Reducing the Cost and Time of Litigation" (1998) 14 Ohio St J Disp Resol 1.

43 J. Lande, "Failing Faith in Litigation? A Survey of Business Lawyers' and Executives' Opinions" (1998) 3 Harv Negot L Rev 1 at 20–21.

44 Ibid. at 18–19.

45 General Counsel Consulting, "Evolving Role of In-House Counsel: Adding Value to the Business" (n.d.), online: General Counsel Consulting <http://www.gcconsulting.com/articles/120280/73/Evolving-Role-of-In-House-Counsel-Adding-Value-to-the-Business/>.

46 Macfarlane, *National SRL Study,* see note 29 above at 29.

47 Ibid. at 78.

48 Ibid. at 42. The study data showed that over half (53 percent) of the SRL sample had retained a lawyer at some point in their case.

49 J. Macfarlane, K. Trask, and E. Chesney, *The Use of Summary Judgment Procedures against Self-Represented Litigants: Effective Case Management or Denial of Access to Justice?* (Windsor, ON: Windsor Law, 2015), online: National Self-Represented Litigants Project <https://representingyourselfcanada.files.wordpress.com/2015/11/nsrlp-the-use-of-summary-judgment-procedures-against-srls1.pdf>. Research in the Canadian Legal Information Institute (CanLII) database shows that summary judgments are being used to dismiss cases involving SRLs as plaintiffs or defendants before they reach trial. While the courts struggle to weed out cases without merit that might take up valuable court time, there is an emerging access to justice issue when the success rate of such applications against (non-"vexatious") SRLs reaches 95 percent.

50 J. Macfarlane, "Ontario Family Legal Services Review Offers Opportunity for Legal Profession to Show the Public It Is Listening – and Cares" (May 16, 2016), online: National Self-Represented Litigants Project Blog <http://representingyourselfcanada.com/ontario-family-legal-services-review-offers-opportunity-for-legal-profession-to-show-the-public-it-is-listening-and-cares/>.

51 For example, in *Ontario Rules of Civil Procedure,* RRO 1990, Reg. 194, amended to O. Reg. 260/05, Rule 24.1; *Ontario Rules of Civil Procedure,* RRO 1990, Reg. 194, Rule 76.10 (simplified procedure); and *Intake and Case Flow Management Rules,* Alta. Reg. 163/2001, s. 3(1).

52 Unpublished data from the Collaborative Lawyering Research Project.

53 Macfarlane, *The Emerging Phenomenon of Collaborative Family Law,* see note 8 above at 43.

54 Ibid.

55 Unpublished data from the Collaborative Lawyering Research Project.

56 See further discussion later in this chapter under the section "Decision Making and Control."

57 See the meta-analysis in R.L. Wissler, "Court-Connected Mediation in General Civil Cases: What We Know from Empirical Research" (2002) 17 Ohio St J Disp Resol 641 at 650–51.

58 Macfarlane, *National SRL Study,* see note 29 at 10, 102, 115.

59 See R.L. Wissler, "The Effectiveness of Court-Connected Dispute Resolution in Civil Cases" (2004) 22 Conflict Resolution Quarterly 55 at 69; and Wissler, "Court-Connected Mediation," see note 57 above at 682.

60 J. Macfarlane and M. Keet, "Civil Justice Reform and Mandatory Civil Mediation in Saskatchewan: Lessons from a Maturing Program" (2004) 42 Alta L Rev 677 at 691.

61 Unpublished data from J. Macfarlane and M. Keet, *Learning from Experience: An Evaluation of the Saskatchewan Queen's Bench Mediation Program* (Regina: Saskatchewan Justice, April 2003).

62 Ibid.

63 Macfarlane, *National SRL Study*, see note 29 above at 45.

64 See, for example, D.A. Binder, P. Bergman, S.C. Price, and P.R. Tremblay, *Lawyers as Counsellors: A Client-Centered Approach*, 2nd ed. (St. Paul, MN: West Publishing, 2004).

65 Thistoo – Your Personal Divorce Assistant <https://thistoo.co/>.

66 M. Patry, D. Stolle, D. Wexler, and A. Tompkins, "Better Legal Counseling through Empirical Research: Identifying Psycholegal Soft Spots and Strategies" in D. Stolle, D. Wexler, and B. Winick, eds., *Practicing Therapeutic Jurisprudence* (Durham, NC: Carolina Academic Press, 2000) 69 at 73–39.

67 Susskind, *Tomorrow's Lawyers*, see note 28 above at 68–70.

68 I take this expression from Linda Mills, in her essay "Affective Lawyering: Emotional Dimensions of the Lawyer-Client Relationship" in Stolle, Wexler, and Winick, *Practicing Therapeutic Jurisprudence*, see note 66 above at 419. She writes: "I learned in my legal practice to rely on my psychological skills to improve my effectiveness as a lawyer" (at 421).

69 Unpublished data from the Collaborative Lawyering Research Project.

70 Unpublished data from the Culture Change Project.

71 See, for example, J. Macfarlane, *Court-Based Mediation in Civil Cases: An Evaluation of the Toronto General Division ADR Centre* (Ottawa: Queen's Printer, 1995) at 8–9 (showing that 15 percent of cases referred to mandatory mediation settled before mediation).

72 Unpublished data from the Culture Change Project.

73 Ibid.

74 White, "The Transformative Potential," see note 1 above at 610.

75 J. Macfarlane, *Analysis Project of the Federal Experience with the Use of Mediation and Other Dispute Resolution Processes* (Ottawa: Department of Justice Canada, 2009) at 43.

76 Ibid.

77 Macfarlane, *The Emerging Phenomenon of Collaborative Family Law*, see note 8 above at 43.

78 Ibid. at 30 [emphasis added].

79 J. Macfarlane, "Experiences of Collaborative Law: Preliminary Results from the Collaborative Lawyering Research Project" (2004) 1 J Disp Resol 179 at 27–28.

80 Macfarlane, *The Emerging Phenomenon of Collaborative Family Law*, see note 8 above at 43.

81 Unpublished data from the Collaborative Lawyering Research Project.

82 Macfarlane, "Experiences of Collaborative Law," see note 79 above at 210.

83 See the cautionary tale in W. Simon, "Lawyer Advice and Client Autonomy: Mrs Jones's Case" in D. Rhodes, ed., *Ethics in Practice: Lawyers Roles, Responsibilities and Regulation* (Oxford: Oxford University Press, 2000) at 165.

84 See, for example, F.S. Mosten, "Unbundled Services to Enhance Peacemaking for Divorcing Families" (2015) 53 Fam Ct Rev 439; A.L. Kirker and J. Blanchard, "Limiting the Risk of Limited Scope Retainers" in Canadian Bar Association, Alberta Branch, *The Limited Scope Retainer* (Calgary: Canadian Bar Association, Alberta Branch, 2013), online: <https://static1.squarespace.com/static/511bd4e0e4b0cecdc77b114b/t/5473a 881e4b02494ba943576/1416865921334/limited+scope+retainers_FINAL.pdf>; and J. Macfarlane and L. Imbrogno, "The Nuts and Bolts of Unbundling: A NSRLP Resource for Lawyers Considering Offering Unbundled Legal Services," online: National Self-Represented Litigants Project <http://representingyourselfcanada.com/wp-content/uploads/2016/11/Nuts-and-Bolts-FINAL.pdf>.

85 Macfarlane, "Seriously?" see note 20 above; Macfarlane, "Providing Legal Services in a Coaching Model," see note 20 above.

86 There are growing numbers of template retainers available online, developed by law societies and other professional organizations. See, for example, a collection provided online by LAWPRO, at <http://www.practicepro.ca/practice/limitedscope.asp>.

87 A.L. Kirker and J. Blanchard, "Limiting the Risk of Limited Scope Retainers" in Canadian Bar Association, Alberta Branch, *The Limited Scope Retainer* (Calgary: Canadian Bar Association, Alberta Branch, 2013), online: <https://static1.squarespace.com/static/511bd4e0e4b0cecdc77b114b/t/5473a881e4b02494ba943576/1416865921334/limited+scope+retainers_FINAL.pdf>.

88 S. Goldberg, "The Time for Action," *CBA National* (June 2013), online: CBA National <http://www.nationalmagazine.ca/Articles/Recent4/The_time_for_action.aspx>.

89 R. Harvie, "Why Me, Why Now?" in Canadian Bar Association, Alberta Branch, *The Limited Scope Retainer,* see note 87 above, 6.

90 "Access to Justice All-Star: Victoria Foster" (May 6, 2015), online: National Self-Represented Litigants Project <https://representingyourselfcanada.com/2015/05/06/access-to-justice-all-star-victoria-foster/>.

91 See, for example, from Canada's leading legal insurer, "Unbundled Legal Services: Pitfalls to Avoid," *LawPRO Magazine* 11:1 (January 2012), online: practicePRO <http://www.practicepro.ca/LAWPROMag/Unbundled_Legal_Services.pdf>.

92 *Practical and Ethical Considerations to Integrating Unbundled Legal Services* (2015), online: Colorado Bar Association <http://www.cobar.org/Portals/COBAR/Repository/modeateIncome/Practical_and_Ethical_ModerateIncome.pdf?ver=2015-08-26 -120950-387>.

93 For example, the Florida Bar Association concluded that "the Florida Bar has not received any complaints regarding lawyers providing unbundled legal services" (M.-R. Crowell, "Report of the Unbundled Legal Services Monitoring Committee" [March 3, 2005], online: Florida Bar Association <http://www.floridabar.org/TFB/TFBResources. nsf/0/B591E315F65F20FC85256FE1007766E3/$FILE/SpecialUnbunLegalServ MonitorRpt.pdf> at 9). Similarly, the New York Bar Association concluded that malpractice suits were avoidable if an adequate letter of engagement was provided (New

York State Bar Association, "Report and Recommendations on 'Unbundled' Legal Services" [December 2002], online: <https://www.nysba.org/WorkArea/DownloadAsset.aspx?id=26674>).

94 J. Macfarlane, "Unbundling 'Unbundling': Separating the Myths from the Realities" (April 11, 2016), online: National Self-Represented Litigants Project <https://representingyourselfcanada.com/2016/04/11/unbundling-unbundling-separating-the-myths-from-the-realities/>.

95 Macfarlane, *National SRL Study,* see note 29 above at 43.

96 Ibid. at 93.

97 Unpublished data from the National Self-Represented Litigants Study database.

98 See, for example, the Client Fact Sheets developed by the New South Wales Law Society, requiring every lawyer to provide each client with specified information about costs in advance of signing a retainer agreement, and regular detailed billings. "Client Fact Sheets," online: The Law Society of New South Wales <https://www.lawsociety.com.au/ForSolicitors/professionalstandards/Costs/Clientfactsheets/index.htm>.

99 See, for example, N. Welsh, "The Thinning Vision of Self-Determination in Court-Connected Mediation: The Inevitable Price of Institutionalization?" (2001) 6 Harv Negot L Rev 101, and the further discussion later in this chapter.

100 Unpublished data from the Collaborative Lawyering Research Project.

101 J. Nolan-Haley, "Lawyers, Clients and Mediation" (1998) 73 Notre Dame L Rev 1369 at 1379.

102 One client in the original Toronto alternative dispute resolution pilot told the evaluators that the first time his lawyer told him they were going to a mediation meeting that day and not, as he expected, to a hearing before a judge was when they were driving into the city that morning. Macfarlane, *Court-Based Mediation in Civil Cases,* see note 71 above at 41.

103 Macfarlane, "Culture Change?" see note 9 above at 275.

104 Ibid.

105 Ibid.

106 Welsh, "The Thinning Vision of Self-Determination," see note 99 above at 125. Welsh argues that this is the price that has been paid for the legitimacy bought with the institutionalization of mediation within the court system.

107 N. Welsh, "Disputants' Decision Control in Court-Connected Mediation: A Hollow Promise without Procedural Justice" (2002) 1 J Disp Resol 179 at 184–86.

108 Macfarlane and Keet, "Civil Justice Reform," see note 60 above at 692.

109 Alternative Dispute Resolution Centre clients, quoted in Macfarlane, *Court-Based Mediation in Civil Cases,* see note 71 above at 55. Many similar comments were made by clients in the evaluation of the Saskatchewan Queen's Bench mandatory mediation program, reported in Macfarlane and Keet, *Learning from Experience,* see note 61 above at 24–26. There are also signs that lawyers who represent corporate clients increasingly recognize that some types of settlement discussion actually work better

without the lawyers being present to "chill" the climate or, worse, to increase the tension and hostility.

110 Macfarlane, "Culture Change?" see note 9 above at 272.

111 Unpublished data from the Culture Change Project.

112 Ibid.

113 Ibid.

114 See, for example, Macfarlane and Keet, *Learning from Experience,* note 61 above at 12–14; Wissler, "The Effectiveness of Court-Connected Dispute Resolution in Civil Cases," see note 59 above; and B. McAdoo, "A Report to the Minnesota Supreme Court: The Impact of Rule 114 on Civil Litigation Practice in Minnesota" (2002) 25 Hamline L Rev 401.

115 M. Silver, "Love, Hate and Other Emotional Interference in the Lawyer/Client Relationship" in Stolle, Wexler, and Winick, *Practicing Therapeutic Jurisprudence,* see note 66 above, 357 at 360.

116 For example, by counter-transference in which the lawyer takes on emotions on the client's behalf. Ibid. at 370–74.

117 See, for example, D. Stolle, D. Wexler, B. Winick, and E. Dauer, "Integrating Preventive Law and Therapeutic Jurisprudence: A Law and Psychology-Based Approach to Lawyering" (1997) 34 Cal WL Rev 15; A. Watson, *Psychiatry for Lawyers* (New York: International Universities Press, 1978); and A.S. Watson, *The Lawyer in the Interviewing and Counselling Process* (Indianapolis: Bobbs-Merrill, 1976).

118 G. Spence, *Win Your Case: How to Present, Persuade and Prevail: Every Place, Every Time* (New York: St. Martin's Press, 2005), cited in D. Linder and N. Levit, *The Good Lawyer: Seeking Quality in the Practice of Law* (New York: Oxford University Press, 2014) at 9.

119 A poignant example is the description of the lawyer/client interaction in Sarat and Felstiner, "Law and Strategy in the Divorce Lawyer's Office," see note 11 above at 47.

120 A. Kronman, *The Lost Lawyer: Failing Ideals of the Legal Profession* (Cambridge, MA: Harvard University Press, 1993).

121 Linder and Levit, *The Good Lawyer,* see note 118 above at 7.

122 Ibid. at 17.

123 Ibid. at 7. See also, J. Macfarlane, "The Empathy Deficit: Why So Many Lawyers Believe Their Job Is to Be a Jerk" (February 10, 2015), online: National Self-Represented Litigants Project <https://representingyourselfcanada.com/2015/02/10/the-empathy-deficit-why-so-many-lawyers-think-their-job-is-to-be-a-jerk/>.

124 Mills, "Affective Lawyering," see note 68 above at 422.

125 Unpublished data from the Collaborative Lawyering Research Project.

126 Macfarlane, *The Emerging Phenomenon of Collaborative Family Law,* see note 8 above at 8.

127 C. Fried, "The Lawyer as Friend: The Moral Foundations of the Lawyer-Client Relation" (1976) 85 Yale LJ 1060 (justifying the role of zealous advocacy as a form of loyalty).

128 See S. Morris, "The Lawyer as Friend: An Aristotelian Inquiry" (2001) 26 Journal of the Legal Profession 55 at 58–61, who locates this idea within Aristotle's writings on friendship. See Aristotle, *Nicomachean Ethics*, trans. M. Ostwald (Englewood Cliffs, NJ: Prentice Hall, 1962).

129 Kronman, *The Lost Lawyer,* see note 120 above at 130.

130 T.L. Shaffer and R.F. Cochran, "Lawyers as Strangers and Friends: A Reply to Professor Sammons" (1995) 18 U Ark Little Rock L Rev 69. Their text, which sparked the debate, is T. Shaffer and R. Cochran, *Lawyers, Clients and Moral Responsibility* (St. Paul, MN: West Publishing Company, 1994).

131 J. Sammons, "Rank Strangers to Me: Shaffer and Cochran's Friendship Model of Moral Counselling in the Law Office" (1995) 18 U Ark Little Rock L Rev 1.

132 Shaffer and Cochran, "Lawyers as Strangers and Friends," see note 130 above at 83.

133 Macfarlane, *The Emerging Phenomenon of Collaborative Family Law,* see note 8 above at 53.

134 Ibid. at 34–35.

135 Ibid. at 53.

136 Silver, "Love, Hate and Other Emotional Interference," see note 115 above at 361–64.

137 Ibid. at 34.

138 Unpublished data from the Collaborative Lawyering Research Project.

139 Described in J. Macfarlane, "Mediating Ethically: The Limits of Codes of Conduct and the Potential of a Reflective Practice Model" (2002) 39 Osgoode Hall LJ 49 at 68.

140 Yet another new emerging dilemma relates to legal coaching. What, for example, would the New Lawyer do if a client asks for coaching but the lawyer does not feel that this is likely to be successful – yet the client has no resources to pay for full legal representation?

141 Unpublished data from the Culture Change Project.

142 Unpublished data from the Collaborative Lawyering Research Project.

143 Ibid.

144 See the discussion to this effect in J. Sternlight, "Lawyers' Representation of Clients in Mediation: Using Economics and Psychology to Structure Advocacy in a Nonadversarial Setting" (1999) 14 Ohio St J Disp Resol 269 at 297–348.

145 Unpublished data from the Collaborative Lawyering Research Project.

Chapter 7: The Shadow of the Law

1 J. Macfarlane and M. Keet, *Learning from Experience: An Evaluation of the Saskatchewan Queen's Bench Mediation Program* (Regina: Saskatchewan Justice, April 2003) at 28.

2 T. Kuhn, *The Structure of Scientific Revolution* (Chicago: University of Chicago Press, 1962).

3 R. Mnookin and C. Kornhauser, "Bargaining in the Shadow of the Law: The Case of Divorce" (1979) 88 Yale LJ 950.

4 For example, L. Putnam, "Communication and Interaction Patterns" in C. Honeyman and A. Schneider, eds., *The Negotiator's Fieldbook* (Chicago: American Bar Association, 2006) 385 at 389.

5 J. Macfarlane, *The Emerging Phenomenon of Collaborative Family Law (CFL): A Qualitative Study of CFL Cases* (Ottawa: Department of Justice, 2005) at 38, online: Department of Justice Canada <http://www.justice.gc.ca/eng/rp-pr/fl-lf/famil/2005_1/pdf/2005_1.pdf>.

6 A strategy that often disappoints clients in its prediction of outcomes; see R.L. Kiser, M.A. Asher, and B.B. McShane, "Let's Not Make a Deal: An Empirical Study of Decision Making in Unsuccessful Settlement Negotiations" (2008) 5 Journal or Empirical Legal Studies 551, online: <http://www.blakemcshane.com/Papers/jels_settlement.pdf>.

7 An example from my mediation experience is parents who believe that the Ontario Special Education Tribunal can order a school board to offer certain curriculum supports to their special needs child. In fact, the tribunal is only empowered to order a board to reconsider its original decision. Ministry of the Attorney General, *Report of the Ontario Human Rights Review 2012* (Toronto: Queen's Printer, 2012).

8 O.M. Fiss, "Against Settlement" (1984) 93 Yale LJ 1073; and D. Luban, "Settlements and the Erosion of the Public Realm" (1995) 83 Geo LJ 2619.

9 See, for example, E. Waldman, "Identifying the Role of Social Norms in Mediation: A Multiple Model Approach" (1997) 48 Hastings LJ 703. Waldman sets out a model of "norm-generating" mediation, in which parties are encouraged to brainstorm their own values and principles to resolve their dispute rather than appealing to perceived entitlements or norms (at 710–23); and "norm-educating" mediation, commonly used in divorce mediation, which encourages the parties to identify appropriate social norms, including, but not limited to, legal principles with which to resolve their dispute (at 727–42). Waldman also describes a further model, the norm-advocating model, which is discussed in the following section.

10 Mnookin and Kornhauser, "Bargaining in the Shadow of the Law," see note 3 above.

11 P. Ewick and S. Silbey, *The Common Place of the Law: Stories from Everyday Life* (Chicago: University of Chicago Press, 1998).

12 Ibid. at 133.

13 Or, as Silbey and Ewick put it, "reified." Ibid. at 77–82.

14 J. Macfarlane, *Islamic Divorce in North America: A Shari'a Path in a Secular Society* (Oxford: Oxford University Press, 2012) at 7–13.

15 Ewick and Silbey, see note 11 above at 97.

16 See the results of the Civil Litigation Research Project, in J.B. Grossman, H.M. Kritizer, A. Sarat, W.L.F. Felstiner, and D.M. Trubek, "The Costs of Ordinary Litigation" (1983) 31 UCLA L Rev 73.

17 J. Macfarlane, "Working towards Restorative Justice in Ethiopia: Integrating Traditional Conflict Resolution Systems with the Formal Legal System" (2007) 8 Cardozo Journal of Conflict Resolution 487.

18 Macfarlane, *Islamic Divorce in North America*, see note 14 above at 118–19 and 129–30.

19 R. Ellickson, *Order without Law: How Neighbours Settle Disputes* (Cambridge, MA: Harvard University Press, 1991) at 60.

20 Ibid. at 133.

21 Ibid. at 212.

22 See, for example, A. Townley, "The Invisible-ism: Heterosexism and the Implications for Mediation" (1992) 9 Mediation Quarterly 397.

23 M.J. Bailey, "Unpacking the Rational Alternative: A Critical Review of Family Mediation Movement Claims" (1989) 8 Can J Fam L 61 at 76–86.

24 Ibid. at 70–72; P. Bryan, "Collaborative Divorce: Meaningful Reform or Another Quick Fix?" (1999) 5 Psychol Pub Pol'y & L 1001.

25 See G. Smyth, "Social Justice in Informal Dispute Resolution Processes through Cultural Competence" (2009) 27 Windsor YB Access Just 111 at 117.

26 Ibid. at 114–18.

27 Waldman, "Identifying the Role of Social Norms," see note 9 above at 742–56.

28 Family Mediation Canada, *Code of Professional Conduct,* art. 13(4), online: Family Mediation Canada <http://fmc.ca/sites/default/files/sites/all/themes/fmc/images-user/Members%20Code%20of%20Professional%20Conduct_0.pdf>.

29 See the discussion in Chapter 6.

30 See, for example, *Custody Access and Child/Spousal Support: A Pilot Project* (Ottawa: Ellis Research Associates; Department of Justice, 1995), online: <http://publications.gc.ca/collections/collection_2012/jus/J3-7-1996-12-eng.pdf>. As well, the results of the small sample in the Collaborative Lawyering Research Project suggest that parties to consensual agreements are often willing to "leave money on the table" or exceed their legal obligations. See Macfarlane, *The Emerging Phenomenon of Collaborative Family Law,* see note 5 above at 57–59.

31 See Macfarlane, ibid. at 57–60.

32 Ibid. at 57.

33 W. Ury, R. Fisher, and B. Patton, *Getting to Yes,* 2nd ed. (New York: Penguin, 1991).

34 Ibid. at 97–106. Others have argued that the more realistic measure would be "worst case scenario." Yet others propose the "most likely" outcome as the pragmatic choice. Each assessment requires the same basic data elements set out earlier in the chapter.

35 See, for example, M. Williams and J. Hall, "Knowledge of the Law in Texas: Socioeconomic and Ethnic Differences" (1972) 7 Law & Soc'y Rev 99; M. Galanter, "Reading the Landscape of Disputes: What We Know and Don't Know (and Think We Know) about Our Allegedly Contentious and Litigious Society" (1983) 31 UCLA L Rev 4.

36 Kiser, Asher, and McShane, "Let's Not Make a Deal," see note 6 above.

37 J. Cassels, *Remedies: The Law of Damages* (Toronto: Irwin Law, 2000).

38 B. Mayer, *The Dynamics of Conflict Resolution: A Practitioner's Guide* (San Francisco: Jossey-Bass, 2000) at 97–108.

39 A 1995 study that matched a control group of litigants participating in (an advanced stage of) traditional litigation with those offered mediation, found that only 8.5 percent of control group litigants described themselves as completely satisfied with the outcome of their case (either settled between the lawyers or adjudicated). The most frequently given reason for a negative or partly negative assessment of outcome in the

remaining 91.5 percent (including some litigants who won their cases at trial) was the length of time and emotional energy consumed by the process. J. Macfarlane, *Court-Based Mediation in Civil Cases: An Evaluation of the Toronto General Division ADR Centre* (Ottawa: Queen's Printer, 1995) at 22.

40 J. Macfarlane and M. Keet, "Civil Justice Reform and Mandatory Civil Mediation in Saskatchewan: Lessons from a Maturing Program" (2004) 42 Alta L Rev 677 at 690.

41 Unpublished data from Macfarlane and Keet, *Learning from Experience,* see note 1 above.

42 See the examples from real life in J. Macfarlane, "Mediating Ethically: The Limits of Codes of Conduct and the Potential of a Reflective Practice Model (2002) 39 Osgoode Hall LJ 49; and J. Macfarlane, "Why Do People Settle?" (2001) 45 McGill LJ 663.

43 See the further discussion of the role of expectations in settlement in Macfarlane, ibid. at 678–89.

44 See L. Mather and B. Yngvesson, "Language, Audience, and the Transformation of Disputes" (1980–81) 15 Law & Soc'y Rev 775; and C. Menkel-Meadow, "The Transformation of Disputes by Lawyers: What the Dispute Paradigm Does and Does Not Tell Us" (1985) Mo J Disp Resol 25.

45 Mather and Yngvesson, ibid. at 777–79.

46 Macfarlane, "Mediating Ethically," see note 42 above at 678–79.

47 Macfarlane, *Islamic Divorce in North America,* see note 14 above at 211.

48 M. LeBaron, "Intercultural Disputes – Mediation, Conflict Resolution, and Multi-Cultural Reality: Culturally Competent Practice" in E. Kruk, ed., *Mediation and Conflict Resolution in Social Work and the Human Sciences* (Chicago: Nelson Hall, 1997) at 321.

49 Important work on conflict orientation and bargaining style related to gender and ethnicity includes D.M. Kolb, "Her Place at the Table: Gender and Negotiation" in L. Hall, ed., *Negotiation: Strategies for Mutual Gain* (London: Sage Publications, 1993) at 138; C. Rose, "Bargaining and Gender" (1995) 18 Harv JL & Pub Pol'y 547; P. Trubisky, S. Ting-Toomey, and S.-L. Lin, "The Influence of Individualism-Collectivism and Self-Monitoring on Conflict Styles" (1991) 15 International Journal of Intercultural Relations 65; and J. Rubin and F. Sander, "Culture, Negotiation and the Eye of the Beholder" (1991) 7 Negotiation Journal 249.

50 R. Miller and A. Sarat, "Grievances, Claims and Disputes: Assessing the Adversary Culture" (1980–81) 15 Law & Soc'y Rev 525 at 551.

51 Cultural consciousness inevitably shapes communication and is integral to the making of meaning. This constructionist perspective is articulated by early sociologists such as Peter Berger and Thomas Luckman, *The Social Construction of Reality: A Treatise in the Sociology of Knowledge* (New York: Doubleday, 1966), and later by Sally Merry, *Getting Justice and Getting Even: Legal Consciousness among Working Class Americans* (Chicago: University of Chicago Press, 1990), and Susan Silbey, with Patricia Ewick, *The Common Place of Law* (Chicago: University of Chicago Press, 1998), and exemplified in dispute resolution scholarship by the work of John Paul Lederach, *Preparing for Peace: Conflict Transformation across Cultures* (Syracuse, NY: Syracuse University Press, 1995).

52 G.O. Faure, "Conflict Formulation: Going beyond Culture-Bound Views of Conflict" in Rubin Bunker and Associates, eds., *Conflict, Co-operation and Justice: Essays Inspired by the Work of Morton Deutsch* (San Francisco: Jossey-Bass, 1995) 39 at 53.

53 This story is also described and discussed at greater length in J. Macfarlane, "When Cultures Collide," in C. Bell and D. Kahane, eds., *Intercultural Dispute Resolution in Aboriginal Contexts: Canadian and International Perspectives* (Vancouver: UBC Press, 2004) 94 at 100–1.

54 The prevalence of "stock stories" (Mather and Yngvesson, "Language, Audience," see note 44 above), combined with what William Simon calls "ritualist advocacy" (see W. Simon, "The Ideology of Advocacy: Procedural Justice and Professional Ethics" [1978] 29 Wis L Rev 29 at 54) often produces a feeling of detachment for clients. "The burning issue which originally belonged to the disputants, both intellectually and emotionally, becomes detached from them on both levels when it is placed in the hands of the legal system." J. Macfarlane, "The Mediation Alternative" in J. Macfarlane, ed., *Rethinking Disputes: The Mediation Alternative* (Toronto: Emond Montgomery, 1997).

55 Macfarlane, *The Emerging Phenomenon of Collaborative Family Law,* see note 5 above at 37.

56 Unpublished data from the Collaborative Lawyering Research Project.

57 Ibid.

58 Macfarlane, *The Emerging Phenomenon of Collaborative Family Law,* see note 5 above at 37–38. This fits with the assertions of some collaborative lawyers that they provide only "generalist" legal advice.

59 Mayer, *The Dynamics of Conflict Resolution,* see note 38 above at 157.

Chapter 8: Ethical Challenges for the New Lawyer

1 A. Dodek, "Canadian Legal Ethics: A Subject in Search of Scholarship" (2000) 50 UTLJ 115.

2 J. Macfarlane, *The National Self-Represented Litigants Project: Identifying and Meeting the Needs of Self-Represented Litigants: Final Report* (May 2013) at 91, online: <https://representingyourselfcanada.files.wordpress.com/2014/02/reportm15-2.pdf> [hereafter *National SRL Study*].

3 A lawyer who was self-representing; see Macfarlane, ibid. at 92.

4 A. Kronman, "The Law as a Profession" in D. Rhodes, ed., *Ethics in Practice: Lawyers' Roles, Responsibilities and Regulation* (Oxford: Oxford University Press, 2000) 29 at 30.

5 A. Abbot, *The System of Professions: An Essay on the Division of Expert Labor* (Chicago: University of Chicago Press, 1988).

6 B.D. Bills, "To Be or Not to Be: The Civility of the Young Lawyer" (2005) 5 Connecticut Public International Law Journal 31; M.E. Aspen, "Overcoming Barriers to Civility in Litigation" (1999) 69 Miss LJ 1049; and T.A. Baker, "A Survey of Professionalism and Civility" (2005) 38 Ind L Rev 1305.

7 See, for example, F. Zacharias, "Reconciling Professionalism and Client Interests" (1995) 36 Wm & Mary L Rev 1303; D. Wilkins, "Redefining the 'Professional' in Pro-

fessional Ethics: An Interdisciplinary Approach to Teaching Professionalism" (1996) 58 Law & Contemp Probs 241; A. Kronman, "Professionalism" (1999) 2 JISLE 8; J. Sammons, "The Professionalism Movement: The Problems Defined" (1993) 29 Ga L Rev 1035; D. Tanovich, "The Reconstruction of a Distinctly Canadian Role Morality 'In the Interests of Justice' and Its Implications for Reform" (Paper presented at the Fourth Chief Justice of Ontario's Colloquia on the Legal Profession, University of Windsor, March 3, 2005); J.O. Calmore, "'Chasing the Wind': Pursuing Social Justice, Overcoming Legal Mis-Education, and Engaging in Professional Re-Socialization" (2004) 37 Loy LA L Rev 1167; S. Hartwell, "Moral Growth or Moral Angst? A Clinical Approach" (2004) 11 Clinical L Rev 115; N. Semple, "Core Values: Professionalism and Independence Theories in Lawyer Regulation" (2013), online: Social Science Research Network <http://dx.doi.org/10.2139/ssrn.2262518>; W.S. Duffey and R.A. Schneider, *A Life in the Law* (Chicago: American Bar Association, 2009); N. Hamilton and V. Monson, "Positive Empirical Relationship of Professionalism to Effectiveness in the Practice of Law" (2011) 24 Geo J Legal Ethics 137; N. Hamilton, "Profession and Professionalism Are Dead: A Review of Thomas Morgan, *The Vanishing American Lawyer*" (2010) 20 The Professional Lawyer 14.

8 W.B. Cotter, *Professional Responsibility Instruction in Canada: A Coordinated Curriculum for Legal Education* (Montreal: Conceptcom, 1992).

9 H.W. Arthurs, "Why Canadian Law Schools Do Not Teach Legal Ethics" in K. Economides, ed., *Ethical Challenges to Legal Education and Conduct* (Oxford: Hart Publishing, 1998); Dodek, "Canadian Legal Ethics," see note 1 above; S.M. Bundy, "Ethics Education in the First Year: An Experiment" (1995) 58 Law & Contemp Probs 19; and E.B. Spaeth Jr., J.G. Perry, and P.B. Wachs, "Teaching Legal Ethics: Exploring the Continuum" (1995) 58 Law & Contemp Probs 153.

10 A. Kronman, *The Lost Lawyer: Failing Ideals of the Legal Profession* (Cambridge, MA: Harvard University Press, 1993).

11 W. Bennett, *The Lawyer's Myth: Reviving the Ideals of the Legal Profession* (Chicago: University of Chicago Press, 2001).

12 See, for example, James R. Elkins, "Rites de Passage: Law Students 'Telling Their Lives'" (1985) 35 J Legal Educ 27.

13 Kronman, *The Lost Lawyer,* see note 10 above at 113–16.

14 Zacharias, "Reconciling Professionalism and Client Interests," see note 7 above at 1307.

15 R. Nelson, "Ideology, Practice and Professional Autonomy: Social Values and Client Relationships in the Large Law Firm" in R. Abel, ed., *Lawyers: A Critical Reader* (New York: New Press, 1997) 70 at 72.

16 J. Macfarlane, "Making It Legal: Some Simple Steps for Moving Unbundling to the Next Stage" (July 12, 2016), online: National Self-Represented Litigants Project <http://representingyourselfcanada.com/making-it-legal-some-simple-steps-for-moving-unbundling-to-the-next-stage/>.

17 See also J. Macfarlane, "Mediating Ethically: The Limits of Codes of Conduct and the Potential of a Reflective Practice Model" (2002) 39 Osgoode Hall LJ 49.

18 See, for example, G.B. Wetlaufer, "The Ethics of Lying in Negotiations" (1990) 75 Iowa L Rev 1219, for an exposition and a critique of the rule-based approach.

19 In the *Oxford English Dictionary,* "morals" are defined as "the distinction between right and wrong." *The Oxford English Dictionary,* 1st ed (Oxford: Clarendon Press, 1970).

20 Law Society of Upper Canada, *Rules of Professional Conduct* (2014), Encouraging Compromise or Settlement Rule 3.2–4: "A lawyer shall advise and encourage the client to compromise or settle a dispute whenever it is possible to do so on a reasonable basis and shall discourage the client from commencing or continuing useless legal proceedings."

21 There is a growing literature on the issue of good faith in bargaining. See, for example, K. Kovach, "Good Faith in Mediation: Requested, Recommended or Required? A New Ethic" (1997) 38 S Tex L Rev 575. Most jurisdictions are understandably hesitant about legislating such a requirement, although some have attempted such a rule. See J. Lande, "Using Dispute System Decision Methods to Promote Good-Faith Participation in Court-Connected Mediation Program" (2002) 50 UCLA L Rev 69; and the discussion later in this chapter.

22 L. Cooks and C. Hale, "The Construction of Ethics in Mediation" (1994) 2 Mediation Quarterly 55 at 72. The original notion of discourse ethics comes from the work of Jürgen Habermas, particularly his *Theory of Communicative Action* (Frankfurt: Suhrkamp, 1981).

23 K. Barnett, "Feminist Legal Methods" (1990) 102 Harv L Rev 829 at 881.

24 C. Menkel-Meadow, "The Limits of Adversarial Ethics" in D. Rhodes, ed., *Ethics in Practice: Lawyer's Roles, Responsibilities and Regulations* (Oxford: Oxford University Press, 2000) 123 at 135.

25 Unpublished data from the Collaborative Lawyering Research Project.

26 See R. Axelrod, *The Evolution of Co-operation* (New York: Basic Books, 1984).

27 Ibid. at 23.

28 J. Macfarlane, *Court-Based Mediation in Civil Cases: An Evaluation of the Toronto General Division* (Ottawa: Queen's Printer, 1995) at 46.

29 Ibid. at 46–47.

30 J. Macfarlane, *The Emerging Phenomenon of Collaborative Family Law (CFL): A Qualitative Study of CFL Cases* (Ottawa: Department of Justice, 2005) at 26, online: Department of Justice Canada <http://www.justice.gc.ca/eng/rp-pr/fl-lf/famil/2005_1/pdf/2005_1.pdf>.

31 Macfarlane, *Court-Based Mediation in Civil Cases,* see note 28 above at 48.

32 Unpublished data from the Collaborative Lawyering Research Project.

33 Ibid. [emphasis added].

34 Macfarlane, *Court-Based Mediation in Civil Cases,* see note 28 above at 23.

35 Typology developed for the Culture Change Project: see J. Macfarlane, "Culture Change? A Tale of Two Cities and Mandatory Court-Connected Mediation" (2002) 2 J Disp Resol 241 at 253–59.

36 Unpublished data from the Culture Change Project.

37 Ibid.
38 See, for example, J. Macfarlane and M. Keet, "Civil Justice Reform and Mandatory Civil Mediation in Saskatchewan: Lessons from a Maturing Program" (2004) 42 Alta L Rev 677 at 691–93.
39 See, for example, J. Macfarlane and M. Keet, *Learning from Experience: An Evaluation of the Saskatchewan Queen's Bench Mediation Program* (Regina: Saskatchewan Justice, April 2003) at 55–56.
40 Macfarlane, "Culture Change?" see note 35 above at 257.
41 Ibid. at 267.
42 Unpublished data from Macfarlane and Keet, *Learning from Experience,* see note 39 above.
43 According to J. Lande, "Why a Good-Faith Requirement Is a Bad Idea for Mediation" (2005) 23 Alternatives to the High Cost of Litigation 1, at least twenty-two US states now have statutes requiring good faith participation in mediation, along with twenty-one federal district courts and seventeen state courts. Statutes, court rules, mediation referral orders, and the common law establish good faith requirements in mediation. At least twenty-two states and the territory of Guam have such statutory requirements. J. Lande, "Using Dispute System Design Methods to Promote Good-Faith Participation in Court-Connected Mediation Programs" (2002) 50 UCLA L Rev 69 at 78.
44 Macfarlane and Keet, *Learning from Experience,* see note 39 above at 19.
45 See the broad general rule proposed by Kimberlee Kovach in "Good Faith in Mediation: Requested, Recommended or Required a New Ethic?" (1997) 38 S Tex L Rev 575 at 622–23. For a different approach, see Lande, "Using Dispute System Design Methods," note 43 above. Lande argues that consensus building is more effective than a rule.
46 Lande, "Using Dispute System Design Methods," see note 43 above.
47 Lande, "Why a Good-Faith Requirement Is a Bad Idea for Mediation," see note 43 above at 9.
48 Unpublished data from Macfarlane and Keet, *Learning from Experience,* see note 39 above.
49 Macfarlane, "Culture Change?" see note 35 above at 316; and Macfarlane and Keet, ibid. at 30.
50 For example, data collected among Toronto litigators compared with the Ottawa bar. See Macfarlane, "Culture Change?" see note 35 above at 313–16.
51 Unpublished data from the Culture Change Project.
52 Ibid.
53 Axelrod, *The Evolution of Co-operation,* see note 26 above.
54 Macfarlane and Keet, "Civil Justice Reform," see note 38 above at 692–93.
55 Unpublished data from Macfarlane and Keet, *Learning from Experience,* see note 39 above; see also Macfarlane and Keet, "Civil Justice Reform," note 38 above at 694–97.
56 A database of all US federal and state cases that review questions relating to mediation is being maintained at the Hamline University Law School. See J. Coben and N.

Thompson, "Disputing Irony: A Systematic Look at Litigation about Mediation" (2006) 11 Harv Negot L Rev 43.

57 N. Welsh, "The Thinning Vision of Self-Determination in Court-Connected Mediation: The Inevitable Price of Institutionalization?" (2001) 6 Harv Negot L Rev 1 at 87.

58 See also the discussion in Chapter 6 under "Client Participation."

59 Unpublished data from the Culture Change Project.

60 Anthony's story in Macfarlane "Mediating Ethically," see note 17 above at 74–81.

61 B. Mayer, *The Dynamics of Conflict Resolution: A Practitioner's Guide* (San Francisco: Jossey-Bass, 2000) at 97–108.

62 Louis Kriesberg describes this as "circumstances when the conflict is ready for an effort to bring about ... change." L. Kriesberg, "Timing, Conditions, Strategies and Errors" in L. Kriesberg and S. Thorson, eds., *Timing the De-escalation of International Conflicts* (Syracuse, NY: Syracuse University Press, 1991).

63 See J. Macfarlane, "Why Do People Settle?" (2001) 45 McGill LJ 663.

64 Unpublished data from the Collaborative Lawyering Research project.

65 Macfarlane, *The Emerging Phenomenon of Collaborative Family Law*, see note 30 above at 69.

66 J. Alfini, "Trashing, Bashing and Hashing It Out: Is This the End of 'Good Mediation'?" (1991) 19 Fla St UL Rev 47.

67 *In re Patterson*, 969 P.2d 1106 (Wash Ct App, 1999), cited in P. Thompson, "Enforcing Rights Generated in Court-Connected Mediation: Tension between the Aspirations of a Private Facilitative Process and the Reality of Public Adversarial Justice" (2004) 19 Ohio St J Disp Resol 509 at 558. Generally, see F. Sander, "The Obsession with Settlement Rates" (1995) 11 Negotiation Journal 329.

68 B. McAdoo, "A Report to the Minnesota Supreme Court: The Impact of Rule 114 on Civil Litigation in Minnesota" (2002) 25 Hamline L Rev 401 at 428–29.

69 However, it was not clear whether this was pressure from the mediator and/or pressure from counsel on either side, unless the comment specifically indicated the source.

70 Macfarlane, *Court-Based Mediation in Civil Cases,* see note 28 above at 43.

71 J. Lande, "How Will Lawyering and Mediation Practices Transform Each Other?" (1997) 24 Fla St UL Rev 839 at 885.

72 On this point, see the discussion in T. Hedeen and P.G. Coy, "Community Mediation and the Court System: The Ties That Bind" (2000) 17 Mediation Quarterly 351.

73 See, for example, J. Nolan-Haley, "Court Mediation and the Search for Justice through Law" (1996) 74 Wash ULQ 47.

74 See, for example, Law Society of Upper Canada, *Rules of Professional Conduct,* see note 20 above, Rule 2.20(3): "A lawyer should consider the use of alternative dispute resolution (ADR) for every dispute and, if appropriate, the lawyer shall inform the client of ADR options and if so instructed, take steps to pursue those options."

75 See, for example, the accounts in Macfarlane and Keet, *Learning from Experience,* note 39 above at 29–30; and Macfarlane, *Court-Based Mediation in Civil Cases,* note 28 above at 41–42. When asked if they had sent information about the mediation session

on to their clients, 49 percent of lawyers responded in the affirmative, but only 37 percent of their clients said they had received the materials (based on questionnaire data, $n = 707$).

76 Macfarlane, *Court-Based Mediation in Civil Cases*, see note 28 above at 42.

77 Ibid. at 41.

78 See, for example, E. Kruk, "Power Imbalance and Spouse Abuse in Divorce Disputes: Deconstructing Mediation Practice via the 'Simulated Client' Technique" (1998) 12 Int'l JL Pol'y & Fam 1; and T. Grillo, "The Mediation Alternative: Process Dangers for Women" (1991) 100 Yale LJ 1545 esp. at 1590–93.

79 See the review of statistics in Macfarlane, *National SRL Study*, note 2 above 32–35.

80 California reports that in 1971, just 1 percent of family court litigants were self-representing; Ed Sherman, *How to Do Your Own Divorce in California: A Guide for Petitioners and Respondents*, 25th ed. (Occidental, CA: Nolo Press, 2001) at 11. See also B. Hough, "Self-Represented Litigants in Family Law: The Response of California's Courts" (2010) The Circuit Paper 15.

81 Macfarlane, *National SRL Study*, see note 2 above at 102; IAALS – Institute for the Advancement of the American Legal System, *Cases without Counsel: Research on Experiences of Self-Representation in US Family Court* (Denver: IAALS, June 2016), online: IAALS <http://iaals.du.edu/sites/default/files/documents/publications/cases_without_counsel_research_report.pdf> at 31.

82 J.-P. Boyd, "The Self-Represented Litigant's Bill of Rights ... and Responsibilities" (September 30, 2012), online: JP Boyd on Family Law <http://bcfamilylawresource.blogspot.ca/2012/09/the-self-represented-litigants-bill-of.html>.

83 Macfarlane, *National SRL Study*, see note 2 above at 12; IAALS, *Cases without Counsel*, see note 81 above at 12.

84 Macfarlane, ibid. at 39.

85 Ibid. at 44.

86 "Loom Analytics – Legal Analytics" (2016), online: Loomanalytics.com <http://www.loomanalytics.com>. Loom is an online legal analytics system providing structure to the large corpus of unstructured Canadian legal open data.

87 J. Macfarlane, K. Trask, and E. Chesney, *The Use of Summary Judgment Procedures against Self-Represented Litigants: Effective Case Management or Denial of Access to Justice?* (Windsor, ON: Windsor Law, 2015) at 10, online: National Self-Represented Litigants Project <https://representingyourselfcanada.files.wordpress.com/2015/11/nsrlp-the-use-of-summary-judgment-procedures-against-srls1.pdf>.

88 2014 SCC 7, [2014] 1 SCR 87.

89 Macfarlane, *National SRL Study*, see note 2 above at 35.

90 Ibid. at 31, 91–92.

91 Ibid. at 15.

92 G. Carson and M. Stangarone, "Self-Represented Litigants in the Family Courts: Is Self-Representation an Unfair Tactic?" (2016), online: MacDonald & Partners LLP <http://036f9fd.netsolhost.com/article_files/selfrepresentedlitigantsinthefamilycourts.pdf>.

93 Law Society of England and Wales, "Litigants in Person: Guidelines for Lawyers" (2015), online: <http://www.lawsociety.org.uk/support-services/advice/articles/litigants-in-person-new-guidelines-for-lawyers-june-2015/>.

94 See, for example, IAALS, *Cases without Counsel,* note 81 above; Macfarlane, *National SRL Study,* note 2 above at 54, 91.

95 Law Society of Upper Canada, *Rules of Professional Conduct* (2013), Rule 7.2–1.

96 Ibid., Rule 7.2–4.

97 See, for example, ibid., Rule 7.2–9, Subrule 2.04(14); Law Society of British Columbia, *Code of Professional Conduct for BC* (2013), Rule 7.2–9; Law Society of Alberta, *Code of Professional Conduct* (2013), Chapter 6, Rule 6.02(11).

98 J.-P. Boyd, "The Rights and Responsibilities of Self-Represented Litigants," online: (August 28, 2016) Slaw <http://www.slaw.ca/2015/08/28/the-rights-and-responsibilities-of-self-represented-litigants-2/>.

99 D. Farmer, *Representing Yourself in Court* (Vancouver: Self-Counsel Press, 2015) at 58.

100 For example, Law Society of Upper Canada, *Rules of Professional Conduct* (2013), Rule 3.2–4.

101 The Advocates' Society, Institute for Civility and Professionalism, "Best Practices: A Practical Guide to Civility" (2013), online: <http://www.advocates.ca/assets/files/pdf/publications/Best%20Practices.pdf> at 6.

102 Law Society of Upper Canada (2000), Rule 6(03)3: "[A lawyer] shall not take advantage of or act without fair warning upon slips, irregularities, or mistakes on the part of other licensees not going to the merits or involving the sacrifice of a client's rights."

103 Farmer, *Representing Yourself in Court,* see note 99 above at 58.

104 M.A. Wilkinson, C. Walker, and P. Mercer, "Do Codes of Ethics Actually Shape Legal Practice?" (2000) 45 McGill LJ 645.

Chapter 9: Where the Action Is

1 R. Susskind, *The End of Lawyers? Rethinking the Future of Legal Services* (Oxford: Oxford University Press, 2010) at 121–30.

2 See, for example, Natalie Kitroeff, "Law School Admissions Set to Hit 15 Year Low," *Bloomberg News* (March 19, 2015); Noam Scheiber, "An Expensive Law Degree and No Place to Use It," *New York Times* (June 17, 2016).

3 J. Macfarlane, "What Does the Changing Culture of Legal Practice Mean for Legal Education?" (2001) 20 Windsor YB Access Just 191.

4 Unpublished data from the Culture Change Project.

5 See, for example, A. Lerner, "Law and Lawyering in the Workplace: Building Better Lawyers by Teaching Students to Exercise Critical Judgment as Creative Problem-Solvers" (1999) 32 Akron L Rev 107; Janet Reno, "Lawyers as Problem-Solvers" (1999) 49 J Legal Educ 5.

6 For example, the introduction of negotiation and mediation courses into growing numbers of law schools as elective components (for a review, see J. Watson-Hamilton, "The Significance of Mediation for Legal Education" [1999] 17 Windsor YB Access

Just 280); and the introduction of mandatory dispute resolution courses in some law schools, such as the University of Ottawa (see E. Zweibel, "Where Does ADR Fit into the Mainstream Law Curriculum?" [1999] 17 Windsor YB Access Just 295). Some law schools have developed extensive clinical programming in a conscious effort to extend the reach of applied and practical knowledge into the curriculum; see, for example, J. Aiken and J. Wizner "Teaching and Doing: The Role of Law School Clinics in Access to Justice" (2004) 73 Fordham L Rev 997.

7 For the classic statement of this position in Canada, see Consultative Group on Research and Education in Law, *Law and Learning* (Ottawa: Social Sciences and Humanities Research Council of Canada, 1983) (also known as the Arthur Report).

8 J. Macfarlane, "Look before You Leap: Knowledge and Learning in Legal Skills Education" (1992) 19 JL & Soc'y 291 at 294–97.

9 See the classic discussion in W. Twining, "Legal Skills and Legal Education" (1988) 22 Law Teacher 4.

10 Mary Hanna, quoted in E. Myers, "Teaching Good and Teaching Well: Integrating Values with Theory and Practice" (1997) 47 J Legal Educ 401.

11 See, for example, American Bar Association, Section of Legal Education and Admissions to the Bar, *Legal Education and Professional Development – An Educational Continuum: The Report of the Task Force on Law Schools and the Profession: Narrowing the Gap* (Chicago: American Bar Association, 1992), online: American Bar Association <http://www.americanbar.org/content/dam/aba/publications/misc/legal_education/2013_legal_education_and_professional_development_maccrate_report).authcheckdam.pdf> [hereafter *MacCrate Report*]; Marre Committee, *A Time for Change: Report of the Committee on the Future of the Legal Profession* (London: General Council of the Bar; Law Society of Upper Canada, 1988); and Australian Law Reform Commission, *Managing Justice: A Review of the Federal Justice System* (Report No. 89) (Sydney: Australian Law Reform Commission, 2000) at chs. 2 and 3, online: <https://www.alrc.gov.au/sites/default/files/pdfs/publications/ALRC89.pdf>.

12 Canadian Bar Association, *Attitudes, Skills, Knowledge: Proposals for Legal Education to Assist in Implementing a Multi-Option Civil Justice System in the Twenty-First Century – Joint Committee Report on Legal Education* (Ottawa: Canadian Bar Association, 1999).

13 American Bar Association, *MacCrate Report,* see note 11 above.

14 Ibid. at 135–40.

15 American Bar Association, *Twenty Years after the MacCrate Report: A Review of the Current State of the Legal Education Continuum and the Challenges Facing the Academy Bar and Judiciary* (Chicago: American Bar Association, 2013), online: American Bar Association <http://www.americanbar.org/content/dam/aba/administrative/legal_education_and_admissions_to_the_bar/council_reports_and_resolutions/june2013councilmeeting/2013_open_session_e_report_prof_educ_continuum_committee.authcheckdam.pdf>.

16 The origin of the concept of "reflective practice" is generally ascribed to the work of Donald Schon and Chris Argyris. See D. Schon, *The Reflective Practitioner* (San Francisco:

Jossey-Bass, 1983); D. Schon, *Educating the Reflective Practitioner* (San Francisco: Jossey-Bass, 1987); and D. Schon and C. Argyris, *Theory in Practice: Increasing Professional Effectiveness* (San Francisco: Jossey-Bass, 1980). In relation to legal practice, see D. Schon, "Educating the Reflective Legal Practitioner" (1995) 2 Clinical L Rev 231; and the first *Report of the Lord Chancellor's Advisory Committee on Legal Education and Conduct* (London: Lord Chancellor's Department, 1996).

17 See, for example, C. Johns and D. Freshwater, eds., *Transforming Nursing through Reflective Practice*, 2nd ed. (London: Blackwell, 2006); and S. Mamede and H.G. Schmidt, "The Structure of Reflective Practice in Medicine" (2004) 38 Medical Education 1302.

18 See J. Macfarlane, "The Challenge of ADR and Alternative Paradigms of Dispute Resolution: How Should the Law Schools Respond?" (1997) 31 Law Teacher 13 at 19–20.

19 S.E. Merry, "Legal Pluralism" (1988) 22 Law & Soc'y Rev 869.

20 J. Lande, "Getting the Faith: Why Business Lawyers and Executives Believe in Mediation" (2000) 5 Harv Negot L Rev 137.

21 J. Resnick, "Managerial Judges" (1982) 96 Harv L Rev 374; H. Baer Jr., "History, Process, and a Role for Judges in Mediating Their Own Cases" (2001) 28 New York University Annual Survey of American Law 143; E.V. Ludwig, "The Changing Role of the Trial Judge" (2002) 85 Judicature 216; and T. Farrow, "Thinking about Dispute Resolution" (2003) 41 Alta L Rev 559.

22 See the data presented by Bobbi McAdoo in B. McAdoo, "All Rise, the Court Is in Session: What Judges Say about Court-Connected Mediation" (2007) 22 Ohio St J Disp Resol 377 at 430.

23 A point noted by McAdoo, ibid. at 430.

24 See, for example, s. 718.2(e) of the *Criminal Code*, RSC 1985, c. C-46, and ss. 38(2)(d) and 39(2) of the *Youth Criminal Justice Act*, SC 2002, c. 1.

25 See, for example, D. Wexler and B. Winick, eds., *Law in a Therapeutic Key: Developments in Therapeutic Jurisprudence* (Durham, NC: Carolina Academic Press, 1996).

26 Interview with Judge Alex Calabrese, Red Hook Community Justice Center, online: Center for Court Innovation <http://www.courtinnovation.org>.

27 See, for example, the work of the National Association of Drug Court Professionals and details on the expansion of drug courts throughout the United States at <http://www.nadcp.org>.

28 Professor Michelle Flaherty has developed a concept of "substantive impartiality" that gives the third party responsibility for ensuring fair process, without encroaching on traditional impartiality. See M. Flaherty, "Self-Represented Litigants: A Sea Change in Adjudication" (University of Ottawa, Faculty of Law Working Paper No. 1013–07, November 1, 2013); and M. Flaherty, "Self-Represented Litigants, Active Adjudication and the Perception of Bias: Issues in Administrative Law" (2015) 38 Dal LJ 119.

29 The methodology adopted in this survey was a modified Delphi approach. The Delphi method circulates text among panels of experts for their input and generally continues this process for a number of rounds until a consensus emerges. In this case, two Delphi rounds were conducted using a survey that included both closed and open ques-

tions. The survey asked judges to identify judicial skills and abilities, and new areas of need for training and further education, and incrementally developed an inventory of judges' skills and abilities. Three Delphi panels were formed, one representing judges who had served up to five years on the bench, a second for mid-career judges (six to fifteen years since appointment), and a final panel representing senior judges (more than fifteen years on the bench). The panels were fairly evenly divided between federal and provincial appointments and men and women.

30 Perhaps this also reflects a growing interest in judges in providing private mediation and arbitration services after retirement.

31 See R. Wissler, "Barriers to Attorneys Discussion and Use of ADR" (2004) 19 Ohio St J Disp Resol 459 at 488–89.

32 J. Macfarlane, "Culture Change: A Tale of Two Cities and Mandatory Mediation" (2002) 2 J Disp Resol 242 at 315–16.

33 In a survey of Ontario family lawyers developed by the Ontario Family Services Review chaired by Justice Bonkalo in June 2016, 54 percent of respondents said that the "explicit encouragement and endorsement of the judiciary" would encourage more lawyers to offer limited-scope retainers or unbundled family legal services <http://representingyourselfcanada.com/making-it-legal-some-simple-steps-for-moving-unbundling-to-the-next-stage/>.

34 See Institute for the Advancement of the American Legal System (IAALS), "An Uncommon Dialogue: What Do We Want in Our Judges and How Do We Get There?" (September 3, 2013), online: IAALS <http://iaals.du.edu/quality-judges/publications/uncommon-dialogue-what-do-we-want-our-judges-how-do-we-get-there>.

35 See IAALS, "Judicial Performance Evaluation," online: IAALS <http://iaals.du.edu/quality-judges/projects/judicial-performance-evaluation>.

36 Limited License Legal Technicians have been introduced and regulated by the Washington State Bar since 2016. See Washington State Bar Association, "Legal Technicians: A New Option for Affordable Legal Services," online: Washington State Bar Association <http://www.wsba.org/licensing-and-lawyer-conduct/limited-licenses/legal-technicians>.

37 R. Abel, "The Professional as Political: English Lawyers through the 1989 Green Papers through the Access to Justice Act 1999" in W. Felstiner, ed., *Reorganisation and Resistance* (Oxford: Hart Publishing, 2005) 13 at 22.

38 Ibid. at 22–24.

39 See Law Society of Upper Canada, *Task Force on Paralegal Regulation* (Toronto: Law Society of Upper Canada, September 23, 2004); *Access to Justice Act,* SO 2006, c. 21 (assented to October 19, 2006, 2d Sess., 38th Leg., Ontario).

40 In Ontario, the Family Legal Services Review (the Bonkalo Review) is charged with addressing the question of paralegal practice in family cases. See the terms of reference at Ministry of the Attorney General, "Expanding Legal Services Options for Ontario Families" (February 9, 2016), online: Ontario Ministry of the Attorney General <https://

www.attorneygeneral.jus.gov.on.ca/english/family/legal_services_consultation_paper.html>. A report is anticipated in 2017.

41 The Law Society of Upper Canada is in the process of considering whether to permit ABS. A 2014 consultation paper, "Alternative Business Structures: The Future of Legal Services," online: <http://www.lsuc.on.ca/uploadedFiles/abs-discussion-paper.pdf>, sets out the issues. A good example of the controversy stirred by multidisciplinary practices is provided by the history of this debate in British Columbia. A two-year debate culminated in a 2001 report by the Multi-Disciplinary Practice Working Group, which recommended that the recognition of MDPs be rejected by the benchers (see "Benchers Say *No* to Multi-Disciplinary Practice," *Benchers' Bulletin* 6 (2001), online: Law Society of British Columbia <https://www.lawsociety.bc.ca/page.cfm?cid=1854&t=Benchers-say-no-to-multi-disciplinary-practice>.

42 See, for example, *New South Wales Legal Practice Rules* (1987, amended 1997), Rule 40, section 48G. For a more relaxed and unrestricted approach, see the recommendations of the Canadian Bar Association, *Report of the International Practice of Law Committee on Multi-Disciplinary Practices and the Legal Profession* (Ottawa: Canadian Bar Association, 1999) at 31.

43 M. Thornton, "The Australian Legal Profession: Towards a National Identity" in Felstiner, *Reorganisation and Resistance,* see note 37 above, 134 at 138.

44 With a few exceptions. See, for example, N. Semple, "Access to Justice: Is Legal Services Regulation Blocking the Path?" (2013) 20 International Journal of the Legal Profession 267, describing how relaxing regulation on capital ownership might create economies of scale with reduced costs for the consumer and access to non-lawyer labour within legal services firms. See also the study prepared by Professor Jasminka Kalajdzic for the Ontario Trial Lawyers Association (G. Kauth, "Study Questions Access to Justice Benefits of ABS," *Legal Feeds* [January 26, 2015]).

45 See the description of the team model in N. Cameron, *Collaborative Practice: Deepening the Dialogue* (Vancouver: Continuing Legal Education Society of British Columbia, 2004) at 106–15.

46 Ibid.

47 Ibid. at 54.

48 Ibid. at 34–35.

49 Ibid. at 55.

50 Ibid.

51 See Susskind, *The End of Lawyers?* note 1 above at 28–33; and "From Bespoke to Commodity" (2006) 1 Legal Technology Journal 4.

52 See, for example, S. Smolkin, "Some Toronto Law Firms and In-House Lawyers Send Work to India," *Toronto Star* (May 13, 2012); "Bangalore Calling," *Canadian Bar Association National Magazine* (April-May 2011) 16.

53 A.L. Naha, "It's India for Legal Services," *The Hindu* (November 26, 2007).

54 See, for example, LegalWise <http://www.legalwise.ca>.

55 For example, the CanLII case database is open to the public, but a basic understanding of the system of precedent is necessary to use it effectively. See National Self-Represented Litigants Project, *The CanLII Primer: Legal Research Principles and CanLII Navigation for Self-Represented Litigants* (Windsor, ON: Windsor Law, 2015), online: National Self-Represented Litigants Project <https://representingyourselfcanada.files. wordpress.com/2015/03/nsrlp-canlii-primer-v11.pdf>.

56 See, for example, the MyLawBC system, developed by the Legal Services Society of British Columbia. N. Prosser, "MyLawBC Promises Help with Separation, Wills, Foreclosure and More" (August 18, 2016), online: The National Self-Represented Litigants Project Blog <http://representingyourselfcanada.com/mylawbc-promises-help-with -separations-wills-foreclosure-and-more/>.

57 "RePresent: Online Game for Self-Represented Litigants," developed by NuLaw Lab at Northwestern University. See <http://www.nulawlab.org/view/online-simulation-for -self-represented-parties>.

58 The British Columbia Civil Resolutions Tribunal <https://www.civilresolutionbc.ca> was established under the *Civil Resolution Tribunal Act,* SBC 2012, c. 25, and amended by the *Civil Resolution Tribunal Amendment Act,* SBC 2015. The tribunal began operating in July 2016.

59 J. Sorensen, "BC Lawyers Worried about Exclusion from New Civil Resolution Tribunal" (September 2, 2013), online: Legal Feeds Blog <http://www.canadianlawyermag. com/legalfeeds/1653/bc-lawyers-worried-about-exclusion-from-new-civil-resolution -tribunal.html>.

60 Lord Justice Briggs, *Civil Courts Structure Review: Interim Report* (December 2015), online: Judiciary of England and Wales <https://www.judiciary.gov.uk/wp-content/ uploads/2016/01/ccsr-interim-report-dec-15-final1.pdf>.

61 See the review of statistics in J. Macfarlane, *The National Self-Represented Litigants Project: Identifying and Meeting the Needs of Self-Represented Litigants: Final Report* (May 2013) at 32–35, online: <https://representingyourselfcanada.files.wordpress. com/2014/02/reportm15-2.pdf> [hereafter *National SRL Study*].

62 Confirmed by studies in Canada (Macfarlane, ibid.); the United States (*Cases without Counsel: Research on Experiences of Self-Representation in US Family Court* [Denver: IAALS, June 2016], online: IAALS <http://iaals.du.edu/sites/default/files/documents/ publications/cases_without_counsel_research_report.pdf>); and England and Wales (Civil Justice Council, *Access to Justice for Litigants in Person [or Self-Represented Litigants]: A Report and Recommendations to the Lord Chancellor and to the Lord Chief Justice* [November 2011], online: Courts and Tribunals Judiciary <https://www.judi ciary.gov.uk/wp-content/uploads/2014/05/report-on-access-to-justice-for-litigants- in-person-nov2011.pdf>).

63 Macfarlane, ibid. at 111.

64 Ibid. at 70–73; T. Farrow et al., *Addressing the Needs of Self-Represented Litigants in the Canadian Justice System* (White Paper prepared for the Association of Canadian Court Administrators, 2010).

65 A "McKenzie Friend" is a lay person who can sit with self-represented litigants at the front of the court and assist them with documents and note taking, but not address the court. The concept derives from an Australian case, *McKenzie v McKenzie* [1971] P 33; [1970] 3 WLR 472; [1970] 3 All ER 1034, CA. See *Practice Guidance on the McKenzie Friend* (Courts and Tribunals Judiciary of England and Wales, July 2010), online: Courts and Tribunals Judiciary <https://www.judiciary.gov.uk/wpcontent/uploads/JCO/Documents/Guidance/mckenzie-friend>; and J.M. DaSilva and J. Macfarlane, *The McKenzie Friend: Choosing and Presenting a Courtroom Companion* (Windsor, ON: Windsor Law, 2016), online: National Self-Represented Litigants Project <https://representingyourselfcanada.files.wordpress.com/2016/03/mckenzie-combined-21.pdf>.

66 See the exposition of arguments and a range of approaches to regulation and deregulation in N. Semple, *Legal Services at the Crossroads: Justitia's Legions* (London: Edward Elgar, 2015).

Epilogue

1 W. Felstiner, "Reorganisation and Resistance" in W. Felstiner, ed., *Reorganisation and Resistance* (Oxford: Hart Publishing, 2005) 1 at 8.

Index

core values, 21, 22, 48–50, 71–73, 74;
justice-as-process, 48, 56–64, 101–2;
lawyer-in-charge model, 48, 63, 64–71,
91–92, 102, 113–14, 131–33; rights-based
dispute resolution, 48, 50–56, 160; role in
negotiation processes, 74–86, 96–97,
100–4; zealous advocacy and, 108
corporate law. *See* commercial clients; corporate sector
corporate sector, 6–7, 10, 230; case example,
161–62, 163–64; Conflict Prevention and
Resolution Pledge, 98, 266n101; effects of
business objectives on conflict resolution,
3–4, 12, 17, 112, 113, 136–39, 241n3;
in-house counsel, 8, 138–39, 241n3
costs. *See* legal costs
counselling services. *See* multidisciplinary
practices
courts: innovative approaches, 226–27
CPR. *See* Conflict Prevention and Resolution
Pledge
criminal justice system: loss of credibility, 13;
reform, 12–13, 15, 226–27
cultural contexts, 170–71, 180–82, 282n51

Day, Stockwell, 88–89
decision making: changing role of clients in,
20, 25, 27, 62, 65, 102, 127, 143–46, 150.
See also ethical decision making;
lawyer-in-charge model
discovery processes, 17, 82–83; settlement
prior to discovery, 90–91
dispute resolution. *See* conflict resolution
domestic clients. *See* clients

emotional intelligence, 18, 23; lacking in
lawyer-in-charge model, 67, 68, 70, 83;
relationships with clients and, 154–59
empathy. *See* emotional intelligence
ethical decision making, 45–46, 186–87,
192–94, 217; bargaining in good faith,
198–202, 217, 285n21, 286n43; client
interests and consensus building, 100–1,
128, 185, 194–95, 270n48; failure of
rule-based approaches, 191–92; pressure
to settle and, 202–8

fairness. *See* procedural justice
family law, 227, 292n40; clients, 38, 288n80;
role of non-legal professionals, 230, 231;

unbundled services, 37, 292n33. *See also*
collaborative law
fees. *See* legal costs
financial issues. *See* billing practices; legal
costs
First Nations peoples, 13, 245n56
Flaherty, Michelle, 291n28
Florida Bar Association, 276n93

Goddard, Lorne, 88–89

Hamline University Law School, 286n56
Hryniak v Mauldin, 213

information: settlement requirements, 83,
90, 122–23, 143–44; withholding of as
power, 81–83, 122, 262n34
informed consent, 208–12
in-house counsel, 8, 138–39, 241n3
Institute for the Advancement of the
American Legal System, 229
institutional clients. *See* commercial clients
insurance carriers: resistance to change,
251n39
interests-based bargaining, 100–1, 128, 185,
194–95, 270n48
internet resources. *See* web-based resources
interpersonal skills, 19, 26, 119. *See also*
emotional intelligence
inter-professional collaboration, 229–32

judges, 291n29; changing roles, 13, 207–8,
225–29, 237
justice: restorative justice, 12–13, 14. *See also*
justice system reform; procedural justice
justice system reform: bar associations and,
15–16; lack of change in law school
curricula, 16–19, 22–23, 219–25;
resistance to, 15–20, 24, 57, 58, 238–39,
255n27
juvenile offenders, 13

large firms, 6–8, 9, 10, 17, 18, 97, 242n16,
266n100, 266n101
law firms: lack of client complaint
mechanisms, 70, 133; large firms, 6–8, 9,
10, 17, 18, 97, 242n16, 266n100, 266n101;
small firms, 6, 7, 107; sole practitioners,
6, 7. *See also* billing practices; legal
services

law school curricula. *See* legal education

Law Society of British Columbia: *Canon of Legal Ethics*, 44–45

Law Society of Upper Canada: *Paralegal Rules of Conduct*, 245n52; *Rules of Professional Conduct*, 43, 44, 45, 215, 256n41, 285n20, 287n74, 289n102, 293n41

law students: adversarial stereotype and, 30; employment, 250n26; personal moral values, 72; use of social media, 38–39

lawyer-in-charge model: client autonomy tensions, 126–28; as core value, 48, 63, 64–71, 91–92, 102, 113–14, 131–33; discounting of emotional intelligence, 67, 68, 70, 83; legal education, 18, 34, 49, 66, 67, 131, 219

lawyers: adversarial stereotype of, 29–31, 106, 222; career satisfaction, 72–73, 260n88, 260n89; competitiveness, 33, 34–35, 81, 108, 220; earnings, 7, 243n25, 269n31; employment, 6, 18; in-house counsel, 8, 138–39, 241n3; inter-professional collaboration, 229–32; media portrayals of, 29–31, 249n1, 249n2; minority lawyers, 42–43; personal experiences, 39–41; personal values, 71–73, 114, 127–29, 157; role models, 9, 41–42, 47, 252n55; settlement-only counsel, 97–98; as unqualified for therapeutic roles, 158, 232; women lawyers, 9, 10, 16–17, 42–43. *See also* lawyer-in-charge model; legal expertise; professional identity

legal aid, 3

legal coaching, 68–69, 134, 258n68, 272n20, 279n140

legal costs: government litigation and, 86–87, 88–89; procedural justice and, 100, 101–2; self-represented litigants, 265n88; transparency concerning costs, 19, 143, 148–49, 168, 277n98; unaffordability of legal services, 4, 19, 68, 73, 136, 227, 236; "value for money" and, 4, 5, 19, 69, 86, 134, 135–36, 231, 233

legal education, 7, 22, 188, 289n6; adversarial norms, 16, 17–19, 31, 34, 108, 219, 222; bullying among students, 33; competi-tiveness, 33, 34–35, 81, 108, 220; critical legal scholarship and, 33; exclusion of

non-legal concerns, 18, 19, 32, 34, 154–55; failure to address new dispute resolution skills, 16, 19, 22–23, 220–21, 223; framing of clients, 67, 108–9, 131, 219–20; future possibilities, 223–25; lawyer-in-charge model, 18, 34, 49, 66, 67, 131, 219; mentoring programs, 42; problem-solving skills, 51, 220, 223–24; professional identity and, 31–35, 46, 72, 221; reflective practice, 223–24; rights-based advocacy, 34, 50, 51; slow response to change, 219–25

legal expertise: role in negotiation, 167–68, 184–85; role in predictive assessment, 167–68, 174–76, 183

legal process outsourcing. *See* outsourcing

legal profession, 5–6; current evolution of, 218–19; increased diversity within, 9–10, 190; re-evaluation of practice habits, 21–22; resistance to change, 238–39, 255n27; size of bar, 5–6. *See also* advocacy; communities of practice; law firms; lawyers; legal services

legal remedies, 13, 245n56; limits to, 176–79; restorative justice, 12–13, 14

legal services, 3, 190; client complaints concerning, 69–70, 71, 133, 148, 237, 238, 271n15, 281n39, 283n54; legal coaching, 68–69, 134, 258n68, 272n20, 279n140; outsourcing, 6, 55, 235; unbundled services, 12, 37, 49, 68, 96, 147, 210, 276n93, 292n33; "value for money" and, 4, 5, 19, 69, 86, 134, 135–36, 231, 233. *See also* billing practices; legal costs

Legal Services Society of British Columbia, 236

limited-scope retainers, 19, 37, 147–48, 228–29, 292n33

litigation, 209, 281n39; costliness, 5, 168; "litigotiation," 74–86. *See also* negotiation practices; trials

"litigotiation," 74–86

local legal culture. *See* communities of practice

Loom Analytics, 288n86

LPO. *See* outsourcing

mandatory mediation, 5, 275n71; effects on lawyers, 14–15, 40–41; timing, 89–90, 264n63, 264n67. *See also* mediation

McKenzie Friends, 237, 295*n*65
MDPs. *See* multidisciplinary practices
mediation, 12; client preparation, 40,
210–11, 277*n*102, 287*n*75; criminal law,
13; negative attitudes towards, 15–16;
third parties, 171, 172–73, 201–2, 206–8,
291*n*28. *See also* mandatory mediation
mediators, 171, 172–73, 291*n*28; pressure to
settle, 201–2, 206–8
medical profession: changes in practice,
134–35, 190; resistance to change, 251*n*39
mega-firms, 6–8, 9, 10, 17, 18, 242*n*16
mentors, 41–43, 47
minority lawyers: difficulty in finding
mentors, 42–43
moral values: conflict with professional
values, 71–73, 114; imposition on clients,
157. *See also* core values; ethical decision
making; professional identity
multidisciplinary practices, 230–34. *See also*
collaborative law

negotiation practices, 25–26, 261*n*14; agent
bargaining, 91–92; in anticipation of
trials, 74–86; bargaining in good faith,
198–202, 217, 285*n*21, 286*n*43; client
presence and, 93–96; client satisfaction
and, 54–55; control vs sharing of
information, 81–83, 122–23, 262*n*34;
criminal law, 13; failure to achieve
consensus, 174–76, 178–79;
implementing change in, 86–87, 89–91,
96–104, 160–65; intentionality in, 119;
positional bargaining and, 78–81, 107,
111–12, 254*n*14, 262*n*30; power
differentials and, 172–73; Prisoner's
Dilemma, 82, 269*n*45; rights-based
advocacy and, 74–86, 100–1, 112;
strategic bargaining and, 77–78;
zero-sum assumptions and, 76–78. *See
also* collaborative law; conflict resolution
advocacy; settlement processes
New York Bar Association, 276*n*93
normative behaviour: adversarial advocacy,
16, 17–19, 24, 31, 34, 108, 219, 222;
changing of, 24–25, 99–100, 251*n*32,
251*n*34; cultural communities and,
170–71. *See also* adversarial stereotype;
core values

online internet resources. *See* web-based
resources
online tribunals, 236, 242*n*12
Ontario: approaches to mediation, 37,
251*n*34; billing options, 292*n*33; family
law, 292*n*33, 292*n*40; mandatory
mediation, 89–90; negative attitudes
towards mediation, 15–16; Ottawa, 228;
paralegals, 242*n*10; Toronto, 228, 251*n*34.
See also Law Society of Upper Canada
outsourcing, 6, 55, 235

paralegals, 6; enlarged role for, 5, 12, 229–30,
231, 237, 242*n*10, 245*n*52, 292*n*40
Pareto optimality, 78, 261*n*17
pit bull stereotype. *See* adversarial stereotype
popular culture: portrayals of lawyers, 29–31,
249*n*1, 249*n*2
pre-trial resolutions, 85–86; early vs late
settlements, 87–91, 100, 103; rates, 11,
74–75, 84; related to litigation costs, 10,
85, 86, 87, 88–89. *See also* mediation;
negotiation practices; settlement
processes
Prisoner's Dilemma, 82, 269*n*45
problem-solving skills, 12, 112, 224, 233,
239; conflict resolution advocacy, 17, 26,
68, 78, 194–97, 233; legal education and,
51, 220, 223, 224
procedural justice, 56–57, 60, 256*n*38; client
expectations and, 60–64; as controllable,
57–60; settlement processes and, 63–64
professional identity, 28–29, 48, 71–73,
233–34; adversarial stereotype, 29–31,
106, 222; codes of conduct and, 43–46,
47; communities of practice and, 35–38,
47; effect of mega-firm market model on,
8; ethical issues and, 187–200; legal
education and, 31–35, 46, 72; personal
experience and, 39–41; reinvention,
21–22; role of mentors in formation of,
41–43, 47; social media and, 38–39. *See
also* core values
professional values. *See* core values; professional identity
public opinion: negative views of lawyers, 3,
19, 29, 187, 188, 240

Quality Judges Initiative, 229

restorative justice, 12–13, 14
rights-based advocacy, 34, 50–51; client disillusionment with, 54–55; as essential justice component, 55–56, 100–1; as ideology, 52–53, 56, 80; moral principles and, 52, 71–72, 114; negotiation practices and, 74–86, 100–1, 112; ownership of client disputes, 67–68; role of power in, 51–52, 61

Saskatchewan: civil trial rates, 263n40; mandatory mediation, 89, 264n67
self-help culture, 135–36. *See also* self-represented litigants; web-based resources
self-represented litigants, xi, 4, 19, 139–40, 227, 288n80; codes of conduct concerning, 214–16; disadvantaging of, 55, 61–63, 254n7, 265n88; guidelines for lawyers concerning, 214–16, 265n92; legal costs and, 4, 19, 241n7; McKenzie Friends, 237, 295n65; negative attitudes of lawyers to, 94–95, 187, 212, 265n89; negotiation processes and, 94–96; responsibilities of lawyers to, 95–96, 186, 212–16, 265n92; SRL phenomenon as change agent, 236–37; summary judgments and, 213, 274n49; unbundled services and, 12, 148; use of web resources, 4, 55; views on lawyers, 19, 274n48; views on procedural justice, 61–64
settlement processes, xiii; BATNA/WATNA, 175–76; benefits of client knowledge, 93–94; case examples, 161–63; client participation, 149–54; conferences, 5, 12, 228; cooperative pledges, 98, 103; early vs late settlements, 87–91, 100, 103; information requirements, 83, 90, 122–23, 143–44; judicial settlements, 225, 226; mandatory, 93, 97, 103, 143–44, 228; personal rights and, 171–74; procedural justice and, 63–64; settlement-only counsel, 97–98. *See also* collaborative law; conflict resolution advocacy; mediation; negotiation practices

shark stereotype. *See* adversarial stereotype
social media: employment and, 252n43; presence of lawyers on, 38–39
soft skills, xii, 275n68; communication skills, 26, 119, 156, 227–28, 271n15; interpersonal skills, 19, 26, 119; judges, 227–28. *See also* emotional intelligence; problem-solving skills
sole practitioners, 6, 7
SRLs. *See* self-represented litigants
summary judgments, 213, 274n49

Trial Lawyers Association of British Columbia: resistance to justice reform, 255n27, 256n30
trials: cases that end in trials, 11, 74–75, 84, 244n44, 263n40; costs, 10, 241n5; pre-trial activities, 5, 11, 245n47

unbundled services, xii, 12, 37, 49, 68, 96, 147, 210, 276n93, 292n33

visible minorities: marginalization of minority lawyers, 9–10, 16–17; in prison populations, 13

warrior stereotype. *See* adversarial stereotype
WATNA ("worst alternative to a negotiated agreement"), 175–76
web-based resources, 4, 5, 55, 142, 276n86, 294n55; as change agent, 69, 134, 135–36, 234–36; consumer culture and, 64, 66, 69; Loom Analytics, 288n86
women lawyers: difficulty in finding mentors, 42–43; marginalization of, 9, 10, 16–17
World Wide Web. *See* web-based resources
worst alternative to a negotiated agreement. *See* WATNA

Youth Criminal Justice Act (2002), 13

zealous advocacy, 25, 108–9, 268; historical evolution, 109–11; outcomes, 123; tensions within, 111–15. *See also* adversarial advocacy